Computer Aided Verification: Emerging Trends

Computer Aided Verification: Emerging Trends

Editor: Tyler Keating

MURPHY & MOORE
www.murphy-moorepublishing.com

www.murphy-moorepublishing.com

ⓂⓂMURPHY & MOORE

Cataloging-in-publication Data

Computer aided verification : emerging trends / edited by Tyler Keating.
    p. cm.
Includes bibliographical references and index.
ISBN 978-1-63987-693-8
1. Computer software--Verification. 2. Computer programs--Verification.
3. Electronic digital computers--Evaluation. 4. Computer-aided design.
I. Keating, Tyler.
QA76.76.V47 C66 2023
005.14--dc23

Murphy & Moore Publishing
1 Rockefeller Plaza,
New York City,
NY 10020, USA

ISBN 978-1-63987-693-8

Contents

Preface..VII

Chapter 1   **Fast Algorithms for Handling Diagonal Constraints in Timed Automata**..1
Paul Gastin, Sayan Mukherjee and B. Srivathsan

Chapter 2   **Security-Aware Synthesis Using Delayed-Action Games**...........................20
Mahmoud Elfar, Yu Wang and Miroslav Pajic

Chapter 3   **Membership-Based Synthesis of Linear Hybrid Automata**.......................40
Miriam García Soto, Thomas A. Henzinger, Christian Schilling and Luka Zeleznik

Chapter 4   **Verifying Asynchronous Interactions via Communicating Session Automata**..58
Julien Lange and Nobuko Yoshida

Chapter 5   **Symbolic Register Automata**...79
Loris D'Antoni, Tiago Ferreira, Matteo Sammartino and Alexandra Silva

Chapter 6   **Quantitative Mitigation of Timing Side Channels**.....................................97
Saeid Tizpaz-Niari, Pavol Černý and Ashutosh Trivedi

Chapter 7   **Efficient Synthesis with Probabilistic Constraints**..................................117
Samuel Drews, Aws Albarghouthi and Loris D'Antoni

Chapter 8   **Safety and Co-Safety Comparator Automata for Discounted-Sum Inclusion**..136
Suguman Bansal and Moshe Y. Vardi

Chapter 9   **Automated Hypersafety Verification**..155
Azadeh Farzan and Anthony Vandikas

Chapter 10   **Verifying Hyperliveness**...174
Norine Coenen, Bernd Finkbeiner, César Sánchez and Leander Tentrup

Chapter 11   **Abstraction Refinement Algorithms for Timed Automata**.......................193
Victor Roussanaly, Ocan Sankur and Nicolas Markey

Chapter 12   **Overfitting in Synthesis: Theory and Practice**..**212**
Saswat Padhi, Todd Millstein, Aditya Nori and Rahul Sharma

Permissions

List of Contributors

Index

Preface

This book aims to highlight the current researches and provides a platform to further the scope of innovations in this area. This book is a product of the combined efforts of many researchers and scientists, after going through thorough studies and analysis from different parts of the world. The objective of this book is to provide the readers with the latest information of the field.

Computer aided verification strives to improve the quality of digital systems by analyzing their designs with the help of logical reasoning reinforced through automated software techniques. It is helpful in enhancing the reliability, correctness and robustness of the software systems. The goal is to create a mathematical model of a system and then attempt to prove its formal properties that either helps in detecting bugs or certifies the system's correctness. The proofs might be millions of lengthy lines, thereby specifically designed computer algorithms are utilized to find and verify them. This book unravels the recent studies on computer aided verification. It consists of contributions made by international experts. The book will help the readers in keeping pace with the rapid changes and emerging trends in this field of computer science.

I would like to express my sincere thanks to the authors for their dedicated efforts in the completion of this book. I acknowledge the efforts of the publisher for providing constant support. Lastly, I would like to thank my family for their support in all academic endeavors.

Editor

Fast Algorithms for Handling Diagonal Constraints in Timed Automata

Paul Gastin[1], Sayan Mukherjee[2], and B. Srivathsan[2]($\boxtimes$)

[1] LSV, ENS Paris-Saclay, CNRS, Université Paris-Saclay, Cachan, France
paul.gastin@lsv.fr
[2] Chennai Mathematical Institute, Chennai, India
{sayanm,sri}@cmi.ac.in

Abstract. A popular method for solving reachability in timed automata proceeds by enumerating reachable sets of valuations represented as zones. A naïve enumeration of zones does not terminate. Various termination mechanisms have been studied over the years. Coming up with efficient termination mechanisms has been remarkably more challenging when the automaton has diagonal constraints in guards.

In this paper, we propose a new termination mechanism for timed automata with diagonal constraints based on a new simulation relation between zones. Experiments with an implementation of this simulation show significant gains over existing methods.

Keywords: Timed automata · Diagonal constraints · Reachability · Zones · Simulations

1 Introduction

Timed automata have emerged as a popular model for systems with real-time constraints [2]. Timed automata are finite automata extended with real-valued variables called *clocks*. All clocks are assumed to start at 0, and increase at the same rate. Transitions of the automaton can make use of these clocks to disallow behaviours which violate timing constraints. This is achieved by making use of *guards* which are constraints of the form $x \leq 5$, $x - y \geq 3$, $y > 7$, etc. where x, y are clocks. A transition guarded by $x \leq 5$ says that it can be fired only when the value of clock x is ≤ 5. Another important feature is the *reset* of clocks in transitions. Each transition can specify a subset of clocks whose values become 0 once the transition is fired. The combination of guards and resets allows to track timing distance between events. A basic question that forms the core of timed automata technology is *reachability*: given a timed automaton, does there exist an execution from its initial state to a final state. This question is known to be decidable [2]. Various algorithms for this problem have been studied over the years and have been implemented in tools [6, 21, 26, 28, 31, 32].

Since the clocks are real valued variables, the space of configurations of a timed automaton (consisting of a state and a valuation of the clocks) is infinite and an explicit enumeration is not possible. The earliest solution to reachability was to partition this space into a finite number of *regions* and build a region graph that provides a finite abstraction of the behaviour of the timed automaton [2]. However, this solution was not practical. Subsequent works introduced the use of *zones* [14]. Zones are special sets of clock valuations with efficient data structures and manipulation algorithms [6]. Within zone based algorithms, there is a division: forward analysis versus backward analysis. The current industry strength tool UPPAAL [28] implements a forward analysis approach, as this works better in the presence of other discrete data structures used in UPPAAL models [9]. We focus on this forward analysis approach using zones in this paper.

The forward analysis of a timed automaton essentially enumerates sets of reachable configurations stored as zones. Some extra care needs to be taken for this enumeration to terminate. Traditional development of timed automata made use of *extrapolation* operators over zones to ensure termination. These are functions which map a zone to a bigger zone. Importantly, the range of these functions is finite. The goal was to come up with extrapolation operators which are sound: adding these extra valuations should not lead to new behaviours. This is where the role of *simulations* between configurations was studied and extrapolation operators based on such simulations were devised [14]. A certain extrapolation operation, which is now known as Extra_M [5] was proposed and reachability using Extra_M was implemented in tools [14].

A seminal paper by Bouyer [9] revealed that Extra_M is not correct in the presence of *diagonal constraints* in guards. These are constraints of the form $x - y \lhd c$ where $\lhd$ is either $<$ or $\le$, and c is an integer. Moreover, it was proved that no such extrapolation operation would be correct when there are diagonal constraints present. It was shown that for automata without diagonal constraints (henceforth referred to as diagonal-free automata), the extrapolation works. After this result, developments in timed automata reachability focussed on the class of diagonal-free automata [4, 5, 23, 24], and diagonal constraints were mostly sidelined. All these developments have led to quite efficient algorithms for diagonal-free timed automata.

Diagonal constraints are a useful modeling feature and occur naturally in certain problems, especially scheduling [3, 17, 20, 27] and logic-automata translations [16, 25], also in [29]. It is however known that they do not add any expressive power: every timed automaton can be converted into a diagonal-free timed automaton [7]. This conversion suffers from an exponential blowup, which was later shown to be unavoidable: diagonal constraints could potentially give exponentially more succinct models [10]. Therefore, a good forward analysis algorithm that works directly on a timed automaton with diagonal constraints would be handy. This is the subject of this paper.

Related Work. The first attempt at such an algorithm was to split the (extrapolated) zones with respect to the diagonal constraints present in the automaton [6]. This gave a correct procedure, but since zones are split, an enumeration starts from each small zone leading to an exponential blow-up in the number of visited zones. A second attempt was to do a more refined conversion into a diagonal free automaton by detecting "relevant" diagonals [13,30] in an iterative manner. In order to do this, special data structures storing sets of sets of diagonal constraints were utilized. In [18] we extended the works [5] and [23] on diagonal-free automata to the case of diagonal constraints. All the approaches suffer from either a space or time bottleneck and are incomparable to the efficiency and scalability of tools for diagonal-free automata.

Our Contributions. The goal of this paper is to come up with fast algorithms for handling diagonal constraints. Since the extrapolation based approach is a dead end, we work with simulation between zones directly, as in [23] and [18]. We propose a new simulation relation between zones that is correct in the presence of diagonal constraints (Sect. 3). We give an algorithm to test this simulation between zones (Sect. 4). We have incorporated this simulation test in (an older version of) the tool TChecker [21] checking reachability for timed automata, and compared our results with the state-of-the-art tool UPPAAL. Experiments show an encouraging gain, both in the number of zones enumerated and in the time taken by the algorithm, sometimes upto four orders of magnitude (Sect. 6). The main advantage of our approach is that it does not split zones, and furthermore it leverages the optimizations studied for diagonal-free automata.

From a technical point of view, our presentation does not make use of regions and instead works with valuations, zones and simulation relations. We think that this presentation provides a clearer perspective - as a justification of this claim, we extend our simulation to timed automata with general updates of the form $x := c$ and $x := y + d$ in transitions (where x, y are clocks and c, d are constants) in a rather natural manner (Sect. 5). In general, reachability for timed automata with updates is undecidable [12]. Some decidable cases have been proposed for which the algorithms are based on regions. For decidable subclasses containing diagonal constraints, no zone based approach has been studied. Our proposed method includes these classes, and also benefits from zones and standard optimizations studied for diagonal-free automata.

Missing proofs can be found in the full version of this paper [19].

2 Preliminaries

Let $\mathbb{N}$ be the set of natural numbers, $\mathbb{R}_{\geq 0}$ the set of non-negative reals and $\mathbb{Z}$ the set of integers. Let X be a finite set of variables ranging over $\mathbb{R}_{\geq 0}$, called *clocks*. Let $\Phi(X)$ denote the set of constraints φ formed using the following grammar: $\varphi := x \lhd c \mid c \lhd x \mid x - y \lhd d \mid \varphi \wedge \varphi$, where $x, y \in X$, $c \in \mathbb{N}$, $d \in \mathbb{Z}$ and $\lhd \in \{<, \leq\}$. Constraints of the form $x \lhd c$ and $c \lhd x$ are called *non-diagonal constraints* and those of the form $x - y \lhd c$ are called *diagonal constraints*. We have adopted a convention that in non-diagonal constraints $x \lhd c$ and $c \lhd x$, the constant c is restricted to $\mathbb{N}$. A *clock valuation* v is a function which maps every clock $x \in X$ to a real number $v(x) \in \mathbb{R}_{\geq 0}$. A valuation is said to satisfy a guard g, written as $v \models g$ if replacing every x in g with $v(x)$ makes the constraint g true. For $\delta \in \mathbb{R}_{\geq 0}$ we write $v + \delta$ for the valuation which maps every x to $v(x) + \delta$. Given a subset of clocks $R \subseteq X$, we write $[R]v$ for the valuation which maps each $x \in R$ to 0 and each $x \notin R$ to $v(x)$.

A *timed automaton* $\mathcal{A}$ is a tuple (Q, X, q_0, T, F) where Q is a finite set of states, X is a finite set of clocks, $q_0 \in Q$ is the initial state, $F \subseteq Q$ is a set of accepting states and $T \in Q \times \Phi(X) \times 2^X \times Q$ is a set of transitions. Each transition $t \in T$ is of the form (q, g, R, q') where q and q' are respectively the source and target states, g is a constraint called the *guard*, and R is a set of clocks which are *reset* in t. We call a timed automaton *diagonal-free* if guards in transitions do not use diagonal constraints.

A *configuration* of $\mathcal{A}$ is a pair (q, v) where $q \in Q$ and v is a valuation. The semantics of a timed automaton is given by a transition system $\mathcal{S}_{\mathcal{A}}$ whose states are the configurations of $\mathcal{A}$. Transitions in $\mathcal{S}_{\mathcal{A}}$ are of two kinds: *delay* transitions are given by $(q, v) \xrightarrow{\delta} (q, v + \delta)$ for all $\delta \geq 0$, and *action* transitions are given by $(q, v) \xrightarrow{t} (q', v')$ for each $t := (q, g, R, q')$, if $v \models g$ and $v' = [R]v$. We write $\xrightarrow{\delta, t}$ for a sequence of delay δ followed by action t. A run of $\mathcal{A}$ is an alternating sequence of delay-action transitions starting from the initial state q_0 and the initial valuation **0** which maps every clock to 0: $(q_0, \mathbf{0}) \xrightarrow{\delta_0, t_0} (q_1, v_1) \xrightarrow{\delta_1, t_1} \cdots (q_n, v_n)$. A run of the above form is said to be accepting if the last state $q_n \in F$. The *reachability problem* for timed automata is the following: given an automaton $\mathcal{A}$, decide if there exists an accepting run. This problem is known to be PSPACE-complete [2]. Since the semantics $\mathcal{S}_{\mathcal{A}}$ is infinite, solutions to the reachability problem work with a finite abstraction of $\mathcal{S}_{\mathcal{A}}$ that is sound and complete. Before we explain one of the popular solutions to reachability, we state a result which allows to convert every timed automaton into a diagonal-free timed automaton.

Theorem 1. *[7] For every timed automaton $\mathcal{A}$, there exists a diagonal-free timed automaton $\mathcal{A}_{df}$ s.t. there is a bijection between runs of $\mathcal{A}$ and $\mathcal{A}_{df}$. The number of states in $\mathcal{A}_{df}$ is $2^d \cdot n$ where d is the number of diagonal constraints and n is the number of states of $\mathcal{A}$.*

The above theorem allows to solve the reachability of a timed automaton $\mathcal{A}$ by first converting it into the diagonal free automaton $\mathcal{A}_{df}$ and then checking reachability on $\mathcal{A}_{df}$. However, this conversion comes with a systematic exponential blowup (in terms of the number of diagonal constraints present in $\mathcal{A}$). It was shown in [10] that such a blowup is unavoidable in general. We will now recall the general algorithm for analyzing timed automata, and then move into specific details which depend on whether the automaton has diagonal constraints or not.

Zones and Simulations. Fix a timed automaton $\mathcal{A}$ with clock set X for the rest of the discussion in this section. As the space of valuations of $\mathcal{A}$ is infinite, algorithms work with sets of valuations called *zones*. A zone is set of clock valuations given by a conjunction of constraints of the form $x - y \vartriangleleft c$, $x \vartriangleleft c$ and

$c \lhd x$ where $c \in \mathbb{Z}$ and $\lhd \in \{<, \leq\}$, for example the solutions of $x - y < 5 \wedge y \leq 10$ is a zone. The transition relation over configurations (q, v) is extended to (q, Z) where Z is a zone. We define the following operations on zones given a guard g and a set of clocks R: time elapse $\overrightarrow{Z} = \{v + \delta \mid v \in Z, \delta \geq 0\}$; guard intersection $Z \wedge g := \{v \mid v \in Z \text{ and } v \models g\}$ and reset $[R]Z := \{[R]v \mid v \in Z\}$. It can be shown that all these operations result in zones. Zones can be efficiently represented and manipulated using Difference Bound Matrices (DBMs) [15].

The *zone graph* $ZG(\mathcal{A})$ of timed automaton $\mathcal{A}$ is a transition system whose nodes are of the form (q, Z) where q is a state of $\mathcal{A}$ and Z is a zone. For each transition $t := (q, g, R, q')$ of $\mathcal{A}$, and each zone (q, Z) there is a transition $(q, Z) \Rightarrow^t (q', Z')$ where $Z' = \overrightarrow{[R](Z \wedge g)}$. The initial node is (q_0, Z_0) where q_0 is the initial state of $\mathcal{A}$ and $Z_0 = \{\mathbf{0} + \delta \mid \delta \geq 0\}$ is the zone obtained by elapsing an arbitrary delay from the initial valuation. A path in the zone graph is a sequence $(q_0, Z_0) \Rightarrow^{t_0} (q_1, Z_1) \Rightarrow^{t_1} \cdots \Rightarrow^{t_{n-1}} (q_n, Z_n)$ starting from the initial node. The path is said to be accepting if q_n is an accepting state. The zone graph is known to be sound and complete for reachability.

Theorem 2. *[14] $\mathcal{A}$ has an accepting run iff $ZG(\mathcal{A})$ has an accepting path.*

This does not yet give an algorithm as the zone graph $ZG(\mathcal{A})$ is still not finite. Moreover, there are examples of automata for which the reachable part of $ZG(\mathcal{A})$ is also infinite: starting from the initial node, applying the successor computation leads to infinitely many zones. Two different approaches have been studied to get finiteness, both of them based on the usage of *simulation relations*.

A (time-abstract) simulation relation ($\preccurlyeq$) between configurations of $\mathcal{A}$ is a reflexive and transitive relation such that $(q, v) \preccurlyeq (q', v')$ implies $q = q'$ and (1) for every $\delta \geq 0$, there exists $\delta' \geq 0$ such that $(q, v + \delta) \preccurlyeq (q, v' + \delta')$ and (2) for every transition t of $\mathcal{A}$, if $(q, v) \xrightarrow{t} (q_1, v_1)$ then $(q, v') \xrightarrow{t} (q_1, v_1')$ such that $(q_1, v_1) \preccurlyeq (q_1, v_1')$.

We say $v \preccurlyeq v'$, read as v is simulated by v' if $(q, v) \preccurlyeq (q, v')$ for all states q. The simulation relation can be extended to zones: $Z \preccurlyeq Z'$ if for every $v \in Z$ there exists $v' \in Z'$ such that $v \preccurlyeq v'$. We write $\downarrow Z$ for $\{v \mid \exists v' \in Z \text{ s.t. } v \preccurlyeq v'\}$. The simulation relation $\preccurlyeq$ is said to be finite if the function mapping zones Z to the down sets $\downarrow Z$ has finite range. We now recall a specific simulation relation $\preccurlyeq_{LU}$ [5, 23]. Current algorithms and tools for diagonal-free automata are based on this simulation. The conditions required for $v \preccurlyeq_{LU} v'$ ensure that when all lower bound constraints $c \lhd x$ satisfy $c \leq L(x)$ and all upper bound constraints $x \lhd c$ satisfy $c \leq U(x)$, whenever v satisfies a constraint, v' will also satisfy it.

Definition 1 (LU-bounds and the relation $\preccurlyeq_{LU}$ [5,23]). *An LU-bounds function is a pair of functions $L : X \mapsto \mathbb{N} \cup \{-\infty\}$ and $U : X \mapsto \mathbb{N} \cup \{-\infty\}$ that map each clock to either a non-negative constant or $-\infty$. Given an LU-bounds function, we define $v \preccurlyeq_{LU} v'$ for valuations v, v' if for every clock $x \in X$:*

$$v'(x) < v(x) \text{ implies } L(x) < v'(x) \quad \text{and} \quad v(x) < v'(x) \text{ implies } U(x) < v(x).$$

Reachability in Diagonal-Free Timed Automata. A natural method to get finiteness of the zone graph is to prune the zone graph computation through simulations $Z \preccurlyeq Z'$: do not explore a node (q, Z) if there is an already visited node (q, Z') such that $Z \preccurlyeq Z'$. Since these simulation tests need to be done often during the zone graph computation, an efficient algorithm for performing this test is crucial. Note that $Z \preccurlyeq Z'$ iff $Z \subseteq \downarrow Z'$. However, it is known that the set $\downarrow Z'$ is not necessarily a zone (this was proved for $\downarrow_{LU} Z'$ in [5]), and hence no simple zone inclusions are applicable. The first algorithms for timed automata followed a different approach, which we call the *extrapolation* approach. In this approach, whenever a new zone Z is discovered by the algorithm, a new zone $\mathsf{Extra}(Z)(\supseteq Z)$ gets computed and stored in the place of Z.

Reachability Algorithm Using Zone Extrapolation. The input to the algorithm is a timed automaton $\mathcal{A}$. The algorithm maintains two lists, Passed and Waiting. Initially, the node $(q_0, \mathsf{Extra}(Z_0))$ is added to the Waiting list (recall that (q_0, Z_0) is the initial node of the zone graph $ZG(\mathcal{A})$). Wlog. we assume that q_0 is not accepting. The algorithm repeatedly performs the following steps:

Step 1. If Waiting is empty, then return "$\mathcal{A}$ has no accepting run"; else pick (and remove) a node (q, Z) from Waiting. Add (q, Z) to Passed.

Step 2. For each transition $t := (q, g, R, q_1)$, compute the successor $(q, Z) \Rightarrow^t (q_1, Z_1)$: if $Z_1 \neq \emptyset$ perform the following operations - if q_1 is accepting, return "$\mathcal{A}$ has an accepting run"; else compute $\hat{Z}_1 := \mathsf{Extra}(Z_1)$ and check if there exists a node (q_1, Z_1') in Passed or Waiting such that $\hat{Z}_1 \subseteq Z_1'$: if yes, ignore the node $(q_1, \hat{Z}_1)$, otherwise add $(q_1, \hat{Z}_1)$ to Waiting.

Several extrapolation operators (Extra_M, Extra_{LU}, Extra_{LU}^+) were introduced in [5]. The function Extra_{LU}^+ has nice properties - (1) $\mathsf{Extra}_{LU}^+(Z) \subseteq \downarrow_{LU} Z$ and (2) $\mathsf{Extra}_{LU}^+(Z)$ is a zone for all Z. These properties give an algorithm that performs only efficient zone operations: successor computations and zone inclusions.

Reachability Algorithm Using Simulations. The initial node (q_0, Z_0) is added to the Waiting list. Wlog. we assume that q_0 is not accepting. The algorithm repeatedly performs the following steps:

Step 1. If Waiting is empty, then return "$\mathcal{A}$ has no accepting run"; else pick (and remove) a node (q, Z) from Waiting. Add (q, Z) to Passed.

Step 2. For each transition $t := (q, g, R, q_1)$, compute the successor $(q, Z) \Rightarrow^t (q_1, Z_1)$: if $Z_1 \neq \emptyset$ perform the following operations - if q_1 is accepting, return "$\mathcal{A}$ has an accepting run"; else check if there exists a node (q_1, Z_1') in Passed or Waiting such that $Z_1 \preccurlyeq Z_1'$: if yes, ignore the node (q_1, Z_1), otherwise add (q_1, Z_1) to Waiting.

An $\mathcal{O}(|X|^2)$ algorithm for $Z \preccurlyeq_{LU} Z'$ was proposed in [23]. The efficiency of this simulation check makes it well suited for use in practice. Moreover, as $\mathsf{Extra}_{LU}^+(Z) \subseteq \downarrow_{LU} Z$, we expect to get more simulations (and hence quicker termination) through $\preccurlyeq_{LU}$.

Reachability in the Presence of Diagonal Constraints. The $\preccurlyeq_{LU}$ relation is no longer a simulation when diagonal constraints are present. Moreover, it was shown in [9] that no extrapolation operator (along the lines of Extra^+_{LU}) can work in the presence of diagonal constraints. The first option to deal with diagonals is to use Theorem 1 to get a diagonal free automaton and then apply the methods discussed previously. One problem with this is the systematic exponential blowup introduced in the number of states of the resulting automaton. Another problem is to get diagnostic information: counterexamples need to be translated back to the original automaton [6]. Various methods have been studied to circumvent the diagonal free conversion and instead work on the automaton with diagonal constraints directly. We recall the approach used in the state-of-the-art tool UPPAAL below.

Zone Splitting [6]. The paper introducing timed automata gave a notion of equivalence between valuations $v \simeq_M v'$ parameterized by a function M mapping each clock x to the maximum constant M among the guards of the automaton that involve x. This equivalence is a finite simulation for diagonal-free automata. Equivalence classes of $\simeq_M$ are called regions. This was extended to the diagonal case by [6] as: $v \simeq^d_M v'$ if $v \simeq_M v'$ and for all diagonal constraints g present in the automaton, if $v \models g$ then $v' \models g$. The $\simeq^d_M$ relation splits the regions further, such that each region is either entirely included inside g, or entirely outside g for each g. The next step is to use this notion of equivalence in zones. The paper [6] follows the extrapolation approach: to each zone Z, an extrapolation operation $\mathsf{Extra}_M(Z)$ is applied; this adds some valuations which are $\simeq_M$ equivalent to valuations in Z; then it is further split into multiple zones, so that each small zone is either inside g or outside g for each diagonal constraint g. If d is the number of diagonal constraints present in the automaton, this splitting process can give rise to 2^d zones for each zone Z. From each small zone, the zone graph computation is started. Essentially, the exponential blow-up at the state level which appeared in the diagonal-free conversion now appears in the zone level.

In this paper, we propose a new simulation to handle diagonal constraints. This has two advantages - using this avoids the blow-up in the number of nodes arising due to zone splitting, and the simulation test between zones has an efficient implementation and is significantly quicker than the simulation of [18].

3 A New Simulation Relation

We start with a definition of a relation between timed automata configurations, which in some sense "declares" upfront what we need out of a simulation relation that can be used in a reachability algorithm. As we proceed, we will make its description more concrete and give an effective simulation algorithm between zones, that can be implemented. Fix a clock set X. This generates constraints $\Phi(X)$.

Definition 2 (the relation $\sqsubseteq_{\mathcal{G}}$). *Let $\mathcal{G}$ be a (finite or infinite) set of constraints. We say $v \sqsubseteq_{\mathcal{G}} v'$ if for all $\varphi \in \mathcal{G}$ and all $\delta \geq 0$, $v + \delta \models \varphi$ implies $v' + \delta \models \varphi$.*

Our goal is to utilize the above relation in a simulation (as defined in p. xx) for a timed automaton. Directly from the definition, we get the following lemma which shows that the $\sqsubseteq_{\mathcal{G}}$ relation is preserved under time elapse.

Lemma 1. *If $v \sqsubseteq_{\mathcal{G}} v'$, then $v + \delta \sqsubseteq_{\mathcal{G}} v' + \delta$ for all $\delta \geq 0$.*

The other kind of transformation over valuations is resets. Given sets of guards $\mathcal{G}_1$, $\mathcal{G}$ and a set of clocks R, we want to find conditions on $\mathcal{G}_1$ and $\mathcal{G}$ so that if $v \sqsubseteq_{\mathcal{G}_1} v'$ then $[R]v \sqsubseteq_{\mathcal{G}} [R]v'$. To do this, we need to answer this question: what guarantees should we ensure for v, v' (via $\mathcal{G}_1$) so that $[R]v \sqsubseteq_{\mathcal{G}} [R]v'$. This motivates the next definition.

Definition 3 (weakest pre-condition of $\sqsubseteq_{\mathcal{G}}$ over resets). *For a constraint φ and a set of clocks R, we define a set of constraints $\mathrm{wp}(\sqsubseteq_{\varphi}, R)$ as follows: when φ is of the form $x \lhd c$ or $c \lhd x$, then $\mathrm{wp}(\sqsubseteq_{\varphi}, R)$ is empty if $x \in R$ and is $\{\varphi\}$ otherwise; when φ is a diagonal constraint $x - y \lhd c$, then $\mathrm{wp}(\sqsubseteq_{\varphi}, R)$ is:*

- *$\{x - y \lhd c\}$ if $\{x, y\} \cap R = \emptyset$*
- *$\{x \lhd c\}$ if $y \in R$, $x \notin R$ and $c \geq 0$*
- *$\{-c \lhd y\}$ if $x \in R$, $y \notin R$ and $-c \geq 0$*
- *empty, otherwise.*

For a set of guards $\mathcal{G}$, we define $\mathrm{wp}(\sqsubseteq_{\mathcal{G}}, R) := \bigcup_{\varphi \in \mathcal{G}} \mathrm{wp}(\sqsubseteq_{\varphi}, R)$.

Note that the relation $\sqsubseteq_{\mathcal{G}}$ is parameterized by a set of constraints. Additionally, we desire this set to be finite, so that the relation can be used in an algorithm. We need to first link an automaton $\mathcal{A}$ with such a set of constraints. One way to do it is to take the set of all guards present in the automaton and to close it under weakest pre-conditions with respect to all possible subsets of clocks. A better approach is to consider a set of constraints for each state, as in [4] where the parameters for extrapolation (the maximum constants appearing in guards) are calculated at each state.

Definition 4 (State based guards). *Let $\mathcal{A} = (Q, X, q_0, T, F)$ be a timed automaton. We associate a set of guards $\mathcal{G}(q)$ for each state $q \in Q$, which is the least set of guards (for the coordinate-wise subset inclusion order) such that for every transition (q, g, R, q_1): the guard g and the set $\mathrm{wp}(\sqsubseteq_{\mathcal{G}(q_1)}, R)$ are present in $\mathcal{G}(q)$. More precisely, $\{\mathcal{G}(q)\}_{q \in Q}$ is the least solution to the following set of equations written for each $q \in Q$:*

$$\mathcal{G}(q) = \bigcup_{(q,g,R,q_1) \in T} \{g\} \cup \mathrm{wp}(\sqsubseteq_{\mathcal{G}(q_1)}, R)$$

All constraints present in the set $\mathrm{wp}(\sqsubseteq_{\mathcal{G}(q_1)}, R)$ contain constants which are already present in $\sqsubseteq_{\mathcal{G}(q_1)}$. The least solution to the above set of equations can therefore be obtained by a fixed point computation which starts with $\mathcal{G}(q)$ set to $\bigcup_{(q,g,R,q_1) \in T} \{g\}$ and then repeatedly updates the weakest-preconditions. Since no new constants are generated in this process, the fixed point computation terminates. We now have the ingredients to define a simulation relation over configurations of a timed automaton with diagonal constraints.

Definition 5 ($\mathcal{A}$-simulation). *Let $\mathcal{A} = (Q, X, q_0, T, F)$ be a timed automaton and let the set of guards $\mathcal{G}(q)$ of Definition 4 be associated to every state $q \in Q$. We define a relation $\preccurlyeq_\mathcal{A}$ between configurations of $\mathcal{A}$ as $(q, v) \preccurlyeq_\mathcal{A} (q, v')$ if $v \sqsubseteq_{\mathcal{G}(q)} v'$.*

Lemma 2. *The relation $\preccurlyeq_\mathcal{A}$ is a simulation on the configurations of timed automaton $\mathcal{A}$.*

As pointed before, Definition 2 gives a declarative description of the simulation and it is unclear how to work with it algorithmically, even when the set of constraints $\mathcal{G}$ is finite. The main issue is with the $\forall \delta$ quantification, which is not finite. We will first provide a characterization that brings out the fact that this $\forall \delta$ quantification is irrelevant for diagonal constraints (essentially because value of $v(x) - v(y)$ does not change with time elapse). Given a set of constraints $\mathcal{G}$, let $\mathcal{G}^- \subseteq \mathcal{G}$ be the set of non-diagonal constraints in $\mathcal{G}$.

Proposition 1. *$v \sqsubseteq_\mathcal{G} v'$ iff $v \sqsubseteq_{\mathcal{G}^-} v'$ and for all diagonal constraints $\varphi \in \mathcal{G}$, if $v \models \varphi$ then $v' \models \varphi$.*

It now amounts to solving the $\forall \delta$ problem for non-diagonals. It turns out that the $\preccurlyeq_{LU}$ simulation achieves this, almost. We will see this in more detail in the next section.

4 Algorithm for $Z \sqsubseteq_\mathcal{G} Z'$

Fix a finite set of guards $\mathcal{G}$. Restating the definition of $\sqsubseteq_\mathcal{G}$ extended to zones: $Z \sqsubseteq_\mathcal{G} Z'$ if for all $v \in Z$ there exists a $v' \in Z'$ such that $v \sqsubseteq_\mathcal{G} v'$. In this section, we will view the characterization of $\sqsubseteq_\mathcal{G}$ as in Proposition 1 and give an algorithm to check $Z \sqsubseteq_\mathcal{G} Z'$ that uses as an oracle a test $Z \sqsubseteq_{\mathcal{G}^-} Z'$. We discuss the computation of $Z \sqsubseteq_{\mathcal{G}^-} Z'$ later in this section. We start with an observation following from Proposition 1.

Lemma 3. *Let $\varphi := x - y \triangleleft c$ be a diagonal constraint in $\mathcal{G}$. Then $Z \sqsubseteq_\mathcal{G} Z'$ if and only if $Z \cap \varphi \sqsubseteq_{\mathcal{G}'} Z' \cap \varphi$ and $Z \cap \neg\varphi \sqsubseteq_{\mathcal{G}'} Z'$ where $\mathcal{G}' = \mathcal{G} \setminus \{\varphi\}$.*
If $\mathcal{G}$ has no diagonal constraints, $Z \sqsubseteq_\mathcal{G} Z'$ if and only if $Z \sqsubseteq_{\mathcal{G}^-} Z'$.

This leads to the following algorithm consisting of two mutually recursive procedures. This algorithm is essentially an implementation of the above lemma, with two optimizations:

- we start with the non-diagonal check in Line 6 of Algorithm 1 - if this is already violated, then the algorithm returns false;
- suppose $Z \sqsubseteq_{\mathcal{G}^-} Z'$, the next task is to perform the checks in the first statement of Lemma 3 - this is done by Algorithm 2; note however that when Algorithm 2 is called, we already have $Z \sqsubseteq_{\mathcal{G}^-} Z'$, hence $Z \cap \neg\varphi \sqsubseteq_{\mathcal{G}^-} Z'$. Therefore we use an optimization in Line 7 by calling Algorithm 2 directly (as the check in Line 6 of Algorithm 1 will be redundant).

Algorithm 1	Algorithm 2

1 check $Z \sqsubseteq_{\mathcal{G}} Z'$:
 2 **if** $Z = \emptyset$:
 3 $\lfloor$ **return** true
 4 **if** $Z' = \emptyset$:
 5 $\lfloor$ **return** false
 6 **if** $Z \not\sqsubseteq_{\mathcal{G}^-} Z'$:
 7 $\lfloor$ **return** false
 8 **return** $Z \sqsubseteq_{\mathcal{G}}^* Z'$
	1 check $Z \sqsubseteq_{\mathcal{G}}^* Z'$:
	 2 **if** $\mathcal{G}$ *does not contain any*
	     diagonal constraints :
	 3 $\lfloor$ **return** true
	 4 pick a diagonal constraint
	     $\varphi = x - y \lhd c$ from $\mathcal{G}$
	 5 $\mathcal{G}' \longleftarrow \mathcal{G} \setminus \{\varphi\}$
	 6 **if** $Z \cap \neg \varphi \neq \emptyset$:
	 7 **if** $Z \cap \neg \varphi \not\sqsubseteq_{\mathcal{G}'}^* Z'$:
	 8 $\lfloor$ **return** false
	 9 **return** $Z \cap \varphi \sqsubseteq_{\mathcal{G}'} Z' \cap \varphi$

Computing $Z \sqsubseteq_{\mathcal{G}^-} Z'$. We will use $\preccurlyeq_{LU}$ to approximate $\sqsubseteq_{\mathcal{G}^-}$: in our implementation of the above algorithms, we replace $Z \sqsubseteq_{\mathcal{G}^-} Z'$ with $Z \preccurlyeq_{LU} Z'$. This works because for an appropriate choice of LU (explained below), we have $Z \preccurlyeq_{LU(\mathcal{G})} Z' \Rightarrow Z \sqsubseteq_{\mathcal{G}^-} Z'$. The converse is not true as the LU bounds functions cannot distinguish between guards with $<$ and $\le$ comparisons. Therefore, the $\preccurlyeq_{LU}$ simulation does not characterize $v \sqsubseteq_{\mathcal{G}^-} v'$ completely. Although we are aware of the (rather technical) modifications to $\preccurlyeq_{LU}$ simulation that are needed for this characterization, we choose to use the existing $\preccurlyeq_{LU}$ directly as it is safe to do so and it has already been implemented in tools. This gives us a finer simulation than $v \sqsubseteq_{\mathcal{G}^-} v'$.

Definition 6 (LU-bounds from $\mathcal{G}$). *Let $\mathcal{G}$ be a finite set of constraints. We define $LU(\mathcal{G})$ to denote the pair of functions $L_{\mathcal{G}}$ and $U_{\mathcal{G}}$ defined as follows:*

$$L_{\mathcal{G}}(x) = \begin{cases} -\infty & \text{if there is no guard of the form } c \lhd x \text{ in } \mathcal{G} \\ \max\{c \mid c \lhd x \in \mathcal{G}\} & \text{otherwise} \end{cases}$$

$$U_{\mathcal{G}}(x) = \begin{cases} -\infty & \text{if there is no guard of the form } x \lhd c \text{ in } \mathcal{G} \\ \max\{c \mid x \lhd c \in \mathcal{G}\} & \text{otherwise} \end{cases}$$

Lemma 4. *For every set of constraints $\mathcal{G}$, $v \preccurlyeq_{LU(\mathcal{G})} v'$ implies $v \sqsubseteq_{\mathcal{G}^-} v'$.*

The above observations call for the next definition and subsequent lemmas.

Definition 7 (approximating $\sqsubseteq_{\mathcal{G}}$). *Let $\mathcal{G}$ be a finite set of constraints. We define a relation $\sqsubseteq_{\mathcal{G}}^{LU}$ as follows: $v \sqsubseteq_{\mathcal{G}}^{LU} v'$ if $v \preccurlyeq_{LU(\mathcal{G})} v'$ and for all diagonal constraints $\varphi \in \mathcal{G}$, if $v \models \varphi$ then $v' \models \varphi$. Similarly, define $\preccurlyeq_{\mathcal{A}}^{LU}$ as $(q, v) \preccurlyeq_{\mathcal{A}}^{LU} (q, v')$ if $v \sqsubseteq_{\mathcal{G}(q)}^{LU} v'$.*

Lemma 5. *The relation $\preccurlyeq_{\mathcal{A}}^{LU}$ is a finite simulation on the configurations of $\mathcal{A}$.*

The above lemma and the fact that $Z \preccurlyeq_{LU(\mathcal{G})} Z'$ can be checked in $\mathcal{O}(|X|^2)$ [23,33], imply the following theorem.

Theorem 3. *When using $Z \preccurlyeq_{LU(\mathcal{G})} Z'$ in the place of $Z \sqsubseteq_{\mathcal{G}^-} Z'$, the algorithm is correct and it terminates in $\mathcal{O}(2^d \cdot |X|^2)$ where d is the number of diagonal guards in $\mathcal{G}$.*

From a complexity viewpoint, this algorithm is not efficient since it makes an exponential number of calls in the number of diagonal constraints (in fact this may not be avoidable due to Lemma 6, which follows from the NP-hardness result in [18]). Although the above algorithm does involve many calls, the internal operations involved in each call are simple zone manipulations. Moreover, the preliminary checks (for instance line 6 of Algorithm 1) cut short the number of calls. This is visible in our experiments which are very good, especially with respect to running time, as compared to other methods. A similar hardness was shown for a different simulation in [18], but the implementation there indeed witnessed the hardness, as the time taken by that algorithm was unsatisfactory.

Lemma 6. *Deciding $Z \not\sqsubseteq_{\mathcal{G}}^{LU} Z'$ is NP-complete.*

5   Simulations for Updatable Timed Automata

In the timed automata considered so far, clocks are allowed to be reset to 0 along transitions. We consider in this section more sophisticated transformations to clocks in transitions. These are called *updates*. An update $up : \mathbb{R}_{\geq 0}^{|X|} \mapsto \mathbb{R}^{|X|}$ is a function mapping non-negative $|X|$-dimensional reals (valuations) v to general $|X|$-dimensional reals (which may apriori not be valuations as the coordinates may be negative). The syntax of the update function up is given by a set of atomic updates up_x to each $x \in X$, which are of the form $x := c$ or $x := y + d$ where $c \in \mathbb{N}$, $d \in \mathbb{Z}$ and $y \in X$ (possibly equal to x). Note that we want d to be an integer, since we allow for decrementing clocks, and on the other hand $c \in \mathbb{N}$ since we have non-negative clocks. Given a valuation v and an update up, the valuation $up(v)$ is:

$$up(v)(x) := \begin{cases} c & \text{if } up_x \text{ is } x := c \\ v(y) + d & \text{if } up_x \text{ is } x := y + d \end{cases}$$

Note that in general, due to the presence of updates $x := y+d$, the update $up(v)$ may not yield a clock valuation. However, when it does give a valuation, it can be used as a transformation in timed automata transitions. We say $up(v) \geq 0$ if $up(v)(x) \geq 0$ for all clocks $x \in X$.

An *updateable timed automaton (UTA)* $\mathcal{A} = (Q, X, q_0, T, F)$ is an extension of a classic timed automaton with transitions of the form (q, g, up, q') where up is an update. Semantics extend in the natural way: delay transitions remain the same, and for action transitions $t := (q, g, up, q')$ we have $(q, v) \xrightarrow{t} (q', v')$ if $v \models g$, $up(v) \geq 0$, and $v' = up(v)$. We allow the transition only if the update results in a valuation. The reachability problem for these automata is known to be undecidable in general [12]. Various subclasses with decidable reachability have been discussed in the same paper. Decidability proofs in [12] take the following flavour, for a given automaton $\mathcal{A}$: (1) divide the space of all valuations into a finite number of equivalence classes called *regions* (2) to build the parameters for the equivalence, derive a set of diophantine equations from the guards of $\mathcal{A}$; if they have a solution then construct the quotient graph of the equivalence (called region graph) parameterized by the obtained solution and check reachability on it; if the equations have no solution, output that reachability for $\mathcal{A}$ cannot be answered. Sufficient conditions on the nature of the updates that give a solution to the diophantine equations have been tabulated in [12]. When the automaton is diagonal-free, the "region-equivalence" can be used to build an extrapolation operation which in turn can be used in a reachability algorithm with zones. When the automaton contains diagonals, the region-equivalence is used to only build a region graph - no effective zone based approach has been studied.

We use a similar idea, but we have two fundamental differences: (1) we want to obtain reachability through the use of simulations on zones, and (2) we build equations over sets of guards as in Definition 4. The advantage of this approach is that this allows the use of coarser simulations over zones. Even for automata with diagonal constraints and updates, we get a zone based algorithm, instead of resorting to regions which are not efficient in practice.

The notion of simulations as in p. xx remains the same, now using the semantics of transitions with updates. We will re-use the simulation relation $\sqsubseteq_{\mathcal{G}}$. We need to extend Definition 3 to incorporate updates. We do this below. Here is a notation: for an update function up, we write $up(x)$ to be c if up_x is $x := c$, and $up(x)$ to be $y + c$ if up_x is $x := y + c$.

Definition 8 (weakest pre-condition of $\sqsubseteq_{\mathcal{G}}$ over updates).
Let up be an update.

For a constraint φ of the form $x \lhd c$ or $c \lhd x$, we define $\mathrm{wp}(\sqsubseteq_{\varphi}, up)$ to be respectively $\{up(x) \lhd c\}$ or $\{c \lhd up(x)\}$ if these resulting constraints are of the form $z \lhd d$ or $d \lhd z$ with $z \in X$ and $d \geq 0$, otherwise $\mathrm{wp}(\sqsubseteq_{\varphi}, up)$ is empty.

For a constraint $\varphi : x - y \lhd c$, we define $\mathrm{wp}(\sqsubseteq_{\varphi}, up)$ to be $\{up(x) - up(y) \lhd c\}$ if this constraint is either a diagonal using different clocks, or it is of the form $z \lhd d$ or $d \lhd z$ with $d \geq 0$, otherwise $\mathrm{wp}(\sqsubseteq_{\varphi}, up)$ is empty.

For a set of guards $\mathcal{G}$, we define $\mathrm{wp}(\sqsubseteq_{\mathcal{G}}, up) := \bigcup_{\varphi \in \mathcal{G}} \mathrm{wp}(\sqsubseteq_{\varphi}, up)$.

Some examples: $\mathrm{wp}(x \leq 5, x := x + 10)$ is empty, since $up(x)$ is $x + 10$, and the guard $x + 10 \leq 5$ is not satisfiable; $\mathrm{wp}(x \leq 5, x := x - 10)$ is $x \leq 15$, $\mathrm{wp}(x \leq 5, x := c)$ is empty, $\mathrm{wp}(x - y \leq 5, \langle x := z_1, y := z_2 + 10\rangle)$ will be $z_1 - (z_2 + 10) \leq 5$, giving the constraint $z_1 - z_2 \leq 15$, $\mathrm{wp}(x - y \leq 5, \langle x := z + c_1, y := z + c_2\rangle)$ is empty, $\mathrm{wp}(x - y \leq 5, \langle x := c_1, y := z + c_2\rangle)$ is $c = c_1 - 5 - c_2 \leq z$ if $c \geq 0$ and is empty otherwise.

Definition 9 (State based guards). *Let $\mathcal{A} = (Q, X, q_0, T, F)$ be a UTA. We associate a set of constraints $\mathcal{G}(q)$ for each state $q \in Q$, which is the least set of constraints (for the coordinate-wise subset inclusion order) such that for* *every transition* (q, g, up, q_1): *the guard* g *and the set* $\mathrm{wp}(\sqsubseteq_{\mathcal{G}(q_1)}, up)$ *are present in* $\mathcal{G}(q)$, *and in addition constraints that allow the update to happen are also present in* $\mathcal{G}$. *The last condition is given by the weakest precondition of the set of constraints* $\{x \geq 0 \mid x \in X\}$. *Overall,* $\{\mathcal{G}(q)\}_{q \in Q}$ *is the least solution to the following set of equations, for each* $q \in Q$:

$$\mathcal{G}(q) = \bigcup_{(q,g,up,q_1) \in T} \left(\{g\} \cup \mathrm{wp}(\sqsubseteq_{\{x \geq 0 \mid x \in X\}}, up) \cup \mathrm{wp}(\sqsubseteq_{\mathcal{G}(q_1)}, up) \right)$$

The least solution $\{\mathcal{G}(q)\}_{q \in Q}$ *is said to be finite if each* $\mathcal{G}(q)$ *is a finite set of constraints.*

In contrast to the simple reset case, the above set of equations may not have a finite solution. Consider a self-looping transition: $(q, x \triangleleft c, x := x - 1, q)$. We require $x \triangleleft c \in \mathcal{G}(q)$. Now, $\mathrm{wp}(x \triangleleft c, x := x - 1)$ is $x \triangleleft c + 1$ which should be in $\mathcal{G}(q)$ according to the above equation. Continuing this process, we need to add $x \triangleleft d$ for every natural number $d \geq c$. Indeed this is consistent with the undecidability of reachability when subtraction updates are allowed. We deal with the subject of finite solutions to the above equations later in this section. On the other hand, when the above system does have a solution with finite $\mathcal{G}(q)$ at every q, we can use the $\mathcal{A}$ simulation of Definition 5 and its approximation $\preccurlyeq_{\mathcal{A}}^{LU}$ to get an algorithm.

Proposition 2. *Let* $\mathcal{A} = (Q, X, q_0, T, F)$ *be a UTA. Let* $\{\mathcal{G}(q)\}_{q \in Q}$ *be the least solution to the equations given in Definition 9. Then, the relation* $\preccurlyeq_{\mathcal{A}}$ *is a simulation on the configurations of* $\mathcal{A}$.

Lemma 7. *For a UTA* $\mathcal{A}$, *assume that the least solution* $\{\mathcal{G}(q)\}_{q \in Q}$ *to the state-based guards equations is finite. Then the relation* $\preccurlyeq_{\mathcal{A}}^{LU}$ *is a finite simulation on the configurations of* $\mathcal{A}$.

Finite Solution to the State-Based Guards Equations. The least solution to the equations of Definition 9 can be obtained by a standard Kleene iteration for fixed points computation. For each $i \geq 0$ and each state q, define:

$$\mathcal{G}^0(q) = \bigcup_{(q,g,up,q') \in T} \{g\} \cup \mathrm{wp}(\sqsubseteq_{\{x \geq 0 \mid x \in X\}}, up)$$

$$\mathcal{G}^{i+1}(q) = \bigcup_{(q,g,up,q') \in T} \mathcal{G}^i(q) \cup \mathrm{wp}(\sqsubseteq_{\mathcal{G}^i(q')}, up)$$

The iteration stabilizes when there exists a k satisfying $\mathcal{G}^{k+1}(q) = \mathcal{G}^k(q)$ for all q. At stabilization, the values $\mathcal{G}^k(q)$ satisfy the equations of Definition 9, and give the required $\mathcal{G}(q)$. However, as we mentioned earlier, this iteration might not stabilize at any k. We will now develop some observations that will help detect after finitely many steps if the iteration will stabilize or not.

Suppose we colour the set $\mathcal{G}^{i+1}(q)$ to *red* if either there exists a diagonal constraint $x - y \triangleleft c \in \mathcal{G}^{i+1}(q) \setminus \mathcal{G}^i(q)$ (a new diagonal is added) or there exists a non-diagonal constraint $x \triangleleft c$ or $c \triangleleft x$ in $\mathcal{G}^{i+1}(q) \setminus \mathcal{G}^i(q)$ such that the constant c is strictly bigger than c' for respectively every non-diagonal $x \triangleleft c'$ or $c' \triangleleft x$ in $\mathcal{G}^i(q)$ (a non-diagonal with a bigger constant is added). If this condition is not applicable, we colour the set $\mathcal{G}^{i+1}(q)$ *green*. The next observations say that the iteration terminates iff we reach a stage where all sets are green. Intuitively, once we reach green, the only constraints that can be added are non-diagonals having smaller (non-negative) constants and hence the procedure terminates.

Lemma 8. *Let $i > 0$. If $\mathcal{G}^i(q)$ is green for all q, then $\mathcal{G}^{i+1}(q)$ is green for all q.*

Lemma 9. *Let $K = 1 + |Q| \cdot |X| \cdot (|X| + 1)$. If there is a state p such that $\mathcal{G}^K(p)$ is red, then there is no i such that $\mathcal{G}^i(q)$ is green for all q.*

As to why the bound $K = 1 + |Q| \cdot |X| \cdot (|X| + 1)$ in the lemma above: a red state at stage i arises due to the addition of a constraint φ_i at state p_i, which in turn depends on a state p_{i-1} marked red at stage $i - 1$ due to constraint φ_{i-1}. If we iterate sufficiently long, we will hit a state p, a sequence of transitions from p to p and a constraint φ such that computing the weakest precondition over this loop will give a new constraint with the same set of clocks as φ but with a different constant. This part can be iterated infinitely often.

Proposition 3. *The least solution of the local constraint equations for a UTA is finite iff $\mathcal{G}^K(q)$ is green for all q and where $K = 1 + |Q| \cdot |X| \cdot (|X| + 1)$.*

Theorem 4. *Let $\mathcal{A}$ be a UTA. It is decidable whether the equations in Definition 9 have a finite solution. When these equations do have a finite solution, zone graph enumeration using $\preccurlyeq_{\mathcal{A}}^{LU}$ is a sound, complete and terminating procedure for the reachability problem.*

All decidable classes of [12] can be shown decidable with our approach, by showing stabilization of the $\mathcal{G}(q)$ computation.

Lemma 10. *Reachability is decidable in UTA where: guards are non-diagonals and updates are of the form $x := c$, $x := y$, $x := y + c$ where $c \geq 0$ or, guards include diagonal constraints and updates are of the form $x := c$, $x := y$.*

6   Experiments

We have implemented the reachability algorithm for timed automata with diagonal constraints (and only resets as updates) based on the simulation approach (p. xx) using the $\preccurlyeq_{\mathcal{A}}^{LU}$ simulation (Definition 7) for pruning zones. The algorithm for $Z \sqsubseteq_{\mathcal{G}}^{LU} Z'$ comes from Sect. 4. Experiments are reported in Table 1. We take model *Cex* from [8,30] and *Fischer* from [30]. We are not aware of any other "standard" benchmarks containing diagonal constraints. In addition to these two models, we introduce a new benchmark. This is an extension of the job-shop scheduling using (diagonal-free) timed automata [1]. Here the tasks within a job were logically independent. We add some timing dependency between them

Table 1. Experiments: the column $\#\mathcal{D}$ gives the number of diagonal constraints. Four methods have been reported in the table. First two methods, TChecker with our simulation relation $\sqsubseteq_{\mathcal{G}}^{LU}$ and UPPAAL engine for diagonals, have been run on $\mathcal{A}$, the automata containing diagonal constraints. Whereas, the third and fourth methods are running diagonal-free engines of UPPAAL and TChecker on $\mathcal{A}_{df}$, a diagonal-free equivalent of $\mathcal{A}$. Experiments were run on macOS X with 2.3 GHz Intel core i5 processor, and 8 GB RAM. Time is reported in seconds. We set a timeout of 15 min.

Model	$\#\mathcal{D}$	$\mathcal{A}$: contains diagonals				$\mathcal{A}_{df}$: diagonal-free *equivalent* of $\mathcal{A}$			
		TChecker + $\sqsubseteq_{\mathcal{G}}^{LU}$		UPPAAL		UPPAAL		TChecker	
		Time	Nodes count	Time	Nodes count	Time	Nodes count	Time	Nodes count
Cex 2	4	0.047	241	0.026	2180	0.005	1039	0.067	1039
Cex 3	6	7.399	7111	111.168	182394	1.028	60982	40.092	60982
Cex 4	8	857.662	185209	Timeout	-	734.543	3447119	Timeout	-
Fischer 4	4	0.032	452	307.836	357687	0.009	1815	0.100	1815
Fischer 5	5	0.257	1842	Timeout	-	0.116	12511	1.856	12511
Fischer 7	7	15.032	26812	Timeout	-	174.560	693603	Timeout	-
Job Shop 3	12	0.420	278	23.093	31711	0.003	845	0.312	845
Job Shop 5	20	285.421	10592	Timeout	-	4.633	179607	150.811	179607

which gets naturally modeled using diagonal constraints. Each model considered above is a product of a number of k timed automata. In the table we write the name of the model and the number k of automata involved in the product. We also report the number of diagonal constraints in each of them.

Experimental Results. We report the results of four methods of handling diagonal constraints, as mentioned in the caption of Table 1. Under each method, we report on the number of zones enumerated and the time taken. The first method gives a huge gain over the second one (upto four orders of magnitude in the number of nodes, and even better for time) and gives a less marked, but still significant, gain over the third and fourth methods. We provide a brief explanation of this phenomenon. The performance of the reachability algorithm is dependent on three factors:

- parameters of extrapolation or simulation: M-simulations which use the maximum constant appearing in the guards, versus the LU-simulations which make a distinction between lower bound guards $c \lhd x$ and upper bound guards $x \lhd c$ (refer to [5] for the exact definitions of extrapolations based on these parameters, and [23] for simulations based on these parameters); LU-simulations are superior to M-simulations.
- computation of the parameters: global parameters which associate a bound to each clock versus the more local state based parameters as in Definition 4 which associate a set of bounds functions to each state [4]; local bounds are superior to global bounds.
- when diagonal constraints are present, whether zones get split or not: each time a zone gets split, new enumerations start from each of the new nodes; clearly, a no-splitting-of-zones approach is superior to zone splitting.

Algorithm of column 1 uses the superior heuristic in all the three optimizations above. The no-splitting-of-zones was possible thanks to our simulation approach, which temporarily splits zones for checking $Z \sqsubseteq_{\mathcal{G}}^{LU} Z'$, but never starts a new exploration from any of the split nodes. The algorithm of column 2, which is implemented in the current version UPPAAL 4.1 uses the inferior heuristic in all the three above. In particular, it is not clear how the extrapolation approach can avoid the zone splitting in an efficient manner. The superiority of our approach gets amplified (by multiplicative factors) when we consider bigger products with many more diagonals. In the third and fourth methods, we give a diagonal free equivalent of the original model (c.f. Theorem 1) and use the UPPAAL and TChecker engines respectively, for diagonal free timed automata. The UPPAAL diagonal free engine is highly optimized, and makes use of the superior heuristics in the first two optimizations mentioned above (the third heuristic is not applicable now as it is a diagonal free automaton). The third and fourth methods can be considered as a good approximation of the zone splitting approach to diagonal constraints using LU-abstractions and local guards.

The second and the third methods are the only possibilities of verifying timed models coming with diagonal constraints in UPPAAL. Both these approaches are in principle prone to a $2^{\#\mathcal{D}}$ blowup compared to the first approach, where $\#\mathcal{D}$ gives the number of diagonal constraints. The table shows that a good extent of this blowup indeed happens. The UPPAAL diagonal free engine uses "minimal constraint systems" [6] for representing zones, whereas TChecker uses DBMs [15]. This explains why even with the same number of nodes visited, UPPAAL performs better in terms of time. We have not included in the table the comparison with two other works dealing with the same problem: the refined diagonal free conversion [30] and the extension of LU simulation for diagonals [18]. However, our results are better than the tables reported in these papers.

7   Conclusion

We have proposed a new algorithm for handling diagonal constraints in timed automata, and extended it to automata with general updates. Our approach is based on a simulation relation between zones. From our preliminary experiments, we can infer that the use of simulations is indispensable in the presence of diagonal constraints as zone-splitting can be avoided. Moreover, the fact that the simulation approach stores the actual zones (as opposed to abstracted zones in the extrapolation approach) has enabled optimizations for diagonal-free automata that work with dynamically changing simulation parameters (LU-bounds), which are learnt as and when the zones are expanded [22]. Working with actual zones is also convenient for finding cost-optimal paths in priced timed automata [11]. Investigating these in the presence of diagonal constraints is part of future work. Currently, we have not implemented our approach for updateable timed automata. This will also be part of our future work.

Working directly with a model containing diagonal constraints could be convenient (both during modeling, and during extraction of diagnostic traces) and can also potentially give a smaller automaton to begin with. We believe that our experiments provide hope that diagonal constraints can indeed be used.

References

1. Abdeddaim, Y., Asarin, E., Maler, O.: Scheduling with timed automata. Theor. Comput. Sci. **354**(2), 272–300 (2006). https://doi.org/10.1016/j.tcs.2005.11.018
2. Alur, R., Dill, D.L.: A theory of timed automata. Theor. Comput. Sci. **126**(2), 183–235 (1994). https://doi.org/10.1016/0304-3975(94)90010-8
3. Amnell, T., Fersman, E., Mokrushin, L., Pettersson, P., Yi, W.: TIMES b— a tool for modelling and implementation of embedded systems. In: Katoen, J.-P., Stevens, P. (eds.) TACAS 2002. LNCS, vol. 2280, pp. 460–464. Springer, Heidelberg (2002). https://doi.org/10.1007/3-540-46002-0_32
4. Behrmann, G., Bouyer, P., Fleury, E., Larsen, K.G.: Static guard analysis in timed automata verification. In: Garavel, H., Hatcliff, J. (eds.) TACAS 2003. LNCS, vol. 2619, pp. 254–270. Springer, Heidelberg (2003). https://doi.org/10.1007/3-540-36577-X_18
5. Behrmann, G., Bouyer, P., Larsen, K.G., Pelánek, R.: Lower and upper bounds in zone-based abstractions of timed automata. STTT **8**(3), 204–215 (2006). https://doi.org/10.1007/s10009-005-0190-0
6. Bengtsson, J., Yi, W.: Timed automata: semantics, algorithms and tools. In: Desel, J., Reisig, W., Rozenberg, G. (eds.) ACPN 2003. LNCS, vol. 3098, pp. 87–124. Springer, Heidelberg (2004). https://doi.org/10.1007/978-3-540-27755-2_3
7. Bérard, B., Petit, A., Diekert, V., Gastin, P.: Characterization of the expressive power of silent transitions in timed automata. Fundamenta Informaticae **36**(2,3), 145–182 (1998). https://doi.org/10.3233/FI-1998-36233
8. Bouyer, P.: Untameable timed automata!. In: Alt, H., Habib, M. (eds.) STACS 2003. LNCS, vol. 2607, pp. 620–631. Springer, Heidelberg (2003). https://doi.org/10.1007/3-540-36494-3_54
9. Bouyer, P.: Forward analysis of updatable timed automata. Form. Methods Syst. Des. **24**(3), 281–320 (2004). https://doi.org/10.1023/B:FORM.0000026093.21513.31
10. Bouyer, P., Chevalier, F.: On conciseness of extensions of timed automata. J. Autom. Lang. Comb. **10**(4), 393–405 (2005). https://doi.org/10.25596/jalc-2005-393
11. Bouyer, P., Colange, M., Markey, N.: Symbolic optimal reachability in weighted timed automata. In: Chaudhuri, S., Farzan, A. (eds.) CAV 2016. LNCS, vol. 9779, pp. 513–530. Springer, Cham (2016). https://doi.org/10.1007/978-3-319-41528-4_28
12. Bouyer, P., Dufourd, C., Fleury, E., Petit, A.: Updatable timed automata. Theor. Comput. Sci. **321**(2–3), 291–345 (2004). https://doi.org/10.1016/j.tcs.2004.04.003
13. Bouyer, P., Laroussinie, F., Reynier, P.-A.: Diagonal constraints in timed automata: forward analysis of timed systems. In: Pettersson, P., Yi, W. (eds.) FORMATS 2005. LNCS, vol. 3829, pp. 112–126. Springer, Heidelberg (2005). https://doi.org/10.1007/11603009_10
14. Daws, C., Tripakis, S.: Model checking of real-time reachability properties using abstractions. In: Steffen, B. (ed.) TACAS 1998. LNCS, vol. 1384, pp. 313–329. Springer, Heidelberg (1998). https://doi.org/10.1007/BFb0054180

15. Dill, D.L.: Timing assumptions and verification of finite-state concurrent systems. In: Sifakis, J. (ed.) CAV 1989. LNCS, vol. 407, pp. 197–212. Springer, Heidelberg (1990). https://doi.org/10.1007/3-540-52148-8_17

16. Ferrère, T.: The compound interest in relaxing punctuality. In: Havelund, K., Peleska, J., Roscoe, B., de Vink, E. (eds.) FM 2018. LNCS, vol. 10951, pp. 147–164. Springer, Cham (2018). https://doi.org/10.1007/978-3-319-95582-7_9

17. Fersman, E., Pettersson, P., Yi, W.: Timed automata with asynchronous processes: schedulability and decidability. In: Katoen, J.-P., Stevens, P. (eds.) TACAS 2002. LNCS, vol. 2280, pp. 67–82. Springer, Heidelberg (2002). https://doi.org/10.1007/3-540-46002-0_6

18. Gastin, P., Mukherjee, S., Srivathsan, B.: Reachability in timed automata with diagonal constraints. In: Schewe, S., Zhang, L. (eds.) CONCUR 2018. Leibniz International Proceedings in Informatics (LIPIcs), vol. 118, pp. 28:1–28:17. Schloss Dagstuhl - Leibniz-Zentrum fuer Informatik, Dagstuhl, Germany (2018). https://doi.org/10.4230/LIPIcs.CONCUR.2018.28

19. Gastin, P., Mukherjee, S., Srivathsan, B.: Fast algorithms for handling diagonal constraints in timed automata. CoRR abs/1904.08590 (2019). http://arxiv.org/abs/1904.08590

20. Hatvani, L., David, A., Seceleanu, C., Pettersson, P.: Adaptive task automata with earliest-deadline-first scheduling. In: Proceedings of the 14th International Workshop on Automated Verification of Critical Systems (AVoCS 2014), vol. 70. Electronic Communications of the EASST (2014). https://doi.org/10.14279/tuj.eceasst.70.975

21. Herbreteau, F., Point, G.: TChecker, April 2019 https://github.com/fredher/tchecker (v02)

22. Herbreteau, F., Srivathsan, B., Walukiewicz, I.: Lazy abstractions for timed automata. In: Sharygina, N., Veith, H. (eds.) CAV 2013. LNCS, vol. 8044, pp. 990–1005. Springer, Heidelberg (2013). https://doi.org/10.1007/978-3-642-39799-8_71

23. Herbreteau, F., Srivathsan, B., Walukiewicz, I.: Better abstractions for timed automata. Inf. Comput. **251**, 67–90 (2016). https://doi.org/10.1016/j.ic.2016.07.004

24. Herbreteau, F., Tran, T.-T.: Improving search order for reachability testing in timed automata. In: Sankaranarayanan, S., Vicario, E. (eds.) FORMATS 2015. LNCS, vol. 9268, pp. 124–139. Springer, Cham (2015). https://doi.org/10.1007/978-3-319-22975-1_9

25. Ho, H.: Revisiting timed logics with automata modalities. In: Proceedings of the 22nd ACM International Conference on Hybrid Systems: Computation and Control, HSCC 2019, pp. 67–76. ACM, New York (2019). https://doi.org/10.1145/3302504.3311818

26. Kant, G., Laarman, A., Meijer, J., van de Pol, J., Blom, S., van Dijk, T.: LTSmin: high-performance language-independent model checking. In: Baier, C., Tinelli, C. (eds.) TACAS 2015. LNCS, vol. 9035, pp. 692–707. Springer, Heidelberg (2015). https://doi.org/10.1007/978-3-662-46681-0_61

27. Krčál, P., Yi, W.: Decidable and undecidable problems in schedulability analysis using timed automata. In: Jensen, K., Podelski, A. (eds.) TACAS 2004. LNCS, vol. 2988, pp. 236–250. Springer, Heidelberg (2004). https://doi.org/10.1007/978-3-540-24730-2_20

28. Larsen, K.G., Pettersson, P., Yi, W.: UPPAAL in a nutshell. STTT **1**(1–2), 134–152 (1997). https://doi.org/10.1007/s100090050010

29. Ponge, J., Benatallah, B., Casati, F., Toumani, F.: Analysis and applications of timed service protocols. ACM Trans. Softw. Eng. Methodol. **19**(4), 11:1–11:38 (2010). https://doi.org/10.1145/1734229.1734230
30. Reynier, P.A.: Diagonal constraints handled efficiently in UPPAAL. In: Research report LSV-07-02. Laboratoire Spécification et Vérification, ENS Cachan, France (2007)
31. Wang, F.: Efficient verification of timed automata with BDD-like data structures. Int. J. Softw. Tools Technol. Transf. **6**(1), 77–97 (2004). https://doi.org/10.1007/s10009-003-0135-4
32. Yovine, S.: Kronos: a verification tool for real-time systems. (Kronos user's manual release 2.2). STTT **1**, 123–133 (1997). https://doi.org/10.1007/s100090050009
33. Zhao, J., Li, X., Zheng, G.: A quadratic-time dbm-based successor algorithm for checking timed automata. Inf. Process. Lett. **96**(3), 101–105 (2005). https://doi.org/10.1016/j.ipl.2005.05.027

2

Security-Aware Synthesis Using Delayed-Action Games

Mahmoud Elfar$^{(\boxtimes)}$ ⓘ, Yu Wang ⓘ, and Miroslav Pajic ⓘ

Duke University, Durham, NC 27708, USA
{mahmoud.elfar,yu.wang094,miroslav.pajic}@duke.edu

Abstract. Stochastic multiplayer games (SMGs) have gained attention in the field of strategy synthesis for multi-agent reactive systems. However, standard SMGs are limited to modeling systems where all agents have full knowledge of the state of the game. In this paper, we introduce delayed-action games (DAGs) formalism that simulates hidden-information games (HIGs) as SMGs, where hidden information is captured by delaying a player's actions. The elimination of private variables enables the usage of SMG off-the-shelf model checkers to implement HIGs. Furthermore, we demonstrate how a DAG can be decomposed into subgames that can be independently explored, utilizing parallel computation to reduce the model checking time, while alleviating the state space explosion problem that SMGs are notorious for. In addition, we propose a DAG-based framework for strategy synthesis and analysis. Finally, we demonstrate applicability of the DAG-based synthesis framework on a case study of a human-on-the-loop unmanned-aerial vehicle system under stealthy attacks, where the proposed framework is used to formally model, analyze and synthesize security-aware strategies for the system.

1 Introduction

Stochastic multiplayer games (SMGs) are used to model reactive systems where nondeterministic decisions are made by multiple players [4,13,23]. SMGs extend probabilistic automata by assigning a player to each choice to be made in the game. This extension enables modeling of complex systems where the behavior of players is unknown at design time. The *strategy synthesis* problem aims to find a *winning strategy*, i.e., a strategy that guarantees that a set of objectives (or winning conditions) is satisfied [6,21]. Algorithms for synthesis include, for instance, value iteration and strategy iteration techniques, where multiple reward-based objectives are satisfied [2,9,17]. To tackle the state-space explosion problem, [29] presents an *assume-guarantee* synthesis framework that relies on synthesizing strategies on the component level first, before composing them into a global winning strategy. Mean-payoffs and ratio rewards are further investigated in [3] to synthesize ε-optimal strategies. Formal tools that support strategy synthesis via SMGs include PRISM-games [7,19] and Uppaal Stratego [10].

SMGs are classified based on the number of players that can make choices at each state. In *concurrent* games, more than one player is allowed to concurrently make choices at a given state. Conversely, *turn-based* games assign one player at most to each state. Another classification considers the information available to different players across the game [27]. *Complete-information* games (also known as *perfect-information* games [5]) grant all players complete access to the information within the game. In *symmetric* games, some information is equally hidden from all players. On the contrary, *asymmetric* games allow some players to have access to more information than the others [27].

This work is motivated by security-aware systems in which stealthy adversarial actions are potentially hidden from the system, where the latter can probabilistically and intermittently gain full knowledge about the current state. While hidden-information games (HIGs) can be used to model such systems by using private variables to capture hidden information [5], standard model checkers can only synthesize strategies for (full-information) SMGs; thus, demanding for alternative representations. The equivalence between turn-based semi-perfect information games and concurrent perfect-information games was shown [5]. Since a player's strategy mainly rely on full knowledge of the game state [9], using SMGs for synthesis produces strategies that may violate synthesis specifications in cases where required information is hidden from the player. *Partially-observable* stochastic games (POSGs) allow agents to have different belief states by incorporating uncertainty about both the current state and adversarial plans [15]. Techniques such as active sensing for online replanning [14] and grid-based abstractions of belief spaces [24] were proposed to mitigate synthesis complexity arising from partial observability. The notion of *delaying actions* has been studied as means for gaining information about a game to improve future strategies [18,30], but was not deployed as means for hiding information.

To this end, we introduce delayed-action games (DAGs)—a new class of games that simulate HIGs, where information is hidden from one player by delaying the actions of the others. The omission of private variables enables the use of off-the-shelf tools to implement and analyze DAG-based models. We show how DAGs (under some mild and practical assumptions) can be decomposed into subgames that can be independently explored, reducing the time required for synthesis by employing parallel computation. Moreover, we propose a DAG-based framework for strategy synthesis and analysis of security-aware systems. Finally, we demonstrate the framework's applicability through a case study of security-aware planning for an unmanned-aerial vehicle (UAV) system prone to stealthy cyber attacks, where we develop a DAG-based system model and further synthesize strategies with strong probabilistic security guarantees.

The paper is organized as follows. Section 2 presents SMGs, HIGs, and problem formulation. In Sect. 3, we introduce DAGs and show that they can simulate HIGs. Section 4 proposes a DAG-based synthesis framework, which we use for security-aware planning for UAVs in Sect. 5, before concluding the paper in Sect. 6.

2   Stochastic Games

In this section, we present turn-based stochastic games, which assume that all players have full information about the game state. We then introduce hidden-information games and their private-variable semantics.

Notation. We use $\mathbb{N}_0$ to denote the set of non-negative integers. $\mathcal{P}(A)$ denotes the powerset of A (i.e., 2^A). A variable v has a set of valuations $Ev\,(v)$, where $\eta\,(v) \in Ev\,(v)$ denotes one. We use Σ^* to denote the set of all finite words over alphabet Σ, including the empty word ϵ. The mapping $E\!f\!f : \Sigma^* \times Ev\,(v) \to Ev\,(v)$ indicates the effect of a finite word on $\eta\,(v)$. Finally, for general indexing, we use s_i or $s^{(i)}$, for $i \in \mathbb{N}_0$, while PL_γ denotes *Player γ*.

Turn-Based Stochastic Games (SMGs). SMGs can be used to model reactive systems that undergo both stochastic and nondeterministic transitions from one state to another. In a *turn-based* game,[1] actions can be taken at any state by at most one player. Formally, an SMG can be defined as follows [1,28,29].

Definition 1 (Turn-Based Stochastic Game). *A turn-based game (SMG) with players $\Gamma = \{\mathrm{I}, \mathrm{II}, \bigcirc\}$ is a tuple $\mathcal{G} = \langle S, (S_\mathrm{I}, S_\mathrm{II}, S_\bigcirc), A, s_0, \delta \rangle$, where*

- *S is a finite set of states, partitioned into S_I, S_II and $S_\bigcirc$;*
- *$A = A_\mathrm{I} \cup A_\mathrm{II} \cup \{\tau\}$ is a finite set of actions where τ is an empty action;*
- *$s_0 \in S_\mathrm{II}$ is the initial state; and*
- *$\delta : S \times A \times S \to [0,1]$ is a transition function, such that $\delta(s,a,s') \in \{1,0\}$, $\forall s \in S_\mathrm{I} \cup S_\mathrm{II}, a \in A$ and $s' \in S$, and $\delta(s,\tau,s') \in [0,1]$, $\forall s \in S_\bigcirc$ and $s' \in S_\mathrm{I} \cup S_\mathrm{II}$, where $\sum_{s' \in S_\mathrm{I} \cup S_\mathrm{II}} \delta(s,\tau,s') = 1$ holds.*

For all $s \in S_\mathrm{I} \cup S_\mathrm{II}$ and $a \in A_\mathrm{I} \cup A_\mathrm{II}$, we write $s \xrightarrow{a} s'$ if $\delta(s,a,s') = 1$. Similarly, for all $s \in S_\bigcirc$ we write $s \xrightarrow{p} s'$ if s' is randomly sampled with probability $p = \delta(s,\tau,s')$.

Hidden-Information Games. SMGs assume that all players have full knowledge of the current state, and hence provide *perfect-information* models [5]. In many applications, however, this assumption may not hold. A great example are security-aware models where stealthy adversarial actions can be hidden from the system; e.g., the system may not even be aware that it is under attack. On the other hand, *hidden-information* games (HIGs) refer to games where one player does not have complete access to (or knowledge of) the current state. The notion of hidden information can be formalized with the use of *private variables* (PVs) [5]. Specifically, a game state can be encoded using variables v_T and v_B, representing the true information, which is only known to PL_I, and PL_II belief, respectively.

---

[1] The term *turn-based* indicates that at any state only one player can play an action. It does not necessarily imply that players take fair turns.

Definition 2 (Hidden-Information Game). *A hidden-information stochastic game (HIG) with players $\Gamma = \{\text{I}, \text{II}, \bigcirc\}$ over a set of variables $V = \{v_T, v_B\}$ is a tuple $\mathcal{G}_H = \langle S, (S_I, S_{II}, S_{\bigcirc}), A, s_0, \beta, \delta \rangle$, where*

- *set of states $S \subseteq Ev(v_T) \times Ev(v_B) \times \mathcal{P}(Ev(v_T)) \times \Gamma$, partitioned in $S_I, S_{II}, S_{\bigcirc}$;*
- *$A = A_I \cup A_{II} \cup \{\tau, \theta\}$ is a finite set of actions, where τ denotes an empty action, and θ is the action capturing PL_{II} attempt to reveal the true value v_T;*
- *$s_0 \in S_{II}$ is the initial state;*
- *$\beta \colon A_{II} \to \mathcal{P}(A_I)$ is a function that defines the set of available PL_I actions, based on PL_{II} action; and*
- *$\delta \colon S \times A \times S \to [0,1]$ is a transition function such that $\delta(s_I, a, s_{\bigcirc}) = \delta(s_{\bigcirc}, a, s_I) = 0$, and $\delta(s_{II}, \theta, s_{\bigcirc})$, $\delta(s_{II}, a, s_I)$, $\delta(s_I, a, s_{II}) \in \{0,1\}$ for all $s_I \in S_I$, $s_{II} \in S_{II}$, $s_{\bigcirc} \in S_{\bigcirc}$ and $a \in A$, where $\sum_{s' \in S_{II}} \delta(s_{\bigcirc}, \tau, s') = 1$.*

In the above definition, δ only allows transitions s_I to s_{II}, s_{II} to s_I or $s_{\bigcirc}$, with s_{II} to $s_{\bigcirc}$ conditioned by action θ, and probabilistic transitions $s_{\bigcirc}$ to s_{II}. A game state can be written as $s = (t, u, \Omega, \gamma)$, but to simplify notation we use $s_\gamma(t, u, \Omega)$ instead, where $t \in Ev(v_T)$ is the *true* value of the game, $u \in Ev(v_B)$ is PL_{II} current *belief*, $\Omega \in \mathcal{P}(Ev(v_T)) \setminus \{\emptyset\}$ is PL_{II} *belief space*, and $\gamma \in \Gamma$ is the current player's index. When the truth is hidden from PL_{II}, the belief space Ω is the *information set* [27], capturing PL_{II} knowledge about the possible true values.

Example 1 (Belief vs. True Value). Our motivating example is a system that consists of a UAV and a human operator. For localization, the UAV mainly relies on a GPS sensor that can be compromised to effectively steer the UAV away from its original path. While aggressive attacks can be detected, some may remain stealthy by introducing only bounded errors at each

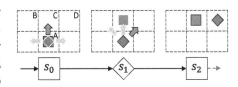

Fig. 1. The UAV belief (solid square) vs. the true value (solid diamond) of its location.

step [16, 20, 22, 26]. For example, Fig. 1 shows a UAV (PL_{II}) occupying zone A and flying north (N). An adversary (PL_I) can launch a stealthy attack targeting its GPS, introducing a bounded error (NE, NW) to remain stealthy. The set of stealthy actions available to the attacker depends on the preceding UAV action, which is captured by the function β, where $\beta(\mathsf{N}) = \{\mathsf{NE}, \mathsf{N}, \mathsf{NW}\}$. Being unaware of the attack, the UAV believes that it is entering zone C, while the true new location is D due to the attack (NE). Initially, $\eta(v_T) = \eta(v_B) = z_A$, and $\Omega = \{z_A\}$ as the UAV is certain it is in zone z_A. In s_2, $\eta(v_B) = z_C$, yet $\eta(v_T) = z_D$. Although v_T is hidden, PL_{II} is aware that $\eta(v_T)$ is in $\Omega = \{z_B, z_C, z_D\}$.

HIG Semantics. $\mathcal{G}_H$ semantics is described using the rules shown in Fig. 2, where H2 and H3 capture PL_{II} and PL_I moves, respectively. The rule H4 specifies that a PL_{II} attempt θ to reveal the true value can succeed with probability p_i where PL_{II} belief is updated (i.e., $u' = t$), and remains unchanged otherwise.

H1: $s_0 = s_{\mathrm{II}}(t_0, u_0, \Omega_0)$ if $t_0 = u_0$, $\Omega_0 = \{t_0\}$

H2: $s_{\mathrm{II}}(t, u, \Omega) \xrightarrow{a_i} s_{\mathrm{I}}(t', u', \Omega')$ if $a_i \in A_{\mathrm{II}}$, $t' = t$, $u' = \mathit{Eff}(a_i, u)$,
$\qquad\qquad\qquad\qquad\qquad\qquad\quad \Omega' = \{t' \mid t' = \mathit{Eff}(b_i, t) \; \forall b_i \in \beta(a_i), t \in \Omega\}$

$\qquad\qquad \xrightarrow{\theta} s_{\bigcirc}(t', u', \Omega')$ if $t' = t$, $u' = u$, $\Omega' = \Omega$

H3: $s_{\mathrm{I}}(t, u, \Omega) \xrightarrow{b_i} s_{\mathrm{II}}(t', u', \Omega')$ if $b_i \in \beta(a_i)$, $t' = \mathit{Eff}(b_i, t)$, $u' = u$, $\Omega' = \Omega$

H4: $s_{\bigcirc}(t, u, \Omega) \xrightarrow{p_i} s_{\mathrm{II}}(t', u', \Omega')$ if $t' = t$, $u' = t$, $\Omega' = \{t\}$, $p_i = \delta(s_{\bigcirc}, \tau, s_{\mathrm{II}})$

$\qquad\qquad \xrightarrow{1-p_i} s_{\mathrm{II}}(t', u', \Omega')$ if $t' = t$, $u' = u$, $\Omega' = \Omega$, $1 - p_i = \delta(s_{\bigcirc}, \tau, s_{\mathrm{II}})$

Fig. 2. Semantic rules for an HIG.

Example 2 (HIG Semantics). Continuing Example 1, let us assume that the set of actions $A_{\mathrm{I}} = A_{\mathrm{II}} = \{\mathsf{N}, \mathsf{S}, \mathsf{E}, \mathsf{W}, \mathsf{NE}, \mathsf{NW}, \mathsf{SE}, \mathsf{SW}\}$, and that $\theta = \mathsf{GT}$ is a geolocation task that attempts to reveal the true value of the game.[2] Now, consider the scenario illustrated in Fig. 3. At the initial state s_0, the UAV attempts to move north (N), progressing the game to the state s_1, where the adversary takes her turn by selecting an action from the set $\beta(\mathsf{N}) = \{\mathsf{NE}, \mathsf{N}, \mathsf{NW}\}$. The players take turns until the UAV performs a geolocation task GT, moving from the state s_4 to s_5. With probability $p = \delta(s_5, \tau, s_6)$, the UAV detects its true location and updates its belief accordingly (i.e., to s_6). Otherwise, the belief remains the same (i.e., equal to s_4).

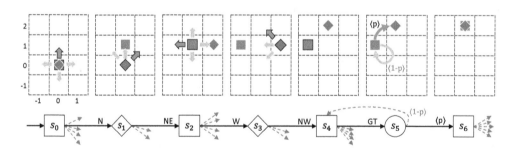

Fig. 3. An example of the UAV motion in a 2D-grid map, modeled as an HIG. Solid squares represent the UAV belief, while solid diamonds represent the ground truth. The UAV action GT denotes performing a geolocation task.

Problem Formulation. Following the system described in Example 2, we now consider the composed HIG $\mathcal{G}_H = \mathcal{M}_{\mathrm{adv}} \| \mathcal{M}_{\mathrm{uav}} \| \mathcal{M}_{\mathrm{as}}$ shown in Fig. 4; the HIG-based model incorporates standard models of a UAV ($\mathcal{M}_{\mathrm{uav}}$), an adversary ($\mathcal{M}_{\mathrm{adv}}$), and a geolocation-task advisory system ($\mathcal{M}_{\mathrm{as}}$) (e.g., as introduced in [11,12]). Here, the probability of a successful detection $p(v_{\mathcal{T}}, v_{\mathcal{B}})$ is a function of both the location the UAV believes to be its current location ($v_{\mathcal{B}}$) as well

---

[2] A geolocation task is an attempt to localize the UAV by examining its camera feed.

as the ground truth location that the UAV actually occupies (v_T). Reasoning about the flight plan using such model becomes problematic since the ground truth v_T is inherently unknown to the UAV (i.e., $\mathrm{PL_{II}}$), and thus so is $p(v_T, v_B)$. Furthermore, such representation, where some information is hidden, is not supported by off-the-shelf SMG model checkers. Consequently, for such HIGs, *our goal is to find an alternative representation that is suitable for strategy synthesis using off-the-shelf SMG model-checkers.*

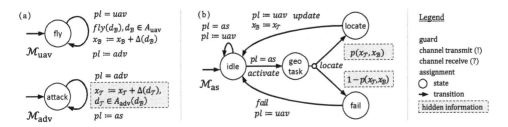

Fig. 4. An example of an HIG-based system model comprised of the UAV $(\mathcal{M}_{\mathrm{uav}})$, the adversary $(\mathcal{M}_{\mathrm{adv}})$, and the AS $(\mathcal{M}_{\mathrm{as}})$. Framed information is hidden from the UAV-AS.

3 Delayed-Action Games

In this section, we provide an alternative representation of HIGs that eliminates the use of private variables—we introduce Delayed-Action Games (DAGs) that exploit the notion of *delayed actions*. Furthermore, we show that for any HIG, a DAG that simulates the former can be constructed.

Delayed Actions. Informally, a DAG reconstructs an HIG such that actions of $\mathrm{PL_I}$ (the player with access to perfect information) follow the actions of $\mathrm{PL_{II}}$, i.e., $\mathrm{PL_I}$ actions are *delayed*. This rearrangement of the players' actions provides a means to hide information from $\mathrm{PL_{II}}$ without the use of private variables, since in this case, at $\mathrm{PL_{II}}$ states, $\mathrm{PL_I}$ actions have not occurred yet. In this way, $\mathrm{PL_{II}}$ can act as though she has complete information at the moment she makes her decision, as the future state has not yet happened and so cannot be known. In essence, the formalism can be seen as a partial ordering of the players' actions, exploiting the (partial) superposition property that a wide class of physical systems exhibit. To demonstrate this notion, let us consider DAG modeling on our running example.

Example 3 (Delaying Actions). Figure 5 depicts the (HIG-based) scenario from Fig. 3, but in the corresponding DAG, where the UAV actions are performed first (in $\hat{s}_0, \hat{s}_1, \hat{s}_2$), followed by the adversary delayed actions (in $\hat{s}_3, \hat{s}_4$). Note that, in the DAG model, at the time the UAV executed its actions $(\hat{s}_0, \hat{s}_1, \hat{s}_2)$ the adversary actions had not occurred (yet). Moreover, $\hat{s}_0$ and $\hat{s}_6$ (Fig. 5) share the same belief and true values as s_0 and s_6 (Fig. 3), respectively, though the transient states do not exactly match. This will be used to show the relationship between the games.

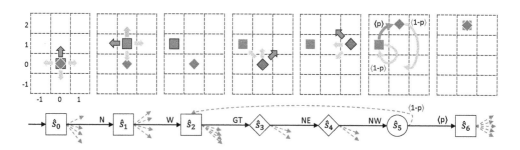

Fig. 5. The same scenario as in Fig. 3, modeled as a DAG. Solid squares represent UAV belief, while solid diamonds represent the ground truth. The UAV action GT denotes performing a geolocation task.

The advantage of this approach is twofold. First, the elimination of private variables enables simulation of an HIG using a full-information game. Thus, the formulation of the strategy synthesis problem using off-the-shelf SMG-based tools becomes feasible. In particular, a PL_{II} synthesized strategy becomes dependent on the knowledge of PL_I behavior (possible actions), rather than the specific (hidden) actions. We formalize a DAG as follows.

Definition 3 (Delayed-Action Game). *A DAG of an HIG* $\mathcal{G}_H = \langle S, (S_I, S_{II}, S_\bigcirc), A, s_0, \beta, \delta \rangle$, *with players* $\Gamma = \{I, II, \bigcirc\}$ *over a set of variables* $V = \{v_T, v_B\}$ *is a tuple* $\mathcal{G}_D = \langle \hat{S}, (\hat{S}_I, \hat{S}_{II}, \hat{S}_\bigcirc), A, \hat{s}_0, \beta, \hat{\delta} \rangle$ *where*

- $\hat{S} \subseteq Ev(v_T) \times Ev(v_B) \times A_{II}^* \times \mathbb{N}_0 \times \Gamma$ *is the set of states, partitioned into* $\hat{S}_I, \hat{S}_{II}$ *and* $\hat{S}_\bigcirc$;
- $\hat{s}_0 \in \hat{S}_{II}$ *is the initial state; and*
- $\hat{\delta} \colon \hat{S} \times A \times \hat{S} \to [0,1]$ *is a transition function such that* $\hat{\delta}(\hat{s}_{II}, a, \hat{s}_\bigcirc) = \hat{\delta}(\hat{s}_I, a, \hat{s}_{II}) = \hat{\delta}(\hat{s}_\bigcirc, a, \hat{s}_I) = 0$, *and* $\hat{\delta}(\hat{s}_{II}, a, \hat{s}_{II}) \in \{0, 1\}$, $\hat{\delta}(\hat{s}_{II}, \theta, \hat{s}_I) \in \{0, 1\}$, $\hat{\delta}(\hat{s}_I, a, \hat{s}_I) \in \{0, 1\}$, $\hat{\delta}(\hat{s}_I, a, \hat{s}_\bigcirc) \in \{0, 1\}$, *for all* $\hat{s}_I \in \hat{S}_I$, $\hat{s}_{II} \in \hat{S}_{II}$, $\hat{s}_\bigcirc \in \hat{S}_\bigcirc$ *and* $a \in A$, *where* $\sum_{\hat{s}' \in \hat{S}_{II}} \delta(\hat{s}_\bigcirc, a, \hat{s}') = 1$.

Note that, in contrast to transition function δ in HIG $\mathcal{G}_H$, $\hat{\delta}$ in DAG $\mathcal{G}_D$ only allows transitions $\hat{s}_{II}$ to $\hat{s}_{II}$ or $\hat{s}_I$, as well as $\hat{s}_I$ to $\hat{s}_I$ or $\hat{s}_\bigcirc$, and probabilistic transitions $\hat{s}_\bigcirc$ to $\hat{s}_{II}$; also note that $\hat{s}_{II}$ to $\hat{s}_I$ is conditioned by the action θ.

DAG Semantics. A DAG state is a tuple $\hat{s} = (\hat{t}, \hat{u}, w, j, \gamma)$, which for simplicity we shorthand as $\hat{s}_\gamma (\hat{t}, \hat{u}, w, j)$, where $\hat{t} \in Ev(v_T)$ is the last known true value, $\hat{u} \in Ev(v_B)$ is PL_{II} belief, $w \in A_{II}^*$ captures PL_{II} actions taken since the last known true value, $j \in \mathbb{N}_0$ is an index on w, and $\gamma \in \Gamma$ is the current player index. The game transitions are defined using the semantic rules from Fig. 6. Note that PL_{II} can execute multiple moves (i.e., actions) before executing θ to attempt to reveal the true value (D2), moving to a PL_I state where PL_I executes all her delayed actions before reaching a 'revealing' state $\hat{s}_\bigcirc$ (D3). Finally, the revealing attempt can succeed with probability p_i where PL_{II} belief is updated (i.e., $\hat{u}' = \hat{t}$), or otherwise remains unchanged (D4).

D1: $\hat{s}_0 = \hat{s}_{\mathrm{II}}(\hat{t}_0, \hat{u}_0, w_0, 0)$ $\qquad$ if $\hat{t}_0 = \hat{u}_0,\ w_0 = \epsilon$

D2: $\hat{s}_{\mathrm{II}}\left(\hat{t}, \hat{u}, w, 0\right) \xrightarrow{a_i} \hat{s}_{\mathrm{II}}\left(\hat{t}', \hat{u}', w', 0\right)$ if $a_i \in A_{\mathrm{II}},\ \hat{t}' = \hat{t},\ \hat{u}' = \mathit{Eff}(a_i, \hat{u}),\ w' = wa_i$

$\qquad\qquad \xrightarrow{\theta} \hat{s}_{\mathrm{I}}\left(\hat{t}', \hat{u}', w', 0\right)$ $\quad$ if $\hat{t}' = \hat{t},\ \hat{u}' = \hat{u},\ w' = w$

D3: $\hat{s}_{\mathrm{I}}\left(\hat{t}, \hat{u}, w, j\right) \xrightarrow{b_i} \hat{s}_{\mathrm{I}}\left(\hat{t}', \hat{u}', w', j{+}1\right)$ if $b_i \in \beta(w_j),\ \hat{t}' = \mathit{Eff}(b_i, \hat{t}),\ \hat{u}' = \hat{u},\ w' = w,\ j < |w| - 1$

$\qquad\qquad \xrightarrow{b_i} \hat{s}_{\bigcirc}\left(\hat{t}', \hat{u}', w', j\right)$ $\quad$ if $b_i \in \beta(w_j),\ \hat{t}' = \mathit{Eff}(b_i, \hat{t}),\ \hat{u}' = \hat{u},\ w' = w,\ j = |w| - 1$

D4: $\hat{s}_{\bigcirc}\left(\hat{t}, \hat{u}, w, j\right) \xrightarrow{p_i} \hat{s}_{\mathrm{II}}\left(\hat{t}', \hat{u}', w', 0\right)$ if $\hat{t}' = \hat{t},\ \hat{u}' = \hat{t},\ w' = \epsilon,\ p_i = \hat{\delta}(\hat{s}_{\bigcirc}, \hat{s}_{\mathrm{II}})$

$\qquad\qquad \xrightarrow{1-p_i} \hat{s}_{\mathrm{II}}\left(\hat{t}', \hat{u}', w', 0\right)$ if $\hat{t}' = \hat{t}_0,\ \hat{u}' = \hat{u},\ w' = w,\ q_i = \hat{\delta}(\hat{s}_{\bigcirc}, \hat{s}_{\mathrm{II}})$

Fig. 6. Semantic rules for DAGs.

In both $\mathcal{G}_{\mathsf{H}}$ and $\mathcal{G}_{\mathsf{D}}$, we label states where all players have full knowledge of the current state as *proper*. We also say that two states are similar if they agree on the belief, and equivalent if they agree on both the belief and ground truth.

Definition 4 (States). *Let* $s_\gamma(t, u, \Omega) \in S$ *and* $\hat{s}_{\hat{\gamma}}(\hat{t}, \hat{u}, w, j) \in \hat{S}$. *We say:*

- s_γ *is proper iff* $\Omega = \{t\}$, *denoted by* $s_\gamma \in \mathrm{Prop}(\mathcal{G}_{\mathsf{H}})$.
- $\hat{s}_{\hat{\gamma}}$ *is proper iff* $w = \epsilon$, *denoted by* $\hat{s}_{\hat{\gamma}} \in \mathrm{Prop}(\mathcal{G}_{\mathsf{D}})$.
- s_γ *and* $\hat{s}_{\hat{\gamma}}$ *are similar iff* $\hat{u} = u$, $\hat{t} \in \Omega$, *and* $\gamma = \hat{\gamma}$, *denoted by* $s_\gamma \sim \hat{s}_{\hat{\gamma}}$.
- s_γ, $\hat{s}_{\hat{\gamma}}$ *are equivalent iff* $t = \hat{t}$, $u = \hat{u}$, $w = \epsilon$, *and* $\gamma = \hat{\gamma}$, *denoted by* $s_\gamma \simeq \hat{s}_{\hat{\gamma}}$.

From the above definition, we have that $s \simeq \hat{s} \implies s \in \mathrm{Prop}(\mathcal{G}_{\mathsf{H}}), \hat{s} \in \mathrm{Prop}(\mathcal{G}_{\mathsf{D}})$. We now define *execution fragments*, possible progressions from a state to another.

Definition 5 (Execution Fragment). *An* execution fragment *(of either an SMG, DAG or HIG) is a finite sequence of states, actions and probabilities*

$$\varrho = s_0 a_1 p_1 s_1 a_2 p_2 s_2 \ldots a_n p_n s_n \text{ such that } (s_i \xrightarrow{a_{i+1}} s_{i+1}) \vee (s_i \xrightarrow{\langle p_{i+1}\rangle} s_{i+1}), \forall i \geq 0.^3$$

We use *first*(ϱ) and *last*(ϱ) to refer to the first and last states of ϱ, respectively. If both states are proper, we say that ϱ is *proper* as well, denoted by $\varrho \in \mathrm{Prop}(\mathcal{G}_{\mathsf{H}})$.[4] Moreover, ϱ is *deterministic* if no probabilities appear in the sequence.

Definition 6 (Move). *A* move m_γ *of an execution* ϱ *from state* $s \in \varrho$, *denoted by* $move_\gamma(s, \varrho)$, *is a sequence of actions* $a_1 a_2 \ldots a_i \in A_\gamma^*$ *that player* γ *performs in* ϱ *starting from* s.

By omitting the player index we refer to the moves of all players. To simplify notation, we use $move(\varrho)$ as a short notation for $move(first(\varrho), \varrho)$. We write $(m)(first(\varrho)) = last(\varrho)$ to denote that the execution of move m from the $first(\varrho)$ leads to the $last(\varrho)$. This allows us to now define the *delay operator* as follows.

---

[3] For deterministic transitions, $p = 1$, hence omitted from ϱ for readability.

[4] An execution fragment lives in the transition system (TS), i.e., $\varrho \in \mathrm{Prop}(\mathrm{TS}(\mathcal{G}))$. We omit TS for readability.

Definition 7 (Delay Operator). *For an $\mathcal{G}_H$, let $m = move(\varrho) = a_1 b_1 \ldots a_n b_n \theta$ be a move for some deterministic $\varrho \in \mathrm{TS}(\mathcal{G}_H)$, where $a_1 \ldots a_n \in A_{II}^*, b_1 \ldots b_n \in A_I^*$. The delay operator, denoted by $\overline{m}$, is defined by the rule $\overline{m} = a_1 \ldots a_n \theta b_1 \ldots b_n$.*

Intuitively, the delay operator shifts PL_I actions to the right of PL_{II} actions up until the next probabilistic state. For example,

$$\text{if} \quad \rho = s_{II}^{(0)} \xrightarrow{a_1} s_I^{(1)} \xrightarrow{b_2} s_{II}^{(2)} \xrightarrow{\theta} s_\bigcirc^{(3)} \xrightarrow{p_3} s_{II}^{(4)} \xrightarrow{a_4} s_I^{(5)} \xrightarrow{b_5} s_{II}^{(6)} \xrightarrow{a_6} s_I^{(7)} \xrightarrow{b_7} s_{II}^{(8)}$$

$$\text{then} \quad m = \quad\quad a_1 \quad\quad b_2 \;\diagdown\!\!\!\!\diagup\; \theta \quad\quad \tau \quad\quad a_4 \quad\quad b_5 \;\diagdown\!\!\!\!\diagup\; a_6 \quad\quad b_7,$$

$$\text{and} \quad \overline{m} = \quad\quad a_1 \quad\quad \theta \;\diagdown\!\!\!\!\diagup\; b_2 \quad\quad \tau \quad\quad a_4 \quad\quad a_6 \;\diagdown\!\!\!\!\diagup\; b_5 \quad\quad b_7.$$

Simulation Relation. Given an HIG $\mathcal{G}_H$, we first define the corresponding DAG $\mathcal{G}_D$.

Definition 8 (Correspondence). *Given an HIG $\mathcal{G}_H$, a corresponding DAG $\mathcal{G}_D = \mathfrak{D}[\mathcal{G}_H]$ is a DAG that follows the semantic rules displayed in Fig. 7.*

$$
\begin{aligned}
s_0 = s_{II}(t_0, u_0, \Omega_0) &\implies \hat{s}_0 = \hat{s}_{II}(\hat{t}_0, \hat{u}_0, w_0, 0) \text{ s.t. } \hat{t}_0 = t_0,\ \hat{u}_0 = u_0 \\
s_{II}(t, u, \Omega) \xrightarrow{a_i} s_I(t', u', \Omega') &\implies \hat{s}_{II}(\hat{t}, \hat{u}, w, 0) \xrightarrow{a_i} \hat{s}_{II}(\hat{t}', \hat{u}', w', 0) \text{ s.t. } \hat{u} = u \\
s_{II}(t, u, \Omega) \xrightarrow{\theta_i} s_\bigcirc(t', u', \Omega') &\implies \hat{s}_{II}(\hat{t}, \hat{u}, w, 0) \xrightarrow{\theta_i} s_I(\hat{t}', \hat{u}', w', 0) \text{ s.t. } \hat{u} = u \\
s_I(t, u, \Omega) \xrightarrow{b_i} s_{II}(t', u', \Omega') &\implies \hat{s}_I(\hat{t}, \hat{u}, w, j) \xrightarrow{b_i} s_I(\hat{t}', \hat{u}', w', j+1) \text{ s.t. } \hat{t} = t, j < |w| \\
s_I(t, u, \Omega) \xrightarrow{b_i} s_{II}(t', u', \Omega') &\implies \hat{s}_I(\hat{t}, \hat{u}, w, j) \xrightarrow{b_i} s_\bigcirc(\hat{t}', \hat{u}', w', j) \text{ s.t. } \hat{t} = t, j = |w| \\
s_\bigcirc(t, u, \Omega) \xrightarrow{p_i} s_{II}(t', u', \Omega') &\implies \hat{s}_\bigcirc(\hat{t}, \hat{u}, w, j) \xrightarrow{p_i} \hat{s}_{II}(\hat{t}', \hat{u}', w', 0) \text{ s.t. } \hat{t} = t,\ \hat{u} = u \\
s_\bigcirc(t, u, \Omega) \xrightarrow{1-p_i} s_{II}(t', u', \Omega') &\implies \hat{s}_\bigcirc(\hat{t}, \hat{u}, w, j) \xrightarrow{1-p_i} \hat{s}_{II}(\hat{t}', \hat{u}', w', 0) \text{ s.t. } \hat{t} = t,\ \hat{u} = u
\end{aligned}
$$

Fig. 7. Semantic rules for HIG-to-DAG transformation.

For the rest of this section, we consider $\mathcal{G}_D = \mathfrak{D}[\mathcal{G}_H]$, and use $\varrho \in \mathrm{TS}(\mathcal{G}_H)$ and $\hat{\varrho} \in \mathrm{TS}(\mathcal{G}_D)$ to denote two execution fragments of the HIG and DAG, respectively. We say that ϱ and $\hat{\varrho}$ are *similar*, denoted by $\varrho \sim \hat{\varrho}$, iff $first(\varrho) \simeq first(\hat{\varrho})$, $last(\varrho) \sim last(\hat{\varrho})$, and $\overline{move(\varrho)} = move(\hat{\varrho})$.

Definition 9 (Game Proper Simulation). *A game $\mathcal{G}_D$ properly simulates $\mathcal{G}_H$, denoted by $\mathcal{G}_D \rightsquigarrow \mathcal{G}_H$, iff $\forall \varrho \in \mathrm{Prop}(\mathcal{G}_H), \exists \hat{\varrho} \in \mathrm{Prop}(\mathcal{G}_D)$ such that $\varrho \sim \hat{\varrho}$.*

Before proving the existence of the simulation relation, we first show that if a move is executed on two equivalent states, then the terminal states are similar.

Lemma 1 (Terminal States Similarity). *For any $s_0 \simeq \hat{s}_0$ and a deterministic $\varrho \in \mathrm{TS}(\mathcal{G}_H)$ where $first(\varrho) = s_0$, $last(\varrho) \in S_{II}$, then $last(\varrho) \sim \left(\overline{move(\varrho)}\right)(\hat{s}_0)$ holds.*

Proof. Let $last(\varrho_i) = s^{(i)}_{\gamma_i}(t_i, u_i, \Omega_i)$ and $\left(\overline{move(\varrho_i)}\right)(\hat{s}_0) = \hat{s}^{(i)}_{\hat{\gamma}_i}(\hat{t}_i, \hat{u}_i, w_i, j_i)$, where $move(\varrho_i) = a_1 b_1 ... a_i b_i \theta$. We then write $\overline{move(\varrho)} = a_1 ... a_i \theta b_1 ... b_i$. We use induction over i as follows:

- Base $(i=0)$: $\varrho_0 = s_0 \implies s^{(0)} \simeq \hat{s}^{(0)}$ where $u_0 = \hat{u}_0$ and $t_0 = \hat{t}_0$.
- Induction $(i > 0)$: Assume that the claim holds for $move(\varrho_{i-1}) = a_1 b_1 ... a_{i-1} b_{i-1} \theta$, i.e., $u_{i-1} = \hat{u}_{i-1}$ and $\hat{t}_{i-1} \in \Omega_{i-1}$. For ϱ_i we have that $u_i = Eff(a_i, u_{i-1})$ and $\hat{u}_i = Eff(a_i, \hat{u}_{i-1})$. Also, $t_i = Eff(b_i, t_{i-1}) \in \Omega_i$ and $\hat{t}_i = Eff(b_i, \hat{t}_{i-1})$. Hence, $u_i = \hat{u}_i$, $\hat{t}_i \in \Omega_i$ and $\hat{\gamma}_i = \gamma_i = \bigcirc$. Thus, $s^{(i)} \sim \hat{s}^{(i)}$ holds. The same can be shown for $move(\varrho) = a_1 b_1 ... a_i b_i$ where no θ occurs. $\qquad\square$

Theorem 1 (Probabilistic Simulation). *For any $s_0 \simeq \hat{s}_0$ and $\varrho \in \mathrm{Prop}(\mathcal{G}_\mathsf{H})$ where $first(\varrho) = s_0$, it holds that*

$$\Pr\left[last(\varrho) = s'\right] = \Pr\left[\left(\overline{move(\varrho)}\right)(\hat{s}_0) = \hat{s}'\right] \quad \forall s', \hat{s}' \ s.t. \ s' \simeq \hat{s}'.$$

Proof. We can rewrite ϱ as $\varrho = \varrho_0 \xrightarrow{p_1} \varrho_1 \cdots \varrho_{n-1} \xrightarrow{p_n} s^{(n)}_{\mathrm{II}}$, where $\varrho_0, \varrho_1, \ldots, \varrho_{n-1}$ are deterministic. Let $first(\varrho_i) = s^{(i)}_{\mathrm{II}}(t_i, u_i, \Omega_i)$, $last(\varrho_i) = s^{(i)}_{\bigcirc}(t'_i, u'_i, \Omega'_i)$, and $\left(\overline{move(\varrho)}\right)(\hat{s}_0) = \hat{s}^{(n)}(\hat{t}_n, \hat{u}_n, w_n, j_n)$. We use induction over n as follows:

- Base $(n=0)$: for ϱ to be deterministic and proper, $\varrho = \varrho_0 = s^{(0)}$ holds.
- Case $(n = 1)$: $p_1 = p(t'_0, u'_0)$. From Lemma 1, $\hat{u}_1 = u_1$ and $\hat{t}_1 = t_1$. Hence, $\Pr\left[last(\varrho) = s^{(1)}_{\mathrm{II}}\right] = \Pr\left[\left(\overline{move(\varrho)}\right)(\hat{s}_0) = \hat{s}^{(1)}_{\mathrm{II}}\right] = p(t'_0, u'_0)$ and $s^{(1)}_{\mathrm{II}} \simeq \hat{s}^{(1)}_{\mathrm{II}}$.
- Induction $(n > 1)$: It is straightforward to infer that $p_n = p\left(t'_{n-1}, u'_{n-1}\right)$, hence $\Pr\left[last(\varrho) = s^{(n)}_{\mathrm{II}}\right] = \Pr\left[\left(\overline{move(\varrho)}\right)(\hat{s}^{(0)}) = \hat{s}^{(n)}\right] = P$, and $s^{(n)}_{\mathrm{II}} \simeq \hat{s}^{(n)}_{\mathrm{II}}$. $\qquad\square$

Note that in case of multiple θ attempts, the above probability P satisfies

$$P = \prod_{i=1}^{n} \sum_{j=1}^{m_i} p_i\left(t'_{i-1}, u'_{i-1}\right)\left(1 - p_{i-1}\left(t'_{i-1}, u'_{i-1}\right)\right)^{(j-1)},$$

where m_i is the number of θ attempts at stage i. Finally, since Theorem 1 imposes no constraints on $move(\varrho)$, a DAG can simulate all proper executions that exist in the corresponding HIG.

Theorem 2 (DAG-HIG Simulation). *For any HIG $\mathcal{G}_\mathsf{H}$ there exists a DAG $\mathcal{G}_\mathsf{D} = \mathfrak{D}[\mathcal{G}_\mathsf{H}]$ such that $\mathcal{G}_\mathsf{D} \rightsquigarrow \mathcal{G}_\mathsf{H}$ (as defined in Definition 9).*

4 Properties of DAG and DAG-based Synthesis

We here discuss DAG features, including how it can be decomposed into sub-games by restricting the simulation to finite executions, and the preservation of safety properties, before proposing a DAG-based synthesis framework.

Transitions. In DAGs, nondeterministic actions of different players underline different semantics. Specifically, PL_I nondeterminism captures what is known about the adversarial behavior, rather than exact actions, where PL_I actions are constrained by the earlier PL_II action. Conversely, PL_II nondeterminism abstracts the player's decisions. This distinction reflects how DAGs can be used for strategy synthesis under hidden information. To illustrate this, suppose that a strategy π_II is to be obtained based on a worst-case scenario. In that case, the game is explored for all possible adversarial behaviors. Yet, if a strategy π_I is known about PL_I, a counter strategy π_II can be found by constructing $\mathcal{G}_\text{D}^{\pi_\text{I}}$.

Probabilistic behaviors in DAGs are captured by $\text{PL}_\bigcirc$, which is characterized by the transition function $\hat{\delta}\colon \hat{S}_\bigcirc \times \hat{S}_\text{II} \to [0,1]$. The specific definition of $\hat{\delta}$ depends on the modeled system. For instance, if the transition function (i.e., the probability) is state-independent, i.e., $\hat{\delta}(\hat{s}_\bigcirc, \hat{s}_\text{II}) = c, c \in [0,1]$, the obtained model becomes trivial. Yet, with a state-dependent transition function, i.e., $\hat{\delta}(\hat{s}_\bigcirc, \hat{s}_\text{II}) = p(\hat{t}, \hat{u})$, the probability that PL_II successfully reveals the true value depends on both the belief and the true value, and the transition function can then be realized since $\hat{s}_\bigcirc$ holds both $\hat{t}$ and $\hat{u}$.

Decomposition. Consider an execution $\hat{\varrho}^* = \hat{s}_0 a_1 \hat{s}_1 a_2 \hat{s}_2 \ldots$ that describes a scenario where PL_II performs infinitely many actions with no attempt to reveal the true value. To simulate $\hat{\varrho}^*$, the word w needs to infinitely grow. Since we are interested in finite executions, we impose *stopping criteria* on the DAG, such that the game is *trapped* whenever $|w| = h_\text{max}$ is true, where $h_\text{max} \in \mathbb{N}$ is an *upper horizon*. We formalize the stopping criteria as a deterministic finite automaton (DFA) that, when composed with the DAG, traps the game whenever the stopping criteria hold. Note that imposing an upper horizon by itself is not a sufficient criterion for a DAG to be considered a stopping game [8]. Conversely, consider a proper (and hence finite) execution $\hat{\varrho} = \hat{s}_0 a_1 \ldots \hat{s}'$, where $\hat{s}_0, \hat{s}' \in \text{Prop}(\mathcal{G}_\text{D})$. From Definition 9, it follows that a DAG initial state is strictly proper, i.e., $\hat{s}_0 \in \text{Prop}(\mathcal{G}_\text{D})$. Hence, when $\hat{s}'$ is reached, the game can be seen as if it is *repeated* with a new initial state $\hat{s}'$. Consequently, a DAG game (complemented with stopping criteria) can be decomposed into a (possibly infinite) countable set of *subgames* that have the same structure yet different initial states.

Definition 10 (DAG Subgames). *The subgames of a $\mathcal{G}_\text{D}$ are defined by the set $\left\{ \hat{\mathcal{G}}_i \mid \hat{\mathcal{G}}_i = \left\langle \hat{S}^{(i)}, (\hat{S}_\text{I}^{(i)}, \hat{S}_\text{II}^{(i)}, \hat{S}_\bigcirc^{(i)}), A, \hat{s}_0^{(i)}, \hat{\delta}^{(i)} \right\rangle, i \in \mathbb{N}_0 \right\}$, where $\hat{S} = \bigcup_i \hat{S}^{(i)}$; $\hat{S}_\gamma = \bigcup_i \hat{S}_\gamma^{(i)} \; \forall \gamma \in \Gamma$; and $\hat{s}_0^{(i)} = \hat{s}_\text{II}^{(i)}$ s.t. $\hat{s}_\text{II}^{(i)} \in \text{Prop}(\mathcal{G}_\text{D}^{(i)})$, $\hat{s}_\text{II}^{(i)} \neq \hat{s}_\text{II}^{(j)} \; \forall i, j \in \mathbb{N}_0$.*

Intuitively, each subgame either reaches a proper state (representing the initial state of another subgame) or terminates by an upper horizon. This decomposition allows for the independent (and parallel) analysis of individual subgames, drastically reducing both the time required for synthesis and the explored state space, and hence improving scalability. An example of this decompositional approach is provided in Sect. 5.

Preservation of Safety Properties. In DAGs, the action θ denotes a transition from PL_{II} to PL_I states and thus the execution of any delayed actions. While this action can simply describe a revealing attempt, it can also serve as a *what-if* analysis of how the true value may evolve at stage i of a subgame. We refer to an execution of the second type as a *hypothetical branch*, where $\mathrm{Hyp}(\hat{\varrho}, h)$ denotes the set of hypothetical branches from $\hat{\varrho}$ at stage $h \in \{1, \dots, n\}$. Let $L_{\mathrm{safe}}(s)$ be a labeling function denoting if a state is safe. The formula $\Phi_{\mathrm{safe}} := [\mathsf{G}\ safe]$ is satisfied by an execution ϱ in HIG iff all $s(t, u, \Omega) \in \varrho$ are safe.

Now, consider $\hat{\varrho}$ of the DAG, with $\hat{\varrho} \sim \varrho$. We identify the following three cases:

(a) $L_{\mathrm{safe}}(s)$ depends only on the belief u, then $\varrho \models \Phi_{\mathrm{safe}}$ iff all $\hat{s}_{II} \in \hat{\varrho}$ are safe;
(b) $L_{\mathrm{safe}}(s)$ depends only on the true value t, then $\varrho \models \Phi_{\mathrm{safe}}$ iff all $\hat{s}_I \in \mathrm{Hyp}(\hat{\varrho}, n)$ are safe; and
(c) $L_{\mathrm{safe}}(s)$ depends on both the true value t and belief u, then $\varrho \models \Phi_{\mathrm{safe}}$ iff $last(\hat{\varrho}_h)$ is safe for all $\hat{\varrho}_h \in \mathrm{Hyp}(\hat{\varrho}, h), h \in \{1, ..., n\}$, where n is the number of PL_{II} actions.

Taking into account such relations, both safety (e.g., never encounter a hazard) and distance-based requirements (e.g., never exceed a subgame horizon) can be specified when using DAGs for synthesis, to ensure their satisfaction in the original model. This can be generalized to other reward-based synthesis objectives, which will be part of our future efforts that we discuss in Sect. 6.

Synthesis Framework. We here propose a framework for strategy synthesis using DAGs, which is summarized in Fig. 8. We start by formulating the automata $\mathcal{M}_I$, $\mathcal{M}_{II}$ and $\mathcal{M}_O$, representing PL_I, PL_{II} and PL_O abstract behaviors, respectively. Next, a FIFO memory stack $(m_i)_{i=1}^n \in A_{II}^n$ is implemented using two automata $\mathcal{M}_{\mathrm{mrd}}$ and $\mathcal{M}_{\mathrm{mwr}}$ to perform reading and writing operations, respectively.[5] The DAG $\mathcal{G}_D$ is constructed by following Algorithm 1. The game starts with PL_{II} moves until she executes a revealing attempt θ, allowing PL_I to play her delayed actions. Once an end criterion is met, the game terminates, resembling conditions such as 'running out of fuel' or 'reaching map boundaries'.

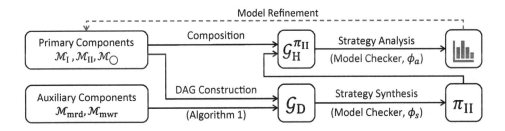

Fig. 8. Synthesis and analysis framework based on the use of DAGs.

---

[5] Specific implementation details are described in Sect. 5.

Algorithm 1. Procedure for DAG construction

Input: Components $\mathcal{M}_I, \mathcal{M}_{II}, \mathcal{M}_O, \mathcal{M}_{mwr}, \mathcal{M}_{mrd}$; initial state $\hat{s}_0$
Result: DAG $\mathcal{G}_D$

1 **while** $\neg(end\ criterion)$ **do**
2   **while** $a \neq \theta$ **do**   ▷ PL_{II} plays until a revealing attempt
3       $\mathcal{M}_{II}.v_B \leftarrow \mathit{Eff}(a, v_B)$, $\mathcal{M}_{mwr}.write(a, \text{++}wr)$
4   **while** $rd \leqslant wr$ **do**   ▷ PL_I plays all delayed actions
5       $\mathcal{M}_{mrd}.read(a, \text{++}rd)$, $\mathcal{M}_I.v_T \leftarrow \mathit{Eff}(\beta(a), v_T)$
6   **if** $draw\ x \sim Brn(p(v_T, v_B))$ **then**   ▷ PL_O plays successful attempt
7       $\mathcal{M}_{II}.v_B \leftarrow \mathcal{M}_I.v_T$, $wr \leftarrow 0$, $rd \leftarrow 0$
8   **else** $rd \leftarrow 0$ ▷ Unsuccessful attempt, forget PL_I actions

---

Algorithm 2 describes the procedure for strategy synthesis based on the DAG $\mathcal{G}_D$, and an rPATL [6] synthesis query ϕ_{syn} that captures, for example, a safety requirement. Starting with the initial location, the procedure checks whether ϕ_{syn} is satisfied if action θ is performed at stage h, and updates the set of feasible strategies Π_i for subgame $\hat{\mathcal{G}}_i$ until h_{max} is reached or ϕ_{syn} is not satisfied.[6] Next, the set Π_i is used to update the list of reachable end locations ℓ with new initial locations of reachable subgames that should be explored. Finally, the composition of both $\mathcal{G}_H$ and Π_{II}^* resolves PL_{II} nondeterminism, where the resulting model $\mathcal{G}_H^{\Pi_{II}^*}$ is a Markov Decision Process (MDP) of complete information that can be easily used for further analysis.

5 Case Study

In this section, we consider a case study where a human operator supervises a UAV prone to stealthy attacks on its GPS sensor. The UAV mission is to visit a number of targets after being airborne from a known base (initial state), while avoiding hazard zones that are known a priori. Moreover, the presence of adversarial stealthy attacks via GPS spoofing is assumed. We use the DAG framework to synthesize strategies for both the UAV and an operator advisory system (AS) that schedules geolocation tasks for the operator.

Modeling. We model the system as a delayed-action game $\mathcal{G}_D$, where PL_I and PL_{II} represent the adversary and the UAV-AS coalition, respectively. Figure 9 shows the model primary and auxiliary components. In the UAV model $\mathcal{M}_{uav}$, $x_B = (\mathsf{x}_B, \mathsf{y}_B)$ encodes the UAV belief, and $A_{uav} = \{N, S, E, W, NE, NW, SE, SW\}$ is the set of available movements. The AS can trigger the action *activate* to initiate a geolocation task, attempting to confirm the current location. The adversary behavior is abstracted by $\mathcal{M}_{adv}$ where $x_T = (\mathsf{x}_T, \mathsf{y}_T)$ encodes the UAV true location. The adversarial actions are limited to one directional

---

[6] Failing to find a strategy at stage i implies the same for all horizons of size $j > i$.

Algorithm 2. Procedure for strategy synthesis

Input: Initial location (x_0, y_0), synthesis query ϕ_{syn}
Output: PL_{II} strategies Π_{II}^*

1   $\ell \leftarrow [(x_0, y_0)]$, $i \leftarrow 0$
2   **while** $i < |\ell|$ **do**   ▷ Explore all reachable subgames
3      $\hat{s}_0 \leftarrow (\ell[i], \ell[i], \epsilon, 0, II)$, $h \leftarrow 1$, $stop \leftarrow \perp$ ▷ Construct initial state
4   **while** $h \leqslant h_{max} \wedge \neg stop$ **do**   ▷ Explore subgame till upper horizon
5         $(\pi_{II}, \varphi) \leftarrow \mathsf{Synth}\left(\hat{\mathcal{G}}_{\hat{s}_0}^{\pi_h}, \phi_{syn} \right)$ ▷ Synthesize strategy for horizon h
6   **if** $\pi_{II} \neq \emptyset$ **then**
7            $\Pi_i \leftarrow \Pi_i \cup (\pi_{II}, \pi_h, \varphi)$, h++   ▷ Save synthesized strategy
8   **else** $stop \leftarrow \top$
9      $\mathsf{Prune}\,(\Pi_t)$, $\Pi_{II}^* \leftarrow \Pi_{II}^* \cup \Pi_t$ ▷ Prune subgame strategies
10      $\ell \leftarrow \ell \cdot (\mathsf{Reachable}\,(\Pi_t) \setminus \ell)$, i++   ▷ update reachability

---

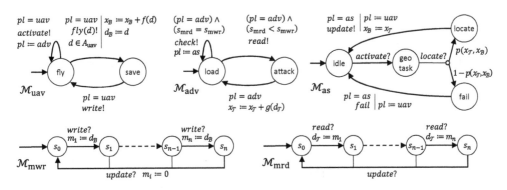

Fig. 9. Primary DAG components: UAV ($\mathcal{M}_{uav}$), adversary ($\mathcal{M}_{adv}$), and AS ($\mathcal{M}_{as}$). Auxiliary DAG components: memory write ($\mathcal{M}_{mwr}$) and memory read ($\mathcal{M}_{mrd}$) models, capturing the DAG representation. At stage i, the next memory location to write/read is m_i.

increment at most.[7] If, for example, the UAV is heading N, then the adversary set of actions is $\beta(\mathsf{N}) = \{\mathsf{N}, \mathsf{NE}, \mathsf{NW}\}$. The auxiliary components $\mathcal{M}_{mwr}$ and $\mathcal{M}_{mrd}$ manage a FIFO memory stack $(m_i)_{i=0}^{n-1} \in A_{uav}^n$. The last UAV movement is saved in m_i by synchronizing $\mathcal{M}_{mwr}$ with $\mathcal{M}_{uav}$ via *write*, while $\mathcal{M}_{mrd}$ synchronizes with $\mathcal{M}_{adv}$ via *read* to read the next UAV action from m_j. The subgame terminates whenever action *write* is attempted and $\mathcal{M}_{mwr}$ is at state n (i.e., out of memory).

The goal is to find strategies for the UAV-AS coalition based on the following:

- *Target reachability.* To overcome cases where targets are unreachable due to hazard zones, the label *reach* is assigned to the set of states with acceptable checkpoint locations (including the target) to render the objective incremen-

---

[7] To detect aggressive attacks, techniques from literature (e.g., [16,25,26]) can be used.

tally feasible. The objective for all encountered subgames is then formalized as $\text{Pr}_{\max}\left[\textsf{F } reach\right] \geqslant p_{\min}$ for some bound $p_{\min}$.

– *Hazard Avoidance.* Similar to target reachability, the label *hazard* is assigned to states corresponding to hazard zones. The objective $\text{Pr}_{\max}\left[\textsf{G } \neg hazard\right] \geqslant p_{\min}$ is then specified for all encountered subgames.

By refining the aforementioned objectives, synthesis queries are used for both the subgames and the supergame. Specifically, the query

$$\phi_{\text{syn}}(k) := \langle\!\langle\text{uav}\rangle\!\rangle\text{Pr}_{\max=?}\left[\neg hazard \; \textsf{U}^{\leqslant k}\left(locate \wedge reach\right)\right] \tag{1}$$

is specified for each encountered subgame $\hat{\mathcal{G}}_i$, where *locate* indicates a successful geolocation task. By following Algorithm 2 for a q number of reachable subgames, the supergame is reduced to an MDP $\mathcal{G}_{\textsf{D}}^{\{\pi_i\}_{i=1}^q}$ (whose states are the reachable subgames), which is checked against the query

$$\phi_{\text{ana}}(n) := \langle\!\langle\text{adv}\rangle\!\rangle\text{Pr}_{\min,\max=?}\left[\textsf{F}^{\leqslant n} \; target\right] \tag{2}$$

to find the bounds on the probability that the target is reached under a maximum number of geolocation tasks n.

Experimental Results. Figure 10(a) shows the map setting used for implementation. The UAV's ability to actively detect an attack depends on both its belief and the ground truth. Specifically, the probability of success in a geolocation task mainly relies on the disparity between the belief and true locations, captured by $f_{\text{dis}}\colon Ev\left(x_{\mathcal{B}}\right) \times Ev\left(x_{\mathcal{T}}\right) \rightarrow [0,1]$, obtained by assigning probabilities for each pair of locations according to their features (e.g., landmarks) and smoothed using a Gaussian 2D filter. A thorough experimental analysis where probabilities are extracted from experiments with human operators is described in [11]. The set of hazard zones include the map boundaries to prevent the UAV from reaching boundary values. Also, the adversary is prohibited from launching attacks for at least the first step, a practical assumption to prevent the UAV model from infinitely bouncing around the target location.

We implemented the model in PRISM-games [7,19] and performed the experiments on an Intel Core i7 4.0 GHz CPU, with 10 GB RAM dedicated to the tool. Figure 10(b) shows the supergame obtained by following the procedure in Algorithm 2. A vertex $\hat{\mathcal{G}}_{\textsf{xy}}$ represents a subgame (composed with its strategy) that starts at location $(\textsf{x}, \textsf{y})$, while the outgoing edges points to subgames reachable from the current one. Note that each edge represents a probabilistic transition. Subgames with more than one outgoing transition imply nondeterminism that is resolved by the adversary actions. Hence, the directed graph depicts an MDP.

The synthesized strategy for $(h_{\text{adv}} = 2, h = 4)$ is demonstrated in Fig. 10(c). For the initial subgame, Fig. 11(a) shows the maximum probability of a successful geolocation task if performed at stage h, and the remaining distance to target. Assuming the adversary can launch attacks after stage $h_{\text{adv}} = 2$, the detection probability is maximized by performing the geolocation task at step 4,

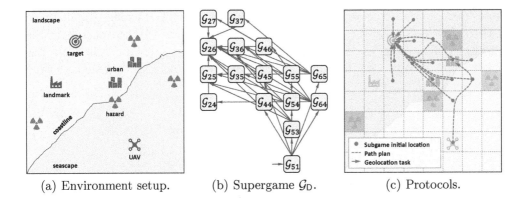

(a) Environment setup.   (b) Supergame $\mathcal{G}_D$.   (c) Protocols.

Fig. 10. (a) The environment setup used for the case study; (b) the induced supergame MDP, where the subgames form its states; and (c) the synthesized protocols.

and hazard areas can still be avoided up till $h = 6$. For $h_{\text{adv}} = 1$, however, $h = 3$ has the highest probability of success, which diminishes at $h = 6$ as no possible flight plan exists without encountering a hazard zone. The effect of the maximum number of geolocation tasks (n) on target reachability is studied by analyzing the supergame against ϕ_{ana} as shown in Fig. 11(b). The minimum number of geolocation tasks to guarantee a non-zero probability of reaching the target (regardless of the adversary strategy) is 3 with probability bounds of $(33.7\%, 94.4\%)$.

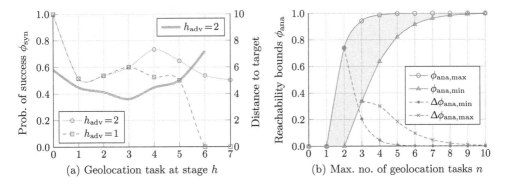

(a) Geolocation task at stage h (b) Max. no. of geolocation tasks n

Fig. 11. Analysis results for (a) subgame $\hat{\mathcal{G}}_{51}$ and (b) supergame $\mathcal{G}_D$.

The experimental data obtained for this case study are listed in Table 1. For the same grid size, more complex maps require more time for synthesis while the state space size remains unaffected. The state space grows exponentially with the explored horizon size, i.e., $\mathcal{O}\left((|A_{\text{uav}}||A_{\text{adv}}|)^h\right)$, and is typically slowed by, e.g., the presence of hazard areas, since the branches of the game transitions are trimmed upon encountering such areas. Interestingly, for $h = 6$ and $h = 7$, while the model construction time (size) for $h_{\mathrm{adv}} = 1$ is almost twice (quadruple) as those for $h_{\mathrm{adv}} = 2$, the time for checking ϕ_{syn} declines in comparison. This reflects the fact that, in case of $h_{\mathrm{adv}} = 1$ compared to $h_{\mathrm{adv}} = 2$, the UAV has higher chances to reach a hazard zone for the same k, leading to a shorter time for model checking.

Table 1. Results for strategy synthesis using queries ϕ_{syn} and ϕ_{ana}.

Subgame $\hat{\mathcal{G}}_{51}$			Model size			Time (sec)		
Map	t_{adv}	k	States	Transitions	Choices	Model	ϕ_{syn}	ϕ_{ana}
8×8	1	4	11,608	17,397	15,950	2.810	0.072	–
		5	57,129	87,865	83,267	14.729	0.602	–
		6	236,714	366,749	359,234	62.582	1.293	–
		7	876,550	1,365,478	1,355,932	231.741	6.021	–
	2	4	6,678	9,230	8,394	2.381	0.042	–
		5	33,904	48,545	45,354	10.251	0.367	–
		6	141,622	204,551	198,640	37.192	1.839	–
		7	524,942	763,144	754,984	145.407	8.850	–
Supergame $\mathcal{G}_{\mathrm{D}}$			6,212	8,306	6,660	2.216	–	2.490

6   Discussion and Conclusion

In this paper, we introduced DAGs and showed how they can simulate HIGs by delaying players' actions. We also derived a DAG-based framework for strategy synthesis and analysis using off-the-shelf SMG model checkers. Under some practical assumptions, we showed that DAGs can be decomposed into independent subgames, utilizing parallel computation to reduce the time needed for model analysis, as well as the size of the state space. We further demonstrated the applicability of the proposed framework on a case study focused on synthesis and analysis of active attack detection strategies for UAVs prone to cyber attacks.

DAGs come at the cost of increasing the total state space size as $\mathcal{M}_{\mathrm{mrd}}$ and $\mathcal{M}_{\mathrm{mwr}}$ are introduced. This does not present a significant limitation due to the compositional approach towards strategy synthesis using subgames. However, the synthesis is still limited to model sizes that off-the-shelf tools can handle.

The concept of delaying actions implicitly assumes that the adversary knows the UAV actions a priori. This does not present a concern in the presented case study as an abstract (i.e., nondeterministic) adversary model is analogous to synthesizing against the worst-case attacking scenario. Nevertheless, strategies synthesized using DAGs (and SMGs in general) are inherently conservative. Depending on the considered system, this can easily lead to no feasible solution.

The proposed synthesis framework ensures preservation of safety properties. Yet, general reward-based strategy synthesis is to be approached with care. For example, rewards dependent on the belief can appear in any state, and exploring hypothetical branches is not required. However, rewards dependent on a state's true value should only appear in proper states, and all hypothetical branches are to be explored. A detailed investigation of how various properties are preserved by DAGs, along with multi-objective synthesis, is a direction for future work.

References

1. Baier, C., Brazdil, T., Grosser, M., Kucera, A.: Stochastic game logic. In: Fourth International Conference on the Quantitative Evaluation of Systems, QEST 2007, pp. 227–236. IEEE (2007). https://doi.org/10.1109/QEST.2007.38
2. Basset, N., Kwiatkowska, M., Topcu, U., Wiltsche, C.: Strategy synthesis for stochastic games with multiple long-run objectives. In: Baier, C., Tinelli, C. (eds.) TACAS 2015. LNCS, vol. 9035, pp. 256–271. Springer, Heidelberg (2015). https://doi.org/10.1007/978-3-662-46681-0_22
3. Basset, N., Kwiatkowska, M., Wiltsche, C.: Compositional strategy synthesis forstochastic games with multiple objectives. Information and Computation (2017). https://doi.org/10.1016/j.ic.2017.09.010
4. Brázdil, T., Chatterjee, K., Křetínský, J., Toman, V.: Strategy representation by decision trees in reactive synthesis. In: Beyer, D., Huisman, M. (eds.) TACAS 2018. LNCS, vol. 10805, pp. 385–407. Springer, Cham (2018). https://doi.org/10.1007/978-3-319-89960-2_21
5. Chatterjee, K., Henzinger, T.A.: Semiperfect-information games. In: Sarukkai, S., Sen, S. (eds.) FSTTCS 2005. LNCS, vol. 3821, pp. 1–18. Springer, Heidelberg (2005). https://doi.org/10.1007/11590156_1
6. Chen, T., Forejt, V., Kwiatkowska, M., Parker, D., Simaitis, A.: Automatic verification of competitive stochastic systems. Form. Methods Syst. Des. 43(1), 61–92 (2013). https://doi.org/10.1007/s10703-013-0183-7
7. Chen, T., Forejt, V., Kwiatkowska, M., Parker, D., Simaitis, A.: PRISM-games: a model checker for stochastic multi-player games. In: Piterman, N., Smolka, S.A. (eds.) TACAS 2013. LNCS, vol. 7795, pp. 185–191. Springer, Heidelberg (2013). https://doi.org/10.1007/978-3-642-36742-7_13
8. Chen, T., Forejt, V., Kwiatkowska, M., Simaitis, A., Wiltsche, C.: On stochastic games with multiple objectives. In: Chatterjee, K., Sgall, J. (eds.) MFCS 2013. LNCS, vol. 8087, pp. 266–277. Springer, Heidelberg (2013). https://doi.org/10.1007/978-3-642-40313-2_25
9. Chen, T., Kwiatkowska, M., Simaitis, A., Wiltsche, C.: Synthesis for multi-objective stochastic games: an application to autonomous urban driving. In: Joshi, K., Siegle, M., Stoelinga, M., D'Argenio, P.R. (eds.) QEST 2013. LNCS, vol. 8054, pp. 322–337. Springer, Heidelberg (2013). https://doi.org/10.1007/978-3-642-40196-1_28
10. David, A., Jensen, P.G., Larsen, K.G., Mikučionis, M., Taankvist, J.H.: UPPAAL STRATEGO. In: Baier, C., Tinelli, C. (eds.) TACAS 2015. LNCS, vol. 9035, pp. 206–211. Springer, Heidelberg (2015). https://doi.org/10.1007/978-3-662-46681-0_16

11. Elfar, M., Zhu, H., Cummings, M.L., Pajic, M.: Security-aware synthesis of human-UAV protocols. In: Proceedings of 2019 IEEE International Conference on Robotics and Automation (ICRA). IEEE (2019)
12. Feng, L., Wiltsche, C., Humphrey, L., Topcu, U.: Synthesis of human-in-the-loop control protocols for autonomous systems. IEEE Trans. Autom. Sci. Eng. **13**(2), 450–462 (2016). https://doi.org/10.1109/TASE.2016.2530623
13. Fremont, D.J., Seshia, S.A.: Reactive control improvisation. In: Chockler, H., Weissenbacher, G. (eds.) CAV 2018. LNCS, vol. 10981, pp. 307–326. Springer, Cham (2018). https://doi.org/10.1007/978-3-319-96145-3_17
14. Fu, J., Topcu, U.: Integrating active sensing into reactive synthesis with temporal logic constraints under partial observations. In: 2015 American Control Conference (ACC), pp. 2408–2413. IEEE (2015). https://doi.org/10.1109/ACC.2015.7171093
15. Hansen, E.A., Bernstein, D.S., Zilberstein, S.: Dynamic programming for partially observable stochastic games. AAAI **4**, 709–715 (2004)
16. Jovanov, I., Pajic, M.: Relaxing integrity requirements for attack-resilient cyber-physical systems. IEEE Trans. Autom. Control (2019). https://doi.org/10.1109/TAC.2019.2898510
17. Kelmendi, E., Krämer, J., Křetínský, J., Weininger, M.: Value iteration for simple stochastic games: stopping criterion and learning algorithm. In: Chockler, H., Weissenbacher, G. (eds.) CAV 2018. LNCS, vol. 10981, pp. 623–642. Springer, Cham (2018). https://doi.org/10.1007/978-3-319-96145-3_36
18. Klein, F., Zimmermann, M.: How much lookahead is needed to win infinite games? In: Halldórsson, M.M., Iwama, K., Kobayashi, N., Speckmann, B. (eds.) ICALP 2015. LNCS, vol. 9135, pp. 452–463. Springer, Heidelberg (2015). https://doi.org/10.1007/978-3-662-47666-6_36
19. Kwiatkowska, M., Parker, D., Wiltsche, C.: Prism-games: verification and strategy synthesis for stochastic multi-player games with multiple objectives. Int. J. Softw. Tools Technol. Transf. **20**(2), 195–210 (2018)
20. Lesi, V., Jovanov, I., Pajic, M.: Security-aware scheduling of embedded control tasks. ACM Trans. Embed. Comput. Syst. (TECS) **16**(5s), 188:1–188:21 (2017). https://doi.org/10.1145/3126518
21. Li, W., Sadigh, D., Sastry, S.S., Seshia, S.A.: Synthesis for human-in-the-loop control systems. In: Ábrahám, E., Havelund, K. (eds.) TACAS 2014. LNCS, vol. 8413, pp. 470–484. Springer, Heidelberg (2014). https://doi.org/10.1007/978-3-642-54862-8_40
22. Mo, Y., Sinopoli, B.: On the performance degradation of cyber-physical systems under stealthy integrity attacks. IEEE Trans. Autom. Control **61**(9), 2618–2624 (2016). https://doi.org/10.1109/TAC.2015.2498708
23. Neider, D., Topcu, U.: An automaton learning approach to solving safety games over infinite graphs. In: Chechik, M., Raskin, J.-F. (eds.) TACAS 2016. LNCS, vol. 9636, pp. 204–221. Springer, Heidelberg (2016). https://doi.org/10.1007/978-3-662-49674-9_12
24. Norman, G., Parker, D., Zou, X.: Verification and control of partially observable probabilistic real-time systems. In: Sankaranarayanan, S., Vicario, E. (eds.) FORMATS 2015. LNCS, vol. 9268, pp. 240–255. Springer, Cham (2015). https://doi.org/10.1007/978-3-319-22975-1_16
25. Pajic, M., Lee, I., Pappas, G.J.: Attack-resilient state estimation for noisy dynamical systems. IEEE Trans. Control Netw. Syst. **4**(1), 82–92 (2017). https://doi.org/10.1109/TCNS.2016.2607420

26. Pajic, M., Weimer, J., Bezzo, N., Sokolsky, O., Pappas, G.J., Lee, I.: Design and implementation of attack-resilient cyberphysical systems: with a focus on attack-resilient state estimators. IEEE Control Syst. **37**(2), 66–81 (2017). https://doi.org/10.1109/MCS.2016.2643239

27. Rasmusen, E., Blackwell, B.: Games and Information, vol. 15. MIT Press, Cambridge (1994)

28. Svoreňová, M., Kwiatkowska, M.: Quantitative verification and strategy synthesis for stochastic games. Eur. J. Control **30**, 15–30 (2016). https://doi.org/10.1016/j.ejcon.2016.04.009

29. Wiltsche, C.: Assume-guarantee strategy synthesis for stochastic games. Ph.D. thesis, Ph.D. dissertation, Department of Computer Science, University of Oxford (2015)

30. Zimmermann, M.: Delay games with WMSO+ U winning conditions. RAIRO Theor. Inform. Appl. **50**(2), 145–165 (2016). https://doi.org/10.1051/ita/2016018

3

Membership-Based Synthesis of Linear Hybrid Automata

Miriam García Soto$^{(\boxtimes)}$ ⓘ, Thomas A. Henzinger ⓘ, Christian Schilling ⓘ,
and Luka Zeleznik

IST Austria, Klosterneuburg, Austria
{miriam.garciasoto,tah,christian.schilling,
luka.zeleznik}@ist.ac.at

Abstract. We present two algorithmic approaches for synthesizing linear hybrid automata from experimental data. Unlike previous approaches, our algorithms work without a template and generate an automaton with nondeterministic guards and invariants, and with an arbitrary number and topology of modes. They thus construct a succinct model from the data and provide formal guarantees. In particular, (1) the generated automaton can reproduce the data up to a specified tolerance and (2) the automaton is tight, given the first guarantee. Our first approach encodes the synthesis problem as a logical formula in the theory of linear arithmetic, which can then be solved by an SMT solver. This approach minimizes the number of modes in the resulting model but is only feasible for limited data sets. To address scalability, we propose a second approach that does not enforce to find a minimal model. The algorithm constructs an initial automaton and then iteratively extends the automaton based on processing new data. Therefore the algorithm is well-suited for online and synthesis-in-the-loop applications. The core of the algorithm is a membership query that checks whether, within the specified tolerance, a given data set can result from the execution of a given automaton. We solve this membership problem for linear hybrid automata by repeated reachability computations. We demonstrate the effectiveness of the algorithm on synthetic data sets and on cardiac-cell measurements.

Keywords: Synthesis · Linear hybrid automaton · Membership

1 Introduction

Natural sciences pursue to understand the mechanisms of real systems and to make this understanding accessible. Achieving these two goals requires observation, analysis, and modeling of the system. Typically, physical components of a system evolve continuously in real time, while the system may switch among a finite set of discrete states. This applies to cyber-physical systems but also to purely analog systems; e.g., an animal's hunger affects its movement. A proper formalism for modeling such types of systems with mixed discrete-continuous behavior is a hybrid automaton [11]. Unlike black-box models such as neural networks, hybrid automata are easy to interpret by humans. However, designing such models is a time-intensive and error-prone process, usually conducted by an expert who analyzes the experimental data and makes decisions.

In this paper, we propose two automatic approaches for synthesizing a linear hybrid automaton [1] from experimental data. The approaches provide two main properties. The first property is *soundness*, which ensures that the generated model has enough executions: these executions approximate the given data up to a predefined accuracy. The second property is *precision*, which ensures that the generated model does not have too many executions. The behavior of a hybrid automaton is constrained by so-called invariants and guards. *Precision* expresses that the boundaries of these invariants and guards are witnessed by the data, which indicates that the constraints cannot be made tighter. Moreover, the proposed synthesis algorithm is *complete* for a general class of linear hybrid automata, i.e., the algorithm can synthesize any given model from this class.

The first approach reduces the synthesis problem to a satisfiability question for a linear-arithmetic formula. The formula allows us to encode a minimality constraint (namely in the number of so-called modes) on the resulting model. This approach is, however, not scalable, which motivates our second approach. Our second approach follows an iterative model-adaptation scheme. Apart from scalability advantages, this *online* algorithm is thus also well-suited for synthesis-in-the-loop applications.

After constructing an initial model, the second approach iteratively improves and expands the model by considering new experiments. After each iteration, the model will capture all behaviors exhibited in the previous experiments. Given an automaton and new experimental data, the algorithm proceeds as follows. First we ask whether the current automaton already captures the data. We pose this question as a membership query for a piecewise-linear function in the set of executions of the automaton. For the membership query, we present an algorithm based on reachability inside a tube around the function. If the data is not captured, we need to modify the automaton accordingly by adding behavior. We first try to relax the above-mentioned invariants and guards, which we reduce to another membership query. If that query is negative as well, we choose a path in the automaton that closely resembles the given data and then modify the automaton along that path by also adding new discrete structure (called modes and transitions). This modification step is again guided by membership queries to identify the aspects of the model that require improvement and expansion.

As the main contributions, (1) we present an online algorithm for automatic synthesis of linear hybrid automata from data that is *sound*, i.e., guarantees that the generated model approximates the data up to a user-defined threshold, *precise*, i.e., the generated model is tight, and *complete* for a general class of models (2) we solve the membership problem of a piecewise-linear function in a linear hybrid automaton. This is a critical step in our synthesis algorithm

Related Work. The synthesis of hybrid systems was initially studied in control theory under the term *identification*, mainly focused on (discrete-time) switched autoregressive exogenous (SARX) and piecewise-affine autoregressive exogenous (PWARX) models [7,18]. SARX models constitute a subclass of linear hybrid automata with deterministic switching behavior. PWARX models are specific SARX models where the mode invariants form a state-space partition. Fixing the number of modes, the identification problem from input-output data can be solved algebraically by inferring template parameters. However, in contrast to linear hybrid automata, the lack of nondeterminism and the underlying assumption that there is no hidden state (mode) limits the applicability of these models. An algorithm by Bemporad et al. constructs a PWARX model that satisfies a *global* error bound [5]. Ozay presents an algorithm for SARX models where the switching is purely time-triggered [17]. There also exist a few *online* algorithms for the recursive synthesis of PWARX models based on pattern recognition [19] or lifting to a high-dimensional identification problem for ARX models [10,22].

Synthesis is also known as *process mining*, and as *learning models from traces*; the latter refers to approaches based on learning finite-state machines [3] or other machine-learning techniques. More recently, synthesis of hybrid automaton models has gained attention. All existing approaches that we are aware of have structural restrictions of some sort, which we describe below. We synthesize, for the first time, a general class of linear hybrid automata which (1) allows nondeterminism to capture many behaviors by a *concise* representation and (2) provides formal soundness and precision guarantees. The algorithm is also the first *online* synthesis approach for linear hybrid automata.

The general synthesis problem for hybrid automata is hard: for deterministic timed automata (a subclass of linear hybrid automata with globally identical continuous dynamics), one may already require data of exponential length [21]. The approach by Niggemann et al. constructs an automaton with acyclic discrete structure [16], while the approach by Grosu et al., intended to model purely periodic behavior, constructs a cyclic-linear hybrid automaton whose discrete structure consists of a loop [8]. Ly and Lipson use symbolic regression to infer a non-linear hybrid automaton [14]. However, their model neither contains state variables (i.e., the model is purely input-driven, comparable to the SARX model) nor invariants, and the number of modes needs to be fixed in advance. Medhat et al. describe an abstract framework, based on heuristics, to learn linear hybrid automata from input/output traces [15]. They first employ Angluin's algorithm for learning a finite-state machine [3], which serves as the discrete structure of the hybrid automaton, before they decorate the automaton with continuous dynamics. This strict separation inherently makes their approach offline. The work by Summerville et al. based on least-squares regression requires an exhaustive construction of all possible models for later optimizing a cost function over all of them [20]. Lamrani et al. learn a completely deterministic model with urgent transitions using ideas from information theory [12].

2   Preliminaries

Sets. Let $\mathbb{R}$, $\mathbb{R}_{\geqslant 0}$, and $\mathbb{N}$ denote the set of real numbers, non-negative real numbers, and natural numbers, respectively. We write $\mathbf{x}$ for points $(x_1, \ldots, x_n)$ in $\mathbb{R}^n$. Let $\mathtt{cpoly}(n)$ be the set of compact and convex polyhedral sets over $\mathbb{R}^n$. A set $X \in \mathtt{cpoly}(n)$ is characterized by its set of vertices $\mathtt{vert}(X)$. For a set of points Y, $\mathtt{chull}(Y) \in \mathtt{cpoly}(n)$ denotes the convex hull. Given a set $X \in \mathtt{cpoly}(n)$ and $\varepsilon \in \mathbb{R}_{\geqslant 0}$, we define the ε-*bloating* of X as $\lceil X \rceil_\varepsilon := \{\mathbf{x} \in \mathbb{R}^n \mid \exists \mathbf{x}_0 \in X : \|\mathbf{x} - \mathbf{x}_0\| \leqslant \varepsilon\} \in \mathtt{cpoly}(n)$, where $\|\cdot\|$ is the infinity norm. Given an interval $I = [l, u] \in \mathtt{cpoly}(1)$, $\mathtt{lb}(I) = l$ and $\mathtt{ub}(I) = u$ denote its lower and upper bound.

Functions and Sequences. Given a function f, let $\mathtt{dom}(f)$ resp. $\mathtt{img}(f)$ denote its domain resp. image. Let $f|_A$ denote the restriction of f to domain $A \subseteq \mathtt{dom}(f)$. We define a *distance* between functions f and g with the same domain and codomain by $d(f, g) := \max_{t \in \mathtt{dom}(f)} \|f(t) - g(t)\|$. A *sequence* of length m is a function $s : D \to A$ over an ordered finite domain $D = \{i_1, \ldots, i_m\} \subseteq \mathbb{N}$ and a set A, and we write $\mathtt{len}(s)$ to denote the length of s. A sequence s is also represented by enumerating its elements, as in $s(i_1), \ldots, s(i_m)$.

Affine and Piecewise-Linear Functions. An *affine piece* is a function $p : I \to \mathbb{R}^n$ over an interval $I = [t_0, t_1] \subseteq \mathbb{R}$ defined as $p(t) = \mathbf{a}t + \mathbf{b}$ where $\mathbf{a}, \mathbf{b} \in \mathbb{R}^n$. Given an affine piece p, $\mathtt{init}(p)$ denotes the start point $p(t_0)$, $\mathtt{end}(p)$ denotes the end point $p(t_1)$, and $\mathtt{slope}(p)$ denotes the slope $\mathbf{a}$. We call two affine pieces p and p' *adjacent* if $\mathtt{end}(p) = \mathtt{init}(p')$ and $\mathtt{ub}(\mathtt{dom}(p)) = \mathtt{lb}(\mathtt{dom}(p'))$. For $m \in \mathbb{N}$, an *m-piecewise-linear (m-PWL) function* $f : I \to \mathbb{R}^n$ over interval $I = [0, \mathsf{T}] \subseteq \mathbb{R}$ consists of m affine pieces $p_1, \ldots, p_m$, such that $I = \cup_{1 \leqslant j \leqslant m} \mathtt{dom}(p_j)$, $f(t) = p_j(t)$ for $t \in \mathtt{dom}(p_j)$, and for every $1 < j \leqslant m$ we have $\mathtt{end}(p_{j-1}) = \mathtt{init}(p_j)$. We show a 3-PWL function in Fig. 1 on the left. Let $\mathtt{pieces}(f)$ denote the set of affine pieces of f. We refer to f and the sequence $p_1, \ldots, p_m$ interchangeably and write "PWL function" if m is clear from the context. A *kink* of a PWL function is the point between two adjacent pieces. Given a PWL function $f : I \to \mathbb{R}^n$ and a value $\varepsilon \in \mathbb{R}_{\geqslant 0}$, the ε-*tube* of f is the function $\mathtt{tube}_{f,\varepsilon} : I \to \mathtt{cpoly}(n)$ such that $\mathtt{tube}_{f,\varepsilon}(t) = \lceil f(t) \rceil_\varepsilon$.

Graphs. A *graph* is a pair (V, E) of a finite set V and a relation $E \subseteq V \times V$. A *path* π in (V, E) is a sequence $v_1, \ldots, v_m$ with $(v_{j-1}, v_j) \in E$ for $1 < j \leqslant m$.

Hybrid Automata. We consider a particular class of hybrid automata [1,11].

Definition 1. *A n-dimensional* linear hybrid automaton (LHA) *is a tuple* $\mathcal{H} = (Q, E, X, Flow, Inv, Grd)$, *where (1)* Q *is a finite set of modes, (2)* $E \subseteq Q \times Q$ *is a transition relation, (3)* $X = \mathbb{R}^n$ *is the continuous state-space, (4)* $Flow : Q \to \mathbb{R}^n$ *is the flow function, (5)* $Inv : Q \to \mathtt{cpoly}(n)$ *is the invariant function, and (6)* $Grd : E \to \mathtt{cpoly}(n)$ *is the guard function*

We sometimes annotate the elements of LHA $\mathcal{H}$ by a subscript, as in $Q_\mathcal{H}$ for the set of modes. We refer to $(Q_\mathcal{H}, E_\mathcal{H})$ as the *graph* of LHA $\mathcal{H}$.

An LHA evolves continuously according to the flow function in each mode. The behavior starts in some mode $q \in Q$ and some continuous state $\mathbf{x} \in Inv(q)$.

For every mode $q \in Q$, the continuous evolution follows the differential equation $\dot{\mathbf{x}} = Flow(q)$ while satisfying the invariant $Inv(q)$. The behavior can switch from one mode q_1 to another mode q_2 if there is a transition $(q_1, q_2) \in E$ and the guard $Grd((q_1, q_2))$ is satisfied. During a switch, the continuous state does not change. This type of system is sometimes called a switched linear hybrid system [13].

Definition 2. *Given an n-dimensional* LHA *$\mathcal{H} = (Q, E, X, Flow, Inv, Grd)$, an execution σ is a triple $\sigma = (\mathcal{I}, \gamma, \delta)$, where $\mathcal{I}$ is a sequence of consecutive intervals $[t_0, t_1], [t_1, t_2], \dots, [t_{m-1}, t_m]$ with $\llbracket \mathcal{I} \rrbracket = \cup_{0 \leqslant j < m}[t_j, t_{j+1}]$, and $\gamma : \llbracket \mathcal{I} \rrbracket \to \mathbb{R}^n$ and $\delta : \{1, \dots, m\} \to Q$ are functions with the following restrictions:*

- *for all $1 \leqslant j < m$, $\gamma(t) \in Inv(\delta(j))$ for $t \in \mathcal{I}(j)$ and $\dot{\gamma}(t') = Flow(\delta(j))$ for all t' in the interior of $\mathcal{I}(j)$, i.e., $\gamma|_{\mathcal{I}(j)}$ is an affine function satisfying the invariant and following the flow, and*
- *for all $1 \leqslant j < m$, $(\delta(j), \delta(j + 1)) \in E$ and $\gamma(t) \in Grd((\delta(j), \delta(j + 1)))$ where $t = \mathtt{ub}(\mathcal{I}(j))$, i.e., if a transition is taken, then the guard is satisfied.*

We denote the set of all executions of $\mathcal{H}$ by $\mathtt{exec}(\mathcal{H})$. Given an LHA $\mathcal{H}$, we say that an execution σ *follows a path* π in $\mathcal{H}$, that is, in the graph $(Q_\mathcal{H}, E_\mathcal{H})$, denoted as $\sigma \overset{\mathcal{H}}{\leadsto} \pi$, if $\mathtt{len}(\mathcal{I}) = \mathtt{len}(\pi)$ and $\delta(j) = \pi(j)$ for every $0 \leqslant j < \mathtt{len}(\mathcal{I})$.

From Time-series Data to PWL *Functions.* Experimental data typically comes as *time series*, i.e., data is only available at sampled points in time. A time series is a sampling $s : D \to \mathbb{R}^n$ over a finite time domain $D \subseteq [0, \mathsf{T}]$. Since the LHA model features piecewise-linear executions, we focus on piecewise-linear approximation of the data. PWL functions can approximate any continuous behavior with arbitrary precision. There are different yet valid choices for approximating data. For a single time series, linear interpolation gives a perfect fit, but contains many kinks; other algorithms minimize the number of kinks for a given error bound [6,9]. One can preprocess multiple time series into a single PWL function using, e.g., linear regression. In this paper, we leave the choice of abstraction open and assume that the input is given as PWL functions.

3   Synthesis of Linear Hybrid Automata

In this section, we specify the synthesis problem, consider two different specifications, synchronous and asynchronous, and present the automated approach for solving the synchronous problem. The overall goal is to synthesize a linear hybrid automaton from a set of PWL functions such that the automaton *captures* the behavior described by each of the PWL functions up to a bound ε.

Definition 3 (Soundness). *Given a* PWL *function f and a value $\varepsilon \in \mathbb{R}_{\geqslant 0}$, we say that an* LHA *$\mathcal{H}$ ε-captures f if there exists an execution $\sigma = (\mathcal{I}, \gamma, \delta)$ in $\mathtt{exec}(\mathcal{H})$ with $d(f, \gamma) \leqslant \varepsilon$.*

The value ε quantifies the acceptable deviation of an execution's continuous function γ from the PWL function f. For $\varepsilon = 0$, γ must precisely follow f. A straightforward formulation of the problem we want to solve is the following.

Problem 1 (Synthesis). Given a finite set of PWL functions $\mathcal{F}$ and $\varepsilon \in \mathbb{R}_{\geqslant 0}$, construct an LHA $\mathcal{H}$ that ε-captures every function $f \in \mathcal{F}$.

Observe that this problem is not well-posed, as it can be satisfied by an automaton that exhibits an excessive amount of behavior. Hence our second goal for the synthesis algorithm is to ensure constraints on the automaton's size. We start with the synthesis of an LHA with minimal number of modes.

3.1 Synchronous Switching Specification

For now, we require that the executions in the LHA switch *synchronously* with the given PWL functions. Under this assumption, we tackle a refinement of Problem 1:

Problem 2 (Synchronous synthesis). Given a finite set of PWL functions $\mathcal{F}$ and a value $\varepsilon \in \mathbb{R}_{\geqslant 0}$, construct an LHA $\mathcal{H}$ that ε-captures every function $f \in \mathcal{F}$ synchronously, and furthermore require that $\mathcal{H}$ has the minimal number of modes.

In the following, we present an algorithm to solve Problem 2. The idea is, given a PWL function f, to synthesize an execution σ that is ε-close to f. Recall that the continuous function γ of an execution is essentially just another PWL function. Any LHA that contains the execution σ has to comprise a mode for each different slope in γ. Thus a minimal number of modes can be achieved by minimizing the number of different slopes in γ. By fixing a number of different slopes, we encode the existence of γ as a logical formula $\phi_{f,\varepsilon}$, which will be satisfiable if and only if there exists a suitable function γ.

Let m be the number of affine pieces $p_1, \ldots, p_m$ in f with $\operatorname{dom}(p_j) = [t_{j-1}, t_j]$ for $1 \leqslant j \leqslant m$. We refer to the time instants t_j as the switching times of f, and to $\mathbf{x}_j = f(t_j)$ as the switching points of f. Fixing a number $\ell \in \mathbb{N}$, we want to construct a PWL function γ_ℓ, consisting of m affine pieces $p'_1, \ldots, p'_m$ with ℓ different slopes, with the same switching times as in f, with switching points $\mathbf{y}_0, \ldots, \mathbf{y}_m$ ε-close to those in f (which is necessary and sufficient for $d(f, \gamma_\ell) \leqslant \varepsilon$), and with unknown slopes $\mathbf{b}_1 = \texttt{slope}(p'_1), \ldots, \mathbf{b}_m = \texttt{slope}(p'_m)$. We define the logical formula

$$\phi_{f,\varepsilon}(\ell) := \bigwedge_{j=1}^{m} \mathbf{y}_j = \mathbf{y}_{j-1} + \mathbf{b}_j(t_j - t_{j-1}) \wedge \bigwedge_{j=0}^{m} \mathbf{y}_j \in \lceil \mathbf{x}_j \rceil_\varepsilon \wedge \bigwedge_{j=1}^{m} \bigvee_{k=1}^{\ell} \mathbf{b}_j = \mathbf{c}_k,$$

which is satisfiable if and only if there exists a suitable PWL function γ_ℓ. For lifting to a set of functions $\mathcal{F}$, we define the formula $\phi_{\mathcal{F},\varepsilon}(\ell) := \bigwedge_{f \in \mathcal{F}} \phi_{f,\varepsilon}(\ell)$. These formulae fall into the theory of linear arithmetic and can be effectively solved by an SMT solver. Now, we can state the following results.

Lemma 1. *Let $\mathcal{F}$ be a finite set of PWL functions and $\varepsilon \in \mathbb{R}_{\geqslant 0}$. If $\phi_{\mathcal{F},\varepsilon}(\ell)$ is satisfiable for some integer value ℓ, then there exists a set of PWL functions $\mathcal{F}'$ such that $|\mathcal{F}'| = |\mathcal{F}|$, each function in $\mathcal{F}$ is ε-close to some function in $\mathcal{F}'$, and the number of distinct slopes in $\mathcal{F}'$ does not exceed ℓ.*

The set $\mathcal{F}'$ can be extracted from a satisfying assignment. We define a hybrid automaton with minimal number of locations 0-capturing a given PWL function.

Definition 4 (Canonical automaton). *Let f be an n-PWL function. The canonical automaton of f is $\mathcal{H}_f := (Q, E, \mathbb{R}^n, Flow, Inv, Grd)$ with*

- $Q = \{q_{\mathbf{a}} \mid \exists p \in pieces(f) : \texttt{slope}(p) = \mathbf{a}\}$,
- $E = \{(q_{\mathbf{a}}, q_{\mathbf{a}'}) \mid \exists p, p' \in pieces(f) \, adjacent : \texttt{slope}(p) = \mathbf{a}, \texttt{slope}(p') = \mathbf{a}'\}$,
- $Flow(q_{\mathbf{a}}) = \mathbf{a}$,
- $Inv(q_{\mathbf{a}}) = \texttt{chull}(\{\texttt{img}(p) \mid p \in pieces(f) : \texttt{slope}(p) = \mathbf{a}\})$, *and*
- $Grd((q_{\mathbf{a}}, q_{\mathbf{a}'})) = \texttt{chull}(\{\texttt{end}(p) \mid \exists p, p' \in pieces(f) \, adjacent : \texttt{slope}(p) = \mathbf{a}, \texttt{slope}(p') = \mathbf{a}'\})$.

Lemma 2. *Given a PWL function f, the canonical automaton $\mathcal{H}_f$ 0-captures f, and every LHA that 0-captures f has at least as many modes as $\mathcal{H}_f$.*

Definition 5 (Merging). *Given two hybrid automata $\mathcal{H}_i = (Q_i, E_i, X, Flow_i, Inv_i, Grd_i)$, $i = 1, 2$ with $Q_1 \cap Q_2 = \emptyset$, let $Q_{\mathbf{a}} = Q_{\mathbf{a}}^{\mathcal{H}_1} \cup Q_{\mathbf{a}}^{\mathcal{H}_2}$ be the locations with flow equal to $\mathbf{a}$. We define the merging of $\mathcal{H}_1$ and $\mathcal{H}_2$ as $\mathcal{H}_1 \sqcup \mathcal{H}_2 := (Q, E, X, Flow, Inv, Grd)$ with $Q = \{q_{\mathbf{a}} \mid \mathbf{a} \in \mathbb{R}^n, Q_{\mathbf{a}} \neq \emptyset\}$, $E = \{(q_{\mathbf{a}}, q_{\mathbf{a}'}) \mid \exists (q, q') \in E_1 \cup E_2, q \in Q_{\mathbf{a}}, q \in Q_{\mathbf{a}'}'\}$, $Flow(q_{\mathbf{a}}) = \mathbf{a}$, $Inv(q_{\mathbf{a}}) = \texttt{chull}(\{Inv_i(q) \mid q \in Q_{\mathbf{a}}, i = 1, 2\})$, and $Grd((q_{\mathbf{a}}, q_{\mathbf{a}'})) = \texttt{chull}(\{Grd_i((q, q')) \mid (q, q') \in E_i, q \in Q_{\mathbf{a}}, q' \in Q_{\mathbf{a}'}, i = 1, 2\})$.*

Theorem 1. *Given a finite set of PWL functions $\mathcal{F}$ and a value $\varepsilon \in \mathbb{R}_{\geqslant 0}$, let ℓ be the smallest integer such that $\phi_{\mathcal{F},\varepsilon}(\ell)$ is satisfiable and let $\mathcal{F}'$ be a set of PWL functions corresponding to a satisfying assignment. Then, the merging of canonical automata $\sqcup_{f \in \mathcal{F}'} \mathcal{H}_f$ solves Problem 2.*

The above synthesis algorithm works well with short and low-dimensional PWL functions but does not scale to realistic problem sizes due to the heavy use of disjunctions. We next address scalability with a new online algorithm.

3.2 Asynchronous Switching Specification

We now change the requirement from the previous subsection (minimality in the models' discrete structure) to tightness in the model's state-space constraints. Intuitively, for every vertex $\mathbf{v}$ of an invariant or guard in $\mathcal{H}$ there should be some witness data $f \in \mathcal{F}$ that is close to $\mathbf{v}$ (at some point in time).

Definition 6 (Precision). *Given an LHA $\mathcal{H} = (Q, E, X, Flow, Inv, Grd)$, let $\mathbf{vert}(\mathcal{H})$ denote the union of the vertices of the invariants and guards:*

$$\mathbf{vert}(\mathcal{H}) = \bigcup_{q \in Q} \mathbf{vert}(Inv(q)) \cup \bigcup_{e \in E} \mathbf{vert}(Grd(e))$$

Given a set of PWL functions $\mathcal{F}$ and a value $\varepsilon \in \mathbb{R}_{\geqslant 0}$, we say that $\mathcal{H}$ is ε-precise (with respect to $\mathcal{F}$) if the following holds:

$$\forall \mathbf{v} \in \mathbf{vert}(\mathcal{H}) \; \exists f \in \mathcal{F} \; \exists t \in \texttt{dom}(f) : \|\mathbf{v} - f(t)\| \leqslant \varepsilon.$$

The restriction to the vertices is reasonable because all sets are compact convex polyhedra. Note that ε-capturing compares functions to the automaton's executions, while ε-precision compares functions to the automaton's state-space.

We also relax the limitation to synchronously switching executions. Instead, we allow *asynchronous* switching, characterized as follows: for every function f ε-captured by $\mathcal{H}$, there exists an execution $\sigma \in \texttt{exec}(\mathcal{H})$ with the same number of switches as there are kinks in f, i.e., $\texttt{len}(\mathcal{I}) = |\texttt{pieces}(f)|$, and where the j-th switch in the execution should take place during the time period between the kinks $j-1$ and $j+1$. We close this section with the new problem statement (a refinement of Problem 1), and present a solution in the next section.

Problem 3 (Asynchronous synthesis). Given a finite set of PWL functions $\mathcal{F}$ and a value $\varepsilon \in \mathbb{R}_{\geqslant 0}$, construct an ε-precise LHA $\mathcal{H}$ that ε-captures every function $f \in \mathcal{F}$ asynchronously.

4 Membership-based Synthesis Approach

In this section, we present an algorithm for solving Problem 3. The core of the algorithm is a reachability computation for providing the polyhedral regions where executions of an LHA that are ε-close to a given PWL function f are allowed to switch. More precisely, given a path π and the ε-tube of f, the algorithm iteratively constructs the set inside the ε-tube where an execution following π can switch, without escaping from the tube. These reachable set are, in general, computed with respect to a starting compact convex polyhedron P, a pair of adjacent affine pieces p and p', and a pair of modes q and q' along π.

Definition 7. *Given an* LHA *$\mathcal{H} = (Q, E, X, Flow, Inv, Grd)$ and a value $\varepsilon \in \mathbb{R}_{\geqslant 0}$, a reachable switching set $switch_{\mathcal{H}}(P, p, p', q, q')$ from a set P with respect to two adjacent affine pieces p, p' and a path $\pi := q, q'$ in $\mathcal{H}$ is defined as*

$$\{\mathbf{x} \in Grd((q, q')) \mid \exists \sigma = (\mathcal{I}, \gamma, \delta) \in \texttt{exec}(\mathcal{H}) : \sigma \overset{\mathcal{H}}{\leadsto} \pi, \text{dom}(\gamma) = \text{dom}(p) \cup \text{dom}(p'),$$
$$\gamma(0) \in P, \gamma(t) \in \textit{tube}_{p,\varepsilon}(t) \cup \textit{tube}_{p',\varepsilon}(t), \ and \ \mathbf{x} = \gamma(\text{ub}(\mathcal{I}(0)))\}.$$

Inductive Reachable Switching Computation. Given an LHA $\mathcal{H}$, an m-PWL function $f = p_1, \ldots, p_m$, a value $\varepsilon \in \mathbb{R}_{\geqslant 0}$ and a path $\pi = q_1, \ldots, q_m$ in the graph $(Q_{\mathcal{H}}, E_{\mathcal{H}})$, we compute the reachable switching set P_j^π for every $0 \leqslant j \leqslant m$:

- $P_0^\pi := Inv_{\mathcal{H}}(q_1) \cap \texttt{tube}_{f,\varepsilon}(0)$,
- $P_j^\pi := switch_{\mathcal{H}}(P_{j-1}^\pi, p_{j-1}, p_j, q_{j-1}, q_j)$ for $1 < j < m$, and
- $P_m^\pi := \{\mathbf{x} \in Inv(q_m) \mid \exists \sigma = (\mathcal{I}, \gamma, \delta) \in \texttt{exec}(\mathcal{H}) : \sigma \overset{\mathcal{H}}{\leadsto} q_m, \gamma(0) \in P_{m-1}^\pi,$
  $\text{dom}(\gamma) = \text{dom}(p_m), \gamma(t) \in \texttt{tube}_{p_m,\varepsilon}(t) \text{ and } \mathbf{x} = \gamma(\text{ub}(\mathcal{I}(m)))\}.$

We denote the set of all reachable switching sets P_j^π by $\mathcal{P}^\pi$. We are now ready to present the complete synthesis algorithm.

Algorithm 1. SYNTHESIS

Input: A set of PWL functions $\mathcal{F} = \{f_0, \ldots, f_N\}$ and a value $\varepsilon \in \mathbb{R}_{\geqslant 0}$
Output: A linear hybrid automaton $\mathcal{H}$ that solves Problem 3
1: $\mathcal{H} := \text{INITLHA}(f_0, \varepsilon)$ ▷ construct initial model for ε-capturing f_0
2: **for** $f \in \mathcal{F} \setminus \{f_0\}$ **do**
3:     $(ans, \pi) := \text{MEMBERSHIP}(f, \mathcal{H}, \varepsilon)$
4:     **if not** ans **then**
5:         $\overline{\mathcal{H}} := \text{RELAXALL}(\mathcal{H}, f, \varepsilon)$ ▷ relax model constraints entirely
6:         $(ans, \pi) := \text{MEMBERSHIP}(f, \overline{\mathcal{H}}, \varepsilon)$
7:         **if** ans **then**
8:             $\mathcal{H} := \text{RELAXPATH}(\mathcal{H}, f, \varepsilon, \pi)$ ▷ relax model constraints for ε-capturing f
9:         **else**
10:            $\mathcal{H} := \text{ADAPT}(\mathcal{H}, f, \varepsilon, \pi)$ ▷ adapt model for ε-capturing f
11: **return** $\mathcal{H}$

4.1   Membership-based Synthesis Algorithm

The synthesis algorithm outlined in Algorithm 1 computes an LHA $\mathcal{H}$ solving Problem 3 for a given finite set of PWL functions $\mathcal{F}$ and a value $\varepsilon \in \mathbb{R}_{\geqslant 0}$. The algorithm initially infers an LHA $\mathcal{H}$ that ε-captures the first function f_0 of $\mathcal{F}$ in an ε-precise manner in line 1. The remaining PWL functions are handled in an iterative loop. For each PWL function f, the algorithm performs a membership query, where it checks if f is ε-captured by the LHA $\mathcal{H}$ in line 3. If the query results in a positive answer ($ans = True$), nothing needs to be done. Otherwise, the query returns a path π and the LHA $\mathcal{H}$ needs to be modified. The modification of the automaton $\mathcal{H}$ is performed in two attempts. The first attempt, in line 5, temporarily increases invariants and guards of $\mathcal{H}$. If such a modification is sufficient to let the membership query succeed, the modifications are made permanent in line 8. Otherwise, in the second attempt the algorithm adds new modes and/or transitions to $\mathcal{H}$ along the path π. Below we describe every procedure of Algorithm 1 in detail.

Initialization. The procedure $\text{INITLHA}(f, \varepsilon)$ constructs an initial LHA $\mathcal{H}$ that ε-captures an m-PWL function f. Observe that by Lemma 2 the canonical automaton $\mathcal{H}_f$ 0-captures (and hence ε-captures) the function f. In order to allow similar dynamical behaviors in a given LHA $\mathcal{H}$, the procedure $\text{INITLHA}(f, \varepsilon)$ ε-bloats both invariant and guards polyhedra. The procedure $\text{INITLHA}(f, \varepsilon)$ outputs the ε-bloated canonical automaton $\mathcal{H}_f^\varepsilon$ and is illustrated in Fig. 1.

Definition 8. *Given an* LHA *$\mathcal{H} = (Q, E, X, Flow, Inv, Grd)$, we define the ε -bloated* LHA *of $\mathcal{H}$ as $\mathcal{H}^\varepsilon = (Q, E, X, Flow, Inv^\varepsilon, Grd^\varepsilon)$ where $Inv^\varepsilon(q) = \lceil Inv(q) \rceil_\varepsilon$ for every $q \in Q$ and $Grd^\varepsilon(e) = \lceil Grd(e) \rceil_\varepsilon$ for every $e \in E$.*

Lemma 3. *Given a* PWL *function f and $\varepsilon \in \mathbb{R}_{\geqslant 0}$, $\mathcal{H}_f^\varepsilon$ ε-captures f.*

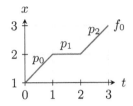 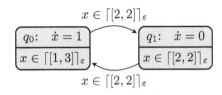

Fig. 1. Example describing the procedure INITLHA(f, ε) for a 3-PWL function $f = f_0$ (depicted on the left). The function f_0 consists of three pieces p_0, p_1, p_2 with slopes $1, 0, 1$, respectively. The LHA on the right is constructed as follows. Mode q_0 corresponds to pieces p_0 and p_2; the invariant is the ε-bloating of interval $[1, 3]$ (which is the convex hull of every start and end point in both pieces). Likewise, mode q_1 corresponds to piece p_1. Transitions and their guards correspond to the kinks of f_0 at $t = 1$ and $t = 2$.

Membership. The procedure MEMBERSHIP$(f, \mathcal{H}, \varepsilon)$ checks whether there exists an *asynchronous* execution $\sigma = (\mathcal{I}, \gamma, \delta)$ in $\mathcal{H}$ such that $d(f, \gamma) \leqslant \varepsilon$ holds. Let us introduce the required notions to formalize the membership problem.

Definition 9. *An execution $\sigma = (\mathcal{I}, \gamma, \delta)$ of an LHA $\mathcal{H}$ is consistent with an m-PWL function f, described by the affine pieces $p_1, \ldots, p_m$, if $\mathrm{len}(\mathcal{I}) = m$, $[\![\mathcal{I}]\!] = \mathrm{dom}(f)$, and $\mathrm{ub}(\mathcal{I}(j)) \in \mathrm{dom}(p_j) \cup \mathrm{dom}(p_{j+1})$ for every $1 \leqslant j < m$.*

Problem 4 (Membership). Given an m-PWL function f, an LHA $\mathcal{H}$, and a value $\varepsilon \in \mathbb{R}_{\geqslant 0}$, decide if there exists an execution $\sigma = (\mathcal{I}, \gamma, \delta)$ in $\mathrm{exec}(\mathcal{H})$ that is consistent with f and such that $d(f, \gamma) \leqslant \varepsilon$ holds.

The procedure MEMBERSHIP$(f, \mathcal{H}, \varepsilon)$ solves Problem 4 by computing the reachable switching sets for every path π of length m in $\mathcal{H}$ until finding a path π where every reachable switching set P_j^π for $0 \leqslant j \leqslant m$ is nonempty. Upon finding a path π satisfying the previous constraints, MEMBERSHIP$(f, \mathcal{H}, \varepsilon)$ returns *True* as answer, together with the path π. If there does not exist such a path π, it returns *False* as answer. We show an example in Fig. 2(a). We remark that, for a fixed path, Problem 4 is a timestamp-generation problem [2] with the restriction to time intervals for switching and the ε-tube as solution corridor.

Lemma 4. *Let $\mathcal{H}$ be an LHA and f be an m-PWL function. Then there exists a path π of length m in $\mathcal{H}$ such that the final reachable switching set P_m^π is not empty if and only if there exists an execution σ in $\mathrm{exec}(\mathcal{H})$ solving Problem 4.*

Relaxation. If MEMBERSHIP$(f, \mathcal{H}, \varepsilon)$ returns *False*, RELAXALL$(\mathcal{H}, f, \varepsilon)$ constructs an automaton $\overline{\mathcal{H}}$ that is equivalent to $\mathcal{H}$ except that its invariants and guards are enlarged to allow additional executions inside the $\mathrm{tube}_{f,\varepsilon}$. Then, the algorithm computes MEMBERSHIP$(f, \overline{\mathcal{H}}, \varepsilon)$. If the answer is *False* again, the algorithm proceeds to the adaptation procedure in line 10. Otherwise (if the answer is *True*), we obtain a path π in $\overline{\mathcal{H}}$. Then the algorithm executes the procedure RELAXPATH$(\mathcal{H}, f, \varepsilon, \pi)$, which extends the constraints of invariants and guards

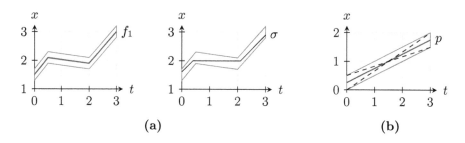

Fig. 2. (a) Example describing the procedure MEMBERSHIP$(f, \mathcal{H}, \varepsilon)$. On the left we depict a 3-PWL function f_1 and its ε-tube. On the right we show a possible execution in the LHA from Fig. 1. **(b)** Given an affine piece p, we say that another piece has a *similar* slope if it does not leave the tube. In the figure, we show the minimal and the maximal allowed slopes by dashed segments.

in $\mathcal{H}$ for the modes in π by taking the convex hull with the corresponding reachable switching sets $P_j^\pi \in \mathcal{P}^\pi$. The relaxation procedure applied on the running example is shown in Fig. 3.

Adaptation. If both the membership query and the relaxation procedure fail, the procedure ADAPT$(\mathcal{H}, f, \varepsilon, \pi)$ modifies the LHA $\mathcal{H}$ for ε-capturing f. Conceptually, we construct a new path π', based on some path π, and modify $\mathcal{H}$ accordingly such that the graph of $\mathcal{H}$ contains π'. Recalling Lemma 4, we need to ensure that every reachable switching set in $\mathcal{P}^{\pi'}$ is nonempty. We construct π' by trying to preserve the modes in path π. If this is not possible, we try to replace them by existing modes in the LHA $\mathcal{H}$ whenever possible, potentially adding new transitions. The last option is to create new modes. Finally, we extend the LHA $\mathcal{H}$ by adding the new transitions and/or modes determined by the new path π'.

In more detail, given an LHA $\mathcal{H}$, an m-PWL function f and a path $\pi = q_1, \ldots, q_m$ in $\mathcal{H}$, we start with path $\pi' = \pi$. Then, the adaptation procedure checks whether there is an empty reachable switching set in $\mathcal{P}^{\pi'}$. Every time we detect emptiness of the set $P_j^{\pi'}$ for some $0 \leqslant j \leqslant m$, a mode in the path π' is replaced in order to make $P_j^{\pi'}$ nonempty. We first try to replace the mode q_{j+1} if it exists. If $P_j^{\pi'}$ is still empty or q_{j+1} does not exist, we repeat the replacement for q_j, q_{i-1}, and so on, until $P_j^{\pi'}$ finally becomes nonempty.

For the replacement of the j-th mode q in the path π' we follow two strategies. The first strategy is to replace the mode q by an existing mode $q' \neq q$ in $\mathcal{H}$ such that $Flow_\mathcal{H}(q')$ is *similar* to $\texttt{slope}(p_j)$. Formally, let T be the duration of piece p_j. $Flow_\mathcal{H}(q')$ is similar to $\texttt{slope}(p_j)$ if $\|\texttt{init}(p_j) + \mathsf{T} \cdot Flow_\mathcal{H}(q') - \texttt{end}(p_j)\| \leqslant 2\varepsilon$. See Fig. 2(b) for an example. If the first strategy fails, the second strategy is to create a new mode q^* with flow $\texttt{newflow}(q^*) = \texttt{slope}(p_j)$ for replacement in π'. We denote the set of existing modes similar to some mode q in π by $\texttt{sim}(\pi')$, and the set of new modes q^* by $\texttt{new}(\pi')$. Once the path π' is constructed, the adaptation of the LHA $\mathcal{H}$ is performed with respect to π'. Figure 4 exemplifies the adaptation of the LHA in Fig. 1.

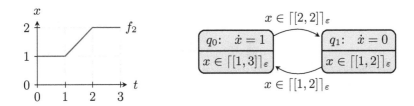

Fig. 3. Example describing the procedure RELAXPATH($\mathcal{H}, f, \varepsilon, \pi$) for $\mathcal{H}$ given in Fig. 1, $f = f_2$ (depicted on the left), and path $\pi = q_1, q_0, q_1$. The algorithm increases the invariant of mode q_1 by computing the convex hull of the old invariant $\lceil\lceil 2,2 \rceil\rceil_\varepsilon$ and the set $\lceil\lceil 1,1 \rceil\rceil_\varepsilon$. Analogously, the guard of the transition (q_1, q_0) is increased.

Definition 10. *The* adaptation *of the* LHA $\mathcal{H} = (Q, E, X, Flow, Inv, Grd)$ *with respect to an* m-PWL *function* f *with affine pieces* $p_1, \ldots, p_m$ *and a path* $\pi = q_1, \ldots, q_m$ *is the* LHA $\mathcal{H}' = (Q', E', X, Flow', Inv', Grd')$ *defined as:*

- $Q' := Q \cup \texttt{new}(\pi')$,
- $E' := E \cup \{(q_j, q_{j+1}) \mid 1 \leqslant j < m\}$,
- $Flow'(q) := \begin{cases} \texttt{newflow}(q) & \text{if } q \in \texttt{new}(\pi'), \\ Flow(q) & \text{otherwise,} \end{cases}$

- $Inv'(q) := \begin{cases} \texttt{chull}(\bigcup_{q=q_j, q \neq q_1} P^{\pi'}_{j-1} \cup \bigcup_{q=q_j} P^{\pi'}_j) & \text{if } q \in \texttt{new}(\pi'), \\ \texttt{chull}(Inv(q) \cup \bigcup_{q=q_j, q \neq q_1} P^{\pi'}_{j-1} \cup \bigcup_{q=q_j} P^{\pi'}_j) & \text{if } q \in \texttt{sim}(\pi'), \\ Inv(q) & \text{otherwise,} \end{cases}$

- $Grd'((q, q')) := \begin{cases} \texttt{chull}(\bigcup_{q=q_j, q'=q_{j+1}} P^{\pi'}_j) & \begin{array}{l}\text{if } q \in \texttt{new}(\pi') \\ \text{or } q' \in \texttt{new}(\pi'), \end{array} \\ \texttt{chull}(Grd((q, q')) \cup \bigcup_{q=q_j, q'=q_{j+1}} P^{\pi'}_j) & \begin{array}{l}\text{if } q \in \texttt{sim}(\pi') \\ \text{or } q' \in \texttt{sim}(\pi'), \end{array} \\ Grd((q, q')) & \text{otherwise.} \end{cases}$

If there is no path of length m in the graph of $\mathcal{H}$, we choose a shorter path π in $\mathcal{H}$ of length m' for the adaptation procedure. Then, for every position $j \geqslant m'$, we define the reachable switching set P^π_j as an empty set and proceed as usual.

4.2 Discussion

The construction of the initial LHA (line 1 in Algorithm 1) can be modified to *clustering* pieces with *similar* slopes. This can help reducing the number of modes in the initial automaton, but does not guarantee that the first PWL function f_0 is ε-captured. To fix this, f_0 can be included in the loop of Algorithm 1.

Algorithm 1 follows a *local* repair strategy, based on a single PWL function. Thanks to this, the algorithm can be used in an online setting where new data arrives after the algorithm has started. However, the resulting model is influenced

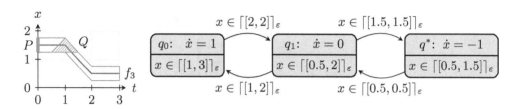

Fig. 4. Example describing the procedure $\text{ADAPT}(\mathcal{H}, f, \pi, \varepsilon)$ for the LHA $\mathcal{H}$ in Fig. 1 with respect to the 3-PWL function $f = f_3$ and the path $\pi = q_1, q_0, q_1$ and $\varepsilon = 0.25$. The initial reachable switching set P_0^π is the projection of the set P on state x. Considering the flows in q_1 and q_0, the next reachable switching set P_1^π is the projection of the set Q on state x. Observe that from Q, using the flow of q_1, the reachable switching set P_2^π is empty. We thus add a new mode q^* and obtain the new path $\pi' = q_1, q^*, q_1$.

by the order in which the algorithm processes the functions $f \in \mathcal{F}$. In the simple case that $\mathcal{F}$ only contains affine functions with the same slope, all models resulting from different processing orders will consist of a single mode with the same flow, and the invariant bounds differ by at most ε. Furthermore, for a precision value $\varepsilon = 0$, the result is always order-independent.

We now discuss the restrictions of the models we obtain from Algorithm 1. We did not include a set of initial states in our presentation, but the generalization is straightforward. Our transitions do not include assignments, which would make executions discontinuous. The usual assumption in many application domains, e.g., life sciences, is that the underlying system is continuous, so having assignments would not be desirable. In the setting where the input is given as time-series data, discrete events would typically be approximated by steep slopes in the PWL function. In the setting where the input is given as discontinuous PWL functions f, in order to ε-capture f, one would generally require that the automaton switches synchronously with f (cf. Sect. 3.1), instead of asynchronous switching as in our algorithm. Under this additional assumption, we can pose the procedures MEMBERSHIP and RELAXPATH as a single linear program (similar to formula $\phi_{f,\varepsilon}$). This linear program can also be used to identify assignments.

The continuous dynamics of our models are defined by constant differential equations. As mentioned before, this class generally suffices to approximate an arbitrary continuous function (by increasing the number of modes). An extension of our approach to use polyhedral differential *inclusions* (also called linear envelopes) is by merging modes of "similar" dynamics. This may, however, lead to the dilemma that several modes are equally similar.

4.3 Theoretical Properties of the Membership-based Synthesis

The following theorem asserts that Algorithm 1 solves Problem 3.

Theorem 2 (Soundness and precision). *Given a finite set of* PWL *functions* $\mathcal{F}$ *and a value* $\varepsilon \in \mathbb{R}_{\geqslant 0}$, *let* $\mathcal{H}$ *be an automaton resulting from* SYNTHESIS$(\mathcal{F}, \varepsilon)$. *Then* $\mathcal{H}$ *both* ε-*captures all functions in* $\mathcal{F}$ *and is* ε-*precise with respect to* $\mathcal{F}$.

Algorithm 1 satisfies a completeness property in the following sense. For every model $\mathcal{H}$ from a certain class we can find a set $\mathcal{F}$ of PWL functions and a value ε such that SYNTHESIS$(\mathcal{F}, \varepsilon)$ results in $\mathcal{H}$. Before we can characterize the class of models, we first need to introduce some terminology.

Definition 11. *Let* $q \in Q$ *be a mode with invariant* $X = Inv(q)$ *and flow* $Flow(q)$. *We call a continuous state* $\mathbf{x}_2 \in X$ *forward reachable in* q *if there is a continuous state* $\mathbf{x}_1 \in X$ *such that* $\mathbf{x}_2$ *is reachable from* $\mathbf{x}_1$ *by just letting time pass, i.e.,* $\exists t > 0 : \mathbf{x}_2 = \mathbf{x}_1 + Flow(q) \cdot t$. *Analogously, we call state* $\mathbf{x}_2 \in X$ *backward reachable in* q *if there is a state* $\mathbf{x}_1 \in X$ *such that* $\mathbf{x}_2$ *is reachable from* $\mathbf{x}_1$. *A continuous state is* dead *in* q *if it is neither forward reachable nor backward reachable in* q.

We characterize the class of automata $\mathcal{H} = (Q, E, X, Flow, Inv, Grd)$ for which the algorithm is complete by considering the following assumptions: (1) no invariant contains a dead continuous state. Furthermore, if $e = (q_1, q_2)$ is a transition, then all continuous states in the guard $Grd(e)$ are forward reachable in q_1 and backward reachable in q_2, and (2) no two modes have the same slope □

Roughly speaking, Assumption (1) asserts that, after every switch, an execution can stay in the new mode for a positive amount of time.

Theorem 3 (Completeness). *Given an* LHA $\mathcal{H}$ *satisfying Assumptions (1) and (2), there exist* PWL *functions* $\mathcal{F}$ *such that* SYNTHESIS$(\mathcal{F}, 0)$ *results in* $\mathcal{H}$.

5 Experimental Results

In this section, we present the experiments used to evaluate our algorithm. The algorithm was implemented in Python and relies on the standard scientific computation packages. For the computations involving polyhedra we used the `pplpy` wrapper to the Parma Polyhedra Library [4].

Case Study: Online Synthesis. We evaluate the precision of our algorithm by collecting data from the executions of existing linear hybrid automata. For each given automaton, we randomly sample ten executions and pass them to our algorithm, which then constructs a new model. After that, we run our algorithm with another 90 executions, but we reuse the intermediate model, thus demonstrating the online feature of the algorithm. We show the different models for two hand-crafted examples in Table 1. We tried both sampling from random states and from a fixed state. The examples show the latter case, which makes sampling the complete state-space and thus learning a precise model harder.

The first example contains a sink with two incoming transitions, which requires at least two simulations to observe both transitions. Consequently, the algorithm had to make use of the *adaptation* step at least once to add one of the

Table 1. Synthesis results for two automaton models. The original model is shown in blue. The synthesis result after 10 iterations is shown in bright red, and after another 90 iterations in dark red. On the bottom left we show three sample executions starting from the same point (top: original model, bottom: synthesized model after 100 iterations). We used $\varepsilon = 0.2$ in all cases. Numbers are rounded to two places.

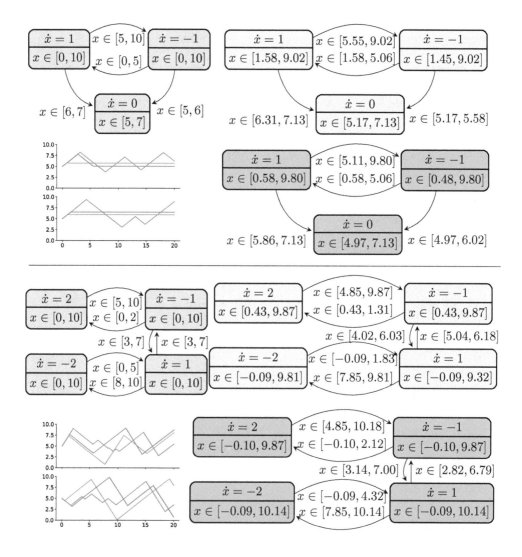

transitions. In the second example, some parts of the state-space are explored less frequently by the sampled executions. Hence the first model obtained after ten iterations does not represent all behavior of the original model yet. After the additional 90 iterations, the remaining parts of the state space have been visited, which is reflected in the precise bounds of the resulting model. In the table, we also show three sample executions from both the original and the final synthesized automaton to illustrate the similarity in the dynamical behavior.

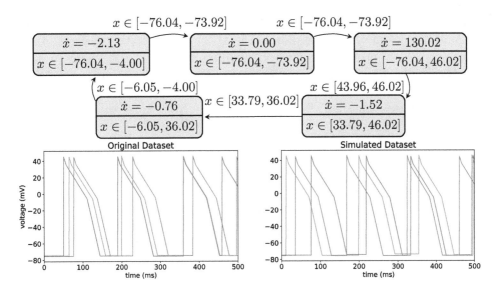

Fig. 5. Results for the cell model. Top: synthesized model using our algorithm. Bottom: three input traces (left) and random simulations of the synthesized model (right).

Case Study: Cell Model. For our case study we synthesize a hybrid automaton from voltage traces of excitable cells. Excitable cells are an important class of cells comprising neurons, cardiac cells, and other muscle cells. The main property of excitable cells is that they exhibit electrical activity which in the case of neurons enables signal transmission and in the case of muscle cells allows them to contract. The excitation signal usually follows distinct dynamics called action potential. Grosu et al. construct a *cyclic-linear hybrid automaton* from action-potential traces of cardiac cells [8]. In their model they identify six modes, two of which exhibit the same dynamics and are just used to model an input signal.

Our algorithm successfully synthesizes a model, depicted in Fig. 5, consisting of five modes that roughly match the normal phases of an action potential. We evaluate the quality of the synthesized model by simulating random executions and visually comparing to the original data (see the bottom of Fig. 5).

6   Conclusion

In this paper we have presented two fully automatic approaches to synthesize a linear hybrid automaton from data. As key features, the synthesized automaton captures the data up to a user-defined bound and is tight. Moreover, the online feature of the membership-based approach allows to combine the approach with alternative synthesis techniques, e.g., for constructing initial models.

A future line of work is to design a methodology for identification of weak generalizations in the model, and use them for driving the experiments and, in consequence, adjusting the model. We would first synthesize a model as before, but then identify the aspects of the model that are least substantiated by the data (e.g., areas in the state space or specific sequences in the executions). Then we would query the system for data about those aspects, and repair the model accordingly. As another line of work, we plan to extend the approach to go from dynamics defined by piecewise-constant differential equations toward linear envelopes. Our approach can be seen as a generalization, to LHA, of Angluin's algorithm for constructing a finite-state machine from finite traces [3], and we plan to pursue this connection further.

References

1. Alur, R., Courcoubetis, C., Henzinger, T.A., Ho, P.-H.: Hybrid automata: an algorithmic approach to the specification and verification of hybrid systems. In: Grossman, R.L., Nerode, A., Ravn, A.P., Rischel, H. (eds.) HS 1991-1992. LNCS, vol. 736, pp. 209–229. Springer, Heidelberg (1993). https://doi.org/10.1007/3-540-57318-6_30

2. Alur, R., Kurshan, R.P., Viswanathan, M.: Membership questions for timed and hybrid automata. In: RTSS, pp. 254–263. IEEE Computer Society (1998). https://doi.org/10.1109/REAL.1998.739751

3. Angluin, D.: Learning regular sets from queries and counterexamples. Inf. Comput. **75**(2), 87–106 (1987). https://doi.org/10.1016/0890-5401(87)90052-6

4. Bagnara, R., Hill, P.M., Zaffanella, E.: The Parma Polyhedra Library: toward a complete set of numerical abstractions for the analysis and verification of hardware and software systems. Sci. Comput. Program. **72**(1–2), 3–21 (2008). https://doi.org/10.1016/j.scico.2007.08.001

5. Bemporad, A., Garulli, A., Paoletti, S., Vicino, A.: A bounded-error approach to piecewise affine system identification. IEEE Trans. Autom. Control **50**(10), 1567–1580 (2005). https://doi.org/10.1109/TAC.2005.856667

6. Douglas, D.H., Peucker, T.K.: Algorithms for the reduction of the number of points required to represent a digitized line or its caricature. Cartographica **10**(2), 112–122 (1973)

7. Garulli, A., Paoletti, S., Vicino, A.: A survey on switched and piecewise affine system identification. IFAC Proc. Vol. **45**(16), 344–355 (2012). https://doi.org/10.3182/20120711-3-BE-2027.00332

8. Grosu, R., Mitra, S., Ye, P., Entcheva, E., Ramakrishnan, I.V., Smolka, S.A.: Learning cycle-linear hybrid automata for excitable cells. In: Bemporad, A., Bicchi, A., Buttazzo, G. (eds.) HSCC 2007. LNCS, vol. 4416, pp. 245–258. Springer, Heidelberg (2007). https://doi.org/10.1007/978-3-540-71493-4_21

9. Hakimi, S.L., Schmeichel, E.F.: Fitting polygonal functions to a set of points in the plane. CVGIP Graph. Model. Image Process. **53**(2), 132–136 (1991). https://doi.org/10.1016/1049-9652(91)90056-P

10. Hashambhoy, Y., Vidal, R.: Recursive identification of switched ARX models with unknown number of models and unknown orders. In: CDC, pp. 6115–6121 (2005). https://doi.org/10.1109/CDC.2005.1583140

11. Henzinger, T.A.: The theory of hybrid automata. In: Inan, M.K., Kurshan, R.P. (eds.) Verification of Digital and Hybrid Systems. NATO ASI Series (Series F: Computer and Systems Sciences), vol. 170, pp. 265–292. Springer, Berlin, Heidelberg (2000). https://doi.org/10.1007/978-3-642-59615-5_13

12. Lamrani, I., Banerjee, A., Gupta, S.K.S.: HyMn: mining linear hybrid automata from input output traces of cyber-physical systems. In: ICPS, pp. 264–269. IEEE (2018). https://doi.org/10.1109/ICPHYS.2018.8387670

13. Liberzon, D.: Switching in Systems and Control. Birkhäuser, Boston (2003). https://doi.org/10.1007/978-1-4612-0017-8

14. Ly, D.L., Lipson, H.: Learning symbolic representations of hybrid dynamical systems. JMLR **13**, 3585–3618 (2012). http://dl.acm.org/citation.cfm?id=2503356

15. Medhat, R., Ramesh, S., Bonakdarpour, B., Fischmeister, S.: A framework for mining hybrid automata from input/output traces. In: EMSOFT, pp. 177–186. IEEE (2015). https://doi.org/10.1109/EMSOFT.2015.7318273

16. Niggemann, O., Stein, B., Vodencarevic, A., Maier, A., Kleine Büning, H.: Learning behavior models for hybrid timed systems. In: AAAI. AAAI Press (2012). http://www.aaai.org/ocs/index.php/AAAI/AAAI12/paper/view/4993

17. Ozay, N.: An exact and efficient algorithm for segmentation of ARX models. In: ACC, pp. 38–41. IEEE (2016). https://doi.org/10.1109/ACC.2016.7524888

18. Paoletti, S., Juloski, A.L., Ferrari-Trecate, G., Vidal, R.: Identification of hybrid systems: a tutorial. Eur. J. Control **13**(2–3), 242–260 (2007). https://doi.org/10.3166/ejc.13.242-260

19. Skeppstedt, A., Lennart, L., Millnert, M.: Construction of composite models from observed data. Int. J. Control **55**(1), 141–152 (1992). https://doi.org/10.1080/00207179208934230

20. Summerville, A., Osborn, J.C., Mateas, M.: CHARDA: causal hybrid automata recovery via dynamic analysis. In: IJCAI, pp. 2800–2806. ijcai.org (2017). https://doi.org/10.24963/ijcai.2017/390

21. Verwer, S.: Efficient identification of timed automata: theory and practice. Ph.D. thesis, Delft University of Technology, Netherlands (2010). http://resolver.tudelft.nl/uuid:61d9f199-7b01-45be-a6ed-04498113a212

22. Vidal, R., Anderson, B.D.O.: Recursive identification of switched ARX hybrid models: exponential convergence and persistence of excitation. In: CDC, vol. 1, pp. 32–37 (2004). https://doi.org/10.1109/CDC.2004.1428602

4

Verifying Asynchronous Interactions via Communicating Session Automata

Julien Lange[1](✉) and Nobuko Yoshida[2]

[1] University of Kent, Canterbury, UK
j.s.lange@kent.ac.uk
[2] Imperial College London, London, UK

Abstract. This paper proposes a sound procedure to verify properties of communicating session automata (CSA), i.e., communicating automata that include multiparty session types. We introduce a new *asynchronous* compatibility property for CSA, called k-multiparty compatibility (k-MC), which is a strict superset of the synchronous multiparty compatibility used in theories and tools based on session types. It is decomposed into two bounded properties: (i) a condition called k-*safety* which guarantees that, within the bound, all sent messages can be received and each automaton can make a move; and (ii) a condition called k-*exhaustivity* which guarantees that all k-reachable send actions can be fired within the bound. We show that k-exhaustivity implies existential boundedness, and *soundly and completely* characterises systems where each automaton behaves equivalently under bounds greater than or equal to k. We show that checking k-MC is PSPACE-complete, and demonstrate its scalability empirically over large systems (using partial order reduction).

1 Introduction

Communicating automata are a Turing-complete model of asynchronous interactions [10] that has become one of the most prominent for studying point-to-point communications over unbounded first-in-first-out channels. This paper focuses on a class of communicating automata, called *communicating session automata* (CSA), which strictly includes automata corresponding to *asynchronous multiparty session types* [28]. Session types originated as a typing discipline for the π-calculus [27,66], where a session type dictates the behaviour of a process wrt. its communications. Session types and related theories have been applied to the verification and specification of concurrent and distributed systems through their integration in several mainstream programming languages, e.g., Haskell [44,55], Erlang [49], F♯ [48], Go [11,37,38,51], Java [30,31,34,65], OCaml [56], C [52], Python [16,47,50], Rust [32], and Scala [61,62]. Communicating automata and asynchronous multiparty session types [28] are closely related: the latter can be seen as a syntactical representation of the former [17] where a sending state corresponds to an internal choice and a receiving state to an external choice. This correspondence between communicating automata and multiparty session types has become the foundation of many tools centred on session types, e.g., for generating communication API from multiparty session (global) types [30,31,48,61], for detecting deadlocks in message-passing programs [51,67], and for monitoring session-enabled programs [5,16,47,49,50]. These tools rely on a property called *multiparty compatibility* [6,18,39], which guarantees that communicating automata representing session types interact correctly, hence enabling the identification of correct protocols or the detection of errors in endpoint programs. Multiparty compatible communicating automata validate two essential requirements for session types frameworks: every message that is sent can be eventually received and each automaton can always eventually make a move. Thus, they satisfy the *abstract* safety invariant φ for session types from [63], a prerequisite for session type systems to guarantee safety of the typed processes. Unfortunately, multiparty compatibility suffers from a severe limitation: it requires that each execution of the system has a synchronous equivalent. Hence, it rules out many correct systems. Hereafter, we refer to this property as *synchronous multiparty compatibility* (SMC) and explain its main limitation with Example 1.

Example 1. The system in Fig. 1 contains an interaction pattern that is *not* supported by any definition of SMC [6,18,39]. It consists of a client (c), a server (s), and a logger (l), which communicate via unbounded FIFO channels. Transition sr!a denotes that sender puts (asynchronously) message a on channel sr; and transition sr?a denotes the consumption of a from channel sr by receiver. The client sends a *request* and some *data* in a fire-and-forget fashion, before waiting for a response from the server. Because of the presence of this simple pattern, the system cannot be executed synchronously (i.e., with the restriction that a send action can only be fired when a matching receive is enabled), hence it is rejected by all definitions of SMC from previous works, even though the system is safe (all sent messages are received and no automaton gets stuck).

Synchronous multiparty compatibility is reminiscent of a strong form of existential boundedness. Among the existing sub-classes of communicating automata (see [46] for a survey), existentially k-bounded communicating automata [22] stand out because they can be model-checked [8,21] and they restrict the model in a natural way: any execution can be rescheduled such that the number of pending messages *that can be received* is bounded by k. However, existential boundedness is generally *undecidable* [22], even for a fixed bound k. This shortcoming makes it impossible to know when theoretical results are applicable.

To address the limitation of SMC and the shortcoming of existential boundedness, we propose a (decidable) sufficient condition for existential boundedness, called k-*exhaustivity*, which serves as a basis for a wider notion of new compatibility, called k-*multiparty compatibility* (k-MC) where $k \in \mathbb{N}_{>0}$ is a bound on the number of pending messages in each channel. A system is k-MC when it is (*i*) k-*exhaustive*, i.e., all k-reachable send actions are enabled within the bound, and (*ii*) k-*safe*, i.e., within the bound k, all sent messages can be received and each automaton can always eventually progress. For example, the system in Fig. 1 is k-multiparty compatible for any $k \in \mathbb{N}_{>0}$, hence it does not lead to communication

Fig. 1. Client-Server-Logger example.

errors, see Theorem 1. The k-MC condition is a natural constraint for real-world systems. Indeed any finite-state system is k-exhaustive (for k sufficiently large), while any system that is not k-exhaustive (resp. k-safe) for any k is unlikely to work correctly. Furthermore, we show that if a system of CSA validates k-exhaustivity, then each automaton locally behaves equivalently under any bound greater than or equal to k, a property that we call *local bound-agnosticity*. We give a *sound and complete* characterisation of k-exhaustivity for CSA in terms of local bound-agnosticity, see Theorem 3. Additionally, we show that the complexity of checking k-MC is PSPACE-complete (i.e., no higher than related algorithms) and we demonstrate empirically that its cost can be mitigated through (sound and complete) partial order reduction.

In this paper, we consider *communicating session automata* (CSA), which cover the most common form of asynchronous multiparty session types [15] (see *Remark* 3), and have been used as a basis to study properties and extensions of session types [6,7,18,30,31,41,42,47,49,50]. More precisely, CSA are deterministic automata, whose every state is either sending (internal choice), receiving (external choice), or final. We focus on CSA that preserve the intent of internal and external choices from session types. In these CSA, whenever an automaton is in a sending state, it can fire any transition, no matter whether channels are bounded; when it is in a receiving state then at most one action must be enabled.

Synopsis. In Sect. 2, we give the necessary background on communicating automata and their properties, and introduce the notions of output/input bound independence which guarantee that internal/external choices are preserved in bounded semantics. In Sect. 3, we introduce the definition of k-multiparty compatibility (k-MC) and show that k-MC systems are safe for systems which validate the bound independence properties. In Sect. 4, we formally relate existential boundedness [22,35], synchronisability [9], and k-exhaustivity. In Sect. 5 we present an implementation (using partial order reduction) and an experimental evaluation of our theory. We discuss related works in Sect. 6 and conclude in Sect. 7.

See [43] for a full version of this paper (including proofs and additional examples). Our implementation and benchmark data are available online [33].

2   Communicating Automata and Bound Independence

This section introduces notations and definitions of communicating automata (following [12,39]), as well as the notion of output (resp. input) bound independence which enforces the intent of internal (resp. external) choice in CSA.

Fix a finite set $\mathcal{P}$ of *participants* (ranged over by p, q, r, s, etc.) and a finite alphabet Σ. The set of *channels* is $\mathcal{C} \stackrel{\text{def}}{=} \{\text{pq} \mid \text{p}, \text{q} \in \mathcal{P} \text{ and p} \neq \text{q}\}$, $\mathcal{A} \stackrel{\text{def}}{=} \mathcal{C} \times \{!, ?\} \times \Sigma$ is the set of *actions* (ranged over by ℓ), Σ^* (resp. $\mathcal{A}^*$) is the set of finite words on Σ (resp. $\mathcal{A}$). Let w range over Σ^*, and ϕ, ψ range over $\mathcal{A}^*$. Also, ϵ ($\notin \Sigma \cup \mathcal{A}$) is the empty word, $|w|$ denotes the length of w, and $w \cdot w'$ is the concatenation of w and w' (these notations are overloaded for words in $\mathcal{A}^*$).

Definition 1 (Communicating automaton). *A communicating automaton is a finite transition system given by a triple $M = (Q, q_0, \delta)$ where Q is a finite set of states, $q_0 \in Q$ is the initial state, and $\delta \subseteq Q \times \mathcal{A} \times Q$ is a set of* transitions.

The transitions of a communicating automaton are labelled by actions in $\mathcal{A}$ of the form sr!a, representing the *emission* of message a from participant s to r, or sr?a representing the *reception* of a by r. Define $subj(\text{pq}!a) = subj(\text{qp}?a) = \text{p}$, $obj(\text{pq}!a) = obj(\text{qp}?a) = \text{q}$, and $chan(\text{pq}!a) = chan(\text{qp}?a) = \text{pq}$. The projection of ℓ onto p is defined as $\pi_{\text{p}}(\ell) = \ell$ if $subj(\ell) = \text{p}$ and $\pi_{\text{p}}(\ell) = \epsilon$ otherwise. Let $\dagger$ range over $\{!, ?\}$, we define: $\pi_{\text{pq}}^{\dagger}(\text{pq} \dagger a) = a$ and $\pi_{\text{pq}}^{\dagger'}(\text{sr} \dagger a) = \epsilon$ if either $\text{pq} \neq \text{sr}$ or $\dagger \neq \dagger'$. We extend these definitions to sequences of actions in the natural way.

A state $q \in Q$ with no outgoing transition is *final*; q is *sending* (resp. *receiving*) if it is not final and all its outgoing transitions are labelled by send (resp. receive) actions, and q is *mixed* otherwise. $M = (Q, q_0, \delta)$ is *deterministic* if $\forall(q, \ell, q'), (q, \ell', q'') \in \delta : \ell = \ell' \implies q' = q''$. $M = (Q, q_0, \delta)$ is *send* (resp. *receive*) *directed* if for all sending (resp. receiving) $q \in Q$ and $(q, \ell, q'), (q, \ell', q'') \in \delta : obj(\ell) = obj(\ell')$. M is *directed* if it is send and receive directed.

Remark 1. In this paper, we consider only deterministic communicating automata without mixed states, and call them *Communicating Session Automata* (CSA). We discuss possible extensions of our results beyond this class in Sect. 7.

Definition 2 (System). *Given a communicating automaton $M_{\text{p}} = (Q_{\text{p}}, q_{0\text{p}}, \delta_{\text{p}})$ for each $\text{p} \in \mathcal{P}$, the tuple $S = (M_{\text{p}})_{\text{p} \in \mathcal{P}}$ is a* system. *A* configuration *of S is a pair $s = (\boldsymbol{q}; \boldsymbol{w})$ where $\boldsymbol{q} = (q_{\text{p}})_{\text{p} \in \mathcal{P}}$ with $q_{\text{p}} \in Q_{\text{p}}$ and where $\boldsymbol{w} = (w_{\text{pq}})_{\text{pq} \in \mathcal{C}}$ with $w_{\text{pq}} \in \Sigma^*$; component $\boldsymbol{q}$ is the* control state *and $q_{\text{p}} \in Q_{\text{p}}$ is the* local state *of automaton M_{p}. The* initial configuration *of S is $s_0 = (\boldsymbol{q_0}; \boldsymbol{\epsilon})$ where $\boldsymbol{q_0} = (q_{0\text{p}})_{\text{p} \in \mathcal{P}}$ and we write $\boldsymbol{\epsilon}$ for the $|\mathcal{C}|$-tuple $(\epsilon, \ldots, \epsilon)$.*

Hereafter, we fix a communicating session automaton $M_{\text{p}} = (Q_{\text{p}}, q_{0\text{p}}, \delta_{\text{p}})$ for each $\text{p} \in \mathcal{P}$ and let $S = (M_{\text{p}})_{\text{p} \in \mathcal{P}}$ be the corresponding system whose initial configuration is s_0. For each $\text{p} \in \mathcal{P}$, we assume that $\forall(q, \ell, q') \in \delta_{\text{p}} : subj(\ell) = \text{p}$. We assume that the components of a configuration are named consistently, e.g., for $s' = (\boldsymbol{q'}; \boldsymbol{w'})$, we implicitly assume that $\boldsymbol{q'} = (q'_{\text{p}})_{\text{p} \in \mathcal{P}}$ and $\boldsymbol{w'} = (w'_{\text{pq}})_{\text{pq} \in \mathcal{C}}$.

Definition 3 (Reachable configuration). *Configuration $s' = (\boldsymbol{q'}; \boldsymbol{w'})$ is* reachable *from configuration $s = (\boldsymbol{q}; \boldsymbol{w})$ by firing transition ℓ, written $s \xrightarrow{\ell} s'$ (or $s \rightarrow s'$ when ℓ is not relevant), if there are $\text{s}, \text{r} \in \mathcal{P}$ and $a \in \Sigma$ such that either:*

1. *(a)* $\ell = \mathrm{sr}!a$ and $(q_{\mathrm{s}}, \ell, q_{\mathrm{s}}') \in \delta_{\mathrm{s}}$, *(b)* $q_{\mathrm{p}}' = q_{\mathrm{p}}$ *for all* $\mathrm{p} \neq \mathrm{s}$, *(c)* $w_{\mathrm{sr}}' = w_{\mathrm{sr}} \cdot a$ and $w_{\mathrm{pq}}' = w_{\mathrm{pq}}$ *for all* $\mathrm{pq} \neq \mathrm{sr}$*; or*
2. *(a)* $\ell = \mathrm{sr}?a$ and $(q_{\mathrm{r}}, \ell, q_{\mathrm{r}}') \in \delta_{\mathrm{r}}$, *(b)* $q_{\mathrm{p}}' = q_{\mathrm{p}}$ *for all* $\mathrm{p} \neq \mathrm{r}$, *(c)* $w_{\mathrm{sr}} = a \cdot w_{\mathrm{sr}}'$, and $w_{\mathrm{pq}}' = w_{\mathrm{pq}}$ *for all* $\mathrm{pq} \neq \mathrm{sr}$.

Remark 2. Hereafter, we assume that any bound k is finite and $k \in \mathbb{N}_{>0}$.

We write $\to^*$ for the reflexive and transitive closure of $\to$. Configuration $(\boldsymbol{q}; \boldsymbol{w})$ is k-bounded if $\forall \mathrm{pq} \in \mathcal{C} : |w_{\mathrm{pq}}| \leqslant k$. We write $s_1 \xrightarrow{\ell_1 \cdots \ell_n} s_{n+1}$ when $s_1 \xrightarrow{\ell_1} s_2 \cdots s_n \xrightarrow{\ell_n} s_{n+1}$, for some $s_2, \ldots, s_n$ (with $n \geqslant 0$); and say that the execution $\ell_1 \cdots \ell_n$ is *k-bounded from* s_1 if $\forall 1 \leqslant i \leqslant n+1 : s_i$ is k-bounded. Given $\phi \in \mathcal{A}^*$, we write $\mathrm{p} \notin \phi$ iff $\phi = \phi_0 \cdot \ell \cdot \phi_1 \implies subj(\ell) \neq \mathrm{p}$. We write $s \xrightarrow{\phi}_k s'$ if s' is reachable with a k-bounded execution ϕ from s. The set of *reachable configurations of* S is $RS(S) = \{s \mid s_0 \to^* s\}$. The *k-reachability set of* S is the largest subset $RS_k(S)$ of $RS(S)$ within which each configuration s can be reached by a k-bounded execution from s_0.

Definition 4 streamlines notions of safety from previous works [6,12,18,39] (absence of deadlocks, orphan messages, and unspecified receptions).

Definition 4 (*k*-Safety). *S is* k-safe *if the following holds* $\forall (\boldsymbol{q}; \boldsymbol{w}) \in RS_k(S)$:

(**ER**) $\forall \mathrm{pq} \in \mathcal{C}$, *if* $w_{\mathrm{pq}} = a \cdot w'$, *then* $(\boldsymbol{q}; \boldsymbol{w}) \to_k^* \xrightarrow{\mathrm{pq}?a}_k$.

(**PG**) $\forall \mathrm{p} \in \mathcal{P}$, *if* q_{p} *is receiving, then* $(\boldsymbol{q}; \boldsymbol{w}) \to_k^* \xrightarrow{\mathrm{qp}?a}_k$ *for* $\mathrm{q} \in \mathcal{P}$ *and* $a \in \Sigma$.

We say that S *is* safe *if it validates the unbounded version of k-safety (∞-safe).*

Property (ER), called *eventual reception*, requires that any sent message can always eventually be received (i.e., if a is the head of a queue then there must be an execution that consumes a), and Property (PG), called *progress*, requires that any automaton in a receiving state can eventually make a move (i.e., it can always eventually receive an *expected* message).

We say that a configuration s is *stable* iff $s = (\boldsymbol{q}; \boldsymbol{\epsilon})$, i.e., all its queues are empty. Next, we define the *stable property* for systems of communicating automata, following the definition from [18].

Definition 5 (Stable). *S has the* stable property *(SP) if* $\forall s \in RS(S) : \exists (\boldsymbol{q}; \boldsymbol{\epsilon}) \in RS(S) : s \to^* (\boldsymbol{q}; \boldsymbol{\epsilon})$.

A system has the stable property if it is possible to reach a stable configuration from any reachable configuration. This property is called *deadlock-free* in [22]. The stable property implies the eventual reception property, but not safety (e.g., an automaton may be waiting for an input in a stable configuration, see Example 2), and safety does not imply the stable property, see Example 4.

Example 2. The following system has the stable property, but it is not safe.

$$M_{\mathrm{s}} : \quad \xleftarrow{\mathrm{pq}!a} \downarrow \xrightarrow{\mathrm{pq}!b} \qquad M_{\mathrm{q}} : \quad \xleftarrow{\mathrm{pq}?a} \downarrow \xrightarrow{\mathrm{pq}?b} \xrightarrow{\mathrm{qr}!c} \qquad M_{\mathrm{r}} : \quad \downarrow \xrightarrow{\mathrm{qr}?c}$$

Next, we define two properties related to *bound independence*. They specify classes of CSA whose branching behaviours are not affected by channel bounds.

Definition 6 (k-OBI). *S is k-output bound independent (k-OBI), if $\forall s = (\boldsymbol{q}; \boldsymbol{w}) \in RS_k(S)$ and $\forall p \in \mathcal{P}$, if $s \xrightarrow{pq!a}_k$, then $\forall(q_p, pr!b, q_p') \in \delta_p : s \xrightarrow{pr!b}_k$.*

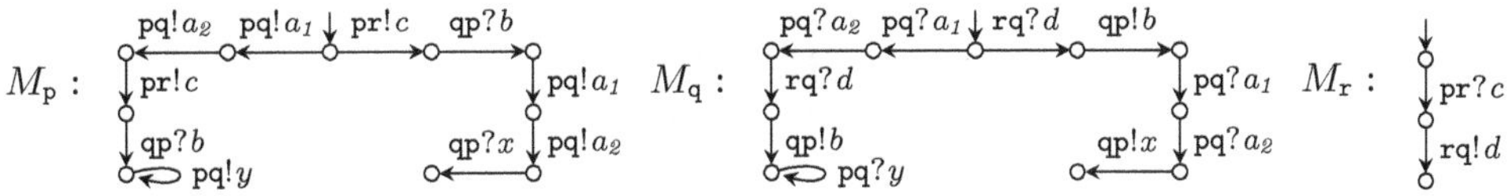

Fig. 2. Example of a *non*-IBI and *non*-safe system.

Definition 7 (k-IBI). *S is k-input bound independent (k-IBI), if $\forall s = (\boldsymbol{q}; \boldsymbol{w}) \in RS_k(S)$ and $\forall p \in \mathcal{P}$, if $s \xrightarrow{qp?a}_k$, then $\forall \ell \in \mathcal{A} : s \xrightarrow{\ell}_k \wedge subj(\ell) = p \implies \ell = qp?a$.*

If S is k-OBI, then any automaton that reaches a sending state is able to fire any of its available transitions, i.e., sending states model *internal choices* which are not constrained by bounds greater than or equal to k. Note that the unbounded version of k-OBI ($k = \infty$) is trivially satisfied for any system due to unbounded asynchrony. If S is k-IBI, then any automaton that reaches a receiving state is able to fire at most one transition, i.e., receiving states model *external choices* where the behaviour of the receiving automaton is controlled exclusively by its environment. We write IBI for the unbounded version of k-IBI ($k = \infty$).

Checking the IBI property is generally undecidable. However, systems consisting of (send and receive) *directed* automata are trivially k-IBI and k-OBI for all k, this subclass of CSA was referred to as *basic* in [18]. We introduce larger decidable approximations of IBI with Definitions 10 and 11.

Proposition 1. *(1) If S is send directed, then S is k-OBI for all $k \in \mathbb{N}_{>0}$. (2) If S is receive directed, then S is IBI (and k-IBI for all $k \in \mathbb{N}_{>0}$).*

Remark 3. CSA validating k-OBI and IBI strictly include the most common forms of asynchronous multiparty session types, e.g., the directed CSA of [18], and systems obtained by projecting Scribble specifications (global types) which need to be receive directed (this is called "consistent external choice subjects" in [31]) and which validate 1-OBI by construction since they are projections of synchronous specifications where choices must be located at a unique sender.

3   Bounded Compatibility for CSA

In this section, we introduce k-*multiparty compatibility* (k-MC) and study its properties wrt. Safety of communicating session automata (CSA) which are k-OBI and IBI. Then, we soundly and completely characterise k-exhaustivity in terms of local bound-agnosticity, a property which guarantees that communicating automata behave equivalently under any bound greater than or equal to k.

3.1 Multiparty Compatibility

The definition of k-MC is divided in two parts: (i) k-*exhaustivity* guarantees that the set of k-reachable configurations contains enough information to make a sound decision wrt. safety of the system; and (ii) k-*safety* (Definition 4) guarantees that a subset of all possible executions is free of any communication errors. Next, we define k-exhaustivity, then k-multiparty compatibility. Intuitively, a system is k-exhaustive if for all k-reachable configurations, whenever a send action is enabled, then it can be fired within a k-bounded execution.

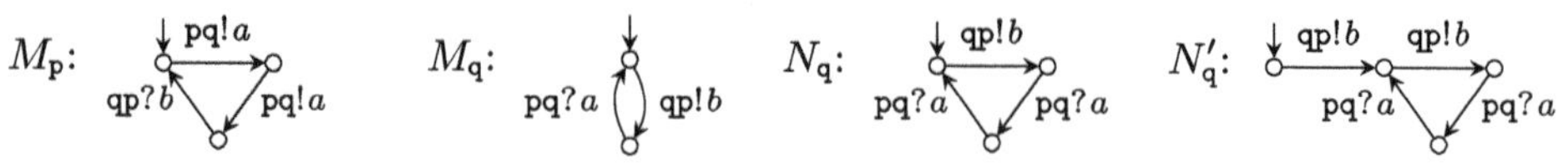

$$M_\mathsf{p}: \qquad M_\mathsf{q}: \qquad N_\mathsf{q}: \qquad N_\mathsf{q}':$$

Fig. 3. $(M_\mathsf{p}, M_\mathsf{q})$ is non-exhaustive, $(M_\mathsf{p}, N_\mathsf{q})$ is 1-exhaustive, $(M_\mathsf{p}, N_\mathsf{q}')$ is 2-exhaustive.

Definition 8 (k-Exhaustivity). S *is* k-exhaustive *if* $\forall (\boldsymbol{q}; \boldsymbol{w}) \in RS_k(S)$ *and* $\forall \mathsf{p} \in \mathcal{P}$, *if* q_p *is sending, then* $\forall (q_\mathsf{p}, \ell, q_\mathsf{p}') \in \delta_\mathsf{p} : \exists \phi \in \mathcal{A}^* : (\boldsymbol{q}; \boldsymbol{w}) \xrightarrow{\phi}_k \xrightarrow{\ell}_k \wedge \mathsf{p} \notin \phi$.

Definition 9 (k-Multiparty compatibility). S *is* k-multiparty compatible (k-MC) *if it is* k-safe *and* k-exhaustive.

Definition 9 is a natural extension of the definitions of *synchronous* multiparty compatibility given in [18, Definition 4.2] and [6, Definition 4]. The common key requirements are that *every send* action must be matched by a receive action (i.e., send actions are universally quantified), while *at least one receive* action must find a matching send action (i.e., receive actions are existentially quantified). Here, the universal check on send actions is done via the eventual reception property (ER) and the k-exhaustivity condition; while the existential check on receive actions is dealt with by the progress property (PG).

Whenever systems are k-OBI and IBI, then k-exhaustivity implies that k-bounded executions are sufficient to make a sound decision wrt. safety. This is not necessarily the case for systems outside of this class, see Examples 3 and 5.

Example 3. The system $(M_\mathsf{p}, M_\mathsf{q}, M_\mathsf{r})$ in Fig. 2 is k-OBI for any k, but not IBI (it is 1-IBI but not k-IBI for any $k \geqslant 2$). When executing with a bound strictly greater than 1, there is a configuration where M_q is in its initial state and *both* its *receive* transitions are enabled. The system is 1-safe and 1-exhaustive (hence 1-MC) but it is *not* 2-exhaustive nor 2-safe. By constraining the automata to execute with a channel bound of 1, the left branch of M_p is prevented to execute together with the right branch of M_q. Thus, the fact that the y messages are not received in this case remains invisible in 1-bounded executions. This example can be easily extended so that it is n-exhaustive (resp. safe) but not $n{+}1$-exhaustive (resp. safe) by sending/receiving $n{+}1$ a_i messages.

Example 4. The system in Fig. 1 is *directed* and 1-MC. The system (M_p, M_q) in Fig. 3 is safe but *not* k-MC for any finite $k \in \mathbb{N}_{>0}$. Indeed, for any execution of this system, at least one of the queues grows arbitrarily large. The system (M_p, N_q) is 1-MC while the system (M_p, N'_q) is *not* 1-MC but it is 2-MC.

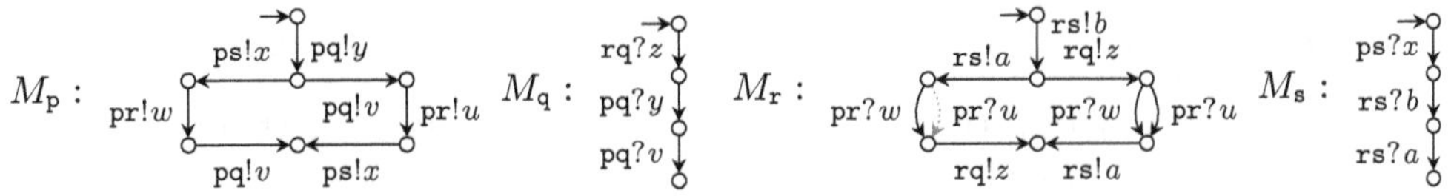

Fig. 4. Example of a system which is not 1-OBI.

Example 5. The system in Fig. 4 (without the dotted transition) is 1-MC, but not 2-safe; it is not 1-OBI but it is 2-OBI. In 1-bounded executions, M_r can execute $\mathtt{rs}!b \cdot \mathtt{rp}!z$, but it cannot fire $\mathtt{rs}!b \cdot \mathtt{rs}!a$ (queue $\mathtt{rs}$ is full), which violates the 1-OBI property. The system with the dotted transition is not 1-OBI, but it is 2-OBI and k-MC for any $k \geqslant 1$. Both systems are receive directed, hence IBI.

Theorem 1. *If S is k-OBI, IBI, and k-MC, then it is safe.*

Remark 4. It is undecidable whether there exists a bound k for which an arbitrary system is k-MC. This is a consequence of the Turing completeness of communicating (session) automata [10, 20, 42].

Although the IBI property is generally undecidable, it is possible to identify sound approximations, as we show below. We adapt the dependency relation from [39] and say that action ℓ' depends on ℓ from $s = (q; w)$, written $s \vdash \ell < \ell'$, iff $subj(\ell) = subj(\ell') \vee (chan(\ell) = chan(\ell') \wedge w_{chan(\ell)} = \epsilon)$. Action ℓ' depends on ℓ in ϕ from s, written $s \vdash \ell <_\phi \ell'$, if the following holds:

$$s \vdash \ell <_\phi \ell' \iff \begin{cases} (s \vdash \ell < \ell'' \wedge s \vdash \ell'' <_\psi \ell') \vee s \vdash \ell <_\psi \ell' & \text{if } \phi = \ell'' \cdot \psi \\ s \vdash \ell < \ell' & \text{otherwise} \end{cases}$$

Definition 10. *S is k-chained input bound independent (k-CIBI) if $\forall s = (q; w) \in RS_k(S)$ and $\forall p \in \mathcal{P}$, if $s \xrightarrow{\mathtt{qp}?a}_k s'$, then $\forall (q_p, \mathtt{sp}?b, q'_p) \in \delta_p : s \neq q \implies \neg(s \xrightarrow{\mathtt{sp}?b}_k) \wedge (\forall \phi \in \mathcal{A}^* : s' \xrightarrow{\phi}_k \xrightarrow{\mathtt{sp}!b}_k \implies s \vdash \mathtt{qp}?a <_\phi \mathtt{sp}!b)$.*

Definition 11. *S is k-strong input bound independent (k-SIBI) if $\forall s = (q; w) \in RS_k(S)$ and $\forall p \in \mathcal{P}$, if $s \xrightarrow{\mathtt{qp}?a}_k s'$, then $\forall (q_p, \mathtt{sp}?b, q'_p) \in \delta_p : s \neq q \implies \neg(s \xrightarrow{\mathtt{sp}?b}_k \vee s' \rightarrow_k^* \xrightarrow{\mathtt{sp}!b}_k)$.*

Definition 10 requires that whenever p can fire a receive action, at most one of its receive actions is enabled at s, and no other receive transition from q_p will be enabled until p has made a move. This is due to the existence of a dependency chain between the reception of a message (qp?a) and the matching send of another possible reception (sp!b). Property k-SIBI (Definition 11) is a stronger version of k-CIBI, which can be checked more efficiently.

Lemma 1. *If S is k-OBI, k-CIBI (resp. k-SIBI) and k-exhaustive, then it is* IBI.

The decidability of k-OBI, k-IBI, k-SIBI, k-CIBI, and k-MC is straightforward since both $RS_k(S)$ (which has an exponential number of states wrt. k) and $\rightarrow_k$ are finite, given a finite k. Theorem 2 states the space complexity of the procedures, except for k-CIBI for which a complexity class is yet to be determined. We show that the properties are PSPACE by reducing to an instance of the reachability problem over a transition system built following the construction of Bollig et al. [8, Theorem 6.3]. The rest of the proof follows from similar arguments in Genest et al. [22, Proposition 5.5] and Bouajjani et al. [9, Theorem 3].

Theorem 2. *The problems of checking the k-OBI, k-IBI, k-SIBI, k-safety, and k-exhaustivity properties are all decidable and PSPACE-complete (with $k \in \mathbb{N}_{>0}$ given in unary). The problem of checking the k-CIBI property is decidable.*

3.2   Local Bound-Agnosticity

We introduce local bound-agnosticity and show that it fully characterises k-exhaustive systems. Local bound-agnosticity guarantees that each communicating automaton behave in the same manner for any bound greater than or equal to some k. Therefore such systems may be executed transparently under a bounded semantics (a communication model available in Go and Rust).

Definition 12 (Transition system). *The k-bounded transition system of S is the labelled transition system (LTS) $TS_k(S) = (N, s_0, \Delta)$ such that $N = RS_k(S)$, s_0 is the initial configuration of S, $\Delta \subseteq N \times \mathcal{A} \times N$ is the transition relation, and $(s, \ell, s') \in \Delta$ if and only if $s \xrightarrow{\ell}_k s'$.*

Definition 13 (Projection). *Let T be an LTS over $\mathcal{A}$. The projection of T onto p, written $\pi_p^\epsilon(T)$, is obtained by replacing each label ℓ in T by $\pi_p(\ell)$.*

Recall that the projection of action ℓ, written $\pi_p(\ell)$, is defined in Sect. 2. The automaton $\pi_p^\epsilon(TS_k(S))$ is essentially the *local* behaviour of participant p within the transition system $TS_k(S)$. When each automaton in a system S behaves equivalently for any bound greater than or equal to some k, we say that S is locally bound-agnostic. Formally, S is *locally bound-agnostic for k* when $\pi_p^\epsilon(TS_k(S))$ and $\pi_p^\epsilon(TS_n(S))$ are weakly bisimilar ($\approx$) for each participant p and any $n \geqslant k$. For k-OBI and IBI systems, local bound-agnosticity is a *necessary and sufficient* condition for k-exhaustivity, as stated in Theorem 3 and Corollary 1.

Theorem 3. *Let S be a system.*

(1) If $\exists k \in \mathbb{N}_{>0} : \forall \mathrm{p} \in \mathcal{P} : \pi_{\mathrm{p}}^{\epsilon}(TS_k(S)) \approx \pi_{\mathrm{p}}^{\epsilon}(TS_{k+1}(S))$, then S is k-exhaustive.

(2) If S is k-OBI, IBI, and k-exhaustive, then $\forall \mathrm{p} \in \mathcal{P} : \pi_{\mathrm{p}}^{\epsilon}(TS_k(S)) \approx \pi_{\mathrm{p}}^{\epsilon}(TS_{k+1}(S))$.

Corollary 1. *Let S be k-OBI and IBI s.t. $\forall \mathrm{p} \in \mathcal{P} : \pi_{\mathrm{p}}^{\epsilon}(TS_k(S)) \approx \pi_{\mathrm{p}}^{\epsilon}(TS_{k+1}(S))$, then S is locally bound-agnostic for k.*

Theorem 3 (1) is reminiscent of the (PSPACE-complete) checking procedure for existentially bounded systems with the stable property [22] (an *undecidable* property). Recall that k-exhaustivity is not sufficient to guarantee safety, see Examples 3 and 5. We give an effective procedure (based on partial order reduction) to check k-exhaustivity and related properties in [43].

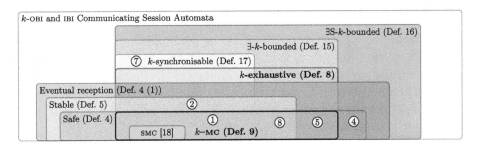

Fig. 5. Relations between k-exhaustivity, existential k-boundedness, and k-synchronisability in k-OBI and IBI CSA (the circled numbers refer to Table 1).

4   Existentially Bounded and Synchronisable Automata

4.1   Kuske and Muscholl's Existential Boundedness

Existentially bounded communicating automata [21, 22, 35] are a class of communicating automata whose executions can always be scheduled in such a way that the number of pending messages is bounded by a given value. Traditionally, existentially bounded communicating automata are defined on communicating automata that feature (local) accepting states and in terms of *accepting runs*. An accepting run is an execution (starting from s_0) which terminates in a configuration $(\boldsymbol{q}; \boldsymbol{w})$ where each q_{p} is a local accepting state. In our setting, we simply consider that every local state q_{p} is an accepting state, hence any execution ϕ starting from s_0 is an accepting run. We first study existential boundedness as defined in [35] as it matches more closely k-exhaustivity, we study the "classical" definition of existential boundedness [22] in Sect. 4.2.

Following [35], we say that an execution $\phi \in \mathcal{A}^*$ is *valid* if for any prefix ψ of ϕ and any channel $\mathrm{pq} \in \mathcal{C}$, we have that $\pi_{\mathrm{pq}}^{?}(\psi)$ is a prefix of $\pi_{\mathrm{pq}}^{!}(\psi)$, i.e., an execution is valid if it models the FIFO semantics of communicating automata.

Definition 14 (Causal equivalence [35]). *Given* $\phi, \psi \in \mathcal{A}^*$, *we define:* $\phi \backsim \psi$
iff ϕ *and* ψ *are* valid *executions and* $\forall p \in \mathcal{P} : \pi_p(\phi) = \pi_p(\psi)$. *We write* $[\phi]_{\backsim}$ *for
the equivalence class of* ϕ *wrt.* $\backsim$.

Definition 15 (Existential boundedness [35]). *We say that a valid execu-
tion* ϕ *is* k-match-bounded *if, for every prefix* ψ *of* ϕ *the difference between the
number of* matched *events of type* pq! *and those of type* pq? *is bounded by* k,
i.e., $\min\{|\pi^!_{pq}(\psi)|, |\pi^?_{pq}(\phi)|\} - |\pi^?_{pq}(\psi)| \leqslant k$.
Write $\mathcal{A}^*|_k$ *for the set of* k-match-bounded *words. An execution* ϕ *is* existentially
k-bounded *if* $[\phi]_{\backsim} \cap \mathcal{A}^*|_k \neq \varnothing$. *A system* S *is* existentially k-bounded, *written* $\exists$-
k-bounded, *if each execution in* $\{\phi \mid \exists s : s_0 \xrightarrow{\phi} s\}$ *is existentially* k-bounded.

Example 6. Consider Fig. 3. (M_p, M_q) is *not* existentially k-bounded, for any k:
at least one of the queues must grow infinitely for the system to progress. Systems
(M_p, N_q) and (M_p, N'_q) are existentially bounded since any of their executions
can be scheduled to an $\backsim$-equivalent execution which is 2-match-bounded.

The relationship between k-exhaustivity and existential boundedness is
stated in Theorem 4 and illustrated in Fig. 5 for k-OBI and IBI CSA, where SMC
refers to synchronous multiparty compatibility [18, Definition 4.2]. The circled
numbers in the figure refer to key examples summarised in Table 1. The strict
inclusion of k-exhaustivity in existential k-boundedness is due to systems that
do not have the eventual reception property, see Example 7.

Example 7. The system below is $\exists$-1-bounded but is *not* k-exhaustive for any k.

$$M_p : \quad \to \circ \multimap \text{sp?}c \qquad M_s : \quad \to \circ \overset{\text{sr!}a}{\underset{\text{sp!}b}{\rightleftharpoons}} \circ \qquad M_r : \quad \to \circ \multimap \text{sr?}a$$

For any k, the channel sp eventually gets full and the send action sp!b can no
longer be fired; hence it does *not* satisfy k-exhaustivity. Note that each execution
can be reordered into a 1-match-bounded execution (the b's are never matched).

Theorem 4. *(1) If* S *is* k-OBI, IBI, *and* k-exhaustive, *then it is* $\exists$-k-bounded.
(2) If S *is* $\exists$-k-bounded *and satisfies eventual reception, then it is* k-exhaustive.

4.2 Existentially Stable Bounded Communicating Automata

The "classical" definition of existentially bounded communicating automata as
found in [22] differs slightly from Definition 15, as it relies on a different notion
of accepting runs, see [22, page 4]. Assuming that all local states are accepting,
we adapt their definition as follows: a *stable accepting run* is an execution ϕ
starting from s_0 which terminates in a *stable* configuration.

Definition 16 (Existential stable boundedness [22]). *A system* S *is* existentially stable k-bounded, *written* $\exists S$-k-bounded, *if for each execution* ϕ *in*
$\{\phi \mid \exists (q; \epsilon) \in RS(S) : s_0 \xrightarrow{\phi} (q; \epsilon)\}$ *there is* ψ *such that* $s_0 \xrightarrow{\psi}_k$ *with* $\phi \backsim \psi$.

A system is existentially stable k-bounded if each of its executions leading to a *stable* configuration can be re-ordered into a k-bounded execution (from s_0).

Theorem 5. *(1) If S is existentially k-bounded, then it is existentially stable k-bounded. (2) If S is existentially stable k-bounded and has the stable property, then it is existentially k-bounded.*

We illustrate the relationship between existentially stable bounded communicating automata and the other classes in Fig. 5. The example below further illustrates the strictness of the inclusions, see Table 1 for a summary.

Example 8. Consider the systems in Fig. 3. (M_p, M_q) and (M_p, N'_q) are (trivially) existentially stable 1-bounded since none of their (non-empty) executions terminate in a stable configuration. The system (M_p, N_q) is existentially stable 2-bounded since each of its executions can be re-ordered into a 2-bounded one. The system in Example 7 is (trivially) ∃S-1-bounded: none of its (non-empty) executions terminate in a stable configuration (the b's are never received).

Theorem 6. *Let S be an ∃(S)-k-bounded system with the stable property, then it is k-exhaustive.*

Table 1. Properties for key examples, where direct. stands for directed, OBI for k-OBI, SIBI for k-SIBI, ER for eventual reception property, SP for stable property, exh. for k-exhaustive, ∃(S)-b for ∃(S)-bounded, and syn. for n-synchronisable (for some $n \in \mathbb{N}_{>0}$).

#	System	Ref.	k	direct.	OBI	SIBI	safe	ER	SP	exh.	∃S-b	∃-b	syn.
1	(M_c, M_s, M_1)	Figure 1	1	yes	yes	yes	yes	yes	yes	yes	yes	yes	yes
2	(M_s, M_q, M_r)	Example 2	1	yes	yes	yes	no	yes	yes	yes	yes	yes	yes
3	(M_p, M_q, M_r)	Figure 2	$\geqslant 2$	no	yes	no	no	no	no	no	yes	yes	no
4	(M_p, M_q)	Figure 3	any	yes	yes	yes	yes	yes	no	no	yes	no	no
5	(M_p, N'_q)	Figure 3	2	yes	yes	yes	yes	yes	no	yes	yes	yes	no
6	(M_p, M_q, M_r, M_s)	Figure 4	2	no	yes	yes	yes	yes	no	yes	yes	yes	no
7	(M_s, M_r, M_p)	Example 7	any	yes	yes	yes	no	no	no	no	yes	yes	yes
8	(M_p, M_q)	Example 9	1	yes	yes	yes	yes	yes	yes	yes	yes	yes	no

4.3 Synchronisable Communicating Session Automata

In this section, we study the relationship between synchronisability [9] and k-exhaustivity via existential boundedness. Informally, communicating automata are synchronisable if each of their executions can be scheduled in such a way that it consists of sequences of "exchange phases", where each phase consists of a bounded number of send actions, followed by a sequence of receive actions. The original definition of k-synchronisable systems [9, Definition 1] is based on

communicating automata with *mailbox* semantics, i.e., each automaton has one
input queue. Here, we adapt the definition so that it matches our point-to-point
semantics. We write $\mathcal{A}_!$ for $\mathcal{A} \cap (\mathcal{C} \times \{!\} \times \Sigma)$, and $\mathcal{A}_?$ for $\mathcal{A} \cap (\mathcal{C} \times \{?\} \times \Sigma)$.

Definition 17 (Synchronisability). *A valid execution* $\phi = \phi_1 \cdots \phi_n$ *is a k-exchange if and only if: (1)* $\forall 1 \leqslant i \leqslant n : \phi_i \in \mathcal{A}_!^* \cdot \mathcal{A}_?^* \wedge |\phi_i| \leqslant 2k$; *and*
(2) $\forall pq \in \mathcal{C} : \forall 1 \leqslant i \leqslant n : \pi_{pq}^!(\phi_i) \neq \pi_{pq}^?(\phi_i) \implies \forall i < j \leqslant n : \pi_{pq}^?(\phi_j) = \epsilon$.

We write $\mathcal{A}^* \|_k$ *for the set of executions that are k-exchanges and say that
an execution ϕ is k-synchronisable if* $[\phi]_{\simeq} \cap \mathcal{A}^* \|_k \neq \varnothing$. *A system S is k-synchronisable if each execution in* $\{\phi \mid \exists s : s_0 \xrightarrow{\phi} s\}$ *is k-synchronisable.*

Table 2. Experimental evaluation. $|\mathcal{P}|$ is the number of participants, k is the bound,
$|RTS|$ is the number of transitions in the *reduced* $TS_k(S)$ (see [43]), direct. stands for
directed, Time is the time taken to check all the properties shown in this table, and
GMC is **yes** if the system is generalised multiparty compatible [39].

Example	$|\mathcal{P}|$	k	$|RTS|$	direct.	k-OBI	k-CIBI	k-MC	Time	GMC
Client-Server-Logger	3	1	11	yes	yes	yes	yes	0.04 s	no
4 Player game[†] [39]	4	1	20	no	yes	yes	yes	0.05 s	yes
Bargain [39]	3	1	8	yes	yes	yes	yes	0.03 s	yes
Filter collaboration [68]	2	1	10	yes	yes	yes	yes	0.03 s	yes
Alternating bit[†] [59]	2	1	8	yes	yes	yes	yes	0.04 s	no
TPMContract v2[†] [25]	2	1	14	yes	yes	yes	yes	0.04 s	yes
Sanitary agency[†] [60]	4	1	34	yes	yes	yes	yes	0.07 s	yes
Logistic[†] [54]	4	1	26	yes	yes	yes	yes	0.05 s	yes
Cloud system v4 [24]	4	2	16	no	yes	yes	yes	0.04 s	yes
Commit protocol [9]	4	1	12	yes	yes	yes	yes	0.03 s	yes
Elevator[†] [9]	5	1	72	no	yes	no	yes	0.14s	no
Elevator-dashed[†] [9]	5	1	80	no	yes	no	yes	0.16s	no
Elevator-directed[†] [9]	3	1	41	yes	yes	yes	yes	0.07 s	yes
Dev system [58]	4	1	20	yes	yes	yes	yes	0.05 s	no
Fibonacci [48]	2	1	6	yes	yes	yes	yes	0.03 s	yes
SAP-Negot. [48,53]	2	1	18	yes	yes	yes	yes	0.04 s	yes
SH [48]	3	1	30	yes	yes	yes	yes	0.06 s	yes
Travel agency [48,64]	3	1	21	yes	yes	yes	yes	0.05 s	yes
HTTP [29,48]	2	1	48	yes	yes	yes	yes	0.07 s	yes
SMTP [30,48]	2	1	108	yes	yes	yes	yes	0.08 s	yes
gen_server (buggy) [67]	3	1	56	no	no	yes	no	0.03 s	no
gen_server (fixed) [67]	3	1	45	no	yes	yes	yes	0.03 s	yes
Double buffering [45]	3	2	16	yes	yes	yes	yes	0.01 s	no

Condition (1) says that execution ϕ should be a sequence of an arbitrary number of send-receive phases, where each phase consists of at most $2k$ actions. Condition (2) says that if a message is not received in the phase in which it is sent, then it cannot be received in ϕ. Observe that the bound k is on the number of actions (over possibly different channels) in a phase rather than the number of pending messages in a given channel.

Example 9. The system below (left) is 1-MC and $\exists(S)$-1-bounded, but it is *not* k-synchronisable for any k. The subsequences of send-receive actions in the $\backsimeq$-equivalent executions below are highlighted (right).

$$M_{\mathsf{p}}: \quad \overset{\mathsf{pq}!a}{\to}\circ\overset{\mathsf{qp}?c}{\to}\circ\overset{\mathsf{pq}!b}{\to}\circ\overset{\mathsf{qp}?d}{\to}\circ$$
$$M_{\mathsf{q}}: \quad \overset{\mathsf{qp}!c}{\to}\circ\overset{\mathsf{qp}!d}{\to}\circ\overset{\mathsf{pq}?a}{\to}\circ\overset{\mathsf{pq}?b}{\to}\circ$$

$$\phi_1 = \underline{\mathsf{pq}!a \cdot \mathsf{qp}!c \cdot \mathsf{qp}?c} \cdot \underline{\mathsf{qp}!d \cdot \mathsf{pq}?a} \cdot \underline{\mathsf{pq}!b \cdot \mathsf{qp}?d \cdot \mathsf{pq}?b}$$
$$\phi_2 = \underline{\mathsf{pq}!a \cdot \mathsf{qp}!c \cdot \mathsf{qp}!d} \cdot \underline{\mathsf{qp}?c \cdot \mathsf{pq}?a} \cdot \underline{\mathsf{pq}!b \cdot \mathsf{qp}?d \cdot \mathsf{pq}?b}$$

Execution ϕ_1 is 1-bounded for s_0, but it is not a k-exchange since, e.g., a is received outside of the phase where it is sent. In ϕ_2, message d is received outside of its sending phase. In the terminology of [9], this system is not k-synchronisable because there is a *"receive-send dependency"* between the exchange of message c and b, i.e., p must receive c before it sends b. Hence, there is no k-exchange that is $\backsimeq$-equivalent to ϕ_1 and ϕ_2.

Theorem 7. *(1) If S is k-synchronisable, then it is $\exists$-k-bounded. (2) If S is k-synchronisable and has the eventual reception property, then it is k-exhaustive.*

Figure 5 and Table 1 summarise the results of Sect. 4 wrt. k-OBI and IBI CSA. We note that any finite-state system is k-exhaustive (and $\exists(S)$-k-bounded) for sufficiently large k, while this does not hold for synchronisability, see Example 9.

5   Experimental Evaluation

We have implemented our theory in a tool [33] which takes two inputs: (i) a system of communicating automata and (ii) a bound MAX. The tool iteratively checks whether the system validates the premises of Theorem 1, until it succeeds or reaches $k = $ MAX. We note that the k-OBI and IBI conditions are required for our soundness result (Theorem 1), but are orthogonal for checking k-MC. Each condition is checked on a *reduced bounded transition system*, called $RTS_k(S)$. Each verification procedure for these conditions is implemented in Haskell using a simple (depth-first-search based) reachability check on the paths of $RTS_k(S)$. We give an (optimal) partial order reduction algorithm to construct $RTS_k(S)$ in [43] and show that it preserves our properties.

We have tested our tool on 20 examples taken from the literature, which are reported in Table 2. The table shows that the tool terminates virtually instantaneously on all examples. The table suggests that many systems are indeed k-MC and most can be easily adapted to validate bound independence. The last column refers to the GMC condition, a form of *synchronous* multiparty compatibility (SMC) introduced in [39]. The examples marked with † have been slightly modified to make them CSA that validate k-OBI and IBI. For instance, we take only one of the possible interleavings between mixed actions to remove mixed states (taking send action before receive action to preserve safety), see [43].

We have assessed the scalability of our approach with automatically generated examples, which we report in Fig. 6. Each system considered in these benchmarks consists of $2m$ (directed) CSA for some $m \geqslant 1$ such that $S = (M_{\mathsf{p}_i})_{1 \leqslant i \leqslant 2m}$, and each automaton M_{p_i} is of the form (when i is *odd*):

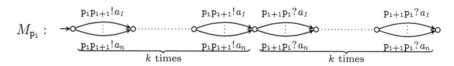

Each M_{p_i} sends k messages to participant p_{i+1}, then receives k messages from p_{i+1}. Each message is taken from an alphabet $\{a_1, \ldots, a_n\}$ $(n \geqslant 1)$. M_{p_i} has the same structure when i is *even*, but interacts with p_{i-1} instead. Observe that any system constructed in this way is k-MC for any $k \geqslant 1$, $n \geqslant 1$, and $m \geqslant 1$. The shape of these systems allows us to assess how our approach fares in the worst case, i.e., large number of paths in $RTS_k(S)$. Figure 6 gives the time taken for our tool to terminate (y axis) wrt. the number of transitions in $RTS_k(S)$ where k is the least natural number for which the system is k-MC. The plot on the left in Fig. 6 gives the timings when k is increasing (every increment from $k = 2$ to $k = 100$) with the other parameters fixed ($n = 1$ and $m = 5$). The middle plot gives the timings when m is increasing (every increment from $m = 1$ to $m = 26$) with $k = 10$ and $n = 1$. The right-hand side plot gives the timings when n is increasing (every increment from $n = 1$ to $n = 10$) with $k = 2$ and $m = 1$. The largest $RTS_k(S)$ on which we have tested our tool has 12222 states and 22220 transitions, and the verification took under 17 min.[1] Observe that partial order reduction mitigates the increasing size of the transition system on which k-MC is checked, e.g., these experiments show that parameters k and m have only a linear effect on the number of transitions (see horizontal distances between data points). However the number of transitions increases exponentially with n (since the number of paths in each automaton increases exponentially with n).

6   Related Work

Theory of communicating automata Communicating automata were introduced, and shown to be Turing powerful, in the 1980s [10] and have since then been studied extensively, namely through their connection with message sequence charts (MSC) [46]. Several works achieved decidability results by using bag or lossy channels [1,2,13,14] or by restricting the topology of the network [36,57].

Existentially bounded communicating automata stand out because they preserve the FIFO semantics of communicating automata, do not restrict the topology of the network, and include infinite state systems. Given a bound k and

---

[1] All the benchmarks in this paper were run on an 8-core Intel i7-7700 machine with 16 GB RAM running a 64-bit Linux.

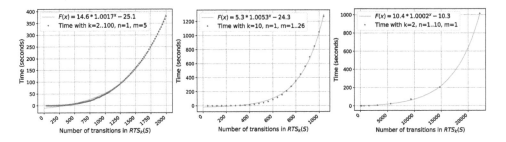

Fig. 6. Benchmarks: increasing k (left), increasing m (middle), and increasing n (right).

an arbitrary system of (deterministic) communicating automata S, it is generally *undecidable* whether S is existentially k-bounded. However, the question becomes decidable (PSPACE-complete) when S has the stable property. The stable property is itself generally *undecidable* (it is called deadlock-freedom in [22,35]). Hence this class is *not* directly applicable to the verification of message passing programs since its membership is overall undecidable. We have shown that k-OBI, IBI, and k-exhaustive CSA systems are (strictly) included in the class of existentially bounded systems. Hence, our work gives a sound *practical* procedure to check whether CSA are existentially k-bounded. To the best of our knowledge, the only tools dedicated to the verification of (unbounded) communicating automata are McScM [26] and Chorgram [40]. Bouajjani et al. [9] study a variation of communicating automata with *mailboxes* (one input queue per automaton). They introduce the class of synchronisable systems and a procedure to check whether a system is k-synchronisable; it relies on executions consisting of k-bounded exchange phases. Given a system and a bound k, it is decidable (PSPACE-complete) whether its executions are equivalent to k-synchronous executions. Section 4.3 states that any k-synchronisable system which satisfies eventual reception is also k-exhaustive, see Theorem 7. In contrast to existential boundedness, synchronisability does not include all finite-state systems. Our characterisation result, based on local bound-agnosticity (Theorem 3), is *unique* to k-exhaustivity. It does not apply to existential boundedness nor synchronisability, see, e.g., Example 7. The term "synchronizability" is used by Basu et al. [3,4] to refer to another verification procedure for communicating automata with mailboxes. Finkel and Lozes [19] have shown that this notion of synchronizability is undecidable. We note that a system that is safe with a point-to-point semantics, may not be safe with a mailbox semantics (due to independent send actions), and vice-versa. For instance, the system in Fig. 2 is safe when executed with mailbox semantics.

Multiparty Compatibility and Programming Languages. The first definition of multiparty compatibility appeared in [18, Definition 4.2], inspired by the work in [23], to characterise the relationship between global types and communicating automata. This definition was later adapted to the setting of communicating timed automata in [6]. Lange et al. [39] introduced a generalised version of multiparty compatibility (GMC) to support communicating automata that feature mixed or non-directed states. Because our results apply to automata without mixed states, k-MC is not a strict extension of GMC, and GMC is not a strict extension of k-MC either, as it requires the existence of *synchronous* executions. In future work, we plan to develop an algorithm to synthesise representative choreographies from k-MC systems, using the algorithm in [39].

The notion of multiparty compatibility is at the core of recent works that apply session types techniques to programming languages. Multiparty compatibility is used in [51] to detect deadlocks in Go programs, and in [30] to study the well-formedness of Scribble protocols [64] through the compatibility of their projections. These protocols are used to generate various endpoint APIs that implement a Scribble specification [30,31,48], and to produce runtime monitoring tools [47,49,50]. Taylor et al. [67] use multiparty compatibility and choreography synthesis [39] to automate the analysis of the `gen_server` library of Erlang/OTP. We can transparently widen the set of safe programs captured by these tools by using k-MC instead of synchronous multiparty compatibility (SMC). The k-MC condition corresponds to a much wider instance of the *abstract* safety invariant φ for session types defined in [63]. Indeed k-MC includes SMC (see [43]) and all finite-state systems (for k sufficiently large).

7   Conclusions

We have studied CSA via a new condition called k-exhaustivity. The k-exhaustivity condition is (i) the basis for a wider notion of multiparty compatibility, k-MC, which captures asynchronous interactions and (ii) the first practical, empirically validated, sufficient condition for existential k-boundedness. We have shown that k-exhaustive systems are fully characterised by local bound-agnosticity (each automaton behaves equivalently for any bound greater than or equal to k). This is a key requirement for asynchronous message passing programming languages where the possibility of having infinitely many orphan messages is undesirable, in particular for Go and Rust which provide *bounded* communication channels.

For future work, we plan to extend our theory beyond CSA. We believe that it is possible to support mixed states and states which do not satisfy IBI, as long as their outgoing transitions are independent (i.e., if they commute). Additionally, to make k-MC checking more efficient, we will elaborate heuristics to find optimal bounds and off-load the verification of k-MC to an off-the-shelf model checker.

Acknowledgements. We thank Laura Bocchi and Alceste Scalas for their comments, and David Castro and Nicolas Dilley for testing the artifact. This work is partially supported by EPSRC EP/K034413/1, EP/K011715/1, EP/L00058X/1, EP/N027833/1, and EP/N028201/1.

References

1. Abdulla, P.A., Bouajjani, A., Jonsson, B.: On-the-fly analysis of systems with unbounded, lossy FIFO channels. In: Hu, A.J., Vardi, M.Y. (eds.) CAV 1998. LNCS, vol. 1427, pp. 305–318. Springer, Heidelberg (1998). https://doi.org/10.1007/BFb0028754
2. Abdulla, P.A., Jonsson, B.: Verifying programs with unreliable channels. In: LICS 1993, pp. 160–170 (1993)
3. Basu, S., Bultan, T.: Automated choreography repair. In: Stevens, P., Wąsowski, A. (eds.) FASE 2016. LNCS, vol. 9633, pp. 13–30. Springer, Heidelberg (2016). https://doi.org/10.1007/978-3-662-49665-7_2
4. Basu, S., Bultan, T., Ouederni, M.: Deciding choreography realizability. In: POPL 2012, pp. 191–202 (2012)
5. Bocchi, L., Chen, T., Demangeon, R., Honda, K., Yoshida, N.: Monitoring networks through multiparty session types. Theor. Comput. Sci. **669**, 33–58 (2017)
6. Bocchi, L., Lange, J., Yoshida, N.: Meeting deadlines together. In: CONCUR 2015, pp. 283–296 (2015)
7. Bocchi, L., Yang, W., Yoshida, N.: Timed multiparty session types. In: Baldan, P., Gorla, D. (eds.) CONCUR 2014. LNCS, vol. 8704, pp. 419–434. Springer, Heidelberg (2014). https://doi.org/10.1007/978-3-662-44584-6_29
8. Bollig, B., Kuske, D., Meinecke, I.: Propositional dynamic logic for message-passing systems. Log. Methods Comput. Sci. **6**(3) (2010). https://lmcs.episciences.org/1057
9. Bouajjani, A., Enea, C., Ji, K., Qadeer, S.: On the completeness of verifying message passing programs under bounded asynchrony. In: Chockler, H., Weissenbacher, G. (eds.) CAV 2018. LNCS, vol. 10982, pp. 372–391. Springer, Cham (2018). https://doi.org/10.1007/978-3-319-96142-2_23
10. Brand, D., Zafiropulo, P.: On communicating finite-state machines. J. ACM **30**(2), 323–342 (1983)
11. Castro, D., Hu, R., Jongmans, S., Ng, N., Yoshida, N.: Distributed programming using role-parametric session types in Go: statically-typed endpoint APIs for dynamically-instantiated communication structures. PACMPL **3**(POPL), 29:1–29:30 (2019)
12. Cécé, G., Finkel, A.: Verification of programs with half-duplex communication. Inf. Comput. **202**(2), 166–190 (2005)
13. Cécé, G., Finkel, A., Iyer, S.P.: Unreliable channels are easier to verify than perfect channels. Inf. Comput. **124**(1), 20–31 (1996)
14. Clemente, L., Herbreteau, F., Sutre, G.: Decidable topologies for communicating automata with FIFO and bag channels. In: Baldan, P., Gorla, D. (eds.) CONCUR 2014. LNCS, vol. 8704, pp. 281–296. Springer, Heidelberg (2014). https://doi.org/10.1007/978-3-662-44584-6_20
15. Coppo, M., Dezani-Ciancaglini, M., Padovani, L., Yoshida, N.: A gentle introduction to multiparty asynchronous session types. In: Bernardo, M., Johnsen, E.B. (eds.) SFM 2015. LNCS, vol. 9104, pp. 146–178. Springer, Cham (2015). https://doi.org/10.1007/978-3-319-18941-3_4
16. Demangeon, R., Honda, K., Hu, R., Neykova, R., Yoshida, N.: Practical interruptible conversations: distributed dynamic verification with multiparty session types and Python. Form. Methods Syst. Des. **46**(3), 197–225 (2015)
17. Deniélou, P.-M., Yoshida, N.: Multiparty session types meet communicating automata. In: Seidl, H. (ed.) ESOP 2012. LNCS, vol. 7211, pp. 194–213. Springer, Heidelberg (2012). https://doi.org/10.1007/978-3-642-28869-2_10

18. Deniélou, P.-M., Yoshida, N.: Multiparty compatibility in communicating automata: characterisation and synthesis of global session types. In: Fomin, F.V., Freivalds, R., Kwiatkowska, M., Peleg, D. (eds.) ICALP 2013. LNCS, vol. 7966, pp. 174–186. Springer, Heidelberg (2013). https://doi.org/10.1007/978-3-642-39212-2_18

19. Finkel, A., Lozes, É.: Synchronizability of communicating finite state machines is not decidable. In: ICALP 2017, pp. 122:1–122:14 (2017)

20. Finkel, A., McKenzie, P.: Verifying identical communicating processes is undecidable. Theor. Comput. Sci. **174**(1–2), 217–230 (1997)

21. Genest, B., Kuske, D., Muscholl, A.: A Kleene theorem and model checking algorithms for existentially bounded communicating automata. Inf. Comput. **204**(6), 920–956 (2006)

22. Genest, B., Kuske, D., Muscholl, A.: On communicating automata with bounded channels. Fundam. Inform. **80**(1–3), 147–167 (2007)

23. Gouda, M.G., Manning, E.G., Yu, Y.: On the progress of communications between two finite state machines. Inf. Control **63**(3), 200–216 (1984)

24. Güdemann, M., Salaün, G., Ouederni, M.: Counterexample guided synthesis of monitors for realizability enforcement. In: Chakraborty, S., Mukund, M. (eds.) ATVA 2012. LNCS, pp. 238–253. Springer, Heidelberg (2012). https://doi.org/10.1007/978-3-642-33386-6_20

25. Hallé, S., Bultan, T.: Realizability analysis for message-based interactions using shared-state projections. In: SIGSOFT 2010, pp. 27–36 (2010)

26. Heußner, A., Le Gall, T., Sutre, G.: McScM: a general framework for the verification of communicating machines. In: Flanagan, C., König, B. (eds.) TACAS 2012. LNCS, vol. 7214, pp. 478–484. Springer, Heidelberg (2012). https://doi.org/10.1007/978-3-642-28756-5_34

27. Honda, K., Vasconcelos, V.T., Kubo, M.: Language primitives and type discipline for structured communication-based programming. In: Hankin, C. (ed.) ESOP 1998. LNCS, vol. 1381, pp. 122–138. Springer, Heidelberg (1998). https://doi.org/10.1007/BFb0053567

28. Honda, K., Yoshida, N., Carbone, M.: Multiparty asynchronous session types. In: POPL 2008, pp. 273–284 (2008)

29. Hu, R.: Distributed programming using Java APIs generated from session types. In: Behavioural Types: Trom Theory to Tools. River Publishers, June 2017

30. Hu, R., Yoshida, N.: Hybrid session verification through endpoint API generation. In: Stevens, P., Wąsowski, A. (eds.) FASE 2016. LNCS, vol. 9633, pp. 401–418. Springer, Heidelberg (2016). https://doi.org/10.1007/978-3-662-49665-7_24

31. Hu, R., Yoshida, N.: Explicit connection actions in multiparty session types. In: FASE 2017, pp. 116–133 (2017)

32. Jespersen, T.B.L., Munksgaard, P., Larsen, K.F.: Session types for Rust. In: WGP@ICFP 2015, pp. 13–22 (2015)

33. KMC tool (2019). https://bitbucket.org/julien-lange/kmc-cav19

34. Kouzapas, D., Dardha, O., Perera, R., Gay, S.J.: Typechecking protocols with Mungo and StMungo. In: PPDP 2016, pp. 146–159 (2016)

35. Kuske, D., Muscholl, A.: Communicating automata (2014). http://eiche.theoinf.tu-ilmenau.de/kuske/Submitted/cfm-final.pdf

36. La Torre, S., Madhusudan, P., Parlato, G.: Context-bounded analysis of concurrent queue systems. In: Ramakrishnan, C.R., Rehof, J. (eds.) TACAS 2008. LNCS, vol. 4963, pp. 299–314. Springer, Heidelberg (2008). https://doi.org/10.1007/978-3-540-78800-3_21

37. Lange, J., Ng, N., Toninho, B., Yoshida, N.: Fencing off Go: liveness and safety for channel-based programming. In: POPL 2017, pp. 748–761 (2017)
38. Lange, J., Ng, N., Toninho, B., Yoshida, N.: A static verification framework for message passing in Go using behavioural types. In: ICSE 2018. ACM (2018)
39. Lange, J., Tuosto, E., Yoshida, N.: From communicating machines to graphical choreographies. In: POPL 2015, pp. 221–232 (2015)
40. Lange, J., Tuosto, E., Yoshida, N.: A tool for choreography-based analysis of message-passing software. In: Behavioural Types: from Theory to Tools. River Publishers, June 2017
41. Lange, J., Yoshida, N.: Characteristic formulae for session types. In: Chechik, M., Raskin, J.-F. (eds.) TACAS 2016. LNCS, vol. 9636, pp. 833–850. Springer, Heidelberg (2016). https://doi.org/10.1007/978-3-662-49674-9_52
42. Lange, J., Yoshida, N.: On the undecidability of asynchronous session subtyping. In: Esparza, J., Murawski, A.S. (eds.) FoSSaCS 2017. LNCS, vol. 10203, pp. 441–457. Springer, Heidelberg (2017). https://doi.org/10.1007/978-3-662-54458-7_26
43. Lange, J., Yoshida, N.: Verifying asynchronous interactions via communicating session automata. CoRR, abs/1901.09606 (2019). https://arxiv.org/abs/1901.09606
44. Lindley, S., Morris, J.G.: Embedding session types in Haskell. In: Haskell 2016, pp. 133–145 (2016)
45. Mostrous, D., Yoshida, N., Honda, K.: Global principal typing in partially commutative asynchronous sessions. In: Castagna, G. (ed.) ESOP 2009. LNCS, vol. 5502, pp. 316–332. Springer, Heidelberg (2009). https://doi.org/10.1007/978-3-642-00590-9_23
46. Muscholl, A.: Analysis of communicating automata. In: Dediu, A.-H., Fernau, H., Martín-Vide, C. (eds.) LATA 2010. LNCS, vol. 6031, pp. 50–57. Springer, Heidelberg (2010). https://doi.org/10.1007/978-3-642-13089-2_4
47. Neykova, R., Bocchi, L., Yoshida, N.: Timed runtime monitoring for multiparty conversations. In: FAOC, pp. 1–34 (2017)
48. Neykova, R., Hu, R., Yoshida, N., Abdeljallal, F.: A session type provider: compile-time API generation for distributed protocols with interaction refinements in F♯. In: CC 2018. ACM (2018)
49. Neykova, R., Yoshida, N.: Let it recover: multiparty protocol-induced recovery. In: CC 2017, pp. 98–108. ACM (2017)
50. Neykova, R., Yoshida, N.: Multiparty session actors. In: LMCS, pp. 13:1–30 (2017)
51. Ng, N., Yoshida, N.: Static deadlock detection for concurrent Go by global session graph synthesis. In: CC 2016, pp. 174–184 (2016)
52. Ng, N., Yoshida, N., Honda, K.: Multiparty session C: safe parallel programming with message optimisation. In: Furia, C.A., Nanz, S. (eds.) TOOLS 2012. LNCS, vol. 7304, pp. 202–218. Springer, Heidelberg (2012). https://doi.org/10.1007/978-3-642-30561-0_15
53. Ocean Observatories Initiative. www.oceanobservatories.org
54. OMG: Business Process Model and Notation (2018). https://www.omg.org/spec/BPMN/2.0/
55. Orchard, D.A., Yoshida, N.: Effects as sessions, sessions as effects. In: POPL 2016, pp. 568–581 (2016)
56. Padovani, L.: A simple library implementation of binary sessions. J. Funct. Program. **27**, e4 (2017)
57. Peng, W., Purushothaman, S.: Analysis of a class of communicating finite state machines. Acta Inf. **29**(6/7), 499–522 (1992)
58. Perera, R., Lange, J., Gay, S.J.: Multiparty compatibility for concurrent objects. In: PLACES 2016, pp. 73–82 (2016)

59. Introduction to protocol engineering (2006). http://cs.uccs.edu/~cs522/pe/pe.htm
60. Salaün, G., Bordeaux, L., Schaerf, M.: Describing and reasoning on web services using process algebra. IJBPIM **1**(2), 116–128 (2006)
61. Scalas, A., Dardha, O., Hu, R., Yoshida, N.: A linear decomposition of multiparty sessions for safe distributed programming. In: ECOOP 2017, pp. 24:1–24:31 (2017)
62. Scalas, A., Yoshida, N.: Lightweight session programming in scala. In: ECOOP 2016, pp. 21:1–21:28 (2016)
63. Scalas, A., Yoshida, N.: Less is more: multiparty session types revisited. PACMPL **3**(POPL), 30:1–30:29 (2019)
64. Scribble Project homepage (2018). www.scribble.org
65. Sivaramakrishnan, K.C., Qudeisat, M., Ziarek, L., Nagaraj, K., Eugster, P.: Efficient sessions. Sci. Comput. Program. **78**(2), 147–167 (2013)
66. Takeuchi, K., Honda, K., Kubo, M.: An interaction-based language and its typing system. In: Halatsis, C., Maritsas, D., Philokyprou, G., Theodoridis, S. (eds.) PARLE 1994. LNCS, vol. 817, pp. 398–413. Springer, Heidelberg (1994). https://doi.org/10.1007/3-540-58184-7_118
67. Taylor, R., Tuosto, E., Walkinshaw, N., Derrick, J.: Choreography-based analysis of distributed message passing programs. In: PDP 2016, pp. 512–519 (2016)
68. Yellin, D.M., Strom, R.E.: Protocol specifications and component adaptors. ACM Trans. Program. Lang. Syst. **19**(2), 292–333 (1997)

5

Symbolic Register Automata

Loris D'Antoni[1], Tiago Ferreira[2], Matteo Sammartino[2(✉)],
and Alexandra Silva[2]

[1] University of Wisconsin–Madison, Madison, WI 53706-1685, USA
loris@cs.wisc.edu
[2] University College London, Gower Street, London WC1E 6BT, UK
me@tiferrei.com, {m.sammartino,a.silva}@ucl.ac.uk

Abstract. Symbolic Finite Automata and Register Automata are two orthogonal extensions of finite automata motivated by real-world problems where data may have unbounded domains. These automata address a demand for a model over large or infinite alphabets, respectively. Both automata models have interesting applications and have been successful in their own right. In this paper, we introduce Symbolic Register Automata, a new model that combines features from both symbolic and register automata, with a view on applications that were previously out of reach. We study their properties and provide algorithms for emptiness, inclusion and equivalence checking, together with experimental results.

1 Introduction

Finite automata are a ubiquitous formalism that is simple enough to model many real-life systems and phenomena. They enjoy a large variety of theoretical properties that in turn play a role in practical applications. For example, finite automata are closed under Boolean operations, and have decidable emptiness and equivalence checking procedures. Unfortunately, finite automata have a fundamental limitation: they can only operate over finite (and typically small) alphabets. Two *orthogonal* families of automata models have been proposed to overcome this: *symbolic automata* and *register automata*. In this paper, we show that these two models can be combined yielding a new powerful model that can cover interesting applications previously out of reach for existing models.

Symbolic finite automata (SFAs) allow transitions to carry predicates over rich first-order alphabet theories, such as linear arithmetic, and therefore extend classic automata to operate over infinite alphabets [12]. For example, an SFA can define the language of all lists of integers in which the first and last elements are positive integer numbers. Despite their increased expressiveness, SFAs enjoy the same closure and decidability properties of finite automata—e.g., closure under Boolean operations and decidable equivalence and emptiness.

Register automata (RA) support infinite alphabets by allowing input characters to be stored in registers during the computation and to be compared against existing values that are already stored in the registers [17]. For example, an RA can define the language of all lists of integers in which all numbers appearing in even positions are the same. RAs do not have some of the properties of finite automata (e.g., they cannot be determinized), but they still enjoy many useful properties that have made them a popular model in static analysis, software verification, and program monitoring [15].

In this paper, we combine the best features of these two models—first order alphabet theories and registers—into a new model, *symbolic register automata* (SRA). SRAs are strictly more expressive than SFAs and RAs. For example, an SRA can define the language of all lists of integers in which the first and last elements are positive rational numbers and all numbers appearing in even positions are the same. This language is not recognizable by either an SFA nor by an RA.

While other attempts at combining symbolic automata and registers have resulted in undecidable models with limited closure properties [11], we show that SRAs enjoy the same closure and decidability properties of (non-symbolic) register automata. We propose a new application enabled by SRAs and implement our model in an open-source automata library.

In summary, our contributions are:

- Symbolic Register Automata (SRA): a new automaton model that can handle complex alphabet theories while allowing symbols at arbitrary positions in the input string to be compared using equality (Sect. 3).
- A thorough study of the properties of SRAs. We show that SRAs are closed under intersection, union and (deterministic) complementation, and provide algorithms for emptiness and forward (bi)simulation (Sect. 4).
- A study of the effectiveness of our SRA implementation on handling regular expressions with back-references (Sect. 5). We compile a set of benchmarks from existing regular expressions with back-references (e.g., `(\d)[a-z]*\1`) and show that SRAs are an effective model for such expressions and existing models such as SFAs and RAs are not. Moreover, we show that SRAs are more efficient than the `java.util.regex` library for matching regular expressions with back-references.

2   Motivating Example

In this section, we illustrate the capabilities of symbolic register automata using a simple example. Consider the regular expression r_p shown in Fig. 1a. This expression, given a sequence of product descriptions, checks whether the products have the same code and lot number. The reader might not be familiar with some of the unusual syntax of this expression. In particular, r_p uses two back-references \1 and \2. The semantics of this construct is that the string matched by the regular expression for \1 (resp. \2) should be exactly the string that matched the subregular expression r appearing between the first (resp. second)

```
C:(.{3}) L:(.) D:[^\s]+( C:\1 L:\2 D:[^\s]+)+
```
(a) Regular expression r_p (with back-reference).

C:X4a L:4 D:bottle C:X4a L:4 D:jar   C:X4a L:4 D:bottle C:X5a L:4 D:jar

(b) Example text matched by r_p.   (c) Example text *not* matched by r_p.

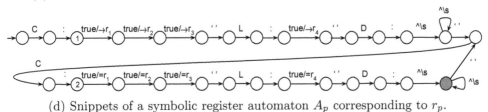

(d) Snippets of a symbolic register automaton A_p corresponding to r_p.

Fig. 1. Regular expression for matching products with same code and lot number—i.e., the characters of C and L are the same in all the products.

two parenthesis, in this case (.{3}) (resp. (.)). Back-references allow regular expressions to check whether the encountered text is the same or is different from a string/character that appeared earlier in the input (see Figs. 1b and c for examples of positive and negative matches).

Representing this complex regular expression using an automaton model requires addressing several challenges. The expression r_p:

1. operates over large input alphabets consisting of upwards of 2^{16} characters;
2. uses complex character classes (e.g., \s) to describe different sets of characters in the input;
3. adopts back-references to detect repeated strings in the input.

Existing automata models do not address one or more of these challenges. Finite automata require one transition for each character in the input alphabet and blow-up when representing large alphabets. Symbolic finite automata (SFA) allow transitions to carry predicates over rich structured first-order alphabet theories and can describe, for example, character classes [12]. However, SFAs cannot directly check whether a character or a string is repeated in the input. An SFA for describing the regular expression r_p would have to store the characters after C: directly in the states to later check whether they match the ones of the second product. Hence, the smallest SFA for this example would require billions of states! Register automata (RA) and their variants can store characters in registers during the computation and compare characters against values already stored in the registers [17]. Hence, RAs can check whether the two products have the same code. However, RAs only operate over unstructured infinite alphabets and cannot check, for example, that a character belongs to a given class.

The model we propose in this paper, *symbolic register automata* (SRA), combines the best features of SFAs and RAs—first-order alphabet theories and registers—and can address all the three aforementioned challenges. Figure 1d shows a snippet of a symbolic register automaton A_p corresponding to r_p. Each transition in A_p is labeled with a predicate that describes what characters can trigger the transition. For example, ^\s denotes that the transition can be triggered by any non-space character, L denotes that the transition can be triggered by the character L, and true denotes that the transition can be triggered by any character. Transitions of the form $\varphi/\!\to r_i$ denote that, if a character x satisfies the predicate φ, the character is then stored in the register r_i. For example, the transition out of state 1 reads any character and stores it in register r_1. Finally, transitions of the form $\varphi/\!=r_i$ are triggered if a character x satisfies the predicate φ and x is the same character as the one stored in r_i. For example, the transition out of state 2 can only be triggered by the same character that was stored in r_1 when reading the transition out state 1—i.e., the first characters in the product codes should be the same.

SRAs are a natural model for describing regular expressions like r_p, where capture groups are of bounded length, and hence correspond to finitely-many registers. The SRA A_p has fewer than 50 states (vs. more than 100 billion for SFAs) and can, for example, be used to check whether an input string matches the given regular expression (e.g., monitoring). More interestingly, in this paper we study the closure and decidability properties of SRAs and provide an implementation for our model. For example, consider the following regular expression r_{pC} that only checks whether the product codes are the same, but not the lot numbers:

$$\texttt{C:(.\{3\}) L:. D:[\textasciicircum\textbackslash s]+(C:\textbackslash1 L:. D:[\textasciicircum\textbackslash s]+)+}$$

The set of strings accepted by r_{pC} is a superset of the set of strings accepted by r_p. In this paper, we present simulation and bisimulation algorithms that can check this property. Our implementation can show that r_p subsumes r_{pC} in 25 s and we could not find other tools that can prove the same property.

3   Symbolic Register Automata

In this section we introduce some preliminary notions, we define symbolic register automata and a variant that will be useful in proving decidability properties.

Preliminaries. An *effective Boolean algebra* $\mathcal{A}$ is a tuple $(\mathcal{D}, \Psi, [\![\_]\!], \bot,$ $\top, \wedge, \vee, \neg)$, where: $\mathcal{D}$ is a set of domain elements; Ψ is a set of predicates closed under the Boolean connectives and $\bot, \top \in \Psi$. The denotation function $[\![\_]\!]: \Psi \to 2^{\mathcal{D}}$ is such that $[\![\bot]\!] = \emptyset$ and $[\![\top]\!] = \mathcal{D}$, for all $\varphi, \psi \in \Psi$, $[\![\varphi \vee \psi]\!] = [\![\varphi]\!] \cup [\![\psi]\!]$, $[\![\varphi \wedge \psi]\!] = [\![\varphi]\!] \cap [\![\psi]\!]$, and $[\![\neg\varphi]\!] = \mathcal{D} \setminus [\![\varphi]\!]$. For $\varphi \in \Psi$, we write isSat(φ) whenever $[\![\varphi]\!] \neq \emptyset$ and say that φ is *satisfiable*. $\mathcal{A}$ is *decidable* if isSat is decidable. For each $a \in \mathcal{D}$, we assume predicates atom(a) such that $[\![\text{atom}(a)]\!] = \{a\}$.

Example 1. The theory of linear integer arithmetic forms an effective BA, where $\mathcal{D} = \mathbb{Z}$ and Ψ contains formulas $\varphi(x)$ in the theory with one fixed integer variable. For example, $\mathsf{div_k} := (x \bmod k) = 0$ denotes the set of all integers divisible by k.

Notation. Given a set S, we write $\mathcal{P}(S)$ for its powerset. Given a function $f\colon A \to B$, we write $f[a \mapsto b]$ for the function such that $f[a \mapsto b](a) = b$ and $f[a \mapsto b](x) = f(x)$, for $x \neq a$. Analogously, we write $f[S \mapsto b]$, with $S \subseteq A$, to map multiple values to the same b. The *pre-image* of f is the function $f^{-1}\colon \mathcal{P}(B) \to \mathcal{P}(A)$ given by $f^{-1}(S) = \{a \mid \exists b \in S\colon b = f(a)\}$; for readability, we will write $f^{-1}(x)$ when $S = \{x\}$. Given a relation $\mathcal{R} \subseteq A \times B$, we write $a\mathcal{R}b$ for $(a, b) \in \mathcal{R}$.

Model Definition. Symbolic register automata have transitions of the form:

$$p \xrightarrow{\varphi/E,I,U} q$$

where p and q are states, φ is a predicate from a fixed effective Boolean algebra, and E, I, U are subsets of a fixed finite set of registers R. The intended interpretation of the above transition is: an input character a can be read in state q if (i) $a \in [\![\varphi]\!]$, (ii) the content of all the registers in E is *equal* to a, and (iii) the content of all the registers in I is *different* from a. If the transition succeeds then a is stored into all the registers U and the automaton moves to q.

Example 2. The transition labels in Fig. 1d have been conveniently simplified to ease intuition. These labels correspond to full SRA labels as follows:

$$\varphi/{\to}r \implies \varphi/\emptyset, \emptyset, \{r\} \qquad \varphi/{=}r \implies \varphi/\{r\}, \emptyset, \emptyset \qquad \varphi \implies \varphi/\emptyset, \emptyset, \emptyset \ .$$

Given a set of registers R, the transitions of an SRA have labels over the following set: $L_R = \Psi \times \{(E, I, U) \in \mathcal{P}(R) \times \mathcal{P}(R) \times \mathcal{P}(R) \mid E \cap I = \emptyset\}$. The condition $E \cap I = \emptyset$ guarantees that register constraints are always satisfiable.

Definition 1 (Symbolic Register Automaton). *A symbolic register automaton (SRA) is a 6-tuple $(R, Q, q_0, v_0, F, \Delta)$, where R is a finite set of registers, Q is a finite set of states, $q_0 \in Q$ is the* initial state, *$v_0\colon R \to \mathcal{D} \cup \{\sharp\}$ is the* initial register assignment *(if $v_0(r) = \sharp$, the register r is considered empty), $F \subseteq Q$ is a finite set of* final *states, and $\Delta \subseteq Q \times L_R \times Q$ is the transition relation. Transitions $(p, (\varphi, \ell), q) \in \Delta$ will be written as $p \xrightarrow{\varphi/\ell} q$.*

An SRA can be seen as a finite description of a (possibly infinite) labeled transition system (LTS), where states have been assigned concrete register values, and transitions read a single symbol from the potentially infinite alphabet. This so-called *configuration LTS* will be used in defining the semantics of SRAs.

Definition 2 (Configuration LTS). *Given an SRA $\mathcal{S}$, the configuration LTS $\mathsf{CLTS}(\mathcal{S})$ is defined as follows. A* configuration *is a pair (p, v) where $p \in Q$ is a state in $\mathcal{S}$ and a $v\colon R \to \mathcal{D} \cup \{\sharp\}$ is register assignment; (q_0, v_0) is called the* initial configuration; *every (q, v) such that $q \in F$ is a* final configuration. *The set of transitions between configurations is defined as follows:*

$$\frac{p \xrightarrow{\varphi/E,I,U} q \in \Delta \qquad E \subseteq v^{-1}(a) \qquad I \cap v^{-1}(a) = \emptyset}{(p, v) \xrightarrow{a} (q, v[U \mapsto a]) \in \mathsf{CLTS}(\mathcal{S})}$$

Intuitively, the rule says that a SRA transition from p can be instantiated to one from (p, v) that reads a when the registers containing the value a, namely $v^{-1}(a)$, satisfy the constraint described by E, I (a is contained in registers E but not in I). If the constraint is satisfied, all registers in U are assigned a.

A *run* of the SRA $\mathcal{S}$ is a sequence of transitions in $\mathsf{CLTS}(\mathcal{S})$ starting from the initial configuration. A configuration is *reachable* whenever there is a run ending up in that configuration. The *language* of an SRA $\mathcal{S}$ is defined as

$$\mathcal{L}(\mathcal{S}) := \{a_1 \ldots a_n \in \mathcal{D}^n \mid \exists (q_0, v_0) \xrightarrow{a_1} \ldots \xrightarrow{a_n} (q_n, v_n) \in \mathsf{CLTS}(\mathcal{S}), q_n \in F\}$$

An SRA $\mathcal{S}$ is *deterministic* if its configuration LTS is; namely, for every word $w \in \mathcal{D}^\star$ there is at most one run in $\mathsf{CLTS}(\mathcal{S})$ spelling w. Determinism is important for some application contexts, e.g., for runtime monitoring. Since SRAs subsume RAs, nondeterministic SRAs are strictly more expressive than deterministic ones, and language equivalence is undecidable for nondeterministic SRAs [27].

We now introduce the notions of *simulation* and *bisimulation* for SRAs, which capture whether one SRA behaves "at least as" or "exactly as" another one.

Definition 3 ((Bi)simulation for SRAs). *A simulation $\mathcal{R}$ on SRAs $\mathcal{S}_1$ and $\mathcal{S}_2$ is a binary relation $\mathcal{R}$ on configurations such that $(p_1, v_1)\mathcal{R}(p_2, v_2)$ implies:*

- *if $p_1 \in F_1$ then $p_2 \in F_2$;*
- *for each transition $(p_1, v_1) \xrightarrow{a} (q_1, w_1)$ in $\mathsf{CLTS}(\mathcal{S}_1)$, there exists a transition $(p_2, v_2) \xrightarrow{a} (q_2, w_2)$ in $\mathsf{CLTS}(\mathcal{S}_2)$ such that $(q_1, w_1)\mathcal{R}(q_2, w_2)$.*

A simulation $\mathcal{R}$ is a bisimulation *if $\mathcal{R}^{-1}$ is a also a simulation. We write $\mathcal{S}_1 \prec \mathcal{S}_2$ (resp. $\mathcal{S}_1 \sim \mathcal{S}_2$) whenever there is a simulation (resp. bisimulation) $\mathcal{R}$ such that $(q_{01}, v_{01})\mathcal{R}(q_{02}, v_{02})$, where (q_{0i}, v_{0i}) is the initial configuration of $\mathcal{S}_i$, for $i = 1, 2$.*

We say that an SRA is *complete* whenever for every configuration (p, v) and $a \in \mathcal{D}$ there is a transition $(p, v) \xrightarrow{a} (q, w)$ in $\mathsf{CLTS}(\mathcal{S})$. The following results connect similarity and language inclusion.

Proposition 1. *If $\mathcal{S}_1 \prec \mathcal{S}_2$ then $\mathcal{L}(\mathcal{S}_1) \subseteq \mathcal{L}(\mathcal{S}_2)$. If $\mathcal{S}_1$ and $\mathcal{S}_2$ are deterministic and complete, then the other direction also holds.*

It is worth noting that given a deterministic SRA we can define its *completion* by adding transitions so that every value $a \in \mathcal{D}$ can be read from any state.

Remark 1. RAs and SFAs can be encoded as SRAs on the same state-space:

- An RA is encoded as an SRA with all transition guards $\top$;
- an SFA can be encoded as an SRA with $R = \emptyset$, with each SFA transition $p \xrightarrow{\varphi} q$ encoded as $p \xrightarrow{\varphi/\emptyset,\emptyset,\emptyset} q$. Note that the absence of registers implies that the CLTS always has finitely many configurations.

SRAs are *strictly more expressive* than both RAs and SFAs. For instance, the language $\{n_0 n_1 \ldots n_k \mid n_0 = n_k, \mathsf{even}(n_i), n_i \in \mathbb{Z}, i = 1, \ldots, k\}$ of finite sequences of even integers where the first and last one coincide, can be recognized by an SRA, but not by an RA or by an SFA.

Boolean Closure Properties. SRAs are closed under intersection and union. Intersection is given by a standard product construction whereas union is obtained by adding a new initial state that mimics the initial states of both automata.

Proposition 2 (Closure under intersection and union). *Given SRAs* S_1 *and* S_2, *there are SRAs* $S_1 \cap S_2$ *and* $S_1 \cup S_2$ *such that* $\mathscr{L}(S_1 \cap S_2) = \mathscr{L}(S_1) \cap \mathscr{L}(S_2)$ *and* $\mathscr{L}(S_1 \cup S_2) = \mathscr{L}(S_1) \cup \mathscr{L}(S_2)$.

SRAs in general are not closed under complementation, because RAs are not. However, we still have closure under complementation for a subclass of SRAs.

Proposition 3. *Let* S *be a complete and deterministic SRA, and let* $\overline{S}$ *be the SRA defined as* S, *except that its final states are* $Q \setminus F$. *Then* $\mathscr{L}(\overline{S}) = \mathcal{D}^\star \setminus \mathscr{L}(S)$.

4   Decidability Properties

In this section we will provide algorithms for checking determinism and emptiness for an SRA, and (bi)similarity of two SRAs. Our algorithms leverage *symbolic* techniques that use the finite syntax of SRAs to indirectly operate over the underlying configuration LTS, which can be infinite.

Single-Valued Variant. To study decidability, it is convenient to restrict register assignments to *injective* ones on non-empty registers, that is functions $v \colon R \to \mathcal{D} \cup \{\sharp\}$ such that $v(r) = v(s)$ and $v(r) \neq \sharp$ implies $r = s$. This is also the approach taken for RAs in the seminal papers [17,27]. Both for RAs and SRAs, this restriction does not affect expressivity. We say that an SRA is *single-valued* if its initial assignment v_0 is injective on non-empty registers. For single-valued SRAs, we only allow two kinds of transitions:

Read transition: $p \xrightarrow{\varphi/r^=} q$ triggers when $a \in [\![\varphi]\!]$ and a is already stored in r.

Fresh transition: $p \xrightarrow{\varphi/r^\bullet} q$ triggers when the input $a \in [\![\varphi]\!]$ and a is *fresh*, i.e., is not stored in any register. After the transition, a is stored into r.

SRAs and their single-valued variants have the same expressive power. Translating single-valued SRAs to ordinary ones is straightforward:

$$p \xrightarrow{\varphi/r^=} q \implies p \xrightarrow{\varphi/\{r\},\emptyset,\emptyset} q \qquad p \xrightarrow{\varphi/r^\bullet} q \implies p \xrightarrow{\varphi/\emptyset,R,\{r\}} q$$

The opposite translation requires a state-space blow up, because we need to encode register equalities in the states.

Theorem 1. *Given an SRA* S *with* n *states and* r *registers, there is a single-valued SRA* S' *with* $\mathcal{O}(nr^r)$ *states and* $r + 1$ *registers such that* $S \sim S'$. *Moreover, the translation preserves determinism.*

Normalization. While our techniques are inspired by analogous ones for non-symbolic RAs, SRAs present an additional challenge: they can have arbitrary predicates on transitions. Hence, the values that each transition can read, and thus which configurations it can reach, depend on the history of past transitions and their predicates. This problem emerges when checking reachability and similarity, because a transition may be *disabled* by particular register values, and so lead to unsound conclusions, a problem that does not exist in register automata.

Example 3. Consider the SRA below, defined over the BA of integers.

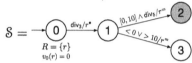

All predicates on transitions are satisfiable, yet $\mathscr{L}(\mathcal{S}) = \emptyset$. To go from 0 to 1, $\mathcal{S}$ must read a value n such that $\mathsf{div}_3(n)$ and $n \neq 0$ and then n is stored into r. The transition from 1 to 2 can only happen if the content of r also satisfies $\mathsf{div}_5(n)$ and $n \in [0, 10]$. However, there is no n satisfying $\mathsf{div}_3(n) \wedge n \neq 0 \wedge \mathsf{div}_5(n) \wedge n \in [0, 10]$, hence the transition from 1 to 2 never happens.

To handle the complexity caused by predicates, we introduce a way of *normalizing* an SRA to an equivalent one that *stores additional information about input predicates*. We first introduce some notation and terminology.

A register abstraction θ for $\mathcal{S}$, used to "keep track" of the domain of registers, is a family of predicates indexed by the registers R of $\mathcal{S}$. Given a register assignment v, we write $v \models \theta$ whenever $v(r) \in [\![\theta_r]\!]$ for $v(r) \neq \sharp$, and $\theta_r = \bot$ otherwise. Hereafter we shall only consider "meaningful" register abstractions, for which there is at least one assignment v such that $v \models \theta$.

With the contextual information about register domains given by θ, we say that a transition $p \xrightarrow{\varphi/\ell} q \in \Delta$ is *enabled by* θ whenever it has at least an instance $(p, v) \xrightarrow{a} (q, w)$ in $\mathsf{CLTS}(\mathcal{S})$, for all $v \models \theta$. Enabled transitions are important when reasoning about reachability and similarity.

Checking whether a transition has at least one realizable instance in the CLTS is difficult in practice, especially when $\ell = r^\bullet$, because it amounts to checking whether $[\![\varphi]\!] \setminus \mathsf{img}(v) \neq \emptyset$, for all injective $v \models \theta$.

To make the check for enabledness practical we will use minterms. For a set of predicates Φ, a *minterm* is a minimal satisfiable Boolean combination of all predicates that occur in Φ. Minterms are the analogue of atoms in a complete atomic Boolean algebra. E.g. the set of predicates $\Phi = \{x > 2, x < 5\}$ over the theory of linear integer arithmetic has minterms $\mathsf{mint}(\Phi) = \{x > 2 \wedge x < 5, \neg x > 2 \wedge x < 5, x > 2 \wedge \neg x < 5\}$. Given $\psi \in \mathsf{mint}(\Phi)$ and $\varphi \in \Phi$, we will write $\varphi \sqsubset \psi$ whenever φ appears non-negated in ψ, for instance $(x > 2) \sqsubset (x > 2 \wedge \neg x < 5)$. A crucial property of minterms is that they do not overlap, i.e., $\mathsf{isSat}(\psi_1 \wedge \psi_2)$ if and only if $\psi_1 = \psi_2$, for ψ_1 and ψ_2 minterms.

Lemma 1 (Enabledness). *Let θ be a register abstraction such that θ_r is a minterm, for all $r \in R$. If φ is a minterm, then $p \xrightarrow{\varphi/\ell} q$ is enabled by θ iff:*

(1) if $\ell = r^=$, then $\varphi = \theta_r$;   (2) if $\ell = r^\bullet$, then $|[\![\varphi]\!]| > \mathscr{E}(\theta, \varphi)$,
where $\mathscr{E}(\theta, \varphi) = |\{r \in R \mid \theta_r = \varphi\}|$ is the # of registers with values from $[\![\varphi]\!]$.

Intuitively, (1) says that if the transition reads a symbol stored in r satisfying φ, the symbol must also satisfy θ_r, the range of r. Because φ and θ_r are minterms, this only happens when $\varphi = \theta_r$. (2) says that the enabling condition $[\![\varphi]\!] \setminus$ img$(v) \neq \emptyset$, for all injective $v \models \theta$, holds if and only if there are fewer registers storing values from φ than the cardinality of φ. That implies we can always find a fresh element in $[\![\varphi]\!]$ to enable the transition. Registers holding values from φ are exactly those $r \in R$ such that $\theta_r = \varphi$. Both conditions can be effectively checked: the first one is a simple predicate-equivalence check, while the second one amounts to checking whether φ holds for at least a certain number k of distinct elements. This can be achieved by checking satisfiability of $\varphi \wedge \neg\mathsf{atom}(a_1) \wedge \cdots \wedge \neg\mathsf{atom}(a_{k-1})$, for $a_1, \ldots, a_{k-1}$ distinct elements of $[\![\varphi]\!]$.

Remark 2. Using single-valued SRAs to check enabledness might seem like a restriction. However, if one would start from a generic SRA, the process to check enabledness would contain an extra step: for each state p, we would have to keep track of all possible equations among registers. In fact, register equalities determine whether (i) register constraints of an outgoing transition are satisfiable; (ii) how many elements of the guard we need for the transition to happen, analogously to condition 2 of Lemma 1. Generating such equations is the key idea behind Theorem 1, and corresponds precisely to turning the SRA into a single-valued one.

Given any SRA, we can use the notion of register abstraction to build an equivalent *normalized* SRA, where (i) states keep track of how the domains of registers change along transitions, (ii) transitions are obtained by breaking the one of the original SRA into minterms and discarding the ones that are disabled according to Lemma 1. In the following we write mint$(\mathcal{S})$ for the minterms for the set of predicates $\{\varphi \mid p \xrightarrow{\varphi/\ell} q \in \Delta\} \cup \{\mathsf{atom}(v_0(r)) \mid v_0(r) \in \mathcal{D}, r \in R\}$. Observe that an atomic predicate always has an equivalent minterm, hence we will use atomic predicates to define the initial register abstraction.

Definition 4 (Normalized SRA). *Given an SRA $\mathcal{S}$, its normalization $\mathsf{N}(\mathcal{S})$ is the SRA $(R, \mathsf{N}(Q), \mathsf{N}(q_0), v_0, \mathsf{N}(F), \mathsf{N}(\Delta))$ where:*

- $\mathsf{N}(Q) = \{\theta \mid \theta$ *is a register abstraction over* mint$(\mathcal{S}) \cup \{\perp\}$ $\} \times Q$; *we will write* $\theta \triangleright q$ *for* $(\theta, q) \in \mathsf{N}(Q)$.
- $\mathsf{N}(q_0) = \theta_0 \triangleright q_0$, *where* $(\theta_0)_r = \mathsf{atom}(v_0(r))$ *if* $v_0(r) \in \mathcal{D}$, *and* $(\theta_0)_r = \perp$ *if* $v_0(r) = \sharp$;
- $\mathsf{N}(F) = \{\theta \triangleright p \in \mathsf{N}(Q) \mid p \in F\}$
- $\mathsf{N}(\Delta) = \{\theta \triangleright p \xrightarrow{\theta_r/r^=} \theta \triangleright q \mid p \xrightarrow{\varphi/r^=} q \in \Delta, \varphi \sqsubseteq \theta_r\} \cup$

$$\{\theta \triangleright p \xrightarrow{\psi/r^\bullet} \theta[r \mapsto \psi] \triangleright q \mid p \xrightarrow{\varphi/r^\bullet} q \in \Delta, \varphi \sqsubseteq \psi, |[\![\psi]\!]| > \mathscr{E}(\theta, \psi)\}$$

The automaton $N(S)$ enjoys the desired property: each transition from $\theta \rhd p$ is enabled by θ, by construction. $N(S)$ is always *finite*. In fact, suppose S has n states, m transitions and r registers. Then $N(S)$ has at most m predicates, and $|\text{mint}(S)|$ is $\mathcal{O}(2^m)$. Since the possible register abstractions are $\mathcal{O}(r2^m)$, $N(S)$ has $\mathcal{O}(nr2^m)$ states and $\mathcal{O}(mr^2 2^{3m})$ transitions.

Example 4. We now show the normalized version of Example 3. The first step is computing the set $\text{mint}(S)$ of minterms for S, i.e., the satisfiable Boolean combinations of $\{\text{atom}(0), \text{div}_3, [0, 10] \wedge \text{div}_5, < 0 \vee > 10\}$. For simplicity, we represent minterms as bitvectors where a 0 component means that the corresponding predicate is negated, e.g., $[1, 1, 1, 0]$ stands for the minterm $\text{atom}(0) \wedge ([0, 10] \wedge \text{div}_3) \wedge \text{div}_5 \wedge \neg(< 0 \vee > 10)$. Minterms and the resulting SRA $N(S)$ are shown below.

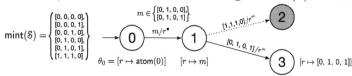

On each transition we show how it is broken down to minterms, and for each state we show the register abstraction (note that state 1 becomes two states in $N(S)$). The transition from 1 to 2 is *not* part of $N(S)$ – this is why it is dotted. In fact, in every register abstraction $[r \mapsto m]$ reachable at state 1, the component for the transition guard $[0, 10] \wedge \text{div}_5$ in the minterm m (3rd component) is 0, i.e., $([0, 10] \wedge \text{div}_5) \not\sqsubseteq m$. Intuitively, this means that r will never be assigned a value that satisfies $[0, 10] \wedge \text{div}_5$. As a consequence, the construction of Definition 4 will not add a transition from 1 to 2.

Finally, we show that the normalized SRA behaves exactly as the original one.

Proposition 4. $(p, v) \sim (\theta \rhd p, v)$, *for all* $p \in Q$ *and* $v \models \theta$. *Hence,* $S \sim N(S)$.

Emptiness and Determinism. The transitions of $N(S)$ are always enabled by construction, therefore every path in $N(S)$ always corresponds to a run in $\text{CLTS}(N(S))$.

Lemma 2. *The state* $\theta \rhd p$ *is reachable in* $N(S)$ *if and only if there is a reachable configuration* $(\theta \rhd p, v)$ *in* $\text{CLTS}(N(S))$ *such that* $v \models \theta$. *Moreover, if* $(\theta \rhd p, v)$ *is reachable, then all configurations* $(\theta \rhd p, w)$ *such that* $w \models \theta$ *are reachable.*

Therefore, using Proposition 4, we can reduce the reachability and emptiness problems of S to that of $N(S)$.

Theorem 2 (Emptiness). *There is an algorithm to decide reachability of any configuration of* S, *hence whether* $\mathscr{L}(S) = \emptyset$.

Proof. Let (p, v) be a configuration of S. To decide whether it is reachable in $\text{CLTS}(S)$, we can perform a visit of $N(S)$ from its initial state, stopping when a state $\theta \triangleright p$ such that $v \models \theta$ is reached. If we are just looking for a final state, we can stop at any state such that $p \in F$. In fact, by Proposition 4, there is a run in $\mathsf{CLTS}(S)$ ending in (p, v) if and only if there is a run in $\mathsf{CLTS}(\mathsf{N}(S))$ ending in $(\theta \triangleright p, v)$ such that $v \models \theta$. By Lemma 2, the latter holds if and only if there is a path in $\mathsf{N}(S)$ ending in $\theta \triangleright p$. This algorithm has the complexity of a standard visit of $\mathsf{N}(S)$, namely $\mathcal{O}(nr2^m + mr^2 2^{3m})$. $\qquad\qquad\qquad\qquad \Box$

Now that we characterized which transitions are reachable, we define what it means for a normalized SRA to be deterministic and we show that determinism is preserved by the translation from SRA.

Proposition 5 (Determinism). $\mathsf{N}(S)$ *is* deterministic *if and only if for all* *reachable transitions* $p \xrightarrow{\varphi_1/\ell_1} q_1, p \xrightarrow{\varphi_2/\ell_2} q_2 \in \mathsf{N}(\Delta)$ *the following holds:* $\varphi_1 \neq \varphi_2$ *whenever either (1)* $\ell_1 = \ell_2$ *and* $q_1 \neq q_2$, *or; (2)* $\ell_1 = r^\bullet$, $\ell_2 = s^\bullet$, *and* $r \neq s$;

One can check determinism of an SRA by looking at its normalized version.

Proposition 6. S *is deterministic if and only if* $\mathsf{N}(S)$ *is deterministic.*

Similarity and Bisimilarity. We now introduce a symbolic technique to decide similarity and bisimilarity of SRAs. The basic idea is similar to *symbolic (bi)simulation* [20,27] for RAs. Recall that RAs are SRAs whose transition guards are all $\top$. Given two RAs S_1 and S_2 a symbolic simulation between them is defined over their state spaces Q_1 and Q_2, not on their configurations. For this to work, one needs to add an extra piece of information about how registers of the two states are related. More precisely, a symbolic simulation is a relation on triples (p_1, p_2, σ), where $p_1 \in Q_1, p_2 \in Q_2$ and $\sigma \subseteq R_1 \times R_2$ is a *partial injective* function. This function encodes constraints between registers: $(r, s) \in \sigma$ is an equality constraint between $r \in R_1$ and $s \in R_2$, and $(r, s) \notin \sigma$ is an inequality constraint. Intuitively, (p_1, p_2, σ) says that all configurations (p_1, v_1) and (p_2, v_2) such that v_1 and v_2 satisfy σ – e.g., $v_1(r) = v_2(s)$ whenever $(r, s) \in \sigma$ – are in the simulation relation $(p_1, v_1) \prec (p_2, v_2)$. In the following we will use $v_1 \bowtie v_2$ to denote the function encoding constraints among v_1 and v_2, explicitly: $\sigma(r) = s$ if and only if $v_1(r) = v_2(s)$ and $v_1(r) \neq \sharp$.

Definition 5 (Symbolic (bi)similarity [27]). *A symbolic simulation is a relation* $\mathcal{R} \subseteq Q_1 \times Q_1 \times \mathcal{P}(R_1 \times R_2)$ *such that if* $(p_1, p_2, \sigma) \in \mathcal{R}$, *then* $p_1 \in F_1$ *implies* $p_2 \in F_2$, *and if* $p_1 \xrightarrow{\ell} q_1 \in \Delta_1{}^1$ *then:*

1. *if* $\ell = r^=$:
   (a) *if* $r \in \mathsf{dom}(\sigma)$, *then there is* $p_2 \xrightarrow{\sigma(r)^=} q_2 \in \Delta_2$ *such that* $(q_1, q_2, \sigma) \in \mathcal{R}$.
   (b) *if* $r \notin \mathsf{dom}(\sigma)$ *then there is* $p_2 \xrightarrow{s^\bullet} q_2 \in \Delta_2$ *s.t.* $(q_1, q_2, \sigma[r \mapsto s]) \in \mathcal{R}$.

---

[1] We will keep the $\top$ guard implicit for succinctness.

2 if $\ell = r^\bullet$:

    (a) for all $s \in R_2 \setminus \mathsf{img}(\sigma)$, there is $p_2 \xrightarrow{s^=} q_2 \in \Delta_2$ such that $(q_1, q_2, \sigma[r \mapsto s]) \in \mathcal{R}$, and;

    (b) there is $p_2 \xrightarrow{s^\bullet} q_2 \in \Delta_2$ such that $(q_1, q_2, \sigma[r \mapsto s]) \in \mathcal{R}$.

Here $\sigma[r \mapsto s]$ stands for $\sigma \setminus (\sigma^{-1}(s), s) \cup (r, s)$, which ensures that σ stays injective when updated.

    Given a symbolic simulation $\mathcal{R}$, its inverse is defined as $\mathcal{R}^{-1} = \{t^{-1} \mid t \in \mathcal{R}\}$, where $(p_1, p_2, \sigma)^{-1} = (p_2, p_1, \sigma^{-1})$. A symbolic bisimulation $\mathcal{R}$ is a relation such that both $\mathcal{R}$ and $\mathcal{R}^{-1}$ are symbolic simulations.

Case 1 deals with cases when p_1 can perform a transition that reads the register r. If $r \in \mathsf{dom}(\sigma)$, meaning that r and $\sigma(r) \in R_2$ contain the same value, then p_2 must be able to read $\sigma(r)$ as well. If $r \notin \mathsf{dom}(\sigma)$, then the content of r is fresh w.r.t. p_2, so p_2 must be able to read any fresh value—in particular the content of r. Case 2 deals with the cases when p_1 reads a fresh value. It ensures that p_2 is able to read all possible values that are fresh for p_1, be them already in some register s – i.e., $s \in R_2 \setminus \mathsf{img}(\sigma)$, case 2(a) – or fresh for p_2 as well – case 2(b). In all these cases, σ must be updated to reflect the new equalities among registers.

    Keeping track of equalities among registers is enough for RAs, because the actual content of registers does not determine the capability of a transition to fire (RA transitions have implicit $\top$ guards). As seen in Example 3, this is no longer the case for SRAs: a transition may or may not happen depending on the register assignment being compatible with the transition guard.

    As in the case of reachability, normalized SRAs provide the solution to this problem. We will reduce the problem of checking (bi)similarity of S_1 and S_2 to that of checking symbolic (bi)similarity on $\mathsf{N}(S_1)$ and $\mathsf{N}(S_2)$, with minor modifications to the definition. To do this, we need to assume that minterms for both $\mathsf{N}(S_1)$ and $\mathsf{N}(S_2)$ are computed over the union of predicates of S_1 and S_2.

Definition 6 (N-simulation). *A N-simulation on S_1 and S_2 is a relation $\mathcal{R} \subseteq \mathsf{N}(Q_1) \times \mathsf{N}(Q_2) \times \mathcal{P}(R_1 \times R_2)$, defined as in Definition 5, with the following modifications:*

(i) we require that $\theta_1 \triangleright p_1 \xrightarrow{\varphi_1/\ell_1} \theta'_1 \triangleright q_1 \in \mathsf{N}(\Delta_1)$ must be matched by transitions $\theta_2 \triangleright p_2 \xrightarrow{\varphi_2/\ell_2} \theta'_2 \triangleright q_2 \in \mathsf{N}(\Delta_2)$ such that $\varphi_2 = \varphi_1$.

(ii) we modify case 2 as follows (changes are underlined):

    2(a)' for all $s \in R_2 \setminus \mathsf{img}(\sigma)$ <u>such that $\varphi_1 = (\theta_2)_s$</u>, there is $\theta_2 \triangleright p_2 \xrightarrow{\varphi_1/s^=} \theta'_2 \triangleright q_2 \in \mathsf{N}(\Delta_2)$ such that $\overline{(\theta'_1 \triangleright q_1, \theta'_2 \triangleright q_2, \sigma[r \mapsto s])} \in \mathcal{R}$, and;

    2(b)' <u>if $\mathscr{E}(\theta_1, \varphi_1) + \mathscr{E}(\theta_2, \varphi_1) < |[\![\varphi_1]\!]|$, then</u> there is $\theta_2 \triangleright p_2 \xrightarrow{\varphi_1/s^\bullet} \theta'_2 \triangleright q_2 \in \mathsf{N}(\Delta_2)$ such that $\overline{(\theta'_1 \triangleright q_1, \theta'_2 \triangleright q_2, \sigma[r \mapsto s])} \in \mathcal{R}$.

A N-bisimulation $\mathcal{R}$ is a relation such that both $\mathcal{R}$ and $\mathcal{R}^{-1}$ are N-simulations. We write $S_1 \overset{\mathsf{N}}{\precsim} S_2$ (resp. $S_1 \overset{\mathsf{N}}{\sim} S_2$) if there is a N-simulation (resp. bisimulation) $\mathcal{R}$ such that $(\mathsf{N}(q_{01}), \mathsf{N}(q_{02}), v_{01} \bowtie v_{02}) \in \mathcal{R}$.

The intuition behind this definition is as follows. Recall that, in a normalized SRA, transitions are defined over minterms, which cannot be further broken down, and are mutually disjoint. Therefore two transitions can read the same values if and only if they have the same minterm guard. Thus condition (i) makes sure that matching transitions can read exactly the same set of values. Analogously, condition (ii) restricts how a fresh transition of $N(S_1)$ must be matched by one of $N(S_2)$: 2(a)' only considers transitions of $N(S_2)$ reading registers $s \in R_2$ such that $\varphi_1 = (\theta_2)_s$ because, by definition of normalized SRA, $\theta_2 \rhd p_2$ has no such transition if this condition is not met. Condition 2(b)' amounts to requiring a fresh transition of $N(S_2)$ that is enabled by both θ_1 and θ_2 (see Lemma 1), i.e., that can read a symbol that is fresh w.r.t. both $N(S_1)$ and $N(S_2)$.

N-simulation is sound and complete for standard simulation.

Theorem 3. $S_1 \prec S_2$ if and only if $S_1 \overset{N}{\prec} S_2$.

As a consequence, we can decide similarity of SRAs via their normalized versions. N-simulation is a relation over a finite set, namely $N(Q_1) \times N(Q_2) \times \mathcal{P}(R_1 \times R_2)$, therefore N-similarity can always be decided in finite time. We can leverage this result to provide algorithms for checking language inclusion/equivalence for deterministic SRAs (recall that they are undecidable for non-deterministic ones).

Theorem 4. *Given two deterministic SRAs S_1 and S_2, there are algorithms to decide $\mathscr{L}(S_1) \subseteq \mathscr{L}(S_2)$ and $\mathscr{L}(S_1) = \mathscr{L}(S_2)$.*

Proof. By Proposition 1 and Theorem 3, we can decide $\mathscr{L}(S_1) \subseteq \mathscr{L}(S_2)$ by checking $S_1 \overset{N}{\prec} S_2$. This can be done algorithmically by iteratively building a relation $\mathcal{R}$ on triples that is an N-simulation on $N(S_1)$ and $N(S_2)$. The algorithm initializes $\mathcal{R}$ with $(N(q_{01}), N(q_{02}), v_{01} \bowtie v_{02})$, as this is required to be in $\mathcal{R}$ by Definition 6. Each iteration considers a candidate triple t and checks the conditions for N-simulation. If satisfied, it adds t to $\mathcal{R}$ and computes the next set of candidate triples, i.e., those which are required to belong to the simulation relation, and adds them to the list of triples still to be processed. If not, the algorithm returns $\mathscr{L}(S_1) \not\subseteq \mathscr{L}(S_2)$. The algorithm terminates returning $\mathscr{L}(S_1) \subseteq \mathscr{L}(S_2)$ when no triples are left to process. Determinism of S_1 and S_2, and hence of $N(S_1)$ and $N(S_2)$ (by Proposition 6), ensures that computing candidate triples is deterministic. To decide $\mathscr{L}(S_1) = \mathscr{L}(S_2)$, at each iteration we need to check that both t and t^{-1} satisfy the conditions for N-simulation.

If S_1 and S_2 have, respectively, n_1, n_2 states, m_1, m_2 transitions, and r_1, r_2 registers, the normalized versions have $\mathcal{O}(n_1 r_1 2^{m_1})$ and $\mathcal{O}(n_2 r_2 2^{m_2})$ states. Each triple, taken from the finite set $N(Q_1) \times N(Q_2) \times \mathcal{P}(R_1 \times R_2)$, is processed exactly once, so the algorithm iterates $\mathcal{O}(n_1 n_2 r_1 r_2 2^{m_1+m_2+r_1 r_2})$ times. $\qquad\square$

5 Evaluation

We have implemented SRAs in the open-source Java library SVPALib [26]. In our implementation, constructions are computed lazily when possible (e.g., the normalized SRA for emptiness and (bi)similarity checks). All experiments were performed on a machine with 3.5 GHz Intel Core i7 CPU with 16 GB of RAM (JVM 8 GB), with a timeout value of 300 s. The goal of our evaluation is to answer the following research questions:

Q1: Are SRAs more succinct than existing models when processing strings over large but finite alphabets? (Sect. 5.1)

Q2: What is the performance of membership for deterministic SRAs and how does it compare to the matching algorithm in `java.util.regex`? (Sect. 5.2)

Q3: Are SRA decision procedures practical? (Sect. 5.3)

Benchmarks. We focus on regular expressions with back-references, therefore all our benchmarks operate over the Boolean algebra of Unicode characters with interval—i.e., the set of characters is the set of all 2^{16} UTF-16 characters and the predicates are union of intervals (e.g., [a-zA-Z]).[2] Our benchmark set contains 19 SRAs that represent variants of regular expressions with back-references obtained from the regular-expression crowd-sourcing website RegExLib [23]. The expressions check whether inputs have, for example, matching first/last name initials or both (Name-F, Name-L and Name), correct Product Codes/Lot number of total length n (Pr-Cn, Pr-CLn), matching XML tags (XML), and IP addresses that match for n positions (IPn). We also create variants of the product benchmark presented in Sect. 2 where we vary the numbers of characters in the code and lot number. All the SRAs are deterministic.

5.1   Succinctness of SRAs vs SFAs

In this experiment, we relate the size of SRAs over finite alphabets to the size of the smallest equivalent SFAs. For each SRA, we construct the equivalent SFA by equipping the state space with the values stored in the registers at each step (this construction effectively builds the configuration LTS). Figure 2a shows the results. As expected, SFAs tend to blow up in size when the SRA contains multiple registers or complex register values. In cases where the register values range over small sets (e.g., [0-9]) it is often feasible to build an SFA equivalent to the SRA, but the construction always yields very large automata. In cases where the registers can assume many values (e.g., 2^{16}) SFAs become prohibitively large and do not fit in memory. To answer **Q1**, even for finite alphabets, **it is not feasible to compile SRAs to SFAs**. Hence, SRAs are a succinct model.

5.2   Performance of Membership Checking

In this experiment, we measure the performance of SRA membership, and we compare it with the performance of the `java.util.regex` matching algorithm.

---

[2] Our experiments are over finite alphabets, but the Boolean algebra can be infinite by taking the alphabet to be positive integers and allowing intervals to contain ∞ as upper bound. This modification does not affect the running time of our procedures, therefore we do not report it.

	SRA				**SFA**	
	states	tr	reg	|reg|	states	tr
IP2	44	46	3	10	4,013	4,312
IP3	44	46	4	10	39,113	42,112
IP4	44	46	5	10	372,113	402,112
IP6	44	46	7	10	—	—
IP9	44	46	10	10	—	—
Name-F	7	10	2	26	201	300
Name-L	7	10	2	26	129	180
Name	7	10	3	26	3,201	4,500
XML	12	16	4	52	—	—
Pr-C2	26	28	3	2^{16}	—	—
Pr-C3	28	30	4	2^{16}	—	—
Pr-C4	30	32	5	2^{16}	—	—
Pr-C6	34	36	7	2^{16}	—	—
Pr-C9	40	42	10	2^{16}	—	—
Pr-CL2	26	28	3	2^{16}	—	—
Pr-CL3	28	30	4	2^{16}	—	—
Pr-CL4	30	32	5	2^{16}	—	—
Pr-CL6	34	36	7	2^{16}	—	—
Pr-CL9	40	42	10	2^{16}	—	—

(a) Size of SRAs vs SFAs. (—) denotes the SFA didn't fit in memory. |reg| denotes how many different characters a register stored.

SRA $\mathcal{S}_1$	SRA $\mathcal{S}_2$	$\mathscr{L}_1=\emptyset$	$\mathscr{L}_1=\mathscr{L}_1$	$\mathscr{L}_2\subseteq\mathscr{L}_1$
Pr-C2	Pr-CL2	0.125s	0.905s	3.426s
Pr-C3	Pr-CL3	1.294s	5.558s	24.688s
Pr-C4	Pr-CL4	13.577s	55.595s	—
Pr-C6	Pr-CL6	—	—	—
Pr-CL2	Pr-C2	1.067s	0.952s	0.889s
Pr-CL3	Pr-C3	10.998s	11.104s	11.811s
Pr-CL4	Pr-C4	—	—	—
Pr-CL6	Pr-C6	—	—	—
IP-2	IP-3	0.125s	0.408s	1.845s
IP-3	IP-4	1.288s	2.953s	21.627s
IP-4	IP-6	18.440s	42.727s	—
IP-6	IP-9	—	—	—

(b) Performance of decision procedures. In the table $\mathscr{L}_i = \mathscr{L}(\mathcal{S}_i)$, for $i = 1, 2$.

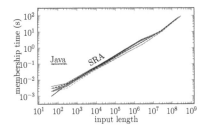

(c) SRA membership and Java `regex` matching performance. Missing data points for Java are stack overflows.

Fig. 2. Experimental results.

For each benchmark, we generate inputs of length varying between approximately 100 and 10^8 characters and measure the time taken to check membership. Figure 2c shows the results. The performance of SRA (resp. Java) is not particularly affected by the size of the expression. Hence, the lines for different expressions mostly overlap. As expected, for SRAs the time taken to check membership grows linearly in the size of the input (axes are log scale). Remarkably, even though our implementation does not employ particular input processing optimizations, it can still check membership for strings with tens of millions of characters in less than 10 s. We have found that our implementation is more efficient than the Java `regex` library, matching the same input an average of 50 times faster than `java.util.regex.Matcher`. `java.util.regex.Matcher` seems to make use of a recursive algorithm to match back-references, which means it does not scale well. Even when given the maximum stack size, the JVM will return a Stack Overflow for inputs as small as 20,000 characters. Our implementation can match such strings in less than 2 s. To answer **Q2**, **deterministic SRAs can be efficiently executed on large inputs and perform better than the `java.util.regex` matching algorithm.**

5.3   Performance of Decision Procedures

In this experiment, we measure the performance of SRAs simulation and bisimulation algorithms. Since all our SRAs are deterministic, these two checks correspond to language equivalence and inclusion. We select pairs of benchmarks for which the above tests are meaningful (e.g., variants of the problem discussed at the end of Sect. 2). The results are shown in Fig. 2b. As expected, due to the translation to single-valued SRAs, our decision procedures do not scale well in the number of registers. This is already the case for classic register automata and it is not a surprising result. However, our technique can still check equivalence and inclusion for regular expressions that no existing tool can handle. To answer **Q3**, **bisimulation and simulation algorithms for SRAs only scale to small numbers of registers**.

6   Conclusions

In this paper we have presented *Symbolic Register Automata*, a novel class of automata that can handle complex alphabet theories while allowing symbol comparisons for equality. SRAs encompass – and are strictly more powerful – than both Register and Symbolic Automata. We have shown that they enjoy the same closure and decidability properties of the former, despite the presence of arbitrary guards on transitions, which are not allowed by RAs. Via a comprehensive set of experiments, we have concluded that SRAs are vastly more succinct than SFAs and membership is efficient on large inputs. Decision procedures do not scale well in the number of registers, which is already the case for basic RAs.

Related Work. RAs were first introduced in [17]. There is an extensive literature on register automata, their formal languages and decidability properties [7, 13, 21, 22, 25], including variants with *global freshness* [20, 27] and totally ordered data [4, 14]. SRAs are based on the original model of [17], but are much more expressive, due to the presence of guards from an arbitrary decidable theory.

In recent work, variants over richer theories have appeared. In [9] RA over rationals were introduced. They allow for a restricted form of linear arithmetic among registers (RAs with arbitrary linear arithmetic subsume two-counter automata, hence are undecidable). SRAs do not allow for operations on registers, but encompass a wider range of theories without any loss in decidability. Moreover, [9] does not study Boolean closure properties. In [8, 16], RAs allowing guards over a range of theories – including (in)equality, total orders and increments/sums – are studied. Their focus is different than ours as they are interested primarily in *active learning* techniques, and several restrictions are placed on models for the purpose of the learning process. We can also relate SRAs with *Quantified Event Automata* [2], which allow for guards and assignments to registers on transitions. However, in QEA guards can be arbitrary, which could lead to several problems, e.g. undecidable equivalence.

Symbolic automata were first introduced in [28] and many variants of them have been proposed [12]. The one that is closer to SRAs is Symbolic Extended Finite Automata (SEFA) [11]. SEFAs are SFAs in which transitions can read more than one character at a time. A transition of arity k reads k symbols which are consumed if they satisfy the predicate $\varphi(x_1, \ldots, x_k)$. SEFAs allow arbitrary k-ary predicates over the input theory, which results in most problems being undecidable (e.g., equivalence and intersection emptiness) and in the model not being closed under Boolean operations. Even when deterministic, SEFAs are not closed under union and intersection. In terms of expressiveness, SRAs and SEFAs are incomparable. SRAs can only use equality, but can compare symbols at arbitrary points in the input while SEFAs can only compare symbols within a constant window, but using arbitrary predicates.

Several works study matching techniques for extended regular expressions [3,5,18,24]. These works introduce automata models with ad-hoc features for extended regular constructs – including back-references – but focus on efficient matching, without studying closure and decidability properties. It is also worth noting that SRAs are not limited to alphanumeric or finite alphabets. On the negative side, SRAs cannot express capturing groups of an unbounded length, due to the finitely many registers. This limitation is essential for decidability.

Future Work. In [21] a polynomial algorithm for checking language equivalence of deterministic RAs is presented. This crucially relies on closure properties of symbolic bisimilarity, some of which are lost for SRAs. We plan to investigate whether this algorithm can be adapted to our setting. Extending SRAs with more complex comparison operators other than equality (e.g., a total order $<$) is an interesting research question, but most extensions of the model quickly lead to undecidability. We also plan to study active automata learning for SRAs, building on techniques for SFAs [1], RAs [6,8,16] and nominal automata [19].

References

1. Argyros, G., D'Antoni, L.: The learnability of symbolic automata. In: CAV, pp. 427–445 (2018)
2. Barringer, H., Falcone, Y., Havelund, K., Reger, G., Rydeheard, D.E.: Quantified event automata: towards expressive and efficient runtime monitors. In: FM, pp. 68–84 (2012)
3. Becchi, M., Crowley, P.: Extending finite automata to efficiently match perl-compatible regular expressions. In: CoNEXT, pp. 25 (2008)
4. Benedikt, M., Ley, C., Puppis, G.: What you must remember when processing data words. In: AMW (2010)
5. Bispo, J., Sourdis, I., Cardoso, J.M.P., Vassiliadis, S.: Regular expression matching for reconfigurable packet inspection. In: FPT, pp. 119–126 (2006)
6. Bollig, B., Habermehl, P., Leucker, M., Monmege, B.: A fresh approach to learning register automata. In: DLT, pp. 118–130 (2013)
7. Cassel, S., Howar, F., Jonsson, B., Merten, M., Steffen, B.: A succinct canonical register automaton model. J. Log. Algebr. Meth. Program. **84**(1), 54–66 (2015)

8. Cassel, S., Howar, F., Jonsson, B., Steffen, B.: Active learning for extended finite state machines. Formal Asp. Comput. **28**(2), 233–263 (2016)
9. Chen, Y., Lengál, O., Tan, T., Wu, Z.: Register automata with linear arithmetic. In: LICS, pp. 1–12 (2017)
10. D'Antoni, L., Ferreira, T., Sammartino, M., Silva, A.: Symbolic register automata. CoRR, abs/1811.06968 (2019). http://arxiv.org/abs/1811.06968
11. D'Antoni, L., Veanes, M.: Extended symbolic finite automata and transducers. Formal Meth. Syst. Des. **47**(1), 93–119 (2015)
12. D'Antoni, L., Veanes, M.: The power of symbolic automata and transducers. In: CAV, pp. 47–67 (2017)
13. Demri, S., Lazic, R.: LTL with the freeze quantifier and register automata. ACM Trans. Comput. Log. **10**(3), 16:1–16:30 (2009)
14. Figueira, D., Hofman, P., Lasota, S.: Relating timed and register automata. Math. Struct. Comput. Sci. **26**(6), 993–1021 (2016)
15. Grigore, R., Distefano, D., Petersen, R.L., Tzevelekos, N.: Runtime verification based on register automata. In: TACAS, pp. 260–276 (2013)
16. Isberner, M., Howar, F., Steffen, B.: Learning register automata: from languages to program structures. Mach. Learn. **96**(1–2), 65–98 (2014)
17. Kaminski, M., Francez, N.: Finite-memory automata. Theor. Comput. Sci. **134**(2), 329–363 (1994)
18. Komendantsky, V.: Matching problem for regular expressions with variables. In: Loidl, H.-W., Peña, R. (eds.) TFP 2012. LNCS, vol. 7829, pp. 149–166. Springer, Heidelberg (2013). https://doi.org/10.1007/978-3-642-40447-4_10
19. Moerman, J., Sammartino, M., Silva, A., Klin, B., Szynwelski, M.: Learning nominal automata. In: POPL, pp. 613–625 (2017)
20. Murawski, A.S., Ramsay, S.J., Tzevelekos, N.: Bisimilarity in fresh-register automata. In: LICS, pp. 156–167 (2015)
21. Murawski, A.S., Ramsay, S.J., Tzevelekos, N.: Polynomial-time equivalence testing for deterministic fresh-register automata. In: MFCS, pp. 72:1–72:14 (2018)
22. Neven, F., Schwentick, T., Vianu, V.: Finite state machines for strings over infinite alphabets. ACM Trans. Comput. Log. **5**(3), 403–435 (2004)
23. RegExLib. Regular expression library (2017). http://regexlib.com/
24. Reidenbach, D., Schmid, M.L.: A polynomial time match test for large classes of extended regular expressions. In: Domaratzki, M., Salomaa, K. (eds.) CIAA 2010. LNCS, vol. 6482, pp. 241–250. Springer, Heidelberg (2011). https://doi.org/10.1007/978-3-642-18098-9_26
25. Sakamoto, H., Ikeda, D.: Intractability of decision problems for finite-memory automata. Theor. Comput. Sci. **231**(2), 297–308 (2000)
26. SVPAlib: Symbolic automata library (2018). https://github.com/lorisdanto/symbolicautomata
27. Tzevelekos, N.: Fresh-register automata. In: POPL, pp. 295–306 (2011)
28. Veanes, M., Halleux, P.D., Tillmann, N.: Rex: symbolic regular expression explorer. In: ICST, pp. 498–507 (2010)

6

Quantitative Mitigation of Timing Side Channels

Saeid Tizpaz-Niari[✉], Pavol Černý,
and Ashutosh Trivedi

University of Colorado Boulder, Boulder, USA
Saeid.TizpazNiari@colorado.edu

Abstract. Timing side channels pose a significant threat to the security
and privacy of software applications. We propose an approach for *mitigating* this problem by decreasing the strength of the side channels as measured by entropy-based objectives, such as min-guess entropy. Our goal
is to minimize the information leaks while guaranteeing a user-specified
maximal acceptable performance overhead. We dub the decision version
of this problem *Shannon mitigation*, and consider two variants, *deterministic* and *stochastic*. First, we show that the deterministic variant is
NP-hard. However, we give a polynomial algorithm that finds an optimal solution from a restricted set. Second, for the stochastic variant, we
develop an approach that uses optimization techniques specific to the
entropy-based objective used. For instance, for min-guess entropy, we
used mixed integer-linear programming. We apply the algorithm to a
threat model where the attacker gets to make *functional observations*,
that is, where she observes the running time of the program for the
same secret value combined with different public input values. Existing
mitigation approaches do not give confidentiality or performance guarantees for this threat model. We evaluate our tool SCHMIT on a number
of micro-benchmarks and real-world applications with different entropy-based objectives. In contrast to the existing mitigation approaches, we
show that in the functional-observation threat model, SCHMIT is scalable
and able to maximize confidentiality under the performance overhead
bound.

1 Introduction

Information leaks through timing side channels remain a challenging problem
[13,16,24,29,35,37,47]. A program leaks secret information through timing side
channels if an attacker can deduce secret values (or their properties) by observing response times. We consider the problem of mitigating timing side channels.
Unlike elimination techniques [7,31,46] that aim to completely remove timing
leaks without considering the performance penalty, the goal of mitigation techniques [10,26,48] is to weaken the leaks, while keeping the penalty low.

We define the *Shannon mitigation* problem that decides whether there is
a mitigation policy to achieve a lower bound on a given security entropy-based

measure while respecting an upper bound on the performance overhead. Consider an example where the program-under-analysis has a secret variable with seven possible values, and has three different timing behaviors, each forming a cluster of secret values. It takes 1 second if the secret value is 1, it takes 5 seconds if the secret is between 2 and 5, and it takes 10 seconds if the secret value is 6 or 7. The *entropy-based measure* quantifies the remaining uncertainty about the secret after timing observations. Min-guess entropy [11,25,41] for this program is 1, because if the observed execution time is 1, the attacker guesses the secret in one try. A *mitigation policy* involves merging some timing clusters by introducing delays. A good solution might be to introduce a 9 second delay if the secret is 1, which merges two timing clusters. But, this might be disallowed by the budget on the performance overhead. Therefore, another solution must be found, such as introducing a 4 seconds delay when the secret is one.

We develop two variants of the Shannon mitigation problem: *deterministic* and *stochastic*. The mitigation policy of the deterministic variant requires us to move all secret values associated to an observation to another observation, while the policy of the stochastic variant allows us to move only a portion of secret values in an observation to another one. We show that the deterministic variant of the Shannon mitigation problem is intractable and propose a dynamic programming algorithm to approximate the optimal solution for the problem by searching through a restricted set of solutions. We develop an algorithm that reduces the problem in the stochastic variant to a well-known optimization problem that depends on the entropy-based measure. For instance, with min-guess entropy, the optimization problem is mixed integer-linear programming.

We consider a threat model where an attacker knows the public inputs (known-message attacks [26]), and furthermore, where the public input changes much more often than the secret inputs (for instance, secrets such as bank account numbers do not change often). As a result, for each secret, the attacker observes a timing function of the public inputs. We call this model *functional observations* of timing side channels.

We develop our tool SCHMIT that has three components: side channel discovery [45], search for the mitigation policy, and the policy enforcement. The side channel discovery builds the functional observations [45] and measures the entropy of secret set after the observations. The mitigation policy component includes the implementation of the dynamic programming and optimization algorithms. The enforcement component is a monitoring system that uses the program internals and functional observations to enforce the policy at runtime. To summarize, we make the following contributions:

- We formalize the *Shannon mitigation* problem with two variants and show that the complexity of finding deterministic mitigation policy is NP-hard.
- We describe two algorithms for synthesizing the mitigation policy: one is based on dynamic programming for the deterministic variant, that is in polynomial time and results in an approximate solution, and the other one solves the stochastic variant of the problem with optimization techniques.

- We consider a threat model that results in functional observations. On a set of micro-benchmarks, we show that existing mitigation techniques are not secure and efficient for this threat model.
- We evaluate our approach on five real-world Java applications. We show that SCHMIT is scalable in synthesizing mitigation policy within a few seconds and significantly improves the security (entropy) of the applications.

```
Example(int high, int low) {
int t_high = high, t_low = low;
  while (t_high > 0) {
    if (t_high % 2 == 1) {
    while (t_low > 0) {
      if (t_low % 2 == 1) {
        res += compute(t_low,t_high);}
        t_low = t_low >> 1;}}
      t_high = t_high >> 1;}
    return res;}
```

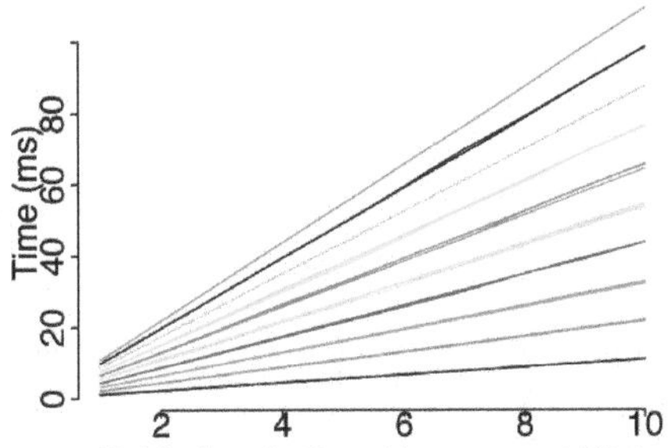

Fig. 1. (a) The example used in Sect. 2. (b) The timing functions for each secret value of the program.

2 Overview

First, we describe the threat model considered in this paper. Second, we describe our approach on a running example. Third, we compare the results of SCHMIT with the existing mitigation techniques [10, 26, 48] and show that SCHMIT achieves the highest entropy (i.e., best mitigation) for all three entropy objectives.

Threat Model. We assume that the attacker has access to the source code and the mitigation model, and she can sample the run-time of the application arbitrarily many times on her own machine. During an attack, she intends to guess a fixed secret of the target machine by observing the mitigated running time. Since we consider the attack models where the attacker knows the public inputs and the secret inputs are less volatile than public inputs, her observations are functional observations, where for each secret value, she learns a function from the public inputs to the running time.

Example 2.1. Consider the program shown in Fig. 1(a). It takes secret and public values as inputs. The running time depends on the number of set bits in both secret and public inputs. We assume that secret and public inputs can be between 1 and 1023. Figure 1(b) shows the running time of different secret values as timing functions, i.e., functions from the public inputs to the running time.

Side channel discovery. One can use existing tools to find the initial functional observations [44,45]. In Example 2.1, functional observations are $\mathcal{F} = \langle y, 2y, \dots, 10y \rangle$ where y is a variable whose value is the number of set bits in the public input. The corresponding secret classes after this observation is $\mathcal{S}_{\mathcal{F}} = \langle 1_1, 1_2, 1_3, \dots, 1_{10} \rangle$ where 1_n shows a set of secret values that have n set bits. The sizes of classes are $B = \{10, 45, 120, 210, 252, 210, 120, 45, 10, 1\}$. We use L_1-norm as metric to calculate the distance between the functional observations $\mathcal{F}$. This distance (penalty) matrix specifies extra performance overhead to move from one functional observation to another. With the assumption of uniform distributions over the secret input, Shannon entropy, guessing entropy, and the min-guessing entropy are 7.3, 90.1, and 1.0, respectively. These entropies are defined in Sect. 3 and measure the remaining entropy of the secret set after the observations. We aim to maximize the entropy measures, while keeping the performance overhead below a threshold, say 60% for this example.

Mitigation with Schmit. We use our tool SCHMIT to mitigate timing leaks of Example 2.1. The mitigation policy for the Shannon entropy objective is shown in Fig. 2(a). The policy results in two classes of observations. The policy requires to move functional observations $\langle y, 2y, \dots, 5y \rangle$ to $\langle 6y \rangle$ and all other observations $\langle 7y, 8y, 9y \rangle$ to $\langle 10y \rangle$. To enforce this policy, we use a monitoring system at run-time. The monitoring system uses a decision tree model of the initial functional observations. The decision tree model characterizes each functional observation with associated program internals such as method calls or basic block invocations [43,44]. The decision tree model for the Example 2.1 is shown in Fig. 2(b). The monitoring system records program internals and matches it with the decision tree model to detect the current functional observation. Then, it adds delays, if necessary, to the execution time in order to enforce the mitigation policy. With this method, the mitigated functional observation is $\mathcal{G} = \langle 6y, 10y \rangle$ and the secret

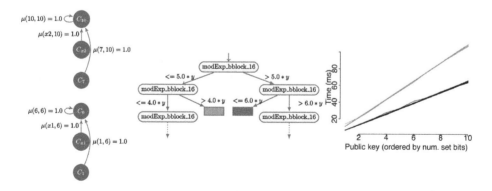

Fig. 2. (a) Mitigation policy calculation with deterministic algorithm (left). The observations $x1$ and $x2$ stands for all observations from $C_2{-}C_5$ and from $C_8{-}C_9$, resp.; (b) Leaned discriminant decision tree (center): it characterizes the functional clusters of Fig. 1(b) with internals of the program in Fig. 1(a); and (c) observations (right) after the mitigation by SCHMIT results in two classes of observations.

class is $\mathcal{S}_\mathcal{G} = \langle\{1_1, 1_2, 1_3, 1_4, 1_5, 1_6\}, \{1_7, 1_8, 1_9, 1_{10}\}\rangle$ as shown in Fig. 2 (c). The performance overhead of this mitigation is 43.1%. The Shannon, guessing, and min-guess entropies have improved to 9.7, 459.6, and 193.5, respectively.

Comparison with state of the art. We compare our mitigation results to black-box mitigation scheme [10] and bucketing [26]. *Black-box double scheme technique.* We use the double scheme technique [10] to mitigate the leaks of Example 2.1. This mitigation uses a prediction model to release events at scheduled times. Let us consider the prediction for releasing the event i at N-th epoch with $S(N, i) = \max(inp_i, S(N, i-1)) + p(N)$, where inp_i is the time arrival of the i-th request, $S(N, i-1)$ is the prediction for the request $i-1$, and $p(N) = 2^{N-1}$ models the basis for the prediction scheme at N-th epoch. We assume that the request are the same type and the sequence of public input requests for each secret are received in the beginning of epoch $N = 1$. Figure 3(a) shows the functional observations after applying the predictive mitigation. With this mitigation, the classes of observations are $\mathcal{S}_\mathcal{G} = \langle 1_1, \{1_2, 1_3\}, \{1_4, 1_5, 1_6, 1_7\}, \{1_8, 1_9, 1_{10}\}\rangle$. The number of classes of observations is reduced from 10 to 4. The performance overhead is 39.9%. The Shannon, guessing, and min-guess entropies have increased to 9.00, 321.5, and 5.5, respectively. *Bucketing.* We consider the mitigation approach with buckets [26]. For Example 2.1, if the attacker does not know the public input (unknown-message attacks [26]), the observations are $\{1.1, 2.1, 3.3, \cdots, 9.9, 10.9, \cdots, 109.5\}$ as shown in Fig. 3(b). We apply the bucketing algorithm in [26] for this observations, and it finds two buckets $\{37.5, 109.5\}$ shown with the red lines in Fig. 3(b). The bucketing mitigation requires to move the observations to the closet bucket. Without functional observations, there are 2 classes of observations. However, with functional observations, there are more than 2 observations. Figure 3(c) shows how the pattern of observations are leaking through functional side channels. There are 7 classes of observations: $\mathcal{S}_\mathcal{G} = \langle\{1_1, 1_2, 1_3\}, \{1_4\}, \{1_5\}, \{1_6\}, \{1_7\}, \{1_8\}, \{1_9\}, \{1_{10}\}\rangle$. The Shannon, guessing, and min-guess entropies are 7.63, 102.3, and 1.0, respectively.

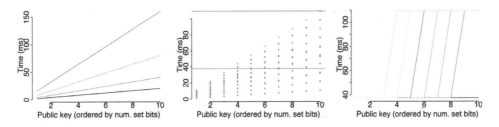

Fig. 3. (a) The execution time after mitigation using the double scheme technique [10]. There are four classes of functional observations after the mitigation. (b) Mitigation with bucketing [26]. All observations require to move to the closet red line. (c) Functional observations distinguish 7 classes of observations after mitigating with bucketing.

Overall, SCHMIT achieves the higher entropy measures for all three objectives under the performance overhead of 60%.

3 Preliminaries

For a finite set Q, we use $|Q|$ for its cardinality. A *discrete probability distribution*, or just distribution, over a set Q is a function $d : Q \to [0,1]$ such that $\sum_{q \in Q} d(q) = 1$. Let $\mathcal{D}(Q)$ denote the set of all discrete distributions over Q. We say a distribution $d \in \mathcal{D}(Q)$ is a *point distribution* if $d(q){=}1$ for a $q \in Q$. Similarly, a distribution $d \in \mathcal{D}(Q)$ is *uniform* if $d(q){=}1/|Q|$ for all $q \in Q$.

Definition 1 (Timing Model). *The timing model of a program $\mathcal{P}$ is a tuple $[\![\mathcal{P}]\!] = (X, Y, \mathcal{S}, \delta)$ where $X = \{x_1, \dots, x_n\}$ is the set of secret-input variables, $Y = \{y_1, \dots, y_m\}$ is the set of public-input variables, $\mathcal{S} \subseteq \mathbb{R}^n$ is a finite set of secret-inputs, and $\delta : \mathbb{R}^n \times \mathbb{R}^m \to \mathbb{R}_{\geq 0}$ is the execution-time function of the program over the secret and public inputs.*

We assume that the adversary knows the program and wishes to learn the value of the secret input. To do so, for some fixed secret value $s \in \mathcal{S}$, the adversary can invoke the program to estimate (to an arbitrary precision) the execution time of the program. If the set of public inputs is empty, i.e. $m = 0$, the adversary can only make *scalar observations* of the execution time corresponding to a secret value. In the more general setting, however, the adversary can arrange his observations in a functional form by estimating an approximation of the *timing function* $\delta(s) : \mathbb{R}^m \to \mathbb{R}_{\geq 0}$ of the program.

A *functional observation* of the program $\mathcal{P}$ for a secret input $s \in \mathcal{S}$ is the function $\delta(s) : \mathbb{R}^m \to \mathbb{R}_{\geq 0}$ defined as $\mathbf{y} \in \mathbb{R}^m \mapsto \delta(s, \mathbf{y})$. Let $\mathcal{F} \subseteq [\mathbb{R}^m \to \mathbb{R}_{\geq 0}]$ be the finite set of all functional observations of the program $\mathcal{P}$. We define an order $\prec$ over the functional observations $\mathcal{F}$: for $f, g \in \mathcal{F}$ we say that $f \prec g$ if $f(y) \leq g(y)$ for all $y \in \mathbb{R}^m$.

The set $\mathcal{F}$ characterizes an equivalence relation $\equiv_\mathcal{F}$, namely secrets with equivalent functional observations, over the set $\mathcal{S}$, defined as following: $s \equiv_\mathcal{F} s'$ if there is an $f \in \mathcal{F}$ such that $\delta(s) = \delta(s') = f$. Let $\mathcal{S}_\mathcal{F} = \langle S_1, S_2, \dots, S_k \rangle$ be the quotient space of $\mathcal{S}$ characterized by the observations $\mathcal{F} = \langle f_1, f_2, \dots, f_k \rangle$. We write $\mathcal{S}_f$ for the secret set $S \in \mathcal{S}_\mathcal{F}$ corresponding to the observations $f \in \mathcal{F}$. Let $\mathcal{B} = \langle B_1, B_2, \dots, B_k \rangle$ be the size of observational equivalence class in $\mathcal{S}_\mathcal{F}$, i.e. $B_i = |\mathcal{S}_{f_i}|$ for $f_i \in \mathcal{F}$ and let $B = |\mathcal{S}| = \sum_{i=1}^{k} B_i$.

Shannon entropy, guessing entropy, and min-guess entropy are three prevalent information metrics to quantify information leaks in programs. Köpf and Basin [25] characterize expressions for various information-theoretic measures on information leaks when there is a uniform distribution on $\mathcal{S}$ given below.

Proposition 1 (Köpf and Basin [25]). *Let $\mathcal{F} = \langle f_1, \dots, f_k \rangle$ be a set of observations and let $\mathcal{S}$ be the set of secret values. Let $\mathcal{B} = \langle B_1, \dots, B_k \rangle$ be the* *corresponding size of secret set in each class of observation and* $B = \sum_{i=1}^{k} B_i$. *Assuming a uniform distribution on* $\mathcal{S}$, *entropies can be characterized as:*

1. **Shannon Entropy:** $SE(\mathcal{S}|\mathcal{F}) \stackrel{\text{def}}{=} (\frac{1}{B}) \sum_{1 \leq i \leq k} B_i \log_2(B_i)$,
2. **Guessing Entropy:** $GE(\mathcal{S}|\mathcal{F}) \stackrel{\text{def}}{=} (\frac{1}{2B}) \sum_{1 \leq i \leq k} B_i^2 + \frac{1}{2}$, *and*
3. **Min-Guess Entropy:** $mGE(\mathcal{S}|\mathcal{F}) \stackrel{\text{def}}{=} \min_{1 \leq i \leq k} \{(B_i + 1)/2\}$.

4   Shannon Mitigation Problem

Our goal is to mitigate the information leakage due to the timing side channels by adding synthetic delays to the program. An aggressive, but commonly-used, mitigation strategy aims to eliminate the side channels by adding delays such that every secret value yields a common functional observation. However, this strategy may often be impractical as it may result in unacceptable performance degradations of the response time. Assuming a well-known penalty function associated with the performance degradation, we study the problem of maximizing entropy while respecting a bound on the performance degradation. We dub the decision version of this problem Shannon mitigation.

Adding synthetic delays to execution-time of the program, so as to mask the side-channel, can give rise to new functional observations that correspond to upper-envelopes of various combinations of original observations. Let $\mathcal{F} = \langle f_1, f_2, \ldots, f_k \rangle$ be the set of functional observations. For $I \subseteq 1, 2, \ldots, k$, let $f_I = \mathbf{y} \in \mathbb{R}^m \mapsto \sup_{i \in I} f_i(\mathbf{y})$ be the functional observation corresponding to upper-envelope of the functional observations in the set I. Let $\mathcal{G}(\mathcal{F}) = \{f_I : I \neq \emptyset \subseteq \{1, 2, \ldots, k\}\}$ be the set of all possible functional observations resulting from the upper-envelope calculations. To change the observation of a secret value with functional observation f_i to a new observation f_I (we assume that $i \in I$), we need to add delay function $f_I^i : \mathbf{y} \in \mathbb{R}^m \mapsto f_I(y) - f_i(y)$.

Mitigation Policies. Let $\mathcal{G} \subseteq \mathcal{G}(\mathcal{F})$ be a set of admissible post-mitigation observations. A *mitigation policy* is a function $\mu : \mathcal{F} \to \mathcal{D}(\mathcal{G})$ that for each secret $s \in \mathcal{S}_f$ suggests the probability distribution $\mu(f)$ over the functional observations. We say that a mitigation policy is *deterministic* if for all $f \in \mathcal{F}$ we have that $\mu(f)$ is a point distribution. Abusing notations, we represent a deterministic mitigation policy as a function $\mu : \mathcal{F} \to \mathcal{G}$. The semantics of a mitigation policy recommends to a program analyst a probability $\mu(f)(g)$ to elevate a secret input $s \in \mathcal{S}_f$ from the observational class f to the class $g \in \mathcal{G}$ by adding $\max\{0, g(p) - f(p)\}$ units delay to the corresponding execution-time $\delta(s, p)$ for all $p \in Y$. We assume that the mitigation policies respect the order, i.e. for every mitigation policy μ and for all $f \in \mathcal{F}$ and $g \in \mathcal{G}$, we have that $\mu(f)(g) > 0$ implies that $f \prec g$. Let $M_{(\mathcal{F} \to \mathcal{G})}$ be the set of mitigation policies from the set of observational clusters $\mathcal{F}$ into the clusters $\mathcal{G}$.

For the functional observations $\mathcal{F} = \langle f_1, \ldots, f_k \rangle$ and a mitigation policy $\mu \in M_{(\mathcal{F} \to \mathcal{G})}$, the resulting observation set $\mathcal{F}[\mu] \subseteq \mathcal{G}$ is defined as:

$$\mathcal{F}[\mu] = \{g \in \mathcal{G} : \text{ there exists } f \in \mathcal{F} \text{ such that } \mu(f)(g) > 0\}.$$

Since the mitigation policy is stochastic, we use average sizes of resulting observations to represent fitness of a mitigation policy. For $\mathcal{F}[\mu] = \langle g_1, g_2, \ldots, g_\ell \rangle$, we define their expected class sizes $\mathcal{B}_\mu = \langle C_1, C_2, \ldots, C_\ell \rangle$ as $C_i = \sum_{j=1}^{i} \mu(f_j)(f_i) \cdot B_j$ (observe that $\sum_{i=1}^{\ell} C_i = B$). Assuming a uniform distribution on $\mathcal{S}$, various entropies for the expected class size after applying a policy $\mu \in M_{(\mathcal{F} \to \mathcal{G})}$ can be characterized by the following expressions:

1. **Shannon Entropy:** $\mathsf{SE}(\mathcal{S}|\mathcal{F}, \mu) \stackrel{\text{def}}{=} (\frac{1}{B}) \sum_{1 \leq i \leq \ell} C_i \log_2(C_i)$,
2. **Guessing Entropy:** $\mathsf{GE}(\mathcal{S}|\mathcal{F}, \mu) \stackrel{\text{def}}{=} (\frac{1}{2B}) \sum_{1 \leq i \leq \ell} C_i^2 + \frac{1}{2}$, and
3. **Min-Guess Entropy:** $\mathsf{mGE}(\mathcal{S}|\mathcal{F}, \mu) \stackrel{\text{def}}{=} \min_{1 \leq i \leq \ell} \{(C_i + 1)/2\}$.

We note that the above definitions do not represent the expected entropies, but rather entropies corresponding to the expected cluster sizes. However, the three quantities provide bounds on the expected entropies after applying μ. Since Shannon and Min-Guess entropies are concave functions, from Jensen's inequality, we get that $\mathsf{SE}(\mathcal{S}|\mathcal{F}, \mu)$ and $\mathsf{mGE}(\mathcal{S}|\mathcal{F}, \mu)$ are upper bounds on expected Shannon and Min-Guess entropies. Similarly, $\mathsf{GE}(\mathcal{S}|\mathcal{F}, \mu)$, being a convex function, give a lower bound on expected guessing entropy.

We are interested in maximizing the entropy while respecting constraints on the overall performance of the system. We formalize the notion of performance by introducing performance penalties: there is a function $\pi : \mathcal{F} \times \mathcal{G} \to \mathbb{R}_{\geq 0}$ such that elevating from the observation $f \in \mathcal{F}$ to the functional observation $g \in \mathcal{G}$ adds an extra $\pi(f, g)$ performance overheads to the program. The expected performance penalty associated with a policy μ, $\pi(\mu)$, is defined as the probabilistically weighted sum of the penalties, i.e. $\sum_{f \in \mathcal{F}, g \in \mathcal{G}: f \prec g} |\mathcal{S}_f| \cdot \mu(f)(g) \cdot \pi(f, g)$. Now, we introduce our key decision problem.

Definition 2 (Shannon Mitigation). *Given a set of functional observations $\mathcal{F} = \langle f_1, \ldots, f_k \rangle$, a set of admissible post-mitigation observations $\mathcal{G} \subseteq \mathcal{G}(\mathcal{F})$, set of secrets $\mathcal{S}$, a penalty function $\pi : \mathcal{F} \times \mathcal{G} \to \mathbb{R}_{\geq 0}$, a performance penalty upper bound $\Delta \in \mathbb{R}_{\geq 0}$, and an entropy lower-bound $E \in \mathbb{R}_{\geq 0}$, the Shannon mitigation problem $\textsc{Shan}_\mathcal{E}(\mathcal{F}, \mathcal{G}, \mathcal{S}, \pi, E, \Delta)$, for a given entropy measure $\mathcal{E} \in \{SE, GE, mGE\}$, is to decide whether there exists a mitigation policy $\mu \in M_{(\mathcal{F} \to \mathcal{G})}$ such that $\mathcal{E}(\mathcal{S}|\mathcal{F}, \mu) \geq E$ and $\pi(\mu) \leq \Delta$. We define the deterministic Shannon mitigation variant where the goal is to find a deterministic such policy.*

5   Algorithms for Shannon Mitigation Problem

5.1   Deterministic Shannon Mitigation

We first establish the intractability of the deterministic variant.

Theorem 1. *Deterministic Shannon mitigation problem is NP-complete.*

Proof. It is easy to see that the deterministic Shannon mitigation problem is in NP: one can guess a certificate as a deterministic mitigation policy $\mu \in M_{(\mathcal{F} \to \mathcal{G})}$

and can verify in polynomial time that it satisfies the entropy and overhead constraints. Next, we sketch the hardness proof for the min-guess entropy measure by providing a reduction from the *two-way partitioning* problem [28]. For the Shannon entropy and guess entropy measures, a reduction can be established from the Shannon capacity problem [18] and the Euclidean sum-of-squares clustering problem [8], respectively.

Given a set $A = \{a_1, a_2, \ldots, a_k\}$ of integer values, the two-way partitioning problem is to decide whether there is a partition $A_1 \uplus A_2 = A$ into two sets A_1 and A_2 with equal sums, i.e. $\sum_{a \in A_1} a = \sum_{a \in A_2} a$. W.l.o.g assume that $a_i \leq a_j$ for $i \leq j$. We reduce this problem to a deterministic Shannon mitigation problem $\text{SHAN}_{\text{mGE}}(\mathcal{F}_A, \mathcal{G}_A, \mathcal{S}_A, \pi_A, E_A, \Delta_A)$ with k clusters $\mathcal{F}_A = \mathcal{G}_A = \langle f_1, f_2, \ldots, f_k \rangle$ with the secret set $\mathcal{S}_A = \langle S_1, S_2, \ldots, S_k \rangle$ such that $|S_i| = a_i$. If $\sum_{1 \leq i \leq k} a_i$ is odd then the solution to the two-way partitioning instance is trivially **no**. Otherwise, let $E_A = (1/2) \sum_{1 \leq i \leq k} a_i$. Notice that any deterministic mitigation strategy that achieves min-guess entropy larger than or equal to E_A must have at most two clusters. On the other hand, the best min-guess entropy value can be achieved by having just a single cluster. To avoid this and force getting two clusters corresponding to the two partitions of a solution to the two-way partitions problem instance A, we introduce performance penalties such that merging more than $k - 2$ clusters is disallowed by keeping performance penalty $\pi_A(f, g) = 1$ and performance overhead $\Delta_A = k - 2$. It is straightforward to verify that an instance of the resulting min-guess entropy problem has a **yes** answer if and only if the two-way partitioning instance does.   □

Since the deterministic Shannon mitigation problem is intractable, we design an approximate solution for the problem. Note that the problem is hard even if we only use existing functional observations for mitigation, i.e., $\mathcal{G} = \mathcal{F}$. Therefore, we consider this case for the approximate solution. Furthermore, we assume the following *sequential dominance* restriction on a deterministic policy μ: for $f, g \in \mathcal{F}$ if $f \prec g$ then either $\mu(f) \prec g$ or $\mu(f) = \mu(g)$. In other words, for any given $f \prec g$, f can not be moved to a higher cluster than g without having g be moved to that cluster. For example, Fig. 4(a) shows Shannon mitigation problem with four functional observations and all possible mitigation policies (we represent $\mu(f_i)(f_j)$ with $\mu(i, j)$). Figure 4(b) satisfies the sequential dominance restriction, while Fig. 4(c) does not.

The search for the deterministic policies satisfying the sequential dominance restriction can be performed efficiently using dynamic programming by effective use of intermediate results' memorizations.

Algorithm (1) provides a pseudocode for the dynamic programming solution to find a deterministic mitigation policy satisfying the sequential dominance. The key idea is to start with considering policies that produce a single cluster for subclasses P_i of the problem with the observation from $\langle f_1, \ldots, f_i \rangle$, and then compute policies producing one additional cluster in each step by utilizing the previously computed sub-problems and keeping track of the performance penalties. The algorithm terminates as soon as the solution of the current step respects the performance bound. The complexity of the algorithm is $O(k^3)$.

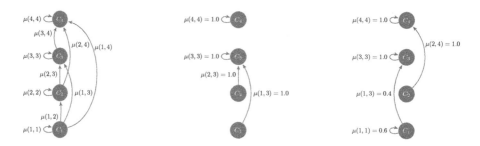

Fig. 4. (a). Example of Shannon mitigation problem with all possible mitigation policies for 4 classes of observations. (b,c) Two examples of the mitigation policies that results in 2 and 3 classes of observations.

5.2 Stochastic Shannon Mitigation Algorithm

Next, we solve the (stochastic) Shannon mitigation problem by posing it as an optimization problem. Consider the stochastic Shannon mitigation problem $\text{SHAN}_{\mathcal{E}}$ $(\mathcal{F}, \mathcal{G} = \mathcal{F}, \mathcal{S}_{\mathcal{F}}, \pi, E, \Delta)$ with a stochastic policy $\mu : \mathcal{F} \to \mathcal{D}(\mathcal{G})$ and

---

Algorithm 1. APPROXIMATE DETERMINISTIC SHANNON MITIGATION

Input: The Shannon entropy problem $\text{SHAN}_{MGE}(\mathcal{F}, \mathcal{G} = \mathcal{F}, \mathcal{S}_{\mathcal{F}}, \pi, E, \Delta)$
Output: The entropy table (T).

1 **for** $i = 1$ *to* k **do**

2 $\quad T(i,1) = \mathcal{E}(\bigcup_{j=1}^{i} S_j)$

3 $\quad$ **if** $\sum_{1 \le j \le i} \pi(j,i)(B_j/B) \le \Delta$ **then** $\Pi(i,1) = \sum_{1 \le j \le i} \pi(j,i)(B_j/B)$

4 $\quad$ **else** $\Pi(i,1) = \infty$

5 **if** $\Pi(k,1) < \infty$ **then return** T;

6 **for** $r = 2$ *to* k **do**

7 $\quad$ **for** $i = 1$ *to* k **do**

8 $\quad\quad \Omega(i,r) = \{j : 1 \le j < i$ and $\Pi(j, r-1) + \sum_{j < q \le i} \pi(q,i)(B_q/B) \le \Delta\}$

9 $\quad\quad$ **if** $\Omega \ne \emptyset$ **then** $T(i,r) = \max_{j \in \Omega(i,r)} \left(\min \left(T(j, r-1), \mathcal{E}(\bigcup_{q=j+1}^{i} S_q) \right) \right)$

10 $\quad\quad$ **else** $T(i,r) = -\infty$

11 $\quad\quad$ Let j be the index that maximizes $T(i,r)$

12 $\quad\quad$ **if** $\Omega \ne \emptyset$ **then** $\Pi(i,r) = \left(\Pi(j, r-1) + \sum_{j < q \le i} \pi(q,i)(B_q/B) \right)$

13 $\quad\quad$ **else** $\Pi(i,r) = \infty$

14 $\quad$ **if** $\Pi(k,r) < \infty$ **then return** T;

15 **return** T;

$\mathcal{S}_{\mathcal{F}} = \langle S_1, S_2, \ldots, S_k \rangle$. The following program characterizes the optimization problem that solves the Shannon mitigation problem with stochastic policy.

Maximize $\mathcal{E}$, subject to:

1. $0 \leq \mu(f_i)(f_j) \leq 1$ for $1 \leq i \leq j \leq k$
2. $\sum_{i \leq j \leq k} \mu(f_i)(f_j) = 1$ for all $1 \leq i \leq k$.
3. $\sum_{i=1}^{k} \sum_{j=i}^{k} |S_i| \cdot \mu(f_i)(f_j) \cdot \pi(f_i, f_j) \leq \Delta$.
4. $C_j = \sum_{i=1}^{j} |S_i| \cdot \mu(f_i)(f_j)$ for $1 \leq j \leq k$.

Here, the objective function $\mathcal{E}$ is one of the following functions:

1. **Guessing Entropy** $\mathcal{E}_{GE} = \sum_{j=1}^{k} C_j^2$
2. **Min-Guess Entropy** $\mathcal{E}_{MGE} = \min_{1 \leq j \leq k} \{C_j \mid C_j > 0\}$
3. **Shannon Entropy** $\mathcal{E}_{SE} = \sum_{j=1}^{k} C_j \cdot \log_2(C_j)$

The linear constraints for the problem are defined as the following. The condition (1) and (2) express that μ provides a probability distributions, condition (3) provides restrictions regarding the performance constraint, and the condition (4) is the entropy specific constraint. The objective function of the optimization problem is defined based on the entropy criteria from $\mathcal{E}$. For the simplicity, we omit the constant terms from the objective function definitions. For the guessing entropy, the problem is an instance of linearly constrained quadratic optimization problem [33]. The problem with Shannon entropy is a non-linear optimization problem [12]. Finally, the optimization problem with min-guess entropy is an instance of mixed integer programming [32]. We evaluate the scalability of these solvers empirically in Sect. 6 and leave the exact complexity as an open problem. We show that the min-guess entropy objective function can be efficiently solved with the branch and bound algorithms [36]. Figure 4(b,c) show two instantiations of the mitigation policies that are possible for the stochastic mitigation.

6 Implementation Details

A. Environmental Setups. All timing measurements are conducted on an Intel NUC5i5RYH. We switch off JIT Compilation and run each experiment multiple times and use the mean running time. This helps to reduce the effects of environmental factors such as the Garbage Collections. All other analyses are conducted on an Intel i5-2.7 GHz machine.

B. Implementation of Side Channel Discovery. We use the technique presented in [45] for the side channel discovery. The technique applies the functional data analysis [38] to create B-spline basis and fit functions to the vector of timing observations for each secret value. Then, the technique applies the functional data clustering [21] to obtain K classes of observations. We use the number of secret values in a cluster as the class size metric and the L_1 distance norm between the clusters as the penalty function.

C. Implementation of Mitigation Policy Algorithms. For the stochastic optimization, we encode the Shannon entropy and guessing entropy with linear constraints in Scipy [22]. Since the objective functions are non-linear (for the Shannon entropy) and quadratic (for the guessing entropy), Scipy uses sequential least square programming (SLSQP) [34] to maximize the objectives. For the stochastic optimization with the min-guess entropy, we encode the problem in Gurobi [19] as a mixed-integer programming (MIP) problem [32]. Gurobi solves the problem efficiently with branch-and-bound algorithms [1]. We use Java to implement the dynamic programming.

D. Implementation of Enforcement. The enforcement of mitigation policy is implemented in two steps. *First*, we use the initial timing functions and characterize them with program internal properties such as basic block calls. To do so, we use the decision tree learning approach presented in [45]. The decision tree model characterizes each functional observations with properties of program internals. *Second*, given the policy of mitigation, we enforce the mitigation policy with a monitoring system implemented on top of the Javassist [15] library. The monitoring system uses the decision tree model and matches the properties enabled during an execution with the tree model (detection of the current cluster). Then, it adds extra delays, based on the mitigation policy, to the current execution-time and enforces the mitigation policy. Note that the dynamic monitoring can result in a few micro-second delays. For the programs with timing differences in the order of micro-seconds, we transform source code using the decision tree model. The transformation requires manual efforts to modify and compile the new program. But, it adds negligible delays.

E. Micro-benchmark Results. Our goal is to compare different mitigation methods in terms of their security and performance. We examine the computation time of our tool SCHMIT in calculating the mitigation policies. See appendix for the relationships between performance bounds and entropy measures.

Applications: Mod_Exp applications [30] are instances of square-and-multiply modular exponentiation ($R = y^k \ mod \ n$) used for secret key operations in RSA [39]. Branch_and_Loop series consist of 6 applications where each application has conditions over secret values and runs a linear loop over the public values. The running time of the applications depend on the slope of the linear loops determined by the secret input.

Computation time comparisons: Fig. 5 shows the computation time for Branch_and _Loop applications (the applications are ordered in x-axis based on the discovered number of observational classes). For the min-guess entropy, we observe that both stochastic and dynamic programming approaches are efficient and fast as shown in Fig. 5(a). For the Shannon and guessing entropies,

Table 1. Micro-benchmark results. M_E and B_L stand for ModExp and Branch_and_Loop applications. Legend: #**S**: no. of secret values, #**P**: no. of public values, Δ: Upper bound over performance penalty, ϵ: clustering parameter, #**K**: classes of observations before mitigation, #$\mathbf{K}_X$: classes of observations after mitigation with X technique, **mGE**: Min-guess entropy before mitigation, $\mathbf{mGE}_X$: Min-guess entropy after mitigation with X. $\mathbf{O}_X$: Performance overhead added after mitigation with X.

App(s)	Initial Characteristics						Double Scheme			Bucketing			SCHMIT (Determ.)			SCHMIT (Stoch.)		
	#S	#P	Δ	ϵ	#K	mGE	#K_{DS}	mGE$_{DS}$	O$_{DS}$(%)	#K_B	mGE$_B$	O$_B$(%)	K$_D$	#mGE$_D$	O$_D$(%)	#K_S	mGE$_S$	O$_S$(%)
M_E_1	32	32	0.5	1.0	1	16.5	1	16.5	0.0	1	16.5	0.0	1	16.5	0.0	1	16.5	0.0
M_E_2	64	64	0.5	1.0	2	16.5	1	32.5	5,221	1	32.5	27.6	1	32.5	21.4	1	32.5	21.4
M_E_3	128	128	0.5	2.0	2	32.5	1	64.5	5,407	1	64.5	33.9	1	64.5	22.7	1	64.5	22.7
M_E_4	256	256	0.5	2.0	4	10.5	1	128.5	6,679	1	128.5	30.7	1	128.5	28.3	1	128.5	28.3
M_E_5	512	512	0.5	5.0	23	1.0	1	256.5	7,294	2	128.5	50.0	1	256.5	31.0	1	253.0	30.3
M_E_6	1,024	1,024	0.5	8.0	40	1.0	1	512.5	7,822	20	1.0	34.5	2	27.5	46.7	5	85.5	50.0
B_L_1	25	50	0.5	10.0	4	3.0	3	3.0	73.0	3	3.0	17.5	2	5.5	26.1	2	6.5	34.9
B_L_2	50	50	0.5	10.0	8	3.0	4	3.0	61.3	5	3.0	21.9	2	10.5	45.3	2	13.0	45.3
B_L_3	100	50	0.5	20.0	16	3.0	4	8.0	42.4	8	3.0	33.4	2	20.5	48.3	2	21.5	50
B_L_4	200	50	0.5	20.0	32	3.0	6	3.0	36.9	16	3.0	28.7	2	48.0	48.7	2	50.5	49.7
B_L_5	400	50	0.5	20.0	64	3.0	8	3.0	35.4	32	3.0	27.2	3	65.5	32.0	2	100.5	50.0
B_L_6	800	50	0.5	20.0	125	3.0	12	8.0	37.8	29	3.0	52.5	3	133.0	34.6	2	200.5	49.6

the dynamic programming is scalable, while the stochastic mitigation is computationally expensive beyond 60 classes of observations as shown in Fig. 5(b,c).

Mitigation Algorithm Comparisons: Table 1 shows micro-benchmark results that compare the four mitigation algorithms with the two program series. Double scheme mitigation technique [10] does not provide guarantees on the performance overhead, and we can see that it is increased by more than 75 times for mod_exp_6. Double scheme method reduces the number of classes of observations. However, we observe that this mitigation has difficulty improving the min-guess entropy. Second, Bucketing algorithm [26] can guarantee the performance overhead, but it is not an effective method to improve the security of functional observations, see the examples mod_exp_6 and Branch_and_Loop_6. Third, in the algorithms, SCHMIT guarantees the performance to be below a certain bound, while it results in the highest entropy values. In most cases, the stochastic optimization technique achieves the highest min-entropy value. Here, we show the results with min-guess entropy measure. Also, we have strong evidences to show that SCHMIT achieves higher Shannon and guessing entropies. For example, in B_L_5, the initial Shannon entropy has improved from 2.72 to 6.62, 4.1, 7.56, and 7.28 for the double scheme, the bucketing, the stochastic, and the deterministic algorithms, respectively.

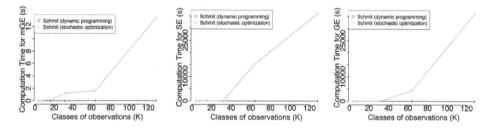

Fig. 5. Computation time for synthesizing mitigation policy over Branch_and_Loop applications. Computation time for min-guess entropy (a) takes only few seconds. Computation time for the Shannon entropy (b) and guessing entropy (c) are expensive using Stochastic optimization. We set time-out to be 10 hours.

7   Case Study

Research Question. Does SCHMIT scale well and improve the security of applications (entropy measures) within the given performance bounds?

Methodology. We use the deterministic and stochastic algorithms for mitigating the leaks. We show our results for the min-guess entropy, but other entropy measures can be applied as well. Since the task is to mitigate existing leakages, we assume that the secret and public inputs are given.

Objects of Study. We consider four real-world applications:

In the inset table, we show the basic characteristics of these benchmarks.

Application	Num methods	Num secret	Num public	ϵ	Initial clusters	Initial. Min-guess
GabFeed	573	1,105	65	6.50	34	1.0
Jetty	63	800	635	0.1	20	4.5
Java Verbal Expressions	61	2,000	10	0.02	9	50.5
Password Checker	6	20	2,620	0.05	6	1.0

GabFeed is a chat server with 573 methods [4]. There is a side channel in the authentication part of the application where the application takes users' public keys and its own private key, and generating a common key [14]. The vulnerability leaks the number of set bits in the secret key. Initial functional observations are shown in Fig. 6a. There are 34 clusters and min-guess entropy is 1. We aim to maximize the min-guess entropy under the performance overhead of 50%.

Jetty. We mitigate the side channels in `util.security` package of Eclipse Jetty web server. The package has `Credential` class which had a timing side channel. This vulnerability was analyzed in [14] and fixed initially in [6]. Then, the developers noticed that the implementation in [6] can still leak information and fixed this issue with a new implementation in [5]. However, this new implementation is still leaking information [45]. We apply SCHMIT to mitigate this timing side channels. Initial functional observations is shown in Fig. 6d. There are 20 classes of observations and the initial min-guess entropy is 4.5. We aim to maximize the min-guess entropy under the performance overhead of 50%.

Java Verbal Expressions is a library with 61 methods that construct regular expressions [2]. There is a timing side channel in the library similar to password comparison vulnerability [3] if the library has secret inputs. In this case, starting from the initial character of a candidate expression, if the character matches with the regular expression, it slightly takes more time to respond the request than otherwise. This vulnerability can leak all the regular expressions. We consider regular expressions to have a maximum size of 9. There are 9 classes of observations and the initial min-guess entropy is 50.5. We aim to maximize the min-guess entropy under the performance overhead of 50%.

Password Checker. We consider the password matching example from loginBad program [9]. The password stored in the server is secret, and the user's guess is a public input. We consider 20 secret (lengths at most 6) and 2,620 public inputs. There are 6 different clusters, and the initial min-guess entropy is 1.

Findings for GabFeed. With the stochastic algorithm, SCHMIT calculates the mitigation policy that results in 4 clusters. This policy improves the min-guess entropy from 1 to 138.5 and adds an overhead of 42.8%. With deterministic algorithm, SCHMIT returns 3 clusters. The performance overhead is 49.7% and the min-guess entropy improves from 1 to 106. The user chooses the deterministic policy and enforces the mitigation. We apply CART decision tree learning and characterizes the classes of observations with GabFeed method calls as shown in

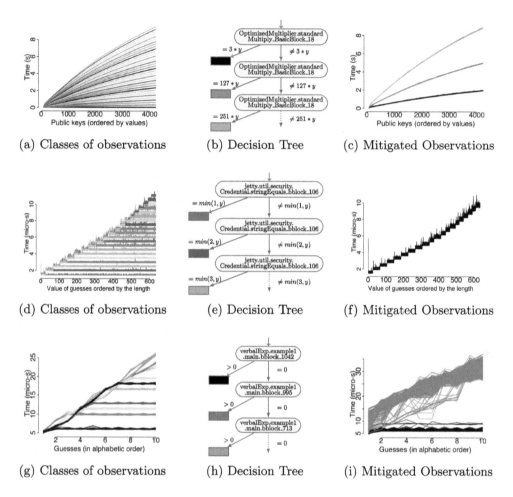

Fig. 6. Initial functional observations, decision tree, and the mitigated observations from left to right for Gabfeed, Jetty, and Verbal Expressions from top to bottom.

Fig. 6b. The monitoring system uses the decision tree model and automatically detects the current class of observation. Then, it adds extra delays based on the mitigation policy to enforce it. The results of the mitigation is shown in Fig. 6c. Answer for our research question. *Scalability*: It takes about 1 second to calculate the stochastic and the deterministic policies. *Security*: Stochastic and deterministic variants improve the min-guess entropy more than 100 times under the given performance overhead of 50%, respectively.

Findings for Jetty. The stochastic algorithm and the deterministic algorithm find the same policy that results in 1 cluster with 39.6% performance overhead. The min-guess entropy improves from 4.5 to 400.5. For the enforcement, SCHMIT first uses the initial clusterings and specifies their characteristics with program internals that result in the decision tree model shown in Fig. 6e. Since the response time is in the order of micro-seconds, we transform the source code using the decision tree model by adding extra counter variables. The results of the mitigation is shown in Fig. 6f. *Scalability*: It takes less than 1 second to calculate the policies for both algorithms. *Security*: Stochastic and deterministic variants improve the min-guess entropy 89 times under the given performance overhead.

Findings for Java Verbal Expressions. For the stochastic algorithm, the policy results in 2 clusters, and the min-guess entropy has improved to 500.5. The performance overhead is 36%. For the dynamic programming, the policy results in 2 clusters. This adds 28% of performance overhead, while it improves the min-guess entropy from 50.5 to 450.5. The user chooses to use the deterministic policy for the mitigation. For the mitigation, we transform the source code using the decision tree model and add the extra delays based on the mitigation policy.

Findings for Password Matching. Both the deterministic and the stochastic algorithms result in finding a policy with 2 clusters where the min-guess entropy has improved from 1 to 5.5 with the performance overhead of 19.6%. For the mitigation, we transform the source code using the decision tree model and add extra delays based on the mitigation policy if necessary.

8 Related Work

Quantitative theory of information have been widely used to measure how much information is being leaked with side-channel observations [11,20,25,41]. Mitigation techniques increase the remaining entropy of secret sets leaked through the side channels, while considering the performance [10,23,26,40,48,49].

Köpf and Dürmuth [26] use a bucketing algorithm to partition programs' observations into intervals. With the unknown-message threat model, Köpf and Dürmuth [26] propose a dynamic programming algorithm to find the optimal number of possible observations under a performance penalty. The works [10,48] introduce different black-box schemes to mitigate leaks. In particular, Askarov et al. [10] show the quantizing time techniques, which permit events to release at scheduled constant slots, have the worst case leakage if the slot is not filled with events. Instead, they introduce the double scheme method that has a schedule of predictions like the quantizing approach, but if the event source fails to deliver events at the predicted time, the failure results in generating a new schedule in which the interval between predictions is doubled. We compare our mitigation technique with both algorithms throughout this paper.

Elimination of timing side channels is a common technique to guarantee the confidentiality of software [7,17,27,30,31,46]. The work [46] aims to eliminate side channels using static analysis enhanced with various techniques to keep the performance overheads low without guaranteeing the amounts of overhead. In contrast, we use dynamic analysis and allow a small amount of information to leak, but we guarantee an upper-bound on the performance overhead.

Machine learning techniques have been used for explaining timing differences between traces [42–44]. Tizpaz-Niari et al. [44] consider performance issues in softwares. They also cluster execution times of programs and then explain what program properties distinguish the different functional clusters. We adopt their techniques for our security problem.

Acknowledgements. The authors would like to thank Mayur Naik for shepherding our paper and providing useful suggestions. This research was supported by DARPA under agreement FA8750-15-2-0096.

References

1. Branch and bound algorithm for mip problems. http://www.gurobi.com/resources/getting-started/mip-basics
2. Verbal expressions library. https://github.com/VerbalExpressions/JavaVerbalExpressions
3. Timing attack in google keyczar library (2009). https://rdist.root.org/2009/05/28/timing-attack-in-google-keyczar-library/
4. Gabfeed application (2016). https://github.com/Apogee-Research/STAC/tree/master/Engagement_Challenges/Engagement_2/gabfeed_1
5. Timing side-channel on the length of password in eclipse jetty May 2017. https://github.com/eclipse/jetty.project/commit/2baa1abe4b1c380a30deacca1ed-367466a1a62ea
6. Timing side-channel on the password in eclipse jetty May 2017. https://github.com/eclipse/jetty.project/commit/f3751d70787fd8ab93932a51c60514c2eb37cb58
7. Agat, J.: Transforming out timing leaks. In: Proceedings of the 27th ACM SIGPLAN-SIGACT Symposium on Principles of Programming Languages, pp. 40–53. ACM (2000)
8. Aloise, D., Deshpande, A., Hansen, P., Popat, P.: Np-hardness of euclidean sum-of-squares clustering. Mach. Learn. **75**(2), 245–248 (2009)
9. Antonopoulos, T., Gazzillo, P., Hicks, M., Koskinen, E., Terauchi, T., Wei, S.: Decomposition instead of self-composition for proving the absence of timing channels. In: PLDI, pp. 362–375. ACM (2017)
10. Askarov, A., Zhang, D., Myers, A.C.: Predictive black-box mitigation of timing channels. In: Proceedings of the 17th ACM Conference on Computer and Communications Security, pp. 297–307. ACM (2010)
11. Backes, M., Köpf, B., Rybalchenko, A.: Automatic discovery and quantification of information leaks. In: 2009 30th IEEE Symposium on Security and Privacy, pp. 141–153. IEEE (2009)
12. Bertsekas, D.P.: Nonlinear programming. Athena Scientific, 2016. Tech. rep., ISBN 978-1-886529-05-2
13. Brumley, D., Boneh, D.: Remote timing attacks are practical. Comput. Netw. **48**(5), 701–716 (2005)
14. Chen, J., Feng, Y., Dillig, I.: Precise detection of side-channel vulnerabilities using quantitative cartesian hoare logic. In: CCS, pp. 875–890 (2017)
15. Chiba, S.: Javassist - a reflection-based programming wizard for java. In: Proceedings of OOPSLA 1998 Workshop on Reflective Programming in C++ and Java, vol. 174 (1998)
16. Dhem, J.-F., Koeune, F., Leroux, P.-A., Mestré, P., Quisquater, J.-J., Willems, J.-L.: A practical implementation of the timing attack. In: Quisquater, J.-J., Schneier, B. (eds.) CARDIS 1998. LNCS, vol. 1820, pp. 167–182. Springer, Heidelberg (2000). https://doi.org/10.1007/10721064_15

17. Eldib, H., Wang, C.: Synthesis of masking countermeasures against side channel attacks. In: Biere, A., Bloem, R. (eds.) CAV 2014. LNCS, vol. 8559, pp. 114–130. Springer, Cham (2014). https://doi.org/10.1007/978-3-319-08867-9_8

18. Fallgren, M.: On the complexity of maximizing the minimum shannon capacity in wireless networks by joint channel assignment and power allocation. In: 2010 IEEE 18th International Workshop on Quality of Service (IWQoS), pp. 1–7 (2010)

19. Gurobi, L.: Optimization: Gurobi optimizer reference manual (2018). http://www.gurobi.com

20. Heusser, J., Malacaria, P.: Quantifying information leaks in software. In: Proceedings of the 26th Annual Computer Security Applications Conference, pp. 261–269. ACM (2010)

21. Jacques, J., Preda, C.: Functional data clustering: a survey. Adv. Data Anal. Classif. **8**(3), 231–255 (2014)

22. Jones, E., Oliphant, T., Peterson, P., et al.: SciPy: open source scientific tools for Python (2001). http://www.scipy.org/

23. Kadloor, S., Kiyavash, N., Venkitasubramaniam, P.: Mitigating timing based information leakage in shared schedulers. In: 2012 Proceedings IEEE Infocom, pp. 1044–1052. IEEE (2012)

24. Kocher, P.C.: Timing attacks on implementations of Diffie-Hellman, RSA, DSS, and other systems. In: Koblitz, N. (ed.) CRYPTO 1996. LNCS, vol. 1109, pp. 104–113. Springer, Heidelberg (1996). https://doi.org/10.1007/3-540-68697-5_9

25. Köpf, B., Basin, D.: An information-theoretic model for adaptive side-channel attacks. In: Proceedings of the 14th ACM Conference on Computer and Communications Security, pp. 286–296. CCS 2007, ACM, New York (2007)

26. Köpf, B., Dürmuth, M.: A provably secure and efficient countermeasure against timing attacks. In: 22nd IEEE Computer Security Foundations Symposium, 2009, CSF 2009, pp. 324–335. IEEE (2009)

27. Köpf, B., Mantel, H.: Transformational typing and unification for automatically correcting insecure programs. Int. J. Inf. Secur. **6**(2–3), 107–131 (2007)

28. Korf, R.E.: A complete anytime algorithm for number partitioning. AI **106**, 181–203 (1998)

29. Lampson, B.W.: A note on the confinement problem. Commun. ACM **16**(10), 613–615 (1973)

30. Mantel, H., Starostin, A.: Transforming out timing leaks, more or less. In: Pernul, G., Ryan, P.Y.A., Weippl, E. (eds.) ESORICS 2015. LNCS, vol. 9326, pp. 447–467. Springer, Cham (2015). https://doi.org/10.1007/978-3-319-24174-6_23

31. Molnar, D., Piotrowski, M., Schultz, D., Wagner, D.: The program counter security model: automatic detection and removal of control-flow side channel attacks. In: Won, D.H., Kim, S. (eds.) ICISC 2005. LNCS, vol. 3935, pp. 156–168. Springer, Heidelberg (2006). https://doi.org/10.1007/11734727_14

32. Nemhauser, G.L., Wolsey, L.A.: Integer programming and combinatorial optimization. In: Nemhauser, G.L., Savelsbergh, M.W.P., Sigismondi, G.S. (1992). Constraint Classification for Mixed Integer Programming Formulations. COAL Bulletin, vol. 20, pp. 8–12. Wiley, Chichester (1988)

33. Nocedal, J., Wright, S.J.: Numerical Optimization 2nd (2006)

34. Nocedal, J., Wright, S.J.: Sequential Quadratic Programming. Springer, New York (2006)

35. Padlipsky, M., Snow, D., Karger, P.: Limitations of End-to-End Encryption in Secure Computer Networks. Tech. rep, MITRE CORP BEDFORD MA (1978)

36. Papadimitriou, C.H., Steiglitz, K.: Combinatorial Optimization: Algorithms and Complexity. Courier Corporation, North Chelmsford (1998)

37. Phan, Q.S., Bang, L., Pasareanu, C.S., Malacaria, P., Bultan, T.: Synthesis of adaptive side-channel attacks. In: 2017 IEEE 30th Computer Security Foundations Symposium (CSF), pp. 328–342. IEEE (2017)
38. Ramsay, J., Hooker, G., Graves, S.: Functional Data Analysis with R and MATLAB. Springer Science & Business Media, Berlin (2009)
39. Rivest, R.L., Shamir, A., Adleman, L.: A method for obtaining digital signatures and public-key cryptosystems. Commun. ACM 21(2), 120–126 (1978)
40. Schinzel, S.: An efficient mitigation method for timing side channels on the web. In: 2nd International Workshop on Constructive Side-Channel Analysis and Secure Design (COSADE) (2011)
41. Smith, G.: On the foundations of quantitative information flow. In: de Alfaro, L. (ed.) FoSSaCS 2009. LNCS, vol. 5504, pp. 288–302. Springer, Heidelberg (2009). https://doi.org/10.1007/978-3-642-00596-1_21
42. Song, L., Lu, S.: Statistical debugging for real-world performance problems. In: Proceedings of the 2014 ACM International Conference on Object Oriented Programming Systems Languages & Applications, pp. 561–578. OOPSLA 2014 (2014). https://doi.org/10.1145/2660193.2660234
43. Tizpaz-Niari, S., Černý, P., Chang, B.-Y.E., Sankaranarayanan, S., Trivedi, A.: Discriminating traces with time. In: Legay, A., Margaria, T. (eds.) TACAS 2017. LNCS, vol. 10206, pp. 21–37. Springer, Heidelberg (2017). https://doi.org/10.1007/978-3-662-54580-5_2
44. Tizpaz-Niari, S., Černý, P., Chang, B.E., Trivedi, A.: Differential performance debugging with discriminant regression trees. In: 32nd AAAI Conference on Artificial Intelligence (AAAI), pp. 2468–2475 (2018)
45. Tizpaz-Niari, S., Černý, P., Trivedi, A.: Data-driven debugging for functional side channels. arXiv preprint. arXiv:1808.10502 (2018)
46. Wu, M., Guo, S., Schaumont, P., Wang, C.: Eliminating timing side-channel leaks using program repair. In: Proceedings of the 27th ACM SIGSOFT International Symposium on Software Testing and Analysis, pp. 15–26. ACM (2018)
47. Yarom, Y., Genkin, D., Heninger, N.: Cachebleed: a timing attack on openssl constant-time rsa. J. Cryptographic Eng. 7(2), 99–112 (2017)
48. Zhang, D., Askarov, A., Myers, A.C.: Predictive mitigation of timing channels in interactive systems. In: Proceedings of the 18th ACM Conference on Computer and Communications Security, pp. 563–574. ACM (2011)
49. Zhang, D., Askarov, A., Myers, A.C.: Language-based control and mitigation of timing channels. PLDI 47(6), 99–110 (2012)

7

Efficient Synthesis with Probabilistic Constraints

Samuel Drews$^{(\boxtimes)}$, Aws Albarghouthi, and Loris D'Antoni

University of Wisconsin-Madison, Madison, USA
sedrews@wisc.edu

Abstract. We consider the problem of synthesizing a program given a probabilistic specification of its desired behavior. Specifically, we study the recent paradigm of *distribution-guided inductive synthesis* (DIGITS), which iteratively calls a synthesizer on finite sample sets from a given distribution. We make theoretical and algorithmic contributions: (*i*) We prove the surprising result that DIGITS only requires a polynomial number of synthesizer calls in the size of the sample set, despite its ostensibly exponential behavior. (*ii*) We present a property-directed version of DIGITS that further reduces the number of synthesizer calls, drastically improving synthesis performance on a range of benchmarks.

1 Introduction

Over the past few years, progress in automatic program synthesis has touched many application domains, including automating data wrangling and data extraction tasks [2,13,15,21,22,30], generating network configurations that meet user intents [10,29], optimizing low-level code [25,28], and more [4,14].

The majority of the current work has focused on synthesis under Boolean constraints. However, often times we require the program to adhere to a probabilistic specification, e.g., a controller that succeeds with a high probability, a decision-making model operating over a probabilistic population model, a randomized algorithm ensuring privacy, etc. In this work, we are interested in (1) investigating probabilistic synthesis from a theoretical perspective and (2) developing efficient algorithmic techniques to tackle this problem.

Our starting point is our recent framework for probabilistic synthesis called *distribution-guided inductive synthesis* (DIGITS) [1]. The DIGITS framework is analogous in nature to the *guess-and-check* loop popularized by counterexample-guided approaches to synthesis and verification (CEGIS and CEGAR). The key idea of the algorithm is reducing the probabilistic synthesis problem to a non-probabilistic one that can be solved using existing techniques, e.g., SAT solvers. This is performed using the following loop: (1) approximating the input probability distribution with a finite sample set; (2) synthesizing a program for various possible output assignments of the finite sample set; and (3) invoking a probabilistic verifier to check if one of the synthesized programs indeed adheres to the given specification.

DIGITS has been shown to theoretically converge to correct programs when they exist—thanks to learning-theory guarantees. The primary bottleneck of DIGITS is the number of expensive calls to the synthesizer, which is ostensibly exponential in the size of the sample set. Motivated by this observation, this paper makes theoretical, algorithmic, and practical contributions:

- On the theoretical side, we present a detailed analysis of DIGITS and prove that it only requires a polynomial number of invocations of the synthesizer, explaining that the strong empirical performance of the algorithm is not merely due to the heuristics presented in [1] (Sect. 3).
- On the algorithmic side, we develop an improved version of DIGITS that is property-directed, in that it only invokes the synthesizer on instances that have a chance of resulting in a correct program, without sacrificing convergence. We call the new approach τ-DIGITS (Sect. 4).
- On the practical side, we implement τ-DIGITS for sketch-based synthesis and demonstrate its ability to converge significantly faster than DIGITS. We apply our technique to a range of benchmarks, including illustrative examples that elucidate our theoretical analysis, probabilistic repair problems of unfair programs, and probabilistic synthesis of controllers (Sect. 5).

2   An Overview of DIGITS

In this section, we present the synthesis problem, the DIGITS [1] algorithm, and fundamental background on learning theory.

2.1   Probabilistic Synthesis Problem

Program Model. As discussed in [1], DIGITS searches through some (infinite) set of programs, but it requires that the set of programs has *finite VC dimension* (we restate this condition in Sect. 2.3). Here we describe one constructive way of obtaining such sets of programs with finite VC dimension: we will consider sets of programs defined as *program sketches* [27] in the simple grammar from [1], where a program is written in a loop-free language, and "holes" defining the sketch replace some constant terminals in expressions.[1] The syntax of the language is defined below:

$$P := V \leftarrow E \mid \texttt{if } B \texttt{ then } P \texttt{ else } P \mid P\ P \mid \texttt{return } V$$

Here, P is a program, V is the set of variables appearing in P, E (resp. B) is the set of linear arithmetic (resp. Boolean) expressions over V (where, again, constants in E and B can be replaced with holes), and $V \leftarrow E$ is an assignment. We assume a vector $\boldsymbol{v}_I$ of variables in V that are inputs to the program. We

---

[1] In the case of loop-free program sketches as considered in our program model, we can convert the input-output relation into a real arithmetic formula that guaranteedly has finite VC dimension [12].

also assume there is a single Boolean variable $v_r \in V$ that is returned by the program.[2] All variables are real-valued or Boolean. Given a vector of constant values $\boldsymbol{c}$, where $|\boldsymbol{c}| = |\boldsymbol{v}_I|$, we use $P(\boldsymbol{c})$ to denote the result of executing P on the input $\boldsymbol{c}$.

In our setting, the inputs to a program are distributed according to some *joint probability distribution* $\mathbb{D}$ over the variables $\boldsymbol{v}_I$. Semantically, a program P is denoted by a *distribution transformer* $[\![P]\!]$, whose input is a distribution over values of $\boldsymbol{v}_I$ and whose output is a distribution over $\boldsymbol{v}_I$ and v_r.

A program also has a *probabilistic postcondition*, *post*, defined as an inequality over terms of the form $\Pr[B]$, where B is a Boolean expression over $\boldsymbol{v}_I$ and v_r. Specifically, a probabilistic postcondition consists of Boolean combinations of the form $e > c$, where $c \in \mathbb{R}$ and e is an arithmetic expression over terms of the form $\Pr[B]$, e.g., $\Pr[B_1] / \Pr[B_2] > 0.75$.

Given a triple $(P, \mathbb{D}, post)$, we say that P is *correct* with respect to $\mathbb{D}$ and *post*, denoted $[\![P]\!](\mathbb{D}) \models post$, *iff* *post* is true on the distribution $[\![P]\!](\mathbb{D})$.

Example 1. Consider the set of intervals of the form $[0, a] \subseteq [0, 1]$ and inputs x uniformly distributed over $[0, 1]$ (i.e. $\mathbb{D} = \text{Uniform}[0, 1]$). We can write inclusion in the interval as a (C-style) program (left) and consider a postcondition stating that the interval must include at least half the input probability mass (right):

```
if (0 <= x && x <= a) {
    return 1;
}
return 0;
```

$$\Pr_{x \sim \mathbb{D}}[P(x) = 1] \geqslant 0.5$$

Let P_c denote the interval program where a is replaced by a constant $c \in [0, 1]$. Observe that $[\![P_c]\!](\mathbb{D})$ describes a joint distribution over (x, v_r) pairs, where $[0, c] \times \{1\}$ is assigned probability measure c and $(c, 1] \times \{0\}$ is assigned probability measure $1 - c$. Therefore, $[\![P_c]\!](\mathbb{D}) \models post$ if and only if $c \in [0.5, 1]$.

Synthesis Problem. DIGITS outputs a program that is approximately "similar" to a given functional specification and that meets a postcondition. This functional specification is some input-output relation which we quantitatively want to match as closely as possible: specifically, we want to minimize the *error* of the output program P from the functional specification $\hat{P}$, defined as $\text{Er}(P) := \Pr_{x \sim \mathbb{D}}[P(x) \neq \hat{P}(x)]$. (Note that we represent the functional specification as a program.) The postcondition is Boolean, and therefore we always want it to be true. DIGITS is guaranteed to converge whenever the space of solutions satisfying the postcondition is *robust* under small perturbations. The following definition captures this notion of robustness:

Definition 1 (α-Robust Programs). *Fix an input distribution $\mathbb{D}$, a postcondition post, and a set of programs $\mathcal{P}$. For any $P \in \mathcal{P}$ and any $\alpha > 0$, denote the*

---

[2] Restricting the output to Boolean is required by the algorithm; other output types can be turned into Boolean by rewriting. See, e.g., thermostat example in Sect. 5.

open α-ball centered at P as $B_\alpha(P) = \{P' \in \mathcal{P} \mid \Pr_{x \sim \mathbb{D}}[P(x) \neq P'(x)] < \alpha\}$. *We say a program P is α-robust if $\forall P' \in B_\alpha(P). [\![P']\!](\mathbb{D}) \models post$.*

We can now state the synthesis problem solved by DIGITS:

Definition 2 (Synthesis Problem). *Given an input distribution $\mathbb{D}$, a set of programs $\mathcal{P}$, a postcondition post, a functional specification $\hat{P} \in \mathcal{P}$, and parameters $\alpha > 0$ and $0 < \varepsilon \leqslant \alpha$, the synthesis problem is to find a program $P \in \mathcal{P}$ such that $[\![P]\!](\mathbb{D}) \models post$ and such that any other α-robust P' has $Er(P) \leqslant Er(P') + \varepsilon$.*

2.2 A Naive DIGITS Algorithm

Algorithm 1 shows a simplified, naive version of DIGITS, which employs a *synthesize-then-verify* approach. The idea of DIGITS is to utilize non-probabilistic synthesis techniques to synthesize a set of programs, and then apply a probabilistic verification step to check if any of the synthesized programs is a solution.

Specifically, this "Naive DIGITS" begins by sampling an appropriate number of inputs from the input distribution and stores them in the set S. Second, it iteratively explores each possible function f that maps the input samples to a Boolean and invokes a synthesis oracle to synthesize a program P that implements f, i.e. that satisfies the set of input–output examples in which each input $x \in S$ is mapped to the output $f(x)$. Naive DIGITS then finds which of the

---

1 Procedure DIGITS $(\hat{P}, \mathbb{D}, post, m)$
2 $\quad S \leftarrow \{x \sim \mathbb{D} \mid i \in [1, \ldots, m]\}$
3 $\quad progs \leftarrow \emptyset$
4 $\quad$ **foreach** $f : S \rightarrow \{0, 1\}$ **do**
5 $\quad\quad P \leftarrow \mathcal{O}_{\mathrm{syn}}(\{(x, f(x)) \mid x \in S\})$
6 $\quad\quad$ **if** $P \neq \bot$ **then**
7 $\quad\quad\quad progs \leftarrow progs \cup \{P\}$
8 $\quad res \leftarrow \{P \in progs \mid \mathcal{O}_{\mathrm{ver}}(P, \mathbb{D}, post)\}$
9 $\quad$ **return** $\mathrm{argmin}_{P \in res}\{\mathcal{O}_{\mathrm{err}}(P)\}$

Algorithm 1: Naive DIGITS

---

synthesized programs satisfy the postcondition (the set *res*); we assume that we have access to a probabilistic verifier $\mathcal{O}_{\mathrm{ver}}$ to perform these computations. Finally, the algorithm outputs the program in the set *res* that has the lowest error with respect to the functional specification, once again assuming access to another oracle $\mathcal{O}_{\mathrm{err}}$ that can measure the error.

Note that the number of such functions $f : S \rightarrow \{0, 1\}$ is exponential in the size of $|S|$. As a "heuristic" to improve performance, the actual DIGITS algorithm as presented in [1] employs an incremental trie-based search, which we describe (alongside our new algorithm, τ-DIGITS) and analyze in Sect. 3. The naive version described here is, however, sufficient to discuss the convergence properties of the full algorithm.

2.3 Convergence Guarantees

DIGITS is only guaranteed to converge when the program model $\mathcal{P}$ has *finite VC dimension*.[3] Intuitively, the VC dimension captures the expressiveness of the set

---

[3] Recall that this is largely a "free" assumption since, again, sketches in our loop-free grammar guaranteedly have finite VC dimension.

of ($\{0, 1\}$-valued) programs $\mathcal{P}$. Given a set of inputs S, we say that $\mathcal{P}$ *shatters* S iff, for every partition of S into sets $S_0 \sqcup S_1$, there exists a program $P \in \mathcal{P}$ such that (*i*) for every $x \in S_0$, $P(x) = 0$, and (*ii*) for every $x \in S_1$, $P(x) = 1$.

Definition 3 (VC Dimension). *The VC dimension of a set of programs $\mathcal{P}$ is the largest integer d such that there exists a set of inputs S with cardinality d that is shattered by $\mathcal{P}$.*

We define the function $\textsc{VCcost}(\varepsilon, \delta, d) = \frac{1}{\varepsilon}(4 \log_2(\frac{2}{\delta}) + 8d \log_2(\frac{13}{\varepsilon}))$ [5], which is used in the following theorem:

Theorem 1 (Convergence). *Assume that there exist an $\alpha > 0$ and program P^* that is α-robust w.r.t. $\mathbb{D}$ and post. Let d be the VC dimension of the set of programs $\mathcal{P}$. For all bounds $0 < \varepsilon \leqslant \alpha$ and $\delta > 0$, for every function $\mathcal{O}_{\mathrm{syn}}$, and for any $m \geqslant \textsc{VCcost}(\varepsilon, \delta, k)$, with probability $\geqslant 1 - \delta$ we have that $\textsc{digits}$ enumerates a program P with $\mathrm{Pr}_{x \sim \mathbb{D}}[P^*(x) \neq P(x)] \leqslant \varepsilon$ and $\llbracket P \rrbracket(\mathbb{D}) \models post$.*

To reiterate, suppose P^* is a correct program with small error $\mathrm{Er}(P^*) = k$; the convergence result follows two main points: (*i*) P^* must be α-*robust*, meaning every P with $\mathrm{Pr}_{x \sim \mathbb{D}}[P(x) \neq P^*(x)] < \alpha$ must also be correct, and therefore (*ii*) by synthesizing *any* P such that $\mathrm{Pr}_{x \sim \mathbb{D}}[P(x) \neq P^*(x)] \leqslant \varepsilon$ where $\varepsilon < \alpha$, then P is a correct program with error $\mathrm{Er}(P)$ within $k \pm \varepsilon$.

2.4 Understanding Convergence

The importance of finite VC dimension is due to the fact that the convergence statement borrows directly from *probably approximately correct (PAC) learning*. We will briefly discuss a core detail of efficient PAC learning that is relevant to understanding the convergence of $\textsc{digits}$ (and, in turn, our analysis of τ-$\textsc{digits}$ in Sect. 4), and refer the interested reader to Kearns and Vazirani's book [16] for a complete overview. Specifically, we consider the notion of an ε-*net*, which establishes the approximate-definability of a target program in terms of points in its input space.

Definition 4 (ε-net). *Suppose $P \in \mathcal{P}$ is a target program, and points in its input domain $\mathcal{X}$ are distributed $x \sim \mathbb{D}$. For a fixed $\varepsilon \in [0, 1]$, we say a set of points $S \subset \mathcal{X}$ is an ε-net for P (with respect to $\mathcal{P}$ and $\mathbb{D}$) if for every $P' \in \mathcal{P}$ with $\mathrm{Pr}_{x \sim \mathbb{D}}[P(x) \neq P'(x)] > \varepsilon$ there exists a witness $x \in S$ such that $P(x) \neq P'(x)$.*

In other words, if S is an ε-net for P, and if P' "agrees" with P on all of S, then P and P' can only differ by at most ε probability mass.

Observe the relevance of ε-nets to the convergence of $\textsc{digits}$: the synthesis oracle is guaranteed not to "fail" by producing only programs ε-far from some ε-robust P^* if the sample set happens to be an ε-net for P^*. In fact, this observation is exactly the core of the PAC learning argument: having an ε-net exactly guarantees the approximate learnability.

A remarkable result of computational learning theory is that whenever $\mathcal{P}$ has finite VC dimension, the probability that m random samples fail to yield an ε-net becomes diminishingly small as m increases. Indeed, the given VCCOST function used in Theorem 1 is a dual form of this latter result—that polynomially many samples are sufficient to form an ε-net with high probability.

3   The Efficiency of Trie-Based Search

After providing details on the search strategy employed by DIGITS, we present our theoretical result on the polynomial bound on the number of synthesis queries that DIGITS requires.

3.1   The Trie-Based Search Strategy of DIGITS

Naive DIGITS, as presented in Algorithm 1, performs a very unstructured, exponential search over the output labelings of the sampled inputs—i.e., the possible Boolean functions f in Algorithm 1. In our original paper [1] we present a "heuristic" implementation strategy that incrementally explores the set of possible output labelings using a trie data structure. In this section, we study the complexity of this technique through the lens of computational learning theory and discover the surprising result that DIGITS requires a polynomial number of calls to the synthesizer in the size of the sample set! Our improved search algorithm (Sect. 4) inherits these results.

For the remainder of this paper, we use DIGITS to refer to this incremental version. A full description is necessary for our analysis: Fig. 1 (non-framed rules only) consists of a collection of guarded rules describing the construction of the trie used by DIGITS to incrementally explore the set of possible output labelings. Our improved version, τ-DIGITS (presented in Sect. 4), corresponds to the addition of the framed parts, but without them, the rules describe DIGITS.

Nodes in the trie represent partial output labelings—i.e., functions f assigning Boolean values to only some of the samples in $S = \{x_1, \ldots, x_m\}$. Each node is identified by a binary string $\sigma = b_1 \cdots b_k$ (k can be smaller than m) denoting the path to the node from the root. The string σ also describes the partial output-labeling function f corresponding to the node—i.e., if the i-th bit b_i is set to 1, then $f(x_i) = true$. The set $explored$ represents the nodes in the trie built thus far; for each node, the algorithm synthesizes a program consistent with the corresponding partial output function ("Explore" rules). The variable $depth$ controls the incremental aspect of the search and represents the maximum length of any σ in $explored$; it is incremented whenever all nodes up to that depth have been explored (the "Deepen" rule). The crucial part of the algorithm is that, if no program can be synthesized for the partial output function of a node identified by σ, the algorithm does not need to issue further synthesis queries for the descendants of σ.

Figure 2 shows how DIGITS builds a trie for an example run on the interval programs from Example 1, where we suppose we begin with an incorrect program describing the interval $[0, 0.3]$. Initially, we set the root program to $[0, 0.3]$ (left

$$\frac{}{explored \leftarrow \{\epsilon\} \quad P_\epsilon \leftarrow \hat{P} \quad depth \leftarrow 0 \quad best \leftarrow \bot} \text{ Initialize}$$

$$\frac{\forall \sigma \in explored.\, \forall b \in \{0,1\}.}{(P_\sigma \neq \bot \wedge |\sigma b| \leqslant depth \boxed{\wedge unblocked(\sigma b)}) \Rightarrow \sigma b \in explored}{sample_{depth+1} \sim \mathbb{D} \quad depth \leftarrow depth + 1} \text{ Deepen}$$

$$\frac{\sigma \in explored \quad P_\sigma \neq \bot \quad b \in \{0,1\}}{\sigma b \notin explored \quad |\sigma b| \leqslant depth \quad \boxed{unblocked(\sigma b)}}{P_{\sigma b} \leftarrow \mathcal{O}_{\text{syn}}(\{(sample_{i+1}, \sigma b(i)) : 0 \leqslant i < |\sigma b|\})}{explored \leftarrow explored \cup \{\sigma b\}} \text{ Explore (Synthesis Query)}$$

$$\frac{\sigma \in explored \quad P_\sigma \neq \bot \quad b \in \{0,1\} \quad \sigma b \notin explored}{|\sigma b| \leqslant depth \quad \boxed{unblocked(\sigma b)} \quad P_\sigma(sample_{|\sigma b|}) = b}{P_{\sigma b} \leftarrow P_\sigma \quad explored \leftarrow explored \cup \{\sigma b\}} \text{ Explore (Solution Propagation)}$$

$$\frac{\sigma^* = \text{argmin}_\sigma \{\mathcal{O}_{\text{err}}(P_\sigma) \mid \sigma \in explored \wedge P_\sigma \neq \bot \wedge \mathcal{O}_{\text{ver}}(P_\sigma) = \text{true}\}}{best \leftarrow P_{\sigma^*}} \text{ Best}$$

$$\boxed{\text{where } unblocked(\sigma) := |\{i : 0 \leqslant i < |\sigma| \wedge \sigma(i) \neq \hat{P}(sample_{i+1})\}| \leqslant \tau \cdot depth}$$

Fig. 1. Full DIGITS description and our new extension, τ-DIGITS, shown in boxes.

figure). The "Deepen" rule applies, so a sample is added to the set of samples—suppose it's 0.4. "Explore" rules are then applied twice to build the children of the root: the child following the 0 branch needs to map $0.4 \mapsto 0$, which $[0, 0.3]$ already does, thus it is propagated to that child without asking $\mathcal{O}_{\text{syn}}$ to perform a synthesis query. For the child following 1, we instead make a synthesis query, using the oracle $\mathcal{O}_{\text{syn}}$, for any value of a such that $[0, a]$ maps $0.4 \mapsto 1$—suppose it returns the solution $a = 1$, and we associate $[0, 1]$ with this node. At this point we have exhausted depth 1 (middle figure), so "Deepen" once again applies, perhaps adding 0.6 to the sample set. At this depth (right figure), only two calls to $\mathcal{O}_{\text{syn}}$ are made: in the case of the call at $\sigma = 01$, there is no value of a that causes both $0.4 \mapsto 0$ and $0.6 \mapsto 1$, so $\mathcal{O}_{\text{syn}}$ returns $\bot$, and we do not try to explore any children of this node in the future. The algorithm continues in this manner until a stopping condition is reached—e.g., enough samples are enumerated.

3.2 Polynomial Bound on the Number of Synthesis Queries

We observed in [1] that the trie-based exploration seems to be efficient in practice, despite potential exponential growth of the number of explored nodes in the trie as the depth of the search increases. The convergence analysis of DIGITS relies on the finite VC dimension of the program model, but VC dimension itself is just a summary of the *growth function*, a function that describes a notion

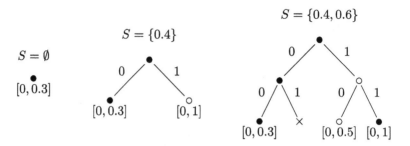

Fig. 2. Example execution of incremental DIGITS on interval programs, starting from $[0, 0.3]$. Hollow circles denote calls to $\mathcal{O}_{\text{syn}}$ that yield new programs; the cross denotes a call to $\mathcal{O}_{\text{syn}}$ that returns $\bot$.

of complexity of the set of programs in question. We will see that the growth function much more precisely describes the behavior of the trie-based search; we will then use a classic result from computational learning theory to derive better bounds on the performance of the search. We define the growth function below, adapting the presentation from [16].

Definition 5 (Realizable Dichotomies). *We are given a set $\mathcal{P}$ of programs representing functions from $\mathcal{X} \to \{0, 1\}$ and a (finite) set of inputs $S \subset \mathcal{X}$. We call any $f : S \to \{0, 1\}$ a dichotomy of S; if there exists a program $P \in \mathcal{P}$ that extends f to its full domain $\mathcal{X}$, we call f a* realizable dichotomy *in $\mathcal{P}$. We denote the set of realizable dichotomies as*

$$\Pi_{\mathcal{P}}(S) := \{f : S \to \{0, 1\} \mid \exists P \in \mathcal{P}. \forall x \in S. P(x) = f(x)\}.$$

Observe that for any (infinite) set $\mathcal{P}$ and any finite set S that $1 \leqslant |\Pi_{\mathcal{P}}(S)| \leqslant 2^{|S|}$. We define the growth function in terms of the realizable dichotomies:

Definition 6 (Growth Function). *The* growth function *is the maximal number of realizable dichotomies as a function of the number of samples, denoted*

$$\hat{\Pi}_{\mathcal{P}}(m) := \max_{\substack{S \subset \mathcal{X}: \\ |S| = m}} \{|\Pi_{\mathcal{P}}(S)|\}.$$

Observe that $\mathcal{P}$ has VC dimension d if and only if d is the largest integer satisfying $\hat{\Pi}_{\mathcal{P}}(d) = 2^d$ (and infinite VC dimension when $\hat{\Pi}_{\mathcal{P}}(m)$ is identically 2^m)— in fact, VC dimension is often defined using this characterization.

Example 2. Consider the set of intervals of the form $[0, a]$ as in Examples 1 and Fig. 2. For the set of two points $S = \{0.4, 0.6\}$, we have that $|\Pi_{[0,a]}(S)| = 3$, since, by example: $a = 0.5$ accepts 0.4 but not 0.6, $a = 0.3$ accepts neither, and $a = 1$ accepts both, thus these three dichotomies are realizable; however, no interval with 0 as a left endpoint can accept 0.6 and not 0.4, thus this dichotomy is not realizable. In fact, for any (finite) set $S \subset [0, 1]$, we have that $|\Pi_{[0,a]}(S)| = |S| + 1$; we then have that $\hat{\Pi}_{[0,a]}(m) = m + 1$.

When DIGITS terminates having used a sample set S, it has considered all the dichotomies of S: the programs it has enumerated exactly correspond to extensions of the realizable dichotomies $\Pi_{\mathcal{P}}(S)$. The trie-based exploration is effectively trying to minimize the number of $\mathcal{O}_{\text{syn}}$ queries performed on non-realizable ones, but doing so without explicit knowledge of the full functional behavior of programs in $\mathcal{P}$. In fact, it manages to stay relatively close to performing queries only on the realizable dichotomies:

Lemma 1. DIGITS *performs at most* $|S||\Pi_{\mathcal{P}}(S)|$ *synthesis oracle queries. More precisely, let* $S = \{x_1, \ldots, x_m\}$ *be indexed by the depth at which each sample was added: the exact number of synthesis queries is* $\sum_{\ell=1}^{m} |\Pi_{\mathcal{P}}(\{x_1, \ldots, x_{\ell-1}\})|$.

Proof. Let T_d denote the total number of queries performed once depth d is completed. We perform no queries for the root,[4] thus $T_0 = 0$. Upon completing depth $d - 1$, the realizable dichotomies of $\{x_1, \ldots, x_{d-1}\}$ exactly specify the nodes whose children will be explored at depth d. For each such node, one child is skipped due to solution propagation, while an oracle query is performed on the other, thus $T_d = T_{d-1} + |\Pi_{\mathcal{P}}(\{x_1, \ldots, x_{d-1}\})|$. Lastly, $|\Pi_{\mathcal{P}}(S)|$ cannot decrease by adding elements to S, so we have that $T_m = \sum_{\ell=1}^{m} |\Pi_{\mathcal{P}}(\{x_1, \ldots, x_{\ell-1}\})| \leqslant \sum_{\ell=1}^{m} |\Pi_{\mathcal{P}}(S)| \leqslant |S||\Pi_{\mathcal{P}}(S)|$. $\quad\square$

Connecting DIGITS to the realizable dichotomies and, in turn, the growth function allows us to employ a remarkable result from computational learning theory, stating that the growth function for any set exhibits one of two asymptotic behaviors: it is either *identically* 2^m (infinite VC dimension) or dominated by a polynomial! This is commonly called the Sauer-Shelah Lemma [24,26]:

Lemma 2 (Sauer-Shelah). *If* $\mathcal{P}$ *has finite VC dimension* d, *then for all* $m \geqslant d$, $\hat{\Pi}_{\mathcal{P}}(m) \leqslant \left(\frac{em}{d}\right)^d$; *i.e.* $\hat{\Pi}_{\mathcal{P}}(m) = O(m^d)$.

Combining our lemma with this famous one yields a surprising result—that for a fixed set of programs $\mathcal{P}$ with finite VC dimension, the number of oracle queries performed by DIGITS *is guaranteedly polynomial* in the depth of the search, where the degree of the polynomial is determined by the VC dimension:

Theorem 2. *If* $\mathcal{P}$ *has VC dimension* d, *then* DIGITS *performs* $O(m^{d+1})$ *synthesis-oracle queries.*

In short, the reason an execution of DIGITS *seems* to enumerate a subexponential number of programs (as a function of the depth of the search) is because it literally must be polynomial. Furthermore, the algorithm performs oracle queries on *nearly* only those polynomially-many realizable dichotomies.

Example 3. A DIGITS run on the $[0, a]$ programs as in Fig. 2 using a sample set of size m will perform $O(m^2)$ oracle queries, since the VC dimension of these intervals is 1. (In fact, every run of the algorithm on these programs will perform exactly $\frac{1}{2}m(m + 1)$ many queries.)

---

[4] We assume the functional specification itself is some $\hat{P} \in \mathcal{P}$ and thus can be used—the alternative is a trivial synthesis query on an empty set of constraints.

4   Property-Directed τ-DIGITS

DIGITS has better convergence guarantees when it operates on larger sets of sampled inputs. In this section, we describe a new optimization of DIGITS that reduces the number of synthesis queries performed by the algorithm so that it more quickly reaches higher depths in the trie, and thus allows to scale to larger samples sets. This optimized DIGITS, called τ-DIGITS, is shown in Fig. 1 as the set of all the rules of DIGITS plus the framed elements. The high-level idea is to skip synthesis queries that are (quantifiably) unlikely to result in optimal solutions. For example, if the functional specification $\hat{P}$ maps every sampled input in S to 0, then the synthesis query on the mapping of every element of S to 1 becomes increasingly likely to result in programs that have maximal distance from $\hat{P}$ as the size of S increases; hence the algorithm could probably avoid performing that query.In the following, we make use of the concept of *Hamming distance* between pairs of programs:

Definition 7 (Hamming Distance). *For any finite set of inputs S and any two programs P_1, P_2, we denote $\mathrm{Hamming}_S(P_1, P_2) := |\{x \in S \mid P_1(x) \neq P_2(x)\}|$ (we will also allow any $\{0, 1\}$-valued string to be an argument of $\mathrm{Hamming}_S$).*

4.1   Algorithm Description

Fix the given functional specification $\hat{P}$ and suppose that there exists an ε-robust solution P^* with (nearly) minimal error $k = \mathrm{Er}(P^*) := \mathrm{Pr}_{x \sim \mathbb{D}}[\hat{P}(x) \neq P^*(x)]$; we would be happy to find *any* program P in P^*'s ε-ball. Suppose we angelically know k a priori, and we thus restrict our search (for each depth m) only to constraint strings (i.e. σ in Fig. 1) that have Hamming distance not much larger than km.

To be specific, we first fix some threshold $\tau \in (k, 1]$. Intuitively, the optimization corresponds to modifying DIGITS to consider only paths σ through the trie such that $\mathrm{Hamming}_S(\hat{P}, \sigma) \leqslant \tau|S|$. This is performed using the *unblocked* function in Fig. 1. Since we are ignoring certain paths through the trie, we need to ask: *How much does this decrease the probability of the algorithm succeeding?*— It depends on the tightness of the threshold, which we address in Sect. 4.2. In Sect. 4.3, we discuss how to adaptively modify the threshold τ as τ-DIGITS is executing, which is useful when a good τ is unknown a priori.

4.2   Analyzing Failure Probability with Thresholding

Using τ-DIGITS, the choice of τ will affect both (i) how many synthesis queries are performed, and (ii) the likelihood that we *miss* optimal solutions; in this section we explore the latter point.[5] Interestingly, we will see that all of the analysis is dependent only on parameters directly related to the threshold; notably, none of this analysis is dependent on the complexity of $\mathcal{P}$ (i.e. its VC dimension).

---

[5] The former point is a difficult combinatorial question that to our knowledge has no precedent in the computational learning literature, and so we leave it as future work.

If we really want to learn (something close to) a program P^*, then we should use a value of the threshold τ such that $\Pr_{S \sim \mathbb{D}^m}[\text{Hamming}_S(\hat{P}, P^*) \leqslant \tau m]$ is large—to do so requires knowledge of the distribution of $\text{Hamming}_S(\hat{P}, P^*)$. Recall the *binomial distribution*: for parameters (n, p), it describes the number of successes in n-many trials of an experiment that has success probability p.

Claim. Fix P and let $k = \Pr_{x \sim \mathbb{D}}[\hat{P}(x) \neq P(x)]$. If S is sampled from $\mathbb{D}^m$, then $\text{Hamming}_S(\hat{P}, P)$ is binomially distributed with parameters (m, k).

Next, we will use our knowledge of this distribution to reason about the *failure probability*, i.e. that τ-DIGITS does not preserve the convergence result of DIGITS. The simplest argument we can make is a union-bound style argument: the thresholded algorithm can "fail" by (i) failing to sample an ε-net, or otherwise (ii) sampling a set on which the optimal solution has a Hamming distance that is not representative of its actual distance. We provide the quantification of this failure probability in the following theorem:

Theorem 3. *Let P^* be a target ε-robust program with $k = \Pr_{x \sim \mathbb{D}}[\hat{P}(x) \neq P^*(x)]$, and let δ be the probability that m samples do not form an ε-net for P^*. If we run the τ-DIGITS with $\tau \in (k, 1]$, then the failure probability is at most $\delta + \Pr[X > \tau m]$ where $X \sim \text{Binomial}(m, k)$.*

In other words, we can use tail probabilities of the binomial distribution to bound the probability that the threshold causes us to "miss" a desirable program we otherwise would have enumerated. Explicitly, we have the following corollary:

Corollary 1. *τ-DIGITS increases failure probability (relative to DIGITS) by at most $\Pr[X > \tau m] = \sum_{i=\lfloor \tau m \rfloor + 1}^{m} \binom{m}{i} k^i (1-k)^{m-i}$.*

Informally, when m is *not too small*, k is *not too large*, and τ is *reasonably forgiving*, these tail probabilities can be quite small. We can even analyze the asymptotic behavior by using any existing upper bounds on the binomial distribution's tail probabilities—importantly, the additional error diminishes exponentially as m increases, dependent on the size of τ relative to k.

Corollary 2. *τ-DIGITS increases failure probability by at most $e^{-2m(\tau - k)^2}$.*[6]

Example 4. Suppose $m = 100$, $k = 0.1$, and $\tau = 0.2$. Then the extra failure probability term in Theorem 3 is less than 0.001.

As stated at the beginning of this subsection, the balancing act is to choose τ (i) small enough so that the algorithm is still fast for large m, yet (ii) large enough so that the algorithm is still likely to learn the desired programs. The further challenge is to relax our initial strong assumption that we know the optimal k a priori when determining τ, which we address in the following subsection.

---

[6] A more precise (though less convenient) bound is $e^{-m(\tau \ln \frac{\tau}{k} + (1-\tau) \ln \frac{1-\tau}{1-k})}$.

4.3   Adaptive Threshold

Of course, we do not have the angelic knowledge that lets us pick an ideal threshold τ; the only absolutely sound choice we can make is the trivial $\tau = 1$. Fortunately, we can begin with this choice of τ and *adaptively* refine it as the search progresses. Specifically, every time we encounter a correct program P such that $k = \mathrm{Er}(P)$, we can refine τ to reflect our newfound knowledge that "the best solution has distance of at most k."

We refer to this refinement as *adaptive τ-DIGITS*. The modification involves the addition of the following rule to Fig. 1:

$$\frac{best \neq \bot}{\tau \leftarrow g(\mathcal{O}_{\mathrm{err}}(best))} \text{ Refine Threshold (for some } g : [0,1] \rightarrow [0,1])$$

We can use any (non-decreasing) function g to update the threshold $\tau \leftarrow g(k)$. The simplest choice would be the identity function (which we use in our experiments), although one could use a looser function so as not to over-prune the search. If we choose functions of the form $g(k) = k + b$, then Corollary 2 allows us to make (slightly weak) claims of the following form:

Claim. Suppose the adaptive algorithm completes a search of up to depth m yielding a best solution with error k (so we have the final threshold value $\tau = k + b$). Suppose also that P^* is an optimal ε-robust program at distance $k - \eta$. The optimization-added failure probability (as in Corollary 1) for a run of (non-adaptive) τ-DIGITS completing depth m and using this τ is at most $e^{-2m(b+\eta)^2}$.

5   Evaluation

Implementation. In this section, we evaluate our new algorithm τ-DIGITS (Fig. 1) and its adaptive variant (Sect. 4.3) against DIGITS (i.e., τ-DIGITS with $\tau = 1$). Both algorithms are implemented in Python and use the SMT solver Z3 [8] to implement a sketch-based synthesizer $\mathcal{O}_{\mathrm{syn}}$. We employ statistical verification for $\mathcal{O}_{\mathrm{ver}}$ and $\mathcal{O}_{\mathrm{err}}$: we use Hoeffding's inequality for estimating probabilities in *post* and Er. Probabilities are computed with 95% confidence, leaving our oracles potentially unsound.

Research Questions. Our evaluation aims to answer the following questions:

RQ1 Is adaptive τ-DIGITS more effective/precise than τ-DIGITS?
RQ2 Is τ-DIGITS more effective/precise than DIGITS?
RQ3 Can τ-DIGITS solve challenging synthesis problems?

We experiment on three sets of benchmarks: (*i*) synthetic examples for which the optimal solutions can be computed analytically (Sect. 5.1), (*ii*) the set of benchmarks considered in the original DIGITS paper (Sect. 5.2), (*iii*) a variant of the thermostat-controller synthesis problem presented in [7] (Sect. 5.3).

5.1 Synthetic Benchmarks

We consider a class of synthetic programs for which we can compute the optimal solution exactly; this lets us compare the results of our implementation to an ideal baseline. Here, the program model $\mathcal{P}$ is defined as the set of axis-aligned hyperrectangles within $[-1, 1]^d$ ($d \in \{1, 2, 3\}$ and the VC dimension is $2d$), and the input distribution $\mathbb{D}$ is such that inputs are distributed uniformly over $[-1, 1]^d$. We fix some probability mass $b \in \{0.05, 0.1, 0.2\}$ and define the benchmarks so that the best error for a correct solution is exactly b (for details, see [9]).

We run our implementation using thresholds $\tau \in \{0.07, 0.15, 0.3, 0.5, 1\}$, omitting those values for which $\tau < b$; additionally, we also consider an adaptive run where τ is initialized as the value 1, and whenever a new best solution is enumerated with error k, we update $\tau \leftarrow k$. Each combination of parameters was run for a period of 2 min. Figure 3 fixates on $d = 1$, $b = 0.1$ and shows each of the following as a function of time: (i) the depth completed by the search (i.e. the current size of the sample set), and (ii) the best solution found by the search. (See our full version of the paper [9] for other configurations of (d, b).)

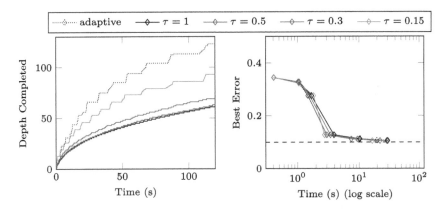

Fig. 3. Synthetic hyperrectangle problem instance with parameters $d = 1$, $b = 0.1$.

By studying Fig. 3 we see that the adaptive threshold search performs at least as well as the tight thresholds fixed a priori because reasonable solutions are found early. In fact, all search configurations find solutions very close to the optimal error (indicated by the horizontal dashed line). Regardless, they reach different depths, and *the main advantage of reaching large depths concerns the strength of the optimality guarantee*. Note, also, that small τ values are necessary to see improvements in the completed depth of the search. Indeed, the discrepancy between the depth-versus-time functions diminishes drastically for the problem instances with larger values of b (See our full version of the paper [9]); the gains of the optimization are contingent on the existence of correct solutions *close* to the functional specification.

Findings (RQ1): τ-DIGITS *does* tend to find *reasonable* solutions at early depths and near-optimal solutions at later depths, thus adaptive τ-DIGITS is more effective than τ-DIGITS, and we use it throughout our remaining experiments.

5.2 Original DIGITS Benchmarks

The original DIGITS paper [1] evaluates on a set of 18 repair problems of varying complexity. The functional specifications are machine-learned decision trees and support vector machines, and each search space $\mathcal{P}$ involves the set of programs formed by replacing some number of real-valued constants in the program with holes. The postcondition is a form of *algorithmic fairness*—e.g., the program should output true on inputs of type A as often as it does on inputs of type B [11]. For each such repair problem, we run both DIGITS and adaptive τ-DIGITS (again, with initial $\tau = 1$ and the identity refinement function). Each benchmark is run for 10 min, where the same sample set is used for both algorithms.

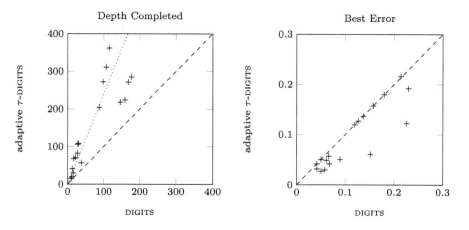

Fig. 4. Improvement of using adaptive τ-DIGITS on the original DIGITS benchmarks. Left: the dotted line marks the 2.4× average increase in depth.

Figure 4 shows, for each benchmark, (*i*) the largest sample set size completed by adaptive τ-DIGITS versus DIGITS (left—above the diagonal line indicates adaptive τ-DIGITS reaches further depths), and (*ii*) the error of the best solution found by adaptive τ-DIGITS versus DIGITS (right—below the diagonal line indicates adaptive τ-DIGITS finds better solutions). We see that adaptive τ-DIGITS reaches further depths on every problem instance, many of which are substantial improvements, and that it finds better solutions on 10 of the 18 problems. For those which did not improve, either the search was already deep enough that DIGITS was able to find near-optimal solutions, or the complexity of the synthesis queries is such that the search is still constrained to small depths.

Findings (RQ2): Adaptive τ-DIGITS can find better solutions than those found by DIGITS and can reach greater search depths.

5.3   Thermostat Controller

We challenge adaptive τ-DIGITS with the task of synthesizing a thermostat controller, borrowing the benchmark from [7]. The input to the controller is the initial temperature of the environment; since the world is uncertain, there is a specified probability distribution over the temperatures. The controller itself is a program sketch consisting primarily of a single main loop: iterations of the loop correspond to timesteps, during which the synthesized parameters dictate an incremental update made by the thermostat based on the current temperature. The loop runs for 40 iterations, then terminates, returning the absolute value of the difference between its final actual temperature and the target temperature.

The postcondition is a Boolean probabilistic correctness property intuitively corresponding to controller safety, e.g. with high probability, the temperature should never exceed certain thresholds. In [7], there is a quantitative objective in the form of minimizing the expected value $\mathrm{E}[\|actual - target\|]$—our setting does not admit optimizing with respect to expectations, so we must modify the problem. Instead, we fix some value N ($N \in \{2, 4, 8\}$) and have the program return 0 when $|actual - target| < N$ and 1 otherwise. Our quantitative objective is to minimize the error from the constant-zero functional specification $\hat{P}(x) := 0$ (i.e. the actual temperature always gets close enough to the target). The full specification of the controller is provided in the full version of our paper [9].

We consider variants of the program where the thermostat runs for fewer timesteps and try loop unrollings of size $\{5, 10, 20, 40\}$. We run each benchmark for 10 min: the final completed search depths and best error of solutions are shown in Fig. 5. For this particular experiment, we use the SMT solver CVC4 [3] because it performs better than Z3 on the occurring SMT instances.

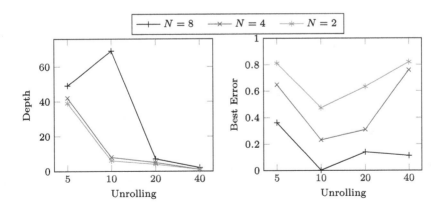

Fig. 5. Thermostat controller results.

As we would expect, for larger values of N it is "easier" for the thermostat to reach the target temperature threshold and thus the quality of the best solution increases in N. However, with small unrollings (i.e. 5) the synthesized controllers do not have enough iterations (time) to modify the temperature enough for the probability mass of extremal temperatures to reach the target: as we increase the number of unrollings to 10, we see that better solutions can be found since the set of programs are capable of stronger behavior.

On the other hand, the completed depth of the search plummets as the unrolling increases due to the complexity of the $\mathcal{O}_{syn}$ queries. Consequently, for 20 and 40 unrollings, adaptive τ-DIGITS synthesizes worse solutions because it cannot reach the necessary depths to obtain better guarantees.

One final point of note is that for $N = 8$ and 10 unrollings, it seems that there is a sharp spike in the completed depth. However, this is somewhat artificial: because $N = 8$ creates a very lenient quantitative objective, an early $\mathcal{O}_{syn}$ query happens to yield a program with an error less than 10^{-3}. Adaptive τ-DIGITS then updates $\tau \leftarrow \approx 10^{-3}$ and skips most synthesis queries.

Findings (RQ3): Adaptive τ-DIGITS can synthesize small variants of a complex thermostat controller, but cannot solve variants with many loop iterations.

6 Related Work

Synthesis and Probability. Program synthesis is a mature area with many powerful techniques. The primary focus is on synthesis under Boolean constraints, and probabilistic specifications have received less attention [1,7,17,19]. We discuss the works that are most related to ours.

DIGITS [1] is the most relevant work. First, we show for the first time that DIGITS only requires a number of synthesis queries polynomial in the number of samples. Second, our adaptive τ-DIGITS further reduces the number of synthesis queries required to solve a synthesis problem without sacrificing correctness.

The technique of *smoothed proof search* [7] approximates a combination of functional correctness and maximization of an expected value as a smooth, continuous function. It then uses numerical methods to find a local optimum of this function, which translates to a synthesized program that is likely to be correct and locally maximal. The benchmarks described in Sect. 5.3 are variants of benchmarks from [7]. Smoothed proof search can minimize expectation; τ-DIGITS minimizes probability only. However, unlike τ-DIGITS, smoothed proof search lacks formal convergence guarantees and cannot support the rich probabilistic postconditions we support, e.g., as in the fairness benchmarks.

Works on synthesis of probabilistic programs are aimed at a different problem [6,19,23]: that of synthesizing a generative model of data. For example, Nori et al. [19] use sketches of probabilistic programs and complete them with a stochastic search. Recently, Saad et al. [23] synthesize an ensemble of probabilistic programs for learning Gaussian processes and other models.

Kůcera et al. [17] present a technique for automatically synthesizing program transformations that introduce uncertainty into a given program with the goal of satisfying given privacy policies—e.g., preventing information leaks. They leverage the specific structure of their problem to reduce it to an SMT constraint solving problem. The problem tackled in [17] is orthogonal to the one targeted in this paper and the techniques are therefore very different.

Stochastic Satisfiability. Our problem is closely related to E-MAJSAT [18], a special case of *stochastic satisfiability* (SSAT) [20] and a means for formalizing probabilistic planning problems. E-MAJSAT is of NP^{PP} complexity. An E-MAJSAT formula has deterministic and probabilistic variables. The goal is to find an assignment of deterministic variables such that the probability that the formula is satisfied is above a given threshold. Our setting is similar, but we operate over complex program statements and have an additional optimization objective (i.e., the program should be close to the functional specification). The deterministic variables in our setting are the holes defining the search space; the probabilistic variables are program inputs.

Acknowledgements. We thank Shuchi Chawla, Yingyu Liang, Jerry Zhu, the entire fairness reading group at UW-Madison, and Nika Haghtalab for all of the detailed discussions. This material is based upon work supported by the National Science Foundation under grant numbers 1566015, 1704117, and 1750965.

References

1. Albarghouthi, A., D'Antoni, L., Drews, S.: Repairing decision-making programs under uncertainty. In: Majumdar, R., Kunčak, V. (eds.) Computer Aided Verification, pp. 181–200. Springer International Publishing, Cham (2017)
2. Barowy, D.W., Gulwani, S., Hart, T., Zorn, B.G.: Flashrelate: extracting relational data from semi-structured spreadsheets using examples. In: Proceedings of the 36th ACM SIGPLAN Conference on Programming Language Design and Implementation, Portland, OR, USA, 15–17 June 2015, pp. 218–228 (2015). https://doi.org/10.1145/2737924.2737952
3. Barrett, C., Conway, C.L., Deters, M., Hadarean, L., Jovanović, D., King, T., Reynolds, A., Tinelli, C.: CVC4. In: Gopalakrishnan, G., Qadeer, S. (eds.) CAV 2011. LNCS, vol. 6806, pp. 171–177. Springer, Heidelberg (2011). https://doi.org/10.1007/978-3-642-22110-1_14
4. Bastani, O., Sharma, R., Aiken, A., Liang, P.: Synthesizing program input grammars. In: Proceedings of the 38th ACM SIGPLAN Conference on Programming Language Design and Implementation, PLDI 2017, Barcelona, Spain, 18–23 June 2017, pp. 95–110 (2017). https://doi.org/10.1145/3062341.3062349
5. Blumer, A., Ehrenfeucht, A., Haussler, D., Warmuth, M.K.: Learnability and the vapnik-chervonenkis dimension. J. ACM (JACM) **36**(4), 929–965 (1989)
6. Chasins, S., Phothilimthana, P.M.: Data-driven synthesis of full probabilistic programs. In: Majumdar, R., Kunčak, V. (eds.) CAV 2017. LNCS, vol. 10426, pp. 279–304. Springer, Cham (2017). https://doi.org/10.1007/978-3-319-63387-9_14
7. Chaudhuri, S., Clochard, M., Solar-Lezama, A.: Bridging boolean and quantitative synthesis using smoothed proof search. In: POPL, vol. 49, pp. 207–220. ACM (2014)
8. de Moura, L., Bjørner, N.: Z3: an efficient SMT solver. In: Ramakrishnan, C.R., Rehof, J. (eds.) TACAS 2008. LNCS, vol. 4963, pp. 337–340. Springer, Heidelberg (2008). https://doi.org/10.1007/978-3-540-78800-3_24
9. Drews, S., Albarghouthi, A., D'Antoni, L.: Efficient synthesis with probabilistic constraints (2019). http://arxiv.org/abs/1905.08364
10. El-Hassany, A., Tsankov, P., Vanbever, L., Vechev, M.: Network-wide configuration synthesis. In: Majumdar, R., Kunčak, V. (eds.) CAV 2017. LNCS, vol. 10427, pp. 261–281. Springer, Cham (2017). https://doi.org/10.1007/978-3-319-63390-9_14

11. Feldman, M., Friedler, S.A., Moeller, J., Scheidegger, C., Venkatasubramanian, S.: Certifying and removing disparate impact. In: Proceedings of the 21th ACM SIGKDD International Conference on Knowledge Discovery and Data Mining, pp. 259–268. ACM (2015)

12. Goldberg, P.W., Jerrum, M.: Bounding the vapnik-chervonenkis dimension of concept classes parameterized by real numbers. Mach. Learn. **18**(2–3), 131–148 (1995). https://doi.org/10.1007/BF00993408

13. Gulwani, S.: Automating string processing in spreadsheets using input-output examples. In: Proceedings of the 38th ACM SIGPLAN-SIGACT Symposium on Principles of Programming Languages, POPL 2011, Austin, TX, USA, 26–28 January 2011, pp. 317–330 (2011). https://doi.org/10.1145/1926385.1926423

14. Gulwani, S.: Program synthesis. In: Software Systems Safety, pp. 43–75 (2014). https://doi.org/10.3233/978-1-61499-385-8-43

15. Gulwani, S.: Programming by examples - and its applications in data wrangling. In: Dependable Software Systems Engineering, pp. 137–158 (2016). https://doi.org/10.3233/978-1-61499-627-9-137

16. Kearns, M.J., Vazirani, U.V.: An Introduction to Computational Learning Theory. MIT Press, Cambridge (1994)

17. Kučera, M., Tsankov, P., Gehr, T., Guarnieri, M., Vechev, M.: Synthesis of probabilistic privacy enforcement. In: Proceedings of the 2017 ACM SIGSAC Conference on Computer and Communications Security, CCS 2017, pp. 391–408. ACM, New York (2017). https://doi.org/10.1145/3133956.3134079

18. Littman, M.L., Goldsmith, J., Mundhenk, M.: The computational complexity of probabilistic planning. J. Artif. Intell. Res. **9**, 1–36 (1998)

19. Nori, A.V., Ozair, S., Rajamani, S.K., Vijaykeerthy, D.: Efficient synthesis ofprobabilistic programs. SIGPLAN Not. **50**(6), 208–217 (2015). https://doi.org/10.1145/2813885.2737982

20. Papadimitriou, C.H.: Games against nature. J. Comput. Syst. Sci. **31**(2), 288–301 (1985)

21. Polozov, O., Gulwani, S.: Flashmeta: a framework for inductive program synthesis. In: Proceedings of the 2015 ACM SIGPLAN International Conference on Object-Oriented Programming, Systems, Languages, and Applications, OOPSLA 2015, part of SPLASH 2015, Pittsburgh, PA, USA, 25–30 October 2015, pp. 107–126 (2015). https://doi.org/10.1145/2814270.2814310

22. Raza, M., Gulwani, S.: Automated data extraction using predictive program synthesis. In: Proceedings of the Thirty-First AAAI Conference on Artificial Intelligence, 4–9 February 2017, San Francisco, California, USA, pp. 882–890 (2017). http://aaai.org/ocs/index.php/AAAI/AAAI17/paper/view/15034

23. Saad, F.A., Cusumano-Towner, M.F., Schaechtle, U., Rinard, M.C., Mansinghka, V.K.: Bayesian synthesis of probabilistic programs for automatic data modeling. Proc. ACM Program. Lang. **3**(POPL), 37 (2019)

24. Sauer, N.: On the density of families of sets. J. Comb. Theory, Seri. A **13**(1), 145–147 (1972)

25. Schkufza, E., Sharma, R., Aiken, A.: Stochastic program optimization. Commun. ACM **59**(2), 114–122 (2016). https://doi.org/10.1145/2863701

26. Shelah, S.: A combinatorial problem; stability and order for models and theories in infinitary languages. Pac. J. Math. **41**(1), 247–261 (1972)

27. Solar-Lezama, A.: Program Synthesis by Sketching. Ph.D. thesis, Berkeley, CA, USA (2008), aAI3353225

28. Srinivasan, V., Reps, T.W.: Synthesis of machine code from semantics. In: Proceedings of the 36th ACM SIGPLAN Conference on Programming Language Design

and Implementation, Portland, OR, USA, 15–17 June 2015, pp. 596–607 (2015). https://doi.org/10.1145/2737924.2737960

29. Subramanian, K., D'Antoni, L., Akella, A.: Genesis: synthesizing forwarding tables in multi-tenant networks. In: Proceedings of the 44th ACM SIGPLAN Symposium on Principles of Programming Languages, POPL 2017, Paris, France, 18–20 January 2017, pp. 572–585 (2017). http://dl.acm.org/citation.cfm?id=3009845

30. Wang, X., Gulwani, S., Singh, R.: FIDEX: filtering spreadsheet data using examples. In: Proceedings of the 2016 ACM SIGPLAN International Conference on Object-Oriented Programming, Systems, Languages, and Applications, OOPSLA 2016, part of SPLASH 2016, Amsterdam, The Netherlands, 30 October - 4 November 2016, pp. 195–213 (2016). https://doi.org/10.1145/2983990.2984030

Safety and Co-safety Comparator Automata for Discounted-Sum Inclusion

Suguman Bansal$^{(\boxtimes)}$ and Moshe Y. Vardi

Rice University, Houston, TX 77005, USA
sugumanb@gmail.com

Abstract. *Discounted-sum inclusion* (DS-inclusion, in short) formalizes the goal of comparing quantitative dimensions of systems such as cost, resource consumption, and the like, when the mode of aggregation for the quantitative dimension is discounted-sum aggregation. *Discounted-sum comparator automata*, or *DS-comparators* in short, are Büchi automata that read two infinite sequences of weights synchronously and relate their discounted-sum. Recent empirical investigations have shown that while DS-comparators enable competitive algorithms for DS-inclusion, they still suffer from the scalability bottleneck of Büchi operations.

Motivated by the connections between discounted-sum and Büchi automata, this paper undertakes an investigation of language-theoretic properties of DS-comparators in order to mitigate the challenges of Büchi DS-comparators to achieve improved scalability of DS-inclusion. Our investigation uncovers that DS-comparators possess safety and co-safety language-theoretic properties. As a result, they enable reductions based on subset construction-based methods as opposed to higher complexity Büchi complementation, yielding tighter worst-case complexity and improved empirical scalability for DS-inclusion.

1 Introduction

The analysis of quantitative dimensions of computing systems such as cost, resource consumption, and distance metrics [6, 10, 28] has been studied thoroughly to design efficient computing systems. Cost-aware program-synthesis [14, 16] and low-cost program-repair [25] have found compelling applications in robotics [24, 29], education [22], and the like. *Quantitative verification* facilitates efficient system design by automatically determining if a system implementation is more efficient than a specification model. Investigations in quantitative verification have demonstrated their high computational complexity and practically intractable [17, 23]. This work addresses practical intractability of quantitative verification.

At the core of quantitative verification lies the problem of *quantitative inclusion* which formalizes the goal of determining which of two given systems is more efficient [17, 23, 31]. In quantitative inclusion, quantitative systems are abstracted as weighted automata [7, 21, 32]. A run in a weighted automaton is associated with a sequence of weights. The quantitative dimension of these runs is determined by the weight of runs, which is computed by taking an aggregate of the run's weight sequence. Quantitative inclusion can be thought of as the quantitative generalization of (qualitative) language inclusion.

A commonly appearing mode of aggregation is that of *Discounted-sum (DS) aggregation* which captures the intuition that weights incurred in the near future are more significant than those incurred later on [19]. The convergence of DS aggregation for all bounded infinite weight-sequences makes it a preferred mode of aggregation across domains: Reinforcement learning [37], planning under uncertainty [34], and game-theory [33]. This work examines the problem of *Discounted-sum inclusion* or *DS-inclusion* that is quantitative inclusion when *discounted sum* is the mode of aggregation.

In theory, DS-inclusion is **PSPACE**-complete [12]. Recent algorithmic approaches have tapped into language-theoretic properties of discounted-sum aggregate function [12,18] to design practical algorithms for DS-inclusion [11,12]. These algorithms use *DS-comparator automata* (*DS-comparator*, in short) as their main technique, and are *purely* automata-theoretic. While these algorithms outperform other existing approaches for DS-inclusion in runtime [15,17], even these do not scale well on weighted-automata with more than few hundreds of states [11]. This work contributes novel techniques and algorithms for DS-inclusion to address the scalability challenge of DS-inclusion

An in-depth examination of the DS-comparator based algorithm exposes their scalability bottleneck. DS-comparator is a Büchi automaton that relates the discounted-sum aggregate of two (bounded) weight-sequences A and B by determining the membership of the interleaved pair of sequences (A, B) in the language of the comparator. As a result, DS-comparators reduce DS-inclusion to language inclusion between (non-deterministic) Büchi automaton. In spite of the fact that many techniques have been proposed to solve Büchi language inclusion efficiently in practice [4,20], none of them can avoid at least an exponential blow-up of $2^{\mathcal{O}(n \log n)}$, for an n-sized input, caused by a direct or indirect involvement of Büchi complementation [36,40].

This work meets the scalability challenge of DS-inclusion by delving deeper into language-theoretic properties of discounted-sum aggregate functions [18] in order to obtain algorithms for DS-inclusion that render both tighter theoretical complexity and improved scalability. Specifically, we prove that DS-comparators are expressed as *safety automata* or *co-safety automata* [26] (Sect. 3.1), and have compact deterministic constructions (Sect. 3.2). Safety and co-safety automata have the property that their complementation is performed by simpler and lower $2^{\mathcal{O}(n)}$-complexity subset-construction methods [27]. As a result, they facilitate a procedure for DS-inclusion that uses subset-construction based intermediate steps instead of Büchi complementation, yielding an improvement in theoretical complexity from $2^{\mathcal{O}(n \cdot \log n)}$ to $2^{\mathcal{O}(n)}$. Our subset-construction based procedure has yet another advantage over Büchi complementation as they support efficient on-the-fly implementations, yielding practical scalability as well (Sect. 4).

An empirical evaluation of our prototype tool **QuIPFly** for the proposed procedure against the prior DS-comparator algorithm and other existing approaches for DS-inclusion shows that **QuIPFly** outperforms them by orders of magnitude both in runtime and the number of benchmarks solved (Sect. 4).

2   Preliminaries and Related Work

A weight-sequence, finite or infinite, is *bounded* if the absolute value of all of its elements are bounded by a fixed number.

Büchi Automaton: A *Büchi automaton* is a tuple $\mathcal{A} = (S, \Sigma, \delta, s_\mathcal{I}, \mathcal{F})$, where S is a finite set of *states*, Σ is a finite *input alphabet*, $\delta \subseteq (S \times \Sigma \times S)$ is the *transition relation*, state $s_\mathcal{I} \in S$ is the *initial state*, and $\mathcal{F} \subseteq S$ is the set of *accepting states* [39]. A Büchi automaton is *deterministic* if for all states s and inputs a, $|\{s' | (s, a, s') \in \delta$ for some $s'\}| \leq 1$. Otherwise, it is *nondeterministic*. A Büchi automaton is *complete* if for all states s and inputs a, $|\{s' | (s, a, s') \in \delta$ for some $s'\}| \geq 1$. For a word $w = w_0 w_1 \cdots \in \Sigma^\omega$, a *run* ρ of w is a sequence of states $s_0 s_1 \ldots$ s.t. $s_0 = s_\mathcal{I}$, and $\tau_i = (s_i, w_i, s_{i+1}) \in \delta$ for all i. Let $inf(\rho)$ denote the set of states that occur infinitely often in run ρ. A run ρ is an *accepting run* if $inf(\rho) \cap \mathcal{F} \neq \emptyset$. A word w is an accepting word if it has an accepting run. The language of Büchi automaton $\mathcal{A}$, denoted by $\mathcal{L}(\mathcal{A})$ is the set of all words accepted by $\mathcal{A}$. By abuse of notation, we write $w \in \mathcal{A}$ and $\rho \in \mathcal{A}$ if w and ρ are an accepting word and an accepting run of $\mathcal{A}$. Büchi automata are closed under set-theoretic union, intersection, and complementation [39].

Safety and Co-safety Properties: Let $\mathcal{L} \subseteq \Sigma^\omega$ be a language over alphabet Σ. A finite word $w \in \Sigma^*$ is a *bad prefix* for $\mathcal{L}$ if for all infinite words $y \in \Sigma^\omega$, $x \cdot y \notin \mathcal{L}$. A language $\mathcal{L}$ is a *safety language* if every word $w \notin \mathcal{L}$ has a bad prefix for $\mathcal{L}$. A language $\mathcal{L}$ is a *co-safety language* if its complement language is a safety language [5]. When a safety or co-safety language is an ω-regular language, the Büchi automaton representing it is called a safety or co-safety automaton, respectively [26]. Wlog, safety and co-safety automaton contain a *sink state* from which every outgoing transitions loops back to the sink state and there is a transition on every alphabet symbol. All states except the sink state are accepting in a safety automaton, while only the sink state is accepting in a co-safety automaton. Unlike Büchi complementation, complementation of safety and co-safety automaton is conducted by simpler subset construction with a lower $2^{\mathcal{O}(n)}$ blow-up. The complementation of safety automaton is a co-safety automaton, and vice-versa. Safety automata are closed under intersection, and co-safety automata are closed under union.

Comparator Automaton: For a finite-set of integers Σ, an aggregate function $f : \mathbb{Z}^\omega \to \mathbb{R}$, and equality or inequality relation $\mathsf{R} \in \{<, >, \leq, \geq, =, \neq\}$, the *comparison language for f with relation* R is a language of infinite words over the alphabet $\Sigma \times \Sigma$ that accepts a pair (A, B) iff $f(A) \mathsf{R} f(B)$ holds. A *comparator automaton (comparator, in short) for aggregate function f and relation* R is an automaton that accepts the comparison language for f with R [12]. A comparator is said to be *regular* if its automaton is a Büchi automaton.

Weighted Automaton: A *weighted automaton* over infinite words is a tuple $\mathcal{A} = (\mathcal{M}, \gamma, f)$, where $\mathcal{M} = (S, \Sigma, \delta, s_\mathcal{I}, S)$ is a complete Büchi automaton with all states as accepting, $\gamma : \delta \rightarrow \mathbb{N}$ is a *weight function*, and $f : \mathbb{N}^\omega \rightarrow \mathbb{R}$ is the *aggregate function* [17,31]. *Words* and *runs* in weighted automata are defined as in Büchi automata. The *weight-sequence* of run $\rho = s_0 s_1 \ldots$ of word $w = w_0 w_1 \ldots$ is given by $wt_\rho = n_0 n_1 n_2 \ldots$ where $n_i = \gamma(s_i, w_i, s_{i+1})$ for all i. The *weight of a run* ρ, denoted by $f(\rho)$, is given by $f(wt_\rho)$. Here the *weight of a word* $w \in \Sigma^\omega$ in weighted automata is defined as $wt_\mathcal{A}(w) = sup\{f(\rho)|\rho$ is a run of w in $\mathcal{A}\}$.

Quantitative Inclusion: Let P and Q be weighted automata with the *same* aggregate function. The *strict quantitative inclusion problem*, denoted by $P \subset Q$, asks whether for all words $w \in \Sigma^\omega$, $wt_P(w) < wt_Q(w)$. The *non-strict quantitative inclusion problem*, denoted by $P \subseteq Q$, asks whether for all words $w \in \Sigma^\omega$, $wt_P(w) \leq wt_Q(w)$. *Comparison language* or *comparator* of a quantitative inclusion problem refer to the comparison language or comparator of the associated aggregate function.

Discounted-sum Inclusion: Let $A = A_0, A_1, \ldots$ be a weight sequence, $d > 1$ be a rational number. The *discounted-sum* (DS in short) of A with *integer* discount-factor $d > 1$ is $DS(A, d) = \Sigma_{i=0}^\infty \frac{A_i}{d^i}$. DS-comparison language and DS-comparator with discount-factor $d > 1$ are the comparison language and comparator obtained for the discounted-sum aggregate function with discount-factor $d > 1$, respectively. Strict or non-strict discounted-sum inclusion is strict or non-strict quantitative inclusion with the discounted-sum aggregate function, respectively. For brevity, we abbreviate discounted-sum inclusion to DS-inclusion.

Related Work. The decidability of DS-inclusion is an open problem when the discount-factor $d > 1$ is arbitrary. Recent work has established that DS-inclusion is PSPACE-complete when the discount-factor is an integer [12]. This work investigates algorithmic approaches to DS-inclusion with integer discount-factors.

Two contrasting solution approaches have been identified for DS-inclusion. The first approach is *hybrid* [17]. It separates out the language-theoretic aspects of weighted-automata from the numerical aspects, and solves each separately [15,17]. More specifically, the hybrid approach solves the language-theoretic aspects by DS-determinization [15] and the numerical aspect is performed by linear programming [8,9] sequentially. To the best of our knowledge, this procedure cannot be performed in parallel. As a result, this approach must always incur the exponential cost of DS-determinization.

The second approach is *purely*-automata theoretic [12]. This approach uses regular DS-comparator to reduce DS-inclusion to language inclusion between non-deterministic Büchi automata [11,12]. While the purely automata-theoretic approach scales better than the hybrid approach in runtime [11], its scalability suffers from fundamental algorithmic limitations of Büchi language inclusion. A key ingredient of Büchi language-inclusion is Büchi complementation [36]. Büchi complementation is $2^{\mathcal{O}(n \log n)}$ in the worst-case, and is practically intractable [40]. These limitations also feature in the theoretical complexity and practical performance of DS-inclusion. The complexity of DS-inclusion between weighted automata P and Q with regular DS-comparator C for integer discount-factor $d > 1$ is $|P| \cdot 2^{\mathcal{O}(|P||Q||C| \cdot \log(|P||Q||C|))}$.

This work improves the worst-case complexity and practical performance of the purely automata theoretic approach for DS-inclusion by a closer investigation of language-theoretic properties of DS-comparators. In particular, we identify that DS-comparator for integer discount-factor form a safety or co-safety automata (depending on the relation R). We show that complementation advantage of safety/co-safety automata not only improves the theoretical complexity of DS-inclusion with integer discount-factor but also facilitate on-the-fly implementations that significantly improve practical performance.

3 DS-inclusion with Integer Discount-Factor

This section covers the core technical contributions of this paper. We uncover novel language-theoretic properties of DS-comparison languages and utilize them to obtain tighter theoretical upper-bound for DS-inclusion with integer discount-factor. Unless mentioned otherwise, the discount-factor is an integer.

In Sect. 3.1 we prove that DS-comparison languages are either safety or co-safety for all rational discount-factors. Since DS-comparison languages are ω-regular for integer discount-factors [12], we obtain that DS-comparators for integer discount-factors form safety or co-safety automata. Next, Sect. 3.2 makes use of newly obtained safety/co-safety properties of DS-comparator to present the first deterministic constructions for DS-comparators. These deterministic construction are compact in the sense that they match their non-deterministic counterparts in number of states [11]. Section 3.3 evaluates the complexity of quantitative inclusion with regular safety/co-safety comparators, and observes that its complexity is lower than the complexity for quantitative inclusion with regular comparators. Finally, since DS-comparators are regular safety/co-safety, our analysis shows that the complexity of DS-inclusion is improved as a consequence of the complexity observed for quantitative-inclusion with regular safety/co-safety comparators.

We begin with formal definitions of safety/co-safety comparison languages and safety/co-safety comparators:

Definition 1 (Safety and co-safety comparison languages). *Let Σ be a finite set of integers, $f : \mathbb{Z}^\omega \to \mathbb{R}$ be an aggregate function, and $\mathsf{R} \in \{\leq, <, \geq, >, =, \neq\}$ be a relation. A comparison language L over $\Sigma \times \Sigma$ for aggregate function f and relation R is said to be a safety comparison language (or a co-safety comparison language) if L is a safety language (or a co-safety language).*

Definition 2 (Safety and co-safety comparators). *Let Σ be a finite set of integers, $f : \mathbb{Z}^\omega \to \mathbb{R}$ be an aggregate function, and $\mathsf{R} \in \{\leq, <, \geq, >, =, \neq\}$ be a relation. A comparator for aggregate function f and relation R is a safety comparator (or co-safety comparator) is the comparison language for f and R is a safety language (or co-safety language).*

A safety comparator is *regular* if its language is ω-regular (equivalently, if its automaton is a safety automaton). Likewise, a co-safety comparator is *regular* if its language is ω-regular (equivalently, automaton is a co-safety automaton).

By complementation duality of safety and co-safety languages, comparison language for an aggregate function f for non-strict inequality $\leq$ is safety iff the comparison language for f for strict inequality $<$ is co-safety. Since safety languages and safety automata are closed under intersection, safety comparison languages and regular safety comparator for non-strict inequality renders the same for equality. Similarly, since co-safety languages and co-safety automata are closed under union, co-safety comparison languages and regular co-safety comparators for non-strict inequality render the same for the inequality relation. Therefore, it suffices to examine the comparison language for one relation only.

It is worth noting that for weight-sequences A and B and all relations R, we have that $DS(A, d)$ R $DS(B, d)$ iff $DS(A - B, d)$ R 0, where $(A - B)_i = A_i - B_i$ for all $i \geq 0$. Prior work [11] shows that we can define *DS-comparison language* with upper bound μ, discount-factor $d > 1$, and relation R to accept infinite and bounded weight-sequence C over $\{-\mu, \ldots, \mu\}$ iff $DS(C, d)$ R 0 holds. Similarly, DS-comparator with the same parameters μ, $d > 1$, accepts the DS-comparison language with parameters μ, d and R. We adopt these definitions for DS-comparison languages and DS-comparators

Throughout this section, the concatenation of finite sequence x with finite or infinite sequence y is denoted by $x \cdot y$ in the following.

3.1 DS-comparison Languages and Their Safety/Co-safety Properties

The central result of this section is that DS-comparison languages are safety or co-safety languages for all (integer and non-integer) discount-factors (Theorem 1). In particular, since DS-comparison languages are ω-regular for integer discount-factors [12], this implies that DS-comparators for integer discount-factors form safety or co-safety automata (Corollary 1).

The argument for safety/co-safety of DS-comparison languages depends on the property that the discounted-sum aggregate of all bounded weight-sequences exists for all discount-factors $d > 1$ [35].

Theorem 1. *Let $\mu > 1$ be the upper bound. For rational discount-factor $d > 1$*

1. *DS-comparison languages are safety languages for relations R $\in \{\leq, \geq, =\}$*
2. *DS-comparison language are co-safety languages for relations R $\in \{<, >, \neq\}$.*

Proof (Proof sketch). Due to duality of safety/co-safety languages, it suffices to show that DS-comparison language with $\leq$ is a safety language.

Let DS-comparison language with upper bound μ, rational discount-factor $d > 1$ and relation $\leq$ be denoted by $\mathcal{L}_{\leq}^{\mu,d}$. Suppose that $\mathcal{L}_{\leq}^{\mu,d}$ is not a safety language. Let W be a weight-sequence in the complement of $\mathcal{L}_{\leq}^{\mu,d}$ such that W does not have a bad prefix. Then the following hold: (a). $DS(W, d) > 0$ (b).

For all $i \geq 0$, the i-length prefix $W[i]$ of W can be extended to an infinite and bounded weight-sequence $W[i] \cdot Y^i$ such that $DS(W[i] \cdot Y^i, d) \leq 0$.

Note that $DS(W, d) = DS(W[i], d) + \frac{1}{d^i} \cdot DS(W[i \ldots], d)$ where $W[i \ldots] = W_i W_{i+1} \ldots$ and $DS(W[i], d)$ is the discounted-sum of the finite sequence $W[i]$ i.e. $DS(W[i], d) = \Sigma_{j=0}^{j=i-1} \frac{W[j]}{d^j}$. Similarly, $DS(W[i] \cdot Y^i, d) = DS(W[i], d) + \frac{1}{d^i} \cdot DS(Y^i, d)$. The contribution of tail sequences $W[i \ldots]$ and Y^i to the discounted-sum of W and $W[i] \cdot Y^i$, respectively, diminishes exponentially as the value of i increases. In addition, since W and $W[i] \cdot Y^i$ share a common i-length prefix $W[i]$, their discounted-sum values must converge to each other. The discounted sum of W is fixed and greater than 0, due to convergence there must be a $k \geq 0$ such that $DS(W[k] \cdot Y^k, d) > 0$. Contradiction to (b).

Therefore, DS-comparison language with $\leq$ is a safety language. $\square$

Semantically this result implies that for a bounded-weight sequence C and rational discount-factor $d > 1$, if $DS(C, d) > 0$ then C must have a finite prefix C_{pre} such that the discounted-sum of the finite prefix is so large that no infinite extension by bounded weight-sequence Y can reduce the discounted-sum of $C_{\mathsf{pre}} \cdot Y$ with the same discount-factor d to zero or below.

Prior work shows that DS-comparison languages are expressed by Büchi automata iff the discount-factor is an integer [13]. Therefore:

Corollary 1. *Let $\mu > 1$ be the upper bound. For integer discount-factor $d > 1$*

1. DS-comparators are regular safety for relations $\mathsf{R} \in \{\leq, \geq, =\}$
2. DS-comparators are regular co-safety for relations $\mathsf{R} \in \{<, >, \neq\}$.

Lastly, it is worth mentioning that for the same reason [13] DS-comparators for non-integer rational discount-factors do not form safety or co-safety automata.

3.2   Deterministic DS-comparator for Integer Discount-Factor

This section issues deterministic safety/co-safety constructions for DS-comparators with integer discount-factors. This is different from prior works since they supply non-deterministic Büchi constructions only [11,12]. An outcome of DS-comparators being regular safety/co-safety (Corollary 1) is a proof that DS-comparators permit deterministic Büchi constructions, since non-deterministic and deterministic safety automata (and co-safety automata) have equal expressiveness [26]. Therefore, one way to obtain deterministic Büchi construction for DS-comparators is to determinize the non-deterministic constructions using standard procedures [26,36]. However, this will result in exponentially larger deterministic constructions. To this end, this section offers direct deterministic safety/co-safety automata constructions for DS-comparator that not only avoid an exponential blow-up but also match their non-deterministic counterparts in number of states (Theorem 3).

Key ideas. Due to duality and closure properties of safety/co-safety automata, we only present the construction of deterministic safety automata for DS-comparator with upper bound μ, integer discount-factor $d > 1$ and relation $\leq$, denoted by $\mathcal{A}_{\leq}^{\mu,d}$. We proceed by obtaining a *deterministic finite automaton*, (DFA), denoted by $\mathsf{bad}(\mu, d, \leq)$, for the language of bad-prefixes of $\mathcal{A}_{\leq}^{\mu,d}$ (Theorem 2). Trivial modifications to $\mathsf{bad}(\mu, d, \leq)$ will furnish the coveted deterministic safety automata for $\mathcal{A}_{\leq}^{\mu,d}$ (Theorem 3).

Construction. We begin with some definitions. Let W be a *finite* weight-sequence. By abuse of notation, the discounted-sum of finite-sequence W with discount-factor d is defined as $DS(W, d) = DS(W \cdot 0^\omega, d)$. The *recoverable-gap* of a finite weight-sequences W with discount factor d, denoted $\mathsf{gap}(W, d)$, is its normalized discounted-sum: If $W = \varepsilon$ (the empty sequence), $\mathsf{gap}(\varepsilon, d) = 0$, and $\mathsf{gap}(W, d) = d^{|W|-1} \cdot DS(W, d)$ otherwise [15]. Observe that the recoverable-gap has an inductive definition i.e. $\mathsf{gap}(\varepsilon, d) = 0$, where ε is the empty weight-sequence, and $\mathsf{gap}(W \cdot v, d) = d \cdot \mathsf{gap}(W, d) + v$, where $v \in \{-\mu, \ldots, \mu\}$.

This observation influences a sketch for $\mathsf{bad}(\mu, d, \leq)$. Suppose all possible values for recoverable-gap of weight sequences forms the set of states. Then, the transition relation of the DFA can mimic the inductive definition of recoverable gap i.e. there is a transition from state s to t on alphabet $v \in \{-\mu, \ldots, \mu\}$ iff $t = d \cdot s + v$, where s and v are recoverable-gap values of weight-sequences. There is one caveat here: There are infinitely many possibilities for the values of recoverable gap. We need to limit the recoverable gap values to finitely many values of interest. The core aspect of this construction is to identify these values.

First, we obtain a lower bound on recoverable gap for bad-prefixes of $\mathcal{A}_{\leq}^{\mu,d}$:

Lemma 1. *Let μ and $d > 1$ be the bound and discount-factor, resp. Let $\mathsf{T} = \frac{\mu}{d-1}$ be the threshold value. Let W be a non-empty, bounded, finite weight-sequence. Weight sequence W is a bad-prefix of $\mathcal{A}_{\leq}^{\mu,d}$ iff $\mathsf{gap}(W, d) > \mathsf{T}$.*

Proof. Let a finite weight-sequence W be a bad-prefix of $\mathcal{A}_{\leq}^{\mu,d}$. Then, $DS(W \cdot Y, d) > 0$ for all infinite and bounded weight-sequences Y. Since $DS(W \cdot Y, d) = DS(W, d) + \frac{1}{d^{|W|}} \cdot DS(Y, d)$, we get $\inf(DS(W, d) + \frac{1}{d^{|W|}} \cdot DS(Y, d)) > 0 \implies DS(W, d) + +\frac{1}{d^{|W|}} \cdot \inf(DS(Y, d)) > 0$ as W is a fixed sequence. Hence $DS(W, d) + \frac{-\mathsf{T}}{d^{|W|-1}} > 0 \implies \mathsf{gap}(W, d) - T > 0$. Conversely, for all infinite, bounded, weight-sequence Y, $DS(W \cdot Y, d) \cdot d^{|W|-1} = \mathsf{gap}(W, d) + \frac{1}{d} \cdot DS(Y, d)$. Since $\mathsf{gap}(W, d) > T$, $\inf(DS(Y, d)) = -\mathsf{T} \cdot d$, we get $DS(W \cdot Y, d) > 0$. □

Since all finite and bounded extensions of bad-prefixes are also bad-prefixes, Lemma 1 implies that if the recoverable-gap of a finite sequence is strictly lower that threshold T, then recoverable gap of all of its extensions also exceed T. Since recoverable gap exceeding threshold T is the precise condition for bad-prefixes, all states with recoverable gap exceeding T can be merged into a single state. Note, this state forms an accepting sink in $\mathsf{bad}(\mu, d, \leq)$.

Next, we attempt to merge very low recoverable gap value into a single state. For this purpose, we define *very-good prefixes* for $\mathcal{A}_{\leq}^{\mu,d}$: A finite and bounded weight-sequence W is a *very good* prefix for language of $\mathcal{A}_{\leq}^{\mu,d}$ if for all infinite, bounded extensions of W by Y, $DS(W \cdot Y, d) \leq 0$. A proof similar to Lemma 1 proves an upper bound for the recoverable gap of very-good prefixes of $\mathcal{A}_{\leq}^{\mu,d}$:

Lemma 2. *Let μ and $d > 1$ be the bound and discount-factor, resp. Let $\mathsf{T} = \frac{\mu}{d-1}$ be the threshold value. Let W be a non-empty, bounded, finite weight-sequence. Weight-sequence W is a very-good prefix of $\mathcal{A}_{\leq}^{\mu,d}$ iff $\mathsf{gap}(W, d) \leq -\mathsf{T}$.*

Clearly, finite extensions of very-good prefixes are also very-good prefixes. Further, $\mathsf{bad}(\mu, d, \leq)$ must not accept very-good prefixes. Thus, by reasoning as earlier we get that all recoverable gap values that are less than or equal to $-\mathsf{T}$ can be merged into one non-accepting sink state in $\mathsf{bad}(\mu, d, \leq)$.

Finally, for an integer discount-factor the recoverable gap is an integer. Let $\lfloor x \rfloor$ denote the floor of $x \in \mathbb{R}$ e.g. $\lfloor 2.3 \rfloor = 2$, $\lfloor -2 \rfloor = -2$, $\lfloor -2.3 \rfloor = -3$. Then,

Corollary 2. *Let μ be the bound and $d > 1$ an integer discount-factor. Let $\mathsf{T} = \frac{\mu}{d-1}$ be the threshold. Let W be a non-empty, bounded, finite weight-sequence.*

- *W is a bad prefix of $\mathcal{A}_{\leq}^{\mu,d}$ iff $\mathsf{gap}(W, d) > \lfloor \mathsf{T} \rfloor$*
- *W is a very-good prefix of $\mathcal{A}_{\leq}^{\mu,d}$ iff $\mathsf{gap}(W, d) \leq \lfloor -\mathsf{T} \rfloor$*

So, the recoverable gap value is either one of $\{\lfloor -\mathsf{T} \rfloor + 1, \ldots, \lfloor \mathsf{T} \rfloor\}$, or less than or equal to $\lfloor -\mathsf{T} \rfloor$, or greater than $\lfloor \mathsf{T} \rfloor$. This curbs the state-space to $\mathcal{O}(\mu)$-many values of interest, as $\mathsf{T} = \frac{\mu}{d-1} < \frac{\mu \cdot d}{d-1}$ and $1 < \frac{d}{d-1} \leq 2$. Lastly, since $\mathsf{gap}(\varepsilon, d) = 0$, state 0 must be the initial state.

Construction of $\mathsf{bad}(\mu, d, \leq)$. Let μ be the upper bound, and $d > 1$ be the integer discount-factor. Let $\mathsf{T} = \frac{\mu}{d-1}$ be the threshold value. The finite-state automata $\mathsf{bad}(\mu, d, \leq) = (S, s_I, \Sigma, \delta, \mathcal{F})$ is defined as follows:

- States $S = \{\lfloor -\mathsf{T} \rfloor + 1, \ldots, \lfloor \mathsf{T} \rfloor\} \cup \{\mathsf{bad}, \mathsf{veryGood}\}$
- Initial state $s_I = 0$, Accepting states $\mathcal{F} = \{\mathsf{bad}\}$
- Alphabet $\Sigma = \{-\mu, -\mu + 1, \ldots, \mu - 1, \mu\}$
- Transition function $\delta \subseteq S \times \Sigma \to S$ where $(s, a, t) \in \delta$ then:
    1. If $s \in \{\mathsf{bad}, \mathsf{veryGood}\}$, then $t = s$ for all $a \in \Sigma$
    2. If $s \in \{\lfloor -\mathsf{T} \rfloor + 1, \ldots, \lfloor \mathsf{T} \rfloor\}$, and $a \in \Sigma$
        (a) If $\lfloor -\mathsf{T} \rfloor < d \cdot s + a \leq \lfloor \mathsf{T} \rfloor$, then $t = d \cdot s + a$
        (b) If $d \cdot s + a > \lfloor \mathsf{T} \rfloor$, then $t = \mathsf{bad}$
        (c) If $d \cdot s + a \leq \lfloor -\mathsf{T} \rfloor$, then $t = \mathsf{veryGood}$

Theorem 2. *Let μ be the upper bound, $d > 1$ be the integer discount-factor. $\mathsf{bad}(\mu, d, \leq)$ accepts finite, bounded, weight-sequence iff it is a bad-prefix of $\mathcal{A}_{\leq}^{\mu,d}$.*

Proof (Proof sketch). First note that the transition relation is deterministic and complete. Therefore, every word has a unique run in $\mathsf{bad}(\mu, d, \leq)$. Let last be the last state in the run of finite, bounded, weight-sequence W in the DFA. Use induction on the length of W to prove the following:

- last $\in \{\lfloor -T \rfloor + 1, \ldots, \lfloor T \rfloor\}$ iff $\mathsf{gap}(W, d) = \mathsf{last}$
- last $= \mathsf{bad}$ iff $\mathsf{gap}(W, d) > \lfloor T \rfloor$
- last $= \mathsf{veryGood}$ iff $\mathsf{gap}(W, d) \leq \lfloor -T \rfloor$

Therefore, a finite, bounded weight-sequence is accepted iff its recoverable gap is greater than $\lfloor T \rfloor$. In other words, iff it is a bad-prefix of $\mathcal{A}_{\leq}^{\mu,d}$. $\qquad\square$

$\mathcal{A}_{\leq}^{\mu,d}$ is obtained from $\mathsf{bad}(\mu, d, \leq)$ by applying co-Büchi acceptance condition.

Theorem 3. *Let μ be the upper bound, and $d > 1$ be the integer discount-factor. DS-comparator for all inequalities and equality are either deterministic safety or deterministic co-safety automata with $\mathcal{O}(\mu)$ states.*

As a matter of fact, the most compact non-deterministic DS-comparator constructions with parameters μ, d and R also contain $\mathcal{O}(\mu)$ states [11].

3.3 Quantitative Inclusion with Safety/Co-safety Comparators

This section investigates quantitative language inclusion with regular safety/co-safety comparators. Unlike quantitative inclusion with regular comparators, quantitative inclusion with regular safety/co-safety comparators is able to circumvent Büchi complementation with intermediate subset-construction steps. As a result, complexity of quantitative inclusion with regular safety/co-safety comparator is lower than the same with regular comparators [12] (Theorem 4). Finally, since DS-comparators are regular safety/co-safety comparators, the algorithm for quantitative inclusion with regular safety/co-safety comparators applies to DS-inclusion yielding a lower complexity algorithm for DS-inclusion (Corollary 5).

Key Ideas A run of word w in a weighted-automaton is *maximal* if its weight is the supremum weight of all runs of w in the weighted-automaton. A run ρ_P of w in P is a *counterexample* for $P \subseteq Q$ (or $P \subset Q$) iff there exists a maximal run sup_Q of w in Q such that $wt(\rho_P) > wt(sup_Q)$ (or $wt(\rho_P) \geq wt(sup_Q)$). Consequently, $P \subseteq Q$ (or $P \subset Q$) iff there are no counterexample runs in P. Therefore, the roadmap to solve quantitative inclusion for regular safety/co-safety comparators is as follows:

1. Use regular safety/co-safety comparators to construct the *maximal automaton* of Q i.e. an automaton that accepts all maximal runs of Q (Corollary 3).
2. Use the regular safety/co-safety comparator and the maximal automaton to construct a *counterexample automaton* that accepts all counterexample runs of the inclusion problem $P \subseteq Q$ (or $P \subset Q$) (Lemma 5).

3. Solve quantitative inclusion for safety/co-safety comparator by checking for emptiness of the counterexample (Theorem 4).
Finally, since DS-comparators are regular safety/co-safety automaton (Corollary 1), apply Theorem 4 to obtain an algorithm for DS-inclusion that uses regular safety/co-safety comparators (Corollary 5).

Let W be a weighted automaton. Then the *annotated automaton* of W, denoted by $\hat{W}$, is the Büchi automaton obtained by transforming transition $s \xrightarrow{a} t$ with weight v in W to transition $s \xrightarrow{a,v} t$ in $\hat{W}$. Observe that $\hat{W}$ is a safety automaton since all its states are accepting. A run on word w with weight sequence wt in W corresponds to an *annotated word* (w, wt) in $\hat{W}$, and vice-versa.

Maximal Automaton. This section covers the construction of the *maximal automaton* from a weighted automaton. Let W and $\hat{W}$ be a weighted automaton and its annotated automaton, respectively. We call an annotated word (w, wt_1) in $\hat{W}$ *maximal* if for all other words of the form (w, wt_2) in $\hat{W}$, $wt(wt_1) \geq wt(wt_2)$. Clearly, (w, wt_1) is a maximal word in $\hat{W}$ iff word w has a run with weight sequence wt_1 in W that is maximal. We define *maximal automaton* of weighted automaton W, denoted $\mathsf{Maximal}(W)$, to be the automaton that accepts all maximal words of its annotated automata $\hat{W}$.

We show that when the comparator is regular safety/co-safety, the construction of the maximal automata incurs a $2^{\mathcal{O}(n)}$ blow-up. This section exposes the construction for maximal automaton when comparator for non-strict inequality is regular safety. The other case when the comparator for strict inequality is regular co-safety has been deferred to the appendix.

Lemma 3. *Let W be a weighted automaton with regular safety comparator for non-strict inequality. Then the language of $\mathsf{Maximal}(W)$ is a safety language.*

Proof (Proof sketch). An annotated word (w, wt_1) is not maximal in $\hat{W}$ for one of the following two reasons: Either (w, wt_1) is not a word in $\hat{W}$, or there exists another word (w, wt_2) in $\hat{W}$ s.t. $wt(wt_1) < wt(wt_2)$ (equivalently (wt_1, wt_2) is not in the comparator non-strict inequality). Both $\hat{W}$ and comparator for non-strict inequality are safety languages, so the language of maximal words must also be a safety language. □

We now proceed to construct the safety automata for $\mathsf{Maximal}(W)$

Intuition. The intuition behind the construction of maximal automaton follows directly from the definition of maximal words. Let $\hat{W}$ be the annotated automaton for weighted automaton W. Let $\hat{\Sigma}$ denote the alphabet of $\hat{W}$. Then an annotated word $(w, wt_1) \in \hat{\Sigma}^\omega$ is a word in $\mathsf{Maximal}(W)$ if (a) $(w, wt_1) \in \hat{W}$, and (b) For all words $(w, wt_2) \in \hat{W}$, $wt(wt_1) \geq wt(wt_2)$.

The challenge here is to construct an automaton for condition (b). Intuitively, this automaton simulates the following action: As the automaton reads word (w, wt_1), it must spawn all words of the form (w, wt_2) in $\hat{W}$, while also ensuring that $wt(wt_1) \geq wt(wt_2)$ holds for every word (w, wt_2) in $\hat{W}$. Since $\hat{W}$ is a safety automaton, for a word $(w, wt_1) \in \hat{\Sigma}^\omega$, all words of the form $(w, wt_2) \in \hat{W}$ can be traced by subset-construction. Similarly since the comparator C for non-strict inequality $(\geq)$ is a safety automaton, all words of the form $(wt_1, wt_2) \in C$ can be traced by subset-construction as well. The construction needs to carefully align the word (w, wt_1) with the all possible $(w, wt_2) \in \hat{W}$ and $(wt_1, wt_2) \in C$.

Construction of $\mathsf{Maximal}(W)$. Let W be a weighted automaton, with annotated automaton $\hat{W}$ and C denote its regular safety comparator for non-strict inequality. Let S_W denote the set of states of W (and $\hat{W}$) and S_C denote the set of states of C. We define $\mathsf{Maximal}(W) = (S, s_I, \hat{\Sigma}, \delta, \mathcal{F})$ as follows:

- Set of states S consists of tuples of the form (s, X), where $s \in S_W$, and $X = \{(t, c)|t \in S_W, c \in S_C\}$
- $\hat{\Sigma}$ is the alphabet of $\hat{W}$
- Initial state $s_I = (s_w, \{(s_w, s_c)\})$, where s_w and s_c are initial states in $\hat{W}$ and C, respectively.
- Let states $(s, X), (s, X') \in S$ such that $X = \{(t_1, c_1), \ldots, (t_n, c_n)\}$ and $X' = \{(t'_1, c'_1), \ldots, (t'_m, c'_m)\}$. Then $(s, X) \xrightarrow{(a,v)} (s', X') \in \delta$ iff

    1. $s \xrightarrow{(a,v)} s'$ is a transition in $\hat{W}$, and
    2. $(t'_j, c'_j) \in X'$ if there exists $(t_i, c_i) \in X$, and a weight v' such that $t_i \xrightarrow{a,v'} t'_j$ and $c_i \xrightarrow{v,v'} c'_j$ are transitions in $\hat{W}$ and C, respectively.

- $(s, \{(t_1, c_1), \ldots, (t_n, c_n)\}) \in \mathcal{F}$ iff s and all t_i are accepting in $\hat{W}$, and all c_i is accepting in C.

Lemma 4. *Let W be a weighted automaton with regular safety comparator C for non-strict inequality. Then the size of $\mathsf{Maximal}(W)$ is $|W| \cdot 2^{\mathcal{O}(|W| \cdot |C|)}$.*

Proof (Proof sketch). A state $(s, \{(t_1, c_1), \ldots, (t_n, c_n)\})$ is non-accepting in the automata if one of s, t_i or c_j is non-accepting in underlying automata $\hat{W}$ and the comparator. Since $\hat{W}$ and the comparator automata are safety, all outgoing transitions from a non-accepting state go to non-accepting state in the underlying automata. Therefore, all outgoing transitions from a non-accepting state in $\mathsf{Maximal}(W)$ go to non-accepting state in $\mathsf{Maximal}(W)$. Therefore, $\mathsf{Maximal}(W)$ is a safety automaton. To see correctness of the transition relation, one must prove that transitions of type (1.) satisfy condition (a), while transitions of type (2.) satisfy condition (b). $\mathsf{Maximal}(W)$ forms the conjunction of (a) and (b), hence accepts the language of maximal words of W.

A similar construction proves that the maximal automata of weighted automata W with regular safety comparator C for strict inequality contains $|W| \cdot 2^{\mathcal{O}(|W| \cdot |C|)}$ states. In this case, however, the maximal automaton may not be a safety automaton. Therefore, Lemma 4 generalizes to:

Corollary 3. *Let W be a weighted automaton with regular safety/co-safety comparator C. Then $\mathsf{Maximal}(W)$ is a Büchi automaton of size $|W| \cdot 2^{\mathcal{O}(|W| \cdot |C|)}$.*

Counterexample Automaton. This section covers the construction of the counterexample automaton. Given weighted-automata P and Q, an annotated word (w, wt_P) in annotated automata $\hat{P}$ is a *counterexample word* of $P \subseteq Q$ (or $P \subset Q$) if there exists (w, wt_Q) in $\mathsf{Maximal}(Q)$ s.t. $wt(wt_P) > wt(wt_Q)$ (or $wt(wt_P) \geq wt(wt_Q)$). Clearly, annotated word (w, wt_P) is a counterexample word iff there exists a counterexample run of w with weight-sequence wt_P in P.

For this section, we abbreviate strict and non-strict to strct and nstrct, respectively. For inc $\in \{\mathsf{strct}, \mathsf{nstrct}\}$, the *counterexample automaton* for inc-quantitative inclusion, denoted by $\mathsf{Counterexample}(\mathsf{inc})$, is the automaton that contains all counterexample words of the problem instance. We construct the counterexample automaton as follows:

Lemma 5. *Let P, Q be weighted-automata with regular safety/co-safety comparators. For inc $\in \{\mathsf{strct}, \mathsf{nstrct}\}$, $\mathsf{Counterexample}(\mathsf{inc})$ is a Büchi automaton.*

Proof. We construct Büchi automaton $\mathsf{Counterexample}(\mathsf{inc})$ for inc $\in \{\mathsf{strct}, \mathsf{nstrct}\}$ that contains the counterexample words of inc-quantitative inclusion. Since the comparator are regular safety/co-safety, $\mathsf{Maximal}(Q)$ is a Büchi automaton (Corollary 3). Construct the product $\hat{P} \times \mathsf{Maximal}(Q)$ such that transition $(p_1, q_1) \xrightarrow{a, v_1, v_2} (p_1, q_2)$ is in the product iff $p_1 \xrightarrow{a, v_1} p_1$ and $q_1 \xrightarrow{a, v_2} q_2$ are transitions in $\hat{P}$ and $\mathsf{Maximal}(Q)$, respectively. A state (p, q) is accepting if both p and q are accepting in $\hat{P}$ and $\mathsf{Maximal}(Q)$. One can show that the product accepts (w, wt_P, wt_Q) iff (w, wt_P) and (w, wt_Q) are words in $\hat{P}$ and $\mathsf{Maximal}(Q)$, respectively.

If inc $=$ strct, intersect $\hat{P} \times \mathsf{Maximal}(Q)$ with comparator for $\geq$. If inc $=$ nstrct, intersect $\hat{P} \times \mathsf{Maximal}(Q)$ with comparator for $>$. Since the comparator is a safety or co-safety automaton, the intersection is taken without the cyclic counter. Therefore, $(s_1, t_1) \xrightarrow{a, v_1, v_2} (s_2, t_2)$ is a transition in the intersection iff $s_1 \xrightarrow{a, v_1, v_2} s_2$ and $t_1 \xrightarrow{v_1, v_2} t_2$ are transitions in the product and the appropriate comparator, respectively. State (s, t) is accepting if both s and t are accepting. The intersection will accept (w, wt_P, wt_Q) iff (w, wt_P) is a counterexample of inc-quantitative inclusion. $\mathsf{Counterexample}(\mathsf{inc})$ is obtained by projecting out the intersection as follows: Transition $m \xrightarrow{a, v_1, v_2} n$ is transformed to $m \xrightarrow{a, v_1} n$. $\square$

Quantitative Inclusion and DS-inclusion. In this section, we give the final algorithm for quantitative inclusion with regular safety/co-safety comparators. Since DS-comparators are regular safety/co-safety comparators, this gives us an algorithm for DS-inclusion with improved complexity than previous results.

Theorem 4. *Let P, Q be weighted-automata with regular safety/co-safety comparators. Let $C_\leq$ and $C_<$ be the comparators for $\leq$ and $<$, respectively. Then*

- *Strict quantitative inclusion $P \subset Q$ is reduced to emptiness checking of a Büchi automaton of size $|P||C_\leq||Q| \cdot 2^{\mathcal{O}(|Q| \cdot |C_<|)}$.*
- *Non-strict quantitative inclusion $P \subseteq Q$ is reduced to emptiness checking of a Büchi automaton of size $|P||C_<||Q| \cdot 2^{\mathcal{O}(|Q| \cdot |C_<|)}$.*

Proof. Strict and non-strict are abbreviated to strct and nstrct, respectively. For inc $\in$ {strct, nstrct}, inc-quantitative inclusion holds iff Counterexample(inc) is empty. Size of Counterexample(inc) is the product of size of P, Maximal(Q) (Corollary 3), and the appropriate comparator as described in Lemma 5.   □

In contrast, quantitative inclusion with regular comparators reduces to emptiness of a Büchi automaton with $|P| \cdot 2^{\mathcal{O}(|P||Q||C| \cdot \log(|P||Q||C|))}$ states [12]. The $2^{\mathcal{O}(n \log n)}$ blow-up is unavoidable due to Büchi complementation. Hence, quantitative inclusion with regular safety/co-safety has lower worst-case complexity.

Lastly, we use the results of developed in previous sections to solve DS-inclusion. Since DS-comparators are regular safety/co-safety (Corollary 1), an immediate consequence of Theorem 4 is an improvement in the worst-case complexity of DS-inclusion in comparison to prior results with regular DS-comparators. Furthermore, since the regular safety/co-safety DS-comparators are of the same size for all inequalities (Theorem 3), we get:

Corollary 4. *Let P, Q be weighted-automata, and C be a regular safety/co-safety DS-comparator with integer discount-factor $d > 1$. Strict DS-inclusion reduces to emptiness checking of a safety automaton of size $|P||C||Q| \cdot 2^{\mathcal{O}(|Q| \cdot |C|)}$.*

Proof (Proof sketch). When comparator for non-strict inequality is safety-automaton, as it is for DS-comparator, the maximal automaton is a safety automaton (Lemma 3). One can then show that the counterexample automata is also a safety automaton.

A similar argument proves *non-strict DS-inclusion* reduces to emptiness of a *weak-Büchi automaton* [27] of size $|P||C||Q| \cdot 2^{\mathcal{O}(|Q| \cdot |C|)}$ (see Appendix).

Corollary 5 ([DS-inclusion with safety/co-safety comparator]). *Let P, Q be weighted-automata, and C be a regular (co)-safety DS-comparator with integer discount-factor $d > 1$. The complexity of DS-inclusion is $|P||C||Q| \cdot 2^{\mathcal{O}(|Q| \cdot |C|)}$.*

4 Implementation and Experimental Evaluation

The goal of the empirical analysis is to examine performance of DS-inclusion with integer discount-factor with safety/co-safety comparators against existing tools to investigate the practical merit of our algorithm. We compare against (a) Regular-comparator based tool QuIP, and (b) DS-determinization and linear-programming tool DetLP.

QuIP is written in C++, and invokes state-of-the-art Büchi language inclusion-solver RABIT [2]. We enable the -fast flag in RABIT, and tune its Java-threads with Xss, Xms, Xmx set to 1GB, 1GB and 8GB, respectively. DetLP is also written in C++, and uses linear programming solver GLPSOL provided by GLPK (GNU Linear Prog. Kit) [1]. We compare these tools along two axes: runtime and number of benchmarks solved.

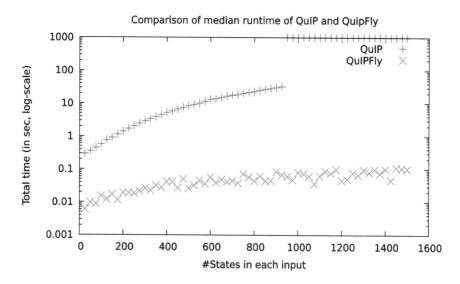

Fig. 1. $s_P = s_Q$ on x-axis, $wt = 4$, $\delta = 3$, $d = 3$, $P \subset Q$

Implementation Details. The algorithm for strict-DS-inclusion with integer discount factor $d > 1$ proposed in Corollary 4 and non-strict DS-inclusion checks for emptiness of the counterexample automata. A naive algorithm will construct the counterexample automata fully, and then check if they are empty by ensuring the absence of an *accepting lasso*.

We implement a more efficient algorithm. In our implementation, we make use of the fact that the constructions for DS-inclusion use subset-construction intermediate steps. This facilitates an *on-the-fly procedure* since successor states of state in the counterexample automata can be determined directly from input weighted automata and the comparator automata. The algorithm terminates as soon as an accepting lasso is detected. When an accepting lasso is absent, the algorithm traverses all states and edges of the counterexample automata.

We implement the optimized on-the-fly algorithm in a prototype QuIPFly. QuIPFly is written in Python 2.7.12. QuIPFly employs basic implementation-level optimizations to avoid excessive re-computation.

Design and Setup for Experiments. Due to lack of standardized benchmarks for weighted automata, we follow a standard approach to performance evaluation of automata-theoretic tools [3,30,38] by experimenting with *randomly generated* benchmarks, using random benchmark generation procedure described in [11].

The parameters for each experiment are number of states s_P and s_Q of weighted automata, transition density δ, maximum weight wt, integer discount-factor d, and inc $\in \{\mathsf{strct}, \mathsf{nstrct}\}$. In each experiment, weighted automata P and Q are randomly generated, and runtime of inc-DS-inclusion for all three tools is reported with a timeout of $900\,\mathrm{s}$. We run the experiment for each parameter tuple 50 times. All experiments are run on a single node of a high-performance cluster consisting of two quad-core Intel-Xeon processor running at $2.83\,\mathrm{GHz}$,

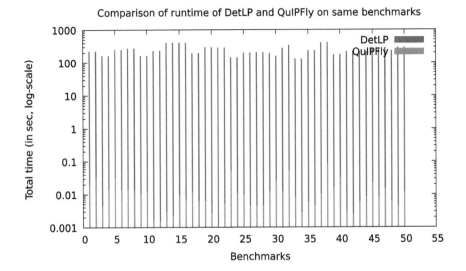

Fig. 2. $s_P = s_Q = 75$, $wt = 4$, $\delta = 3$, $d = 3$, $P \subset Q$

with 8 GB of memory per node. We experiment with $s_P = s_Q$ ranging from 0–1500 in increments of 25, $\delta \in \{3, 3.5, 4\}$, $d = 3$, and $wt \in \{d^1 + 1, d^3 - 1, d^4 - 1\}$.

Observations and Inferences.[1] For clarity of exposition, we present the observations for only one parameter-tuple. Trends and observations for other parameters were similar.

QuIPFly Outperforms. QuIP by at least an order of magnitude in runtime. Figure 1 plots the median runtime of all 50 experiments for the given parameter-values for QuIP and QuIPFly. More importantly, QuIPFly solves all of our benchmarks within a fraction of the timeout, whereas QuIP struggled to solve at least 50% of the benchmarks with larger inputs (beyond $s_P = s_Q = 1000$). Primary cause of failure is memory overflow inside RABIT. We conclude that regular safety/co-safety comparators outperform their regular counterpart, giving credit to the simpler subset-constructions vs. Büchi complementation.

QuIPFly Outperforms. DetLP comprehensively in runtime and in number of benchmarks solved. We were unable to plot DetLP in Fig. 1 since it solved fewer than 50% benchmarks even with small input instances. Figure 2 compares the runtime of both tools on the same set of 50 benchmarks for a representative parameter-tuple on which all 50 benchmarks were solved. The plot shows that QuIPFly beats DetLP by 2–4 orders of magnitude on all benchmarks.

Overall Verdict. Overall, QuIPFly outperforms QuIP and DetLP by a significant margin along both axes, runtime and number of benchmarks solved. This analysis gives unanimous evidence in favor of our safety/co-safety approach to solving DS-inclusion.

---

[1] Figures are best viewed online and in color.

5   Concluding Remarks

The goal of this paper was to build scalable algorithms for DS-inclusion. To this end, this paper furthers the understanding of language-theoretic properties of discounted-sum aggregate function by demonstrating that DS-comparison languages form safety and co-safety languages, and utilizes these properties to obtain a decision procedure for DS-inclusion that offers both tighter theoretical complexity and improved scalability. All in all, the key insights of this work are:

1. Pure automata-theoretic techniques of DS-comparator are better for DS-inclusion;
2. In-depth language-theoretic analysis improve both theoretical complexity and practical scalability of DS-inclusion;
3. DS-comparators are compact deterministic safety or co-safety automata.

To the best of our knowledge, this is the first work that applies language-theoretic properties such as safety/co-safety in the context of quantitative reasoning.

   More broadly, this paper demonstrates that the close integration of language-theoretic and quantitative properties can render novel algorithms for quantitative reasoning that can benefit from advances in qualitative reasoning.

Acknowledgements. We thank anonymous reviewers for their comments. We thank D. Fried, L. M. Tabajara, and A. Verma for their valuable inputs on initial drafts of the paper. This work was partially supported by NSF Grant No. CCF-1704883.

References

1. GLPK. https://www.gnu.org/software/glpk/
2. Rabit-Reduce. http://www.languageinclusion.org/
3. Abdulla, P.A., et al.: Simulation subsumption in ramsey-based büchi automata universality and inclusion testing. In: Proceedings of CAV, pp. 132–147. Springer (2010)
4. Abdulla, P.A., et al.. Advanced ramsey-based büchi automata inclusion testing. In: Proceedings of CONCUR, vol. 11, pp. 187–202. Springer (2011)
5. Alpern, B., Schneider, F.B.: Recognizing safety and liveness. Distrib. Comput. **2**(3), 117–126 (1987)
6. Alur, R., Mamouras, K.: An introduction to the streamqre language. Dependable Softw. Syst. Eng. **50**, 1 (2017)
7. Aminof, B., Kupferman, O., Lampert, R.: Reasoning about online algorithms with weighted automata. Trans. Algorithms **6**(2), 28 (2010)
8. Andersen, G., Conitzer, V.: Fast equilibrium computation for infinitely repeated games. In: Proceedings of AAAI, pp. 53–59 (2013)
9. Andersson, D.: An improved algorithm for discounted payoff games. In: ESSLLI Student Session, pp. 91–98 (2006)
10. Baier, C.: Probabilistic model checking. In: Dependable Software Systems Engineering, pp. 1–23 (2016)
11. Bansal, S., Chaudhuri, S., Vardi, M.Y.: Automata vs linear-programming discounted-sum inclusion. In: Proceedings of International Conference on Computer-Aided Verification (CAV) (2018)

12. Bansal, S., Chaudhuri, S., Vardi, M.Y. : Comparator automata in quantitative verification. In: Proceedings of International Conference on Foundations of Software Science and Computation Structures (FoSSaCS) (2018)
13. Bansal, S., Chaudhuri, S., Vardi, M.Y.: Comparator automata in quantitative verification (full version). CoRR, abs/1812.06569 (2018)
14. Bloem, R., Chatterjee, K., Henzinger, T.A., Jobstmann, B.: Better quality in synthesis through quantitative objectives. In: Bouajjani, A., Maler, O. (eds.) CAV 2009. LNCS, vol. 5643, pp. 140–156. Springer, Heidelberg (2009). https://doi.org/10.1007/978-3-642-02658-4_14
15. Boker, U., Henzinger, T.A.: Exact and approximate determinization of discounted-sum automata. LMCS **10**(1), 1–13 (2014)
16. Chakrabarti, A., Chatterjee, K., Henzinger, T.A., Kupferman, O., Majumdar, R.: Verifying quantitative properties using bound functions. In: Borrione, D., Paul, W. (eds.) CHARME 2005. LNCS, vol. 3725, pp. 50–64. Springer, Heidelberg (2005). https://doi.org/10.1007/11560548_7
17. Chatterjee, K., Doyen, L., Henzinger, T.A.: Quantitative languages. Trans. Computat. Logic **11**(4), 23 (2010)
18. Chaudhuri, S., Sankaranarayanan, S., Vardi, M.Y.: Regular real analysis. In: Proceedings of LICS, pp. 509–518 (2013)
19. de Alfaro, L., Henzinger, T.A., Majumdar, R.: Discounting the future in systems theory. In: Baeten, J.C.M., Lenstra, J.K., Parrow, J., Woeginger, G.J. (eds.) ICALP 2003. LNCS, vol. 2719, pp. 1022–1037. Springer, Heidelberg (2003). https://doi.org/10.1007/3-540-45061-0_79
20. Doyen, L., Raskin, J.-F.: Antichain algorithms for finite automata. In: Esparza, J., Majumdar, R. (eds.) TACAS 2010. LNCS, vol. 6015, pp. 2–22. Springer, Heidelberg (2010). https://doi.org/10.1007/978-3-642-12002-2_2
21. Droste, M., Kuich, W., Vogler, H.: Handbook of Weighted Automata. Springer, Berlin (2009)
22. D'Antoni, L., Samanta, R., Singh, R.: Qlose: program repair with quantitative objectives. In: Proceedings of CAV, pp. 383–401. Springer (2016)
23. Filiot, E., Gentilini, R., Raskin, J.-F.: Quantitative languages defined by functional automata. In: Koutny, M., Ulidowski, I. (eds.) CONCUR 2012. LNCS, vol. 7454, pp. 132–146. Springer, Heidelberg (2012). https://doi.org/10.1007/978-3-642-32940-1_11
24. He, K., Lahijanian, M., Kavraki, L.E., Vardi, M.Y.: Reactive synthesis for finite tasks under resource constraints. In: 2017 IEEE/RSJ International Conference on Intelligent Robots and Systems (IROS), pp. 5326–5332. IEEE (2017)
25. Hu, Q., DAntoni, L.: Syntax-guided synthesis with quantitative syntactic objectives. In: Chockler, H., Weissenbacher, G. (eds.) CAV 2018. LNCS, vol. 10981, pp. 386–403. Springer, Cham (2018). https://doi.org/10.1007/978-3-319-96145-3_21
26. Kupferman, O., Vardi, M.Y.: Model checking of safety properties. In: Halbwachs, N., Peled, D. (eds.) CAV 1999. LNCS, vol. 1633, pp. 172–183. Springer, Heidelberg (1999). https://doi.org/10.1007/3-540-48683-6_17
27. Kupferman, O., Vardi, M.Y.: Weak alternating automata are not that weak. Trans. Computat. Logic **2**(3), 408–429 (2001)
28. Kwiatkowska, M.: Quantitative verification: models, techniques and tools. In: Proceedings 6th Joint Meeting of the European Software Engineering Conference and the ACM SIGSOFT Symposium on the Foundations of Software Engineering (ESEC/FSE), pp. 449–458. ACM Press, September 2007
29. Lahijanian, M., Almagor, S., Fried, D., Kavraki, L.E., Vardi, M.Y.: This time the

robot settles for a cost: a quantitative approach to temporal logic planning with partial satisfaction. In: AAAI, pp. 3664–3671 (2015)

30. Mayr, R., Clemente, L.: Advanced automata minimization. ACM SIGPLAN Not. **48**(1), 63–74 (2013)

31. Mohri, M.: Weighted automata algorithms. In: Droste, M., Kuich, W., Vogler, H. (eds.) Handbook of Weighted Automata. Monographs in Theoretical Computer Science. An EATCS Series. Springer, Berlin (2009). https://doi.org/10.1007/978-3-642-01492-5_6

32. Mohri, M., Pereira, F., Riley, M.: Weighted finite-state transducers in speech recognition. Comput. Speech Lang. **16**(1), 69–88 (2002)

33. Osborne, M.J., Rubinstein, A.: A Course in Game Theory. MIT press, Cambridge (1994)

34. Puterman, M.L.: Markov decision processes. Handbooks Oper. Res. Manag. Sci. **2**, 331–434 (1990)

35. Rudin, W.: Principles of Mathematical Analysis, vol. 3. McGraw-Hill, New York (1964)

36. Safra, S.: On the complexity of ω-automata. In: Proceedings of FOCS, pp. 319–327. IEEE (1988)

37. Sutton, R.S., Barto, A.G.: Introduction to Reinforcement Learning, vol. 135. MIT press, Cambridge (1998)

38. Tabakov, D., Vardi, M.Y.: Experimental evaluation of classical automata constructions. In: Sutcliffe, G., Voronkov, A. (eds.) LPAR 2005. LNCS (LNAI), vol. 3835, pp. 396–411. Springer, Heidelberg (2005). https://doi.org/10.1007/11591191_28

39. Thomas, W., Wilke, T., et al.: Automata, Logics, and Infinite Games: A Guide to Current Research, vol. 2500. Springer Science & Business Media, Berlin (2002)

40. Vardi, M.Y.: The büchi complementation saga. In: Annual Symposium on Theoretical Aspects of Computer Science, pp. 12–22. Springer (2007)

9

Automated Hypersafety Verification

Azadeh Farzan$^{(\boxtimes)}$ and Anthony Vandikas

University of Toronto, Toronto, Canada
azadeh@cs.toronto.edu

Abstract. We propose an automated verification technique for hypersafety properties, which express sets of valid interrelations between multiple finite runs of a program. The key observation is that constructing a proof for a small representative set of the runs of the product program (i.e. the product of the several copies of the program by itself), called a *reduction*, is sufficient to formally prove the hypersafety property about the program. We propose an algorithm based on a counterexample-guided refinement loop that simultaneously searches for a reduction and a proof of the correctness for the reduction. We demonstrate that our tool WEAVER is very effective in verifying a diverse array of hypersafety properties for a diverse class of input programs.

1 Introduction

A hypersafety property describes the set of valid interrelations between multiple finite runs of a program. A k-safety property [7] is a program safety property whose violation is witnessed by at least k finite runs of a program. Determinism is an example of such a property: non-determinism can only be witnessed by two runs of the program on the same input which produce two different outputs. This makes determinism an instance of a 2-safety property.

The vast majority of existing program verification methodologies are geared towards verifying standard (1-)safety properties. This paper proposes an approach to automatically reduce verification of k-safety to verification of 1-safety, and hence a way to leverage existing safety verification techniques for hypersafety verification. The most straightforward way to do this is via *self-composition* [5], where verification is performed on k memory-disjoint copies of the program, sequentially composed one after another. Unfortunately, the proofs in these cases are often very verbose, since the full functionality of each copy has to be captured by the proof. Moreover, when it comes to automated verification, the invariants required to verify such programs are often well beyond the capabilities of modern solvers [26] even for very simple programs and properties.

The more practical approach, which is typically used in manual or automated proofs of such properties, is to compose k memory-disjoint copies of the program *in parallel* (instead of in sequence), and then verify some *reduced* program obtained by removing redundant traces from the program formed in the previous step. This parallel product program can have many such reductions.

For example, the program formed from sequential self-composition is one such reduction of the parallel product program. Therefore, care must be taken to choose a "good" reduction that *admits a simple proof*. Many existing approaches limit themselves to a narrow class of reductions, such as the one where each copy of the program executes in lockstep [3,10,24], or define a general class of reductions, but do not provide algorithms with guarantees of covering the entire class [4,24].

We propose a solution that combines the search for a safety proof with the search for an appropriate reduction, in a counterexample-based refinement loop. Instead of settling on a single reduction in advance, we try to verify the entire (possibly infinite) set of reductions simultaneously and terminate as soon as some reduction is successfully verified. If the proof is not currently strong enough to cover at least one of the represented program reductions, then an appropriate set of counterexamples are generated that guarantee progress towards a proof.

Our solution is language-theoretic. We propose a way to represent sets of reductions using infinite tree automata. The standard safety proofs are also represented using the same automata, which have the desired closure properties. This allows us to check if a candidate proof is in fact a proof for one of the represented program reductions, with reasonable efficiency.

Our approach is not uniquely applicable to hypersafety properties of sequential programs. Our proposed set of reductions naturally work well for concurrent programs, and can be viewed in the spirit of reduction-based methods such as those proposed in [11,21]. This makes our approach particularly appealing when it comes to verification of hypersafety properties of concurrent programs, for example, proving that a concurrent program is deterministic. The parallel composition for hypersafety verification mentioned above and the parallel composition of threads inside the multi-threaded program are treated in a uniform way by our proof construction and checking algorithms. In summary:

- We present a counterexample-guided refinement loop that simultaneously searches for a proof and a program reduction in Sect. 7. This refinement loop relies on an efficient algorithm for proof checking based on the antichain method of [8], and strong theoretical progress guarantees.
- We propose an automata-based approach to representing a class of program reductions for k-safety verification. In Sect. 5 we describe the precise class of automata we use and show how their use leads to an effective proof checking algorithm incorporated in our refinement loop.
- We demonstrate the efficacy of our approach in proving hypersafety properties of sequential and concurrent benchmarks in Sect. 8.

2   Illustrative Example

We use a simple program MULT, that computes the product of two non-negative integers, to illustrate the challenges of verifying hypersafety properties and the type of proof that our approach targets. Consider the multiplication program in Fig. 1(i), and assume we want to prove that it is distributive over addition.

Mult:		**Copy 1:**		**Copy 2:**		**Copy 3:**	
$\ell_1:$	$i \leftarrow 0$	$\ell_1:$	$i_1 \leftarrow 0$	$\ell_1:$	$i_2 \leftarrow 0$	$\ell_1:$	$i_3 \leftarrow 0$
$\ell_2:$	$x \leftarrow 0$	$\ell_2:$	$x_1 \leftarrow 0$	$\ell_2:$	$x_2 \leftarrow 0$	$\ell_2:$	$x_3 \leftarrow 0$
$\ell_3:$	**while** $i < a$	$\ell_3:$	**while** $i_1 < a + b$	$\ell_3:$	**while** $i_2 < a$	$\ell_3:$	**while** $i_3 < b$
$\ell_4:$	$x \leftarrow x + b$	$\ell_4:$	$x_1 \leftarrow x_1 + c$	$\ell_4:$	$x_2 \leftarrow x_2 + c$	$\ell_4:$	$x_3 \leftarrow x_3 + c$
$\ell_5:$	$i \leftarrow i + 1$	$\ell_5:$	$i_1 \leftarrow i_1 + 1$	$\ell_5:$	$i_2 \leftarrow i_2 + 1$	$\ell_5:$	$i_3 \leftarrow i_3 + 1$
$\ell_6:$	(i)	$\ell_6:$		$\ell_6:$		$\ell_6:$	(ii)

Fig. 1. Program MULT (i) and the parallel composition of three copies of it (ii).

In Fig. 1(ii), the parallel composition of MULT with two copies of itself is illustrated. The product program is formed for the purpose of proving distributivity, which can be encoded through the postcondition $x_1 = x_2 + x_3$. Since a, b, and c are not modified in the program, the same variables are used across all copies. One way to prove MULT is distributive is to come up with an inductive invariant ϕ_{ijk} for each location in the product program, represented by a triple of program locations (ℓ_i, ℓ_j, ℓ_k), such that $true \implies \phi_{111}$ and $\phi_{666} \implies x_1 = x_2 + x_3$. The main difficulty lies in finding assignments for locations such as ϕ_{611} that are points in the execution of the program where one thread has finished executing and the next one is starting. For example, at (ℓ_6, ℓ_1, ℓ_1) we need the assignment $\phi_{611} \leftarrow x_1 = (a + b) * c$ which is non-linear. However, the program given in Fig. 1(ii) can be verified with simpler (linear) reasoning.

The program on the right is a semantically equivalent *reduction* of the full composition of Fig. 1(ii). Consider the program $P =$ (Copy 1 || (Copy 2; Copy 3)). The program on the right is equivalent to a lockstep execution of the two parallel components of P. The validity of this reduction is derived from the fact that the statements in each thread are *independent* of the statements in the other. That is, reordering the statements of different threads in an execution leads to an equivalent execution. It is easy to see that $x_1 = x_2 + x_3$ is an invariant of both while loops in the reduced program, and therefore, linear reasoning is sufficient to prove the postcondition for this program. Conceptually, this reduction (and its soundness proof) together with the proof of correctness for the reduced program constitute a proof that the original program MULT is distributive. Our proposed approach can come up with reductions like this and their corresponding proofs fully automatically. Note that a lockstep reduction of the program in Fig. 1(ii) would not yield a solution for this problem and therefore the discovery of the right reduction is an integral part of the solution.

$i_1 \leftarrow 0, i_2 \leftarrow 0, i_3 \leftarrow 0$
$x_1 \leftarrow 0, x_2 \leftarrow 0, x_3 \leftarrow 0$
while $i_2 < a$
    $x_1 \leftarrow x_1 + c$
    $x_2 \leftarrow x_2 + c$
    $i_1 \leftarrow i_1 + 1$
    $i_2 \leftarrow i_2 + 1$
while $i_3 < b$
    $x_1 \leftarrow x_1 + c$
    $x_3 \leftarrow x_3 + c$
    $i_1 \leftarrow i_1 + 1$
    $i_3 \leftarrow i_3 + 1$

3   Programs and Proofs

A non-deterministic finite automaton (NFA) is a tuple $A = (Q, \Sigma, \delta, q_0, F)$ where Q is a finite set of states, Σ is a finite alphabet, $\delta \subseteq Q \times \Sigma \times Q$ is the transition relation, $q_0 \in Q$ is the initial state, and $F \subseteq Q$ is the set of final states. A deterministic finite automaton (DFA) is an NFA whose transition relation is a function $\delta : Q \times \Sigma \to Q$. The language of an NFA or DFA A is denoted $\mathcal{L}(A)$, which is defined in the standard way [18].

3.1   Program Traces

$\mathcal{S}t$ denotes the (possibly infinite) set of *program states*. For example, a program with two integer variables has $\mathcal{S}t = \mathbb{Z} \times \mathbb{Z}$. $\mathcal{A} \subseteq \mathcal{S}t$ is a (possibly infinite) set of *assertions* on program states. Σ denotes a finite alphabet of program *statements*. We refer to a finite string of statements as a (program) *trace*. For each statement $a \in \Sigma$ we associate a *semantics* $[\![a]\!] \subseteq \mathcal{S}t \times \mathcal{S}t$ and extend $[\![-]\!]$ to traces via (relation) composition. A trace $x \in \Sigma^*$ is said to be *infeasible* if $[\![x]\!](\mathcal{S}t) = \emptyset$, where $[\![x]\!](\mathcal{S}t)$ denotes the image of $[\![x]\!]$ under $\mathcal{S}t$. To abstract away from a particular program syntax, we define a *program* as a regular language of traces. The semantics of a program P is simply the union of the semantics of its traces $[\![P]\!] = \bigcup_{x \in P} [\![x]\!]$. Concretely, one may obtain programs as languages by interpreting their edge-labelled control-flow graphs as DFAs: each vertex in the control flow graph is a state, and each edge in the control flow graph is a transition. The control flow graph entry location is the initial state of the DFA and all its exit locations are final states.

3.2   Safety

There are many equivalent notions of program safety; we use non-reachability. A program P is *safe* if all traces of P are infeasible, i.e. $[\![P]\!](\mathcal{S}t) = \emptyset$. Standard partial correctness specifications are then represented via a simple encoding. Given a precondition ϕ and a postcondition ψ, the validity of the Hoare-triple $\{\phi\}P\{\psi\}$ is equivalent to the safety of $[\phi] \cdot P \cdot [\neg \psi]$, where $[]$ is a standard assume statement (or the singleton set containing it), and $\cdot$ is language concatenation.

Example 3.1. We use determinism as an example of how k-safety can be encoded in the framework defined thus far. If P is a program then determinism of P is equivalent to safety of $[\phi] \cdot (P_1 \sqcup\!\sqcup P_2) \cdot [\neg\phi]$ where P_1 and P_2 are copies of P operating on disjoint variables, $\sqcup\!\sqcup$ is a shuffle product of two languages, and $[\phi]$ is an assume statement asserting that the variables in each copy of P are equal.

A *proof* is a finite set of assertions $\Pi \subseteq \mathcal{A}$ that includes *true* and *false*. Each Π gives rise to an NFA $\Pi_{NFA} = (\Pi, \mathcal{S}t, \delta_\Pi, true, \{false\})$ where $\delta_\Pi(\phi_{pre}, a) = \{\phi_{post} \mid [\![a]\!](\phi_{pre}) \subseteq \phi_{post}\}$. We abbreviate $\mathcal{L}(\Pi_{NFA})$ as $\mathcal{L}(\Pi)$. Intuitively, $\mathcal{L}(\Pi)$

consists of all traces that can be proven infeasible using only assertions in Π. Thus the following proof rule is sound [12, 13, 17]:

$$\frac{\exists \Pi \subseteq \mathcal{A}.\, P \subseteq \mathcal{L}(\Pi)}{P \text{ is safe}} \qquad \text{(SAFE)}$$

When $P \subseteq \mathcal{L}(\Pi)$, we say that Π is a proof for P. A proof does not uniquely belong to any particular program; a single Π may prove many programs correct.

4 Reductions

The set of assertions used for a proof is usually determined by a particular language of assertions, and a safe program may not have a (safety) proof in that particular language. Yet, a subset of the program traces may have a proof in that assertion language. If it can be proven that the subset of program runs that have a safety proof are a faithful representation of all program behaviours (with respect to a given property), then the program is correct. This motivates the notion of *program reductions*.

Definition 4.1 (semantic reduction). *If for programs P and P', P' is safe implies that P is safe, then P' is a* semantic reduction *of P (written $P' \preceq P$).*

The definition immediately gives rise to the following proof rule for proving program safety:

$$\frac{\exists P' \preceq P, \Pi \subseteq \mathcal{A}.\, P' \subseteq \mathcal{L}(\Pi)}{P \text{ is safe}} \qquad \text{(SAFERED1)}$$

This generic proof rule is not automatable since, given a proof Π, verifying the existence of the appropriate reduction is *undecidable*. Observe that a program is safe if and only if $\emptyset$ is a valid reduction of the program. This means that discovering a semantic reduction and proving safety are mutually reducible to each other. To have decidable premises for the proof rule, we need to formulate an easier (than proving safety) problem in discovering a reduction. One way to achieve this is by restricting the set of reductions under consideration from all reductions (given in Definition 4.1) to a proper subset which more amenable to algorithmic checking. Fixing a set $\mathcal{R}$ of (semantic) reductions, we will have the rule:

$$\frac{\exists P' \in \mathcal{R}.\, P' \subseteq \mathcal{L}(\Pi) \qquad \forall P' \in \mathcal{R}.\, P' \preceq P}{P \text{ is safe}} \qquad \text{(SAFERED2)}$$

Proposition 4.2. *The proof rule SAFERED2 is sound.*

The core contribution of this paper is that it provides an algorithmic solution inspired by the above proof rule. To achieve this, two subproblems are solved: (1) Given a set $\mathcal{R}$ of reductions of a program P and a candidate proof Π, can we check if there exists a reduction $P' \in \mathcal{R}$ which is covered by the proof Π? In Sect. 5, we propose a new semantic interpretation of an existing notion of infinite tree automata that gives rise to an algorithmic check for this step. (2) Given a program P, is there a general sound set of reductions $\mathcal{R}$ that be effectively represented to accommodate step (1)? In Sect. 6, we propose a construction of an effective set of reductions, representable by our infinite tree automata, using inspirations from existing partial order reduction techniques [15].

5 Proof Checking

Given a set of reductions $\mathcal{R}$ of a program P, and a candidate proof Π, we want to check if there exists a reduction $P' \in \mathcal{R}$ which is covered by Π. We call this *proof checking*. We use tree automata to represent certain classes of languages (i.e sets of sets of strings), and then use operations on these automata for the purpose of proof checking.

The set Σ^* can be represented as an infinite tree. Each $x \in \Sigma^*$ defines a path to a unique node in the tree: the root node is located at the empty string ϵ, and for all $a \in \Sigma$, the node located at xa is a child of the node located at x. Each node is then identified by the string labeling the path leading to it. A language $L \subseteq \Sigma^*$ (equivalently, $L : \Sigma^* \to \mathbb{B}$) can consequently be represented as an infinite tree where the node at each x is labelled with a boolean value $B \equiv (x \in L)$. An example is given in Fig. 2.

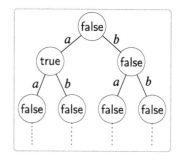

Fig. 2. Language $\{a\}$ as an infinite tree.

It follows that a set of languages is a set of infinite trees, which can be represented using automata over infinite trees. Looping Tree Automata (LTAs) are a subclass of Büchi Tree Automata where all states are accept states [2]. The class of Looping Tree Automata is closed under intersection and union, and checking emptiness of LTAs is decidable. Unlike Büchi Tree Automata, emptiness can be decided in linear time [2].

Definition 5.1. *A Looping Tree Automaton (LTA) over $|\Sigma|$-ary, $\mathbb{B}$-labelled trees is a tuple $M = (Q, \Delta, q_0)$ where Q is a finite set of states, $\Delta \subseteq Q \times \mathbb{B} \times (\Sigma \to Q)$ is the transition relation, and q_0 is the initial state.*

Intuitively, an LTA $M = (Q, \Delta, q_0)$ performs a parallel and depth-first traversal of an infinite tree L while maintaining some local state. Execution begins at the root ϵ from state q_0 and non-deterministically picks a transition $(q_0, B, \sigma) \in \Delta$ such that B matches the label at the root of the tree (i.e. $B = (\epsilon \in L)$). If no such transition exists, the tree is rejected. Otherwise, M recursively works on each child a from state $q' = \sigma(a)$ in parallel. This process continues infinitely, and L is accepted if and only if L is never rejected.

Formally, M's execution over a tree L is characterized by a *run* δ^* : $\Sigma^* \rightarrow Q$ where $\delta^*(\epsilon) = q_0$ and $(\delta^*(x), x \in L, \lambda a. \delta^*(xa)) \in \Delta$ for all $x \in \Sigma^*$. The set of languages accepted by M is then defined as $\mathcal{L}(M) = \{L \mid \exists \delta^*. \delta^*$ is a run of M on $L\}$.

Theorem 5.2. *Given an LTA M and a regular language L, it is decidable whether $\exists P \in \mathcal{L}(M). P \subseteq L$.*

The proof, which appears in [14], reduces the problem to deciding whether $\mathcal{L}(M) \cap \mathcal{P}(L) \neq \emptyset$. LTAs are closed under intersection and have decidable emptiness checks, and the lemma below is the last piece of the puzzle.

Lemma 5.3. *If L is a regular language, then $\mathcal{P}(L)$ is recognized by an LTA.*

Counterexamples. Theorem 5.2 effectively states that proof checking is decidable. For automated verification, beyond checking the validity of a proof, we require counterexamples to fuel the development of the proof when the proof does not check. Note that in the simple case of the proof rule SAFE, when $P \not\subseteq \mathcal{L}(\Pi)$ there exists a counterexample trace $x \in P$ such that $x \notin \mathcal{L}(\Pi)$.

With our proof rule SAFERED2, things get a bit more complicated. First, note that unlike the classic case (SAFE), where a failed proof check coincides with the non-emptiness of an intersection check (i.e. $P \cap \overline{\mathcal{L}(\Pi)} \neq \emptyset$), in our case, a failed proof check coincides with the emptiness of an intersection check (i.e. $\mathcal{R} \cap \mathcal{P}(\mathcal{L}(\Pi)) = \emptyset$). The sets $\mathcal{R}$ and $\mathcal{P}(\mathcal{L}(\Pi))$ are both sets of languages. What does the witness to the emptiness of the intersection look like? Each language member of $\mathcal{R}$ contains at least one string that does not belong to any of the subsets of our proof language. One can collect all such witness strings to guarantee progress across the board in the next round. However, since LTAs can represent an infinite set of languages, one must take care not end up with an infinite set of counterexamples following this strategy. Fortunately, this will not be the case.

Theorem 5.4. *Let M be an LTA and let L be a regular language such that $P \not\subseteq L$ for all $P \in \mathcal{L}(M)$. There exists a finite set of counterexamples C such that, for all $P \in \mathcal{L}(M)$, there exists some $x \in C$ such that $x \in P$ and $x \notin L$.*

The proof appears in [14]. This theorem justifies our choice of using LTAs instead of more expressive formalisms such as Büchi Tree Automata. For example, the Büchi Tree Automaton that accepts the language $\{\{x\} \mid x \in \Sigma^*\}$ would give rise to an infinite number of counterexamples with respect to the empty proof (i.e. $\Pi = \emptyset$). The finiteness of the counterexample set presents an alternate proof that LTAs are strictly less expressive than Büchi Tree Automata [27].

6   Sleep Set Reductions

We have established so far that (1) a set of assertions gives rise to a regular language proof, and (2) given a regular language proof and a set of program reductions recognizable by an LTA, we can check the program (reductions) against the proof. The last piece of the puzzle is to show that a useful class of program reductions can be expressed using LTAs.

Recall our example from Sect. 2. The reduction we obtain is sound because, for every trace in the full parallel-composition program, an equivalent trace exists in the reduced program. By equivalent, we mean that one trace can be obtained from the other by swapping independent statements. Such an equivalence is the essence of the theory of Mazurkiewicz traces [9].

We fix a reflexive symmetric *dependence relation* $D \subseteq \Sigma \times \Sigma$. For all $a, b \in \Sigma$, we say that a and b are *dependent* if $(a, b) \in D$, and say they are *independent* otherwise. We define $\sim_D$ as the smallest congruence satisfying $xaby \sim_D xbay$ for all $x, y \in \Sigma^*$ and independent $a, b \in \Sigma$. The closure of a language $L \subseteq \Sigma^*$ with respect to $\sim_D$ is denoted $[L]_D$. A language L is $\sim_D$-*closed* if $L = [L]_D$. It is worthwhile to note that all input programs considered in this paper correspond to regular languages that are $\sim_D$-closed.

An equivalence class of $\sim_D$ is typically called a (Mazurkiewicz) trace. We avoid using this terminology as it conflicts with our definition of traces as strings of statements in Sect. 3.1. We assume D is *sound*, i.e. $[\![ab]\!] = [\![ba]\!]$ for all independent $a, b \in \Sigma$.

Definition 6.1 (D-reduction). *A program P' is a D-reduction of a program P, that is $P' \preceq_D P$, if $[P']_D = P$.*

Note that the equivalence relation on programs induced by $\sim_D$ is a refinement of the semantic equivalence relation used in Definition 4.1.

Lemma 6.2. *If $P' \preceq_D P$ then $P' \preceq P$.*

Ideally, we would like to define an LTA that accepts all D-reductions of a program P, but unfortunately this is not possible in general.

Proposition 6.3 (corollary of Theorem 67 of [9]). *For arbitrary regular languages $L_1, L_2 \in \Sigma^*$ and relation D, the proposition $\exists L \preceq_D L_1. L \subseteq L_2$ is undecidable.*

The proposition is decidable only when $\overline{D}$ is transitive, which does not hold for a semantically correct notion of independence for a parallel program encoding a k-safety property, since statements from the same thread are dependent and statements from different program copies are independent. Therefore, we have:

Proposition 6.4. *Assume P is a $\sim_D$-closed program and Π is a proof. The proposition $\exists P' \preceq_D P. P' \subseteq \mathcal{L}(\Pi)$ is undecidable.*

In order to have a decidable premise for proof rule SAFERED2 then, we present an approximation of the set of D-reductions, inspired by sleep sets [15]. The idea is to construct an LTA that recognizes *a class of D-reductions* of an input program P, whose language is assumed to be $\sim_D$-closed. This automaton intuitively makes non-deterministic choices about what program traces to *prune* in favour of other $\sim_D$-equivalent program traces for a given reduction. Different non-deterministic choices lead to different D-reductions.

Consider two statements $a, b \in \Sigma$ where $(a, b) \notin D$. Let $x, y \in \Sigma^*$ and consider two program runs $xaby$ and $xbay$. We know $[\![xbay]\!] = [\![xaby]\!]$. If the automaton makes a non-deterministic choice that the successors of xa have been explored, then the successors of xba need not be explored (can be pruned away) as illustrated in Fig. 3. Now assume $(a, c) \in D$, for some $c \in \Sigma$. When the node xbc is being explored, we can no longer safely ignore a-transitions, since the equality $[\![xbcay]\!] = [\![xabcy]\!]$ is not guaranteed. Therefore, the a successor of xbc has to be explored. The nondeterministic choice of what child node to explore is modelled by a choice of order in which we explore each node's children. Different orders yield different reductions. Reductions are therefore characterized as an assignment $R : \Sigma^* \to \mathcal{L}in(\Sigma)$ from nodes to linear orderings on Σ, where $(a, b) \in R(x)$ means we explore child xa after child xb.

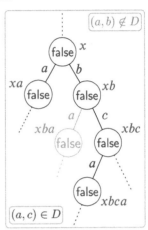

Fig. 3. Exploring from x with sleep sets.

Given $R : \Sigma^* \to \mathcal{L}in(\Sigma)$, the *sleep set* $\text{sleep}_R(x) \subseteq \Sigma$ at node $x \in \Sigma^*$ defines the set of transitions that can be ignored at x:

$$\text{sleep}_R(\epsilon) = \emptyset \tag{1}$$
$$\text{sleep}_R(xa) = (\text{sleep}_R(x) \cup R(x)(a)) \setminus D(a) \tag{2}$$

Intuitively, (1) no transition can be ignored at the root node, since nothing has been explored yet, and (2) at node x, the sleep set of xa is obtained by adding the transitions we explored before a ($R(x)(a)$) and then removing the ones that conflict with a (i.e. are related to a by D). Next, we define the nodes that are ignored. The set of ignored nodes is the smallest set $\text{ignore}_R : \Sigma^* \to \mathbb{B}$ such that

$$x \in \text{ignore}_R \implies xa \in \text{ignore}_R \tag{1}$$
$$a \in \text{sleep}_R(x) \implies xa \in \text{ignore}_R \tag{2}$$

Intuitively, a node xa is ignored if (1) any of its ancestors is ignored ($\text{ignore}_R(x)$), or (2) a is one of the ignored transitions at node x ($a \in \text{sleep}_R(x)$).

Finally, we obtain an actual reduction of a program P from a characterization of a reduction R by removing the ignored nodes from P, i.e. $P \setminus \text{ignore}_R$.

Lemma 6.5. *For all $R : \Sigma^* \to \mathcal{L}in(\Sigma)$, if P is a $\sim_D$-closed program then $P \setminus \text{ignore}_R$ is a D-reduction of P.*

The set of all such reductions is $\text{reduce}_D(P) = \{P \backslash \text{ignore}_R \mid R : \Sigma^* \to \mathcal{L}in(\Sigma)\}$.

Theorem 6.6. *For any regular language P, $\text{reduce}_D(P)$ is accepted by an LTA.*

Interestingly, every reduction in $\text{reduce}_D(P)$ is optimal in the sense that each reduction contains at most one representative of each equivalence class of $\sim_D$.

Theorem 6.7. *Fix some $P \subseteq \Sigma^*$ and $R : \Sigma^* \to \mathcal{L}in(\Sigma)$. For all $(x, y) \in P \backslash \text{ignore}_R$, if $x \sim_D y$ then $x = y$.*

7   Algorithms

Figure 4 illustrates the outline of our verification algorithm. It is a counterexample-guided abstraction refinement loop in the style of [12, 13, 17]. The key difference is that instead of checking whether some proof Π is a proof for the program P, it checks if there exists a

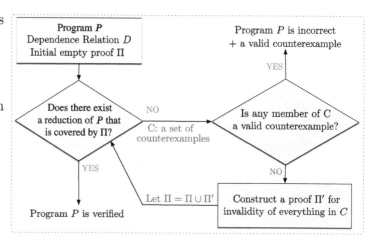

Fig. 4. Counterexample-guided refinement loop.

reduction of the program P that Π proves correct.

The algorithm relies on an oracle INTERPOLATE that, given a finite set of program traces C, returns a proof Π', if one exists, such that $C \subseteq \mathcal{L}(\Pi')$. In our tool, we use Craig interpolation to implement the oracle INTERPOLATE. In general, since program traces are the simplest form of sequential programs (loop and branch free), any automated program prover that can handle proving them may be used.

The results presented in Sects. 5 and 6 give rise to the proof checking sub routine of the algorithm in Fig. 4 (i.e. the light grey test). Given a program DFA $A_P = (Q_P, \Sigma, \delta_P, q_{P0}, F_P)$ and a proof DFA $A_\Pi = (Q_\Pi, \Sigma, \delta_\Pi, q_{\Pi 0}, F_\Pi)$ (obtained by determinizing Π_{NFA}), we can decide $\exists P' \in \text{reduce}_D(\mathcal{L}(A_P)). P' \subseteq \mathcal{L}(A_\Pi)$ by constructing an LTA $M_{P\Pi}$ for $\text{reduce}_D(\mathcal{L}(A_P)) \cap \mathcal{P}(\mathcal{L}(A_\Pi))$ and checking emptiness (Theorem 5.2).

7.1   Progress

The algorithm corresponding to Fig. 4 satisfies a weak progress theorem: none of the counterexamples from a round of the algorithm will ever appear in a future counterexample set. This, however, is not strong enough to guarantee termination. Alternatively, one can think of the algorithm's progress as follows. In each round new assertions are discovered through the oracle INTERPOLATE, and one can optimistically hope that one can finally converge on an existing target proof Π^*. The success of this algorithm depends on two factors: (1) the counterexamples used by the algorithm belong to $\mathcal{L}(\Pi^*)$ and (2) the proof that INTERPOLATE discovers for these counterexamples coincide with Π^*. The latter is a typical known wild card in software model checking, which cannot be guaranteed; there is plenty of empirical evidence, however, that procedures based on Craig Interpolation do well in approximating it. The former is a new problem for our refinement loop.

In a standard algorithm in the style of [12,13,17], the verification proof rule dictates that every program trace must be in $\mathcal{L}(\Pi^*)$. In our setting, we only require a subset (corresponding to some reduction) to be in $\mathcal{L}(\Pi^*)$. This means one cannot simply rely on program traces as *appropriate* counterexamples. Theorem 5.4 presents a solution to this problem. It ensures that we always feed INTERPOLATE some counterexample from Π^* and therefore guarantee progress.

Theorem 7.1 (Strong Progress). *Assume a proof Π^* exists for some reduction $P^* \in \mathcal{R}$ and INTERPOLATE always returns some subset of Π^* for traces in $\mathcal{L}(\Pi^*)$. Then the algorithm will terminate in at most $|\Pi^*|$ iterations.*

Theorem 7.1 ensures that the algorithm will never get into an infinite loop due to a bad choice of counterexamples. The condition on INTERPOLATE ensures that divergence does not occur due to the wrong choice of assertions by INTERPOLATE and without it any standard interpolation-based software model checking algorithm may diverge. The assumption that there exists a proof for a reduction of the program in the fixed set $\mathcal{R}$ ensures that the proof checking procedure can verify the target proof Π^* once it is reached. Note that, in general, a proof may exist for a reduction of the program which is not in $\mathcal{R}$. Therefore, the algorithm is not complete with respect to all reductions, since checking the premises of SAFERED1 is undecidable as discussed in Sect. 4.

7.2 Faster Proof Checking Through Antichains

The state set of M_{P_Π}, the intersection of program and proof LTAs, has size $|Q_P \times \mathbb{B} \times \mathcal{P}(\Sigma) \times Q_\Pi|$, which is exponential in $|\Sigma|$. Therefore, even a linear emptiness test for this LTA can be computationally expensive. Antichains have been previously used [8] to optimize certain operations over NFAs that also suffer from exponential blowups, such as deciding universality and inclusion tests. The main idea is that these operations involve computing downwards-closed and upwards-closed sets according to an appropriate subsumption relation, which can be represented compactly as antichains. We employ similar techniques to propose a new emptiness check algorithm.

Antichains. The set of maximal elements of a set X with respect to some ordering relation $\sqsubseteq$ is denoted $\max(X)$. The downwards-closure of a set X with respect to $\sqsubseteq$ is denoted $\lfloor X \rfloor$. An antichain is a set X where no element of X is related (by $\sqsubseteq$) to another. The maximal elements $\max(X)$ of a finite set X is an antichain. If X is downwards-closed then $\lfloor \max(X) \rfloor = X$.

The emptiness check algorithm for LTAs from [2] computes the set of *inactive* states (i.e. states which generate an empty language) and checks if the initial state is inactive. The set of inactive states of an LTA $M = (Q, \Delta, q_0)$ is defined as the smallest set inactive(M) satisfying

$$\frac{\forall (q, B, \sigma) \in \Delta.\, \exists a.\, \sigma(a) \in \text{inactive}(M)}{q \in \text{inactive}(M)} \qquad \text{(INACTIVE)}$$

Alternatively, one can view inactive(M) as the least fixed-point of a monotone (with respect to $\subseteq$) function $F_M : \mathcal{P}(Q) \to \mathcal{P}(Q)$ where

$$F_M(X) = \{q \mid \forall (q, B, \sigma) \in \Delta.\, \exists a.\, \sigma(a) \in X\}.$$

Therefore, inactive(M) can be computed using a standard fixpoint algorithm.

If inactive(M) is downwards-closed with respect to some *subsumption relation* $(\sqsubseteq) \subseteq Q \times Q$, then we need not represent all of inactive(M). The antichain $\max(\text{inactive}(M))$ of maximal elements of inactive(M) (with respect to $\sqsubseteq$) would be sufficient to represent the entirety of inactive(M), and can be exponentially smaller than inactive(M), depending on the choice of relation $\sqsubseteq$.

A trivial way to compute $\max(\text{inactive}(M))$ is to first compute inactive(M) and then find the maximal elements of the result, but this involves doing strictly more work than the baseline algorithm. However, observe that if F_M also preserves downwards-closedness with respect to $\sqsubseteq$, then

$$\begin{aligned}
\max(\text{inactive}(M)) &= \max(\text{lfp}(F_M)) \\
&= \max(\text{lfp}(F_M \circ \lfloor - \rfloor \circ \max)) = \text{lfp}(\max \circ F_M \circ \lfloor - \rfloor)
\end{aligned}$$

That is, $\max(\text{inactive}(M))$ is the least fixed-point of a function $F_M^{\max} : \mathcal{P}(Q) \to \mathcal{P}(Q)$ defined as $F_M^{\max}(X) = \max(F_M(\lfloor X \rfloor))$. We can calculate $\max(\text{inactive}(M))$ efficiently if we can calculate $F_M^{\max}(X)$ efficiently, which is true in the special case of the intersection automaton for the languages of our proof $\mathcal{P}(\mathcal{L}(\Pi))$ and our program reduce$_D(P)$, which we refer to as $M_{P\Pi}$.

We are most interested in the state space of $M_{P\Pi}$, which is $Q_{P\Pi} = (Q_P \times \mathbb{B} \times \mathcal{P}(\Sigma)) \times Q_\Pi$. Observe that states whose $\mathbb{B}$ part is $\top$ are always active:

Lemma 7.2. $((q_P, \top, S), q_\Pi) \notin \text{inactive}(M_{P\Pi})$ *for all* $q_P \in Q_P$, $q_\Pi \in Q_\Pi$, *and* $S \subseteq \Sigma$.

The state space can then be assumed to be $Q_{P\Pi} = (Q_P \times \{\bot\} \times \mathcal{P}(\Sigma)) \times Q_\Pi$ for the purposes of checking inactivity. The subsumption relation defined as the smallest relation $\sqsubseteq_{P\Pi}$ satisfying

$$S \subseteq S' \implies ((q_P, \bot, S), q_\Pi) \sqsubseteq_{P\Pi} ((q_P, \bot, S'), q_\Pi)$$

for all $q_P \in Q_P$, $q_\Pi \in Q_\Pi$, and $S, S' \subseteq \Sigma$, is a suitable one since:

Lemma 7.3. $F_{M_{P\Pi}}$ *preserves downwards-closedness with respect to* $\sqsubseteq_{P\Pi}$.

The function $F_{M_{P\Pi}}^{\max}$ is a function over relations

$$F_{M_{P\Pi}}^{\max} : \mathcal{P}((Q_P \times \{\bot\} \times \mathcal{P}(\Sigma)) \times Q_\Pi) \to \mathcal{P}((Q_P \times \{\bot\} \times \mathcal{P}(\Sigma)) \times Q_\Pi)$$

but in our case it is more convenient to view it as a function over functions

$$F_{M_{P\Pi}}^{\max} : (Q_P \times \{\bot\} \times Q_\Pi \to \mathcal{P}(\mathcal{P}(\Sigma))) \to (Q_P \times \{\bot\} \times Q_\Pi \to \mathcal{P}(\mathcal{P}(\Sigma)))$$

Through some algebraic manipulation and some simple observations, we can define $F_{M_{P\Pi}}^{\max}$ functionally as follows.

Lemma 7.4. *For all* $q_P \in Q_P$, $q_\Pi \in Q_\Pi$, *and* $X : Q_P \times \{\bot\} \times Q_\Pi \to \mathcal{P}(\mathcal{P}(\Sigma))$,

$$F_{M_{P\Pi}}^{\max}(X)(q_P, \bot, q_\Pi) = \begin{cases} \{\Sigma\} & \text{if } q_P \in F_P \wedge q_\Pi \notin F_\Pi \\ \displaystyle\prod_{R \in \mathcal{L}in(\Sigma)} \bigsqcup_{\substack{a \in \Sigma \\ S \in X(q_P', \bot, q_\Pi')}} S' & \text{otherwise} \end{cases}$$

where

$$q_P' = \delta_P(q_P, a) \qquad X \sqcap Y = \max\{x \cap y \mid x \in X \wedge y \in Y\}$$
$$q_\Pi' = \delta_\Pi(q_\Pi, a) \qquad X \sqcup Y = \max(X \cup Y)$$

$$S' = \begin{cases} \{(S \cup D(a)) \setminus \{a\}\} & \text{if } R(a) \setminus D(a) \subseteq S \\ \emptyset & \text{otherwise} \end{cases}$$

```
function Check(A_P, A_Π, D)
    (Q_P, Σ, δ_P, q_{0P}, F_P) ← A_P
    (Q_Π, Σ, δ_Π, q_{0Π}, F_Π) ← A_Π
    function FMax(X)((q_P, ⊥, q_Π))
        if q_P ∈ F_P ∧ q_Π ∉ F_Π
            return {Σ}
        X^⊓ ← {Σ}
        for R ∈ Lin(Σ)
            X^⊔ ← ∅
            for a ∈ Σ, S ∈ X((δ_P(q_P, a), ⊥, δ_Π(q_Π, a)))
                if R(a) \ D(a) ⊆ S
                    X^⊔ ← X^⊔ ⊔ {(S ∪ D(a)) \ {a}}
            X^⊓ ← X^⊓ ⊓ X^⊔
        return X^⊓
    return Fix(FMax)((q_{0P}, ⊥, q_{0Π})) ≠ ∅
```

Algorithm 1. Proof checking algorithm

A full justification appears in [14]. Formulating $F_{M_{P\Pi}}^{\max}$ as a higher-order function allows us to calculate $\max(\text{inactive}(M_{P\Pi}))$ using efficient fixpoint algorithms like the one in [22]. Algorithm 1 outlines our proof checking routine. $\textsc{Fix} : ((A \to B) \to (A \to B)) \to (A \to B)$ is a procedure that computes the least fixpoint of its input. The algorithm simply computes the fixpoint of the function $F_{M_{P\Pi}}^{\max}$ as defined in Lemma 7.4, which is a compact representation of $\text{inactive}(M_{P\Pi})$ and checks if the start state of $M_{P\Pi}$ is in it.

Counterexamples. Theorem 5.4 states that a finite set of counterexamples exists whenever $\exists P' \in \text{reduce}_D(P). P' \subseteq \mathcal{L}(\Pi)$ does not hold. The proof of emptiness for an LTA, formed using rule INACTIVE above, is a finite tree. Each edge in the tree is labelled by an element of Σ (obtained from the existential in the rule) and the paths through this tree form the counterexample set. To compute this set, then, it suffices to remember enough information during the computation of $\text{inactive}(M)$ to reconstruct the proof tree. Every time a state q is determined to be inactive, we must also record the witness $a \in \Sigma$ for each transition $(q, B, \sigma) \in \Delta$ such that $\sigma(a) \in \text{inactive}(M)$.

In an antichain-based algorithm, once we determine a state q to be inactive, we simultaneously determine everything it subsumes (i.e. $\sqsubseteq q$) to be inactive as well. If we record unique witnesses for each and every state that q subsumes, then the space complexity of our antichain algorithm will be the same as the unoptimized version. The following lemma states that it is sufficient to record witnesses only for q and discard witnesses for states that q subsumes.

Lemma 7.5. *Fix some states q, q' such that $q' \sqsubseteq_{P\Pi} q$. A witness used to prove q is inactive can also be used to prove q' is inactive.*

Note that this means that the antichain algorithm soundly returns potentially fewer counterexamples than the original one.

7.3   Partition Optimization

The LTA construction for $\text{reduce}_D(P)$ involves a nondeterministic choice of linear order at each state. Since $|\mathcal{L}in(\Sigma)|$ has size $|\Sigma|!$, each state in the automaton would have a large number of transitions. As an optimization, our algorithm selects ordering relations out of $\mathcal{P}art(\Sigma)$ (instead of $\mathcal{L}in(\Sigma)$), defined as $\mathcal{P}art(\Sigma) = \{\Sigma_1 \times \Sigma_2 \mid \Sigma_1 \uplus \Sigma_2 = \Sigma\}$ where $\uplus$ is disjoint union. This leads to a sound algorithm which is not complete with respect to sleep set reductions and trades the factorial complexity of computing $\mathcal{L}in(\Sigma)$ for an exponential one.

8   Experimental Results

To evaluate our approach, we have implemented our algorithm in a tool called WEAVER written in Haskell. WEAVER accepts a program written in a simple imperative language as input, where the property is already encoded in the program in the form of *assume* statements, and attempts to prove the program correct. The dependence relation for each input program is computed using a heuristic that ensures $\sim_D$-closedness. It is based on the fact that the shuffle product (i.e. parallel composition) of two $\sim_D$-closed languages is $\sim_D$-closed.

WEAVER employs two verification algorithms: (1) The total order algorithm presented in Algorithm 1, and (2) the variation with the partition optimization discussed in Sect. 7.3. It also implements multiple counterexample generation algorithms: (1) *Naive:* selects the first counterexample in the difference of the program and proof language. (2) *Progress-Ensuring:* selects a set of counterexamples satisfying Theorem 5.4. (3) *Bounded Progress-Ensuring:* selects a few counterexamples (in most cases just one) from the set computed by the progress-ensuring algorithm. Our experimentation demonstrated that in the vast majority of the cases, the bounded progress ensuring algorithm (an instance of the partition algorithm) is the fastest of all options. Therefore, all our reports in this section are using this instance of the algorithm.

For the larger benchmarks, we use a simple sound optimization to reduce the proof size. We declare the basic blocks of code as atomic, so that internal assertions need not be generated for them as part of the proof. This optimization is incomplete with respect to sleep set reductions.

Benchmarks. We use a set of sequential benchmarks from [24] and include additional sequential benchmarks that involve more interesting reductions in their proofs. We have a set of parallel benchmarks, which are beyond the scope of previous hypersafety verification techniques. We use these benchmarks to demonstrate that our technique/tool can seamlessly handle concurrency. These involve proving concurrency specific hypersafety properties such as determinism and equivalence of parallel and sequential implementations of algorithms. Finally, since the proof checking algorithm is the core contribution of this paper, we have a contrived set of instances to stress test our algorithm. These involve proving determinism of simple parallel-disjoint programs with various numbers of threads and statements per thread. These benchmarks have been designed to cause a combinatorial explosion for the proof checker and counterexample generation routines. More information on the benchmarks can be found in [14].

Evaluation

Due to space restrictions, it is not feasible to include a detailed account of all our experiments here, for over 50 benchmarks. A detailed table can be found in [14]. Table 1 includes a summary in the form of averages, and here, we discuss our top findings.

Proof construction time refers to the time spent to construct $\mathcal{L}(\Pi)$ from a given set of assertions Π and excludes the time to produce proofs for the counterexamples in a given round. **Proof checking time** is the time spent to check if the current proof candidate is strong enough for a reduction of the program. In the fastest instances (total time around 0.01 s), roughly equal time is spent in proof checking and proof construction. In the slowest instances, the total time is almost entirely spent in proof construction. In contrast, in our stress

Table 1. Experimental results averages for benchmark groups.

Benchmark group	Group count	Proof size	Number of refinement rounds	Proof construction time	Proof checking time	Total time
Looping programs of [24] 2-safety properties	5	63	12	46.69 s	0.1 s	47.03 s
Looping programs of [24] 3-safety properties	8	155	22	475.78 s	11.79 s	448.36 s
Loop-free programs of [24]	27	5	2	0.13 s	0.0004 s	0.15 s
Our sequential benchmarks	13	30	9	14.27 s	2.5 s	17.94 s
Our parallel benchmarks	7	31	8	17.95	0.56 s	18.63 s

tests (designed to stress the proof checking algorithm) the majority of the time is spent in proof checking. The time spent in proving counterexamples correct is negligible in all instances. **Proof sizes** vary from 4 assertions to 298 for the most complicated instance. Verification times are *correlated* with the final proof size; larger proofs tend to cause longer verification times.

Numbers of refinement rounds vary from 2 for the simplest to 33 for the most complicated instance. A small number of refinement rounds (e.g. 2) implies a fast verification time. But, for the higher number of rounds, a strong positive correlation between the number of rounds and verification time does not exist.

For our **parallel programs** benchmarks (other than our stress tests), the tool spends the majority of its time in proof construction. Therefore, we designed specific (unusual) parallel programs to stress test the proof checker. **Stress test** benchmarks are trivial tests of determinism of disjoint parallel programs, which can be proven correct easily by using the atomic block optimization. However, we force the tool to do the unnecessary hard work. These instances simulate the worst case theoretical complexity where the proof checking time and number of counterexamples grow exponentially with the number of threads and the sizes of the threads. In the largest instance, more than 99% of the total verification time is spent in proof checking. Averages are not very informative for these instances, and therefore are not included in Table 1.

Finally, WEAVER is only slow for verifying 3-safety properties of large looping benchmarks from [24]. Note that unlike the approach in [24], which starts from a default lockstep reduction (that is incidentally sufficient to prove these instances), we do not assume any reduction and consider them all. The extra time is therefore expected when the product programs become quite large.

9　Related Work

The notion of a k-safety hyperproperty was introduced in [7] without consideration for automatic program verification. The approach of reducing k-safety to 1-safety by self-composition is introduced in [5]. While theoretically complete, self-composition is not practical as discussed in Sect. 1. Product programs generalize the self-composition approach and have been used in verifying translation validation [20], non-interference [16,23], and program optimization [25]. A product of two programs P_1 and P_2 is semantically equivalent to $P_1 \cdot P_2$ (sequential composition), but is made easier to verify by allowing parts of each program to be interleaved. The product programs proposed in [3] allow lockstep interleaving exclusively, but only when the control structures of P_1 and P_2 match. This restriction is lifted in [4] to allow some non-lockstep interleavings. However, the given construction rules are non-deterministic, and the choice of product program is left to the user or a heuristic.

Relational program logics [6,28] extend traditional program logics to allow reasoning about relational program properties, however automation is usually not addressed. Automatic construction of product programs is discussed in [10] with the goal of supporting procedure specifications and modular reasoning, but is also restricted to lockstep interleavings. Our approach does not support procedure calls but is fully automated and permits non-lockstep interleavings.

The key feature of our approached is the automation of the discovery of an appropriate program reduction and a proof combined. In this case, the only other method that compares is the one based on Cartesian Hoare Logic (CHL) proposed in [24] along with an algorithm for automatic verification based on CHL. Their proposed algorithm implicitly constructs a product program, using a heuristic that favours lockstep executions as much as possible, and then prioritizes certain rules of the logic over the rest. The heuristic nature of the search for the proof means that no characterization of the search space can be given, and no guarantees about whether an appropriate product program will be found. In contrast, we have a formal characterization of the set of explored product programs in this paper. Moreover, CHL was not designed to deal with concurrency.

Lipton [19] first proposed reduction as a way to simplify reasoning about concurrent programs. His ideas have been employed in a semi-automatic setting in [11]. Partial-order reduction (POR) is a class of techniques that reduces the state space of search by removing redundant paths. POR techniques are concerned with finding a single (preferably minimal) reduction of the input program. In contrast, we use the same underlying ideas to explore many program reductions simultaneously. The class of reductions described in Sect. 6 is based on the sleep set technique of Godefroid [15]. Other techniques exist [1,15] that are used in conjunction with sleep sets to achieve minimality in a normal POR setting. In our setting, reductions generated by sleep sets are already optimal (Theorem 6.7). However, employing these additional POR techniques may propose ways of optimizing our proof checking algorithm by producing a smaller reduction LTA.

References

1. Abdulla, P.A., Aronis, S., Jonsson, B., Sagonas, K.: Source sets: a foundation for optimal dynamic partial order reduction. J. ACM (JACM) **64**(4), 25 (2017)

2. Baader, F., Tobies, S.: The inverse method implements the automata approach for modal satisfiability. In: Goré, R., Leitsch, A., Nipkow, T. (eds.) IJCAR 2001. LNCS, vol. 2083, pp. 92–106. Springer, Heidelberg (2001). https://doi.org/10.1007/3-540-45744-5_8

3. Barthe, G., Crespo, J.M., Kunz, C.: Relational verification using product programs. In: Butler, M., Schulte, W. (eds.) FM 2011. LNCS, vol. 6664, pp. 200–214. Springer, Heidelberg (2011). https://doi.org/10.1007/978-3-642-21437-0_17

4. Barthe, G., Crespo, J.M., Kunz, C.: Beyond 2-safety: asymmetric product programs for relational program verification. In: Artemov, S., Nerode, A. (eds.) LFCS 2013. LNCS, vol. 7734, pp. 29–43. Springer, Heidelberg (2013). https://doi.org/10.1007/978-3-642-35722-0_3

5. Barthe, G., D'argenio, P.R., Rezk, T.: Secure information flow by self-composition. Math. Struct. Comput. Sci. **21**(6), 1207–1252 (2011)

6. Benton, N.: Simple relational correctness proofs for static analyses and program transformations. In: ACM SIGPLAN Notices, vol. 39, pp. 14–25. ACM (2004)

7. Clarkson, M.R., Schneider, F.B.: Hyperproperties. In: 21st IEEE Computer Security Foundations Symposium, pp. 51–65. IEEE (2008)

8. De Wulf, M., Doyen, L., Henzinger, T.A., Raskin, J.-F.: Antichains: a new algorithm for checking universality of finite automata. In: Ball, T., Jones, R.B. (eds.) CAV 2006. LNCS, vol. 4144, pp. 17–30. Springer, Heidelberg (2006). https://doi.org/10.1007/11817963_5

9. Diekert, V., Métivier, Y.: Partial commutation and traces. In: Rozenberg, G., Salomaa, A. (eds.) Handbook of Formal Languages, pp. 457–533. Springer, Heidelberg (1997). https://doi.org/10.1007/978-3-642-59126-6_8

10. Eilers, M., Müller, P., Hitz, S.: Modular product programs. In: Ahmed, A. (ed.) ESOP 2018. LNCS, vol. 10801, pp. 502–529. Springer, Cham (2018). https://doi.org/10.1007/978-3-319-89884-1_18

11. Elmas, T., Qadeer, S., Tasiran, S.: A calculus of atomic actions. In: ACM SIGPLAN Notices, vol. 44, pp. 2–15. ACM (2009)

12. Farzan, A., Kincaid, Z., Podelski, A.: Inductive data flow graphs. In: ACM SIGPLAN Notices, vol. 48, pp. 129–142. ACM (2013)

13. Farzan, A., Kincaid, Z., Podelski, A.: Proof spaces for unbounded parallelism. In: ACM SIGPLAN Notices, vol. 50, pp. 407–420. ACM (2015)

14. Farzan, A., Vandikas, A.: Reductions for automated hypersafety verification (2019)

15. Godefroid, P. (ed.): Partial-Order Methods for the Verification of Concurrent Systems: An Approach to the State-Explosion Problem, vol. 1032. Springer, Heidelberg (1996). https://doi.org/10.1007/3-540-60761-7

16. Goguen, J.A., Meseguer, J.: Security policies and security models. In: 1982 IEEE Symposium on Security and Privacy, p. 11. IEEE (1982)

17. Heizmann, M., Hoenicke, J., Podelski, A.: Refinement of trace abstraction. In: Palsberg, J., Su, Z. (eds.) SAS 2009. LNCS, vol. 5673, pp. 69–85. Springer, Heidelberg (2009). https://doi.org/10.1007/978-3-642-03237-0_7

18. Hopcroft, J.E., Motwani, R., Ullman, J.D.: Introduction to Automata Theory, Languages, and Computation, 3rd edn. Addison-Wesley Longman Publishing Co. Inc., Boston (2006)

19. Lipton, R.J.: Reduction: a method of proving properties of parallel programs. Commun. ACM **18**(12), 717–721 (1975)

20. Pnueli, A., Siegel, M., Singerman, E.: Translation validation. In: Steffen, B. (ed.) TACAS 1998. LNCS, vol. 1384, pp. 151–166. Springer, Heidelberg (1998). https://doi.org/10.1007/BFb0054170

21. Popeea, C., Rybalchenko, A., Wilhelm, A.: Reduction for compositional verification of multi-threaded programs. In: Formal Methods in Computer-Aided Design (FMCAD), 2014, pp. 187–194. IEEE (2014)
22. Pottier, F.: Lazy least fixed points in ML (2009)
23. Sabelfeld, A., Myers, A.C.: Language-based information-flow security. IEEE J. Sel. Areas Commun. **21**(1), 5–19 (2003)
24. Sousa, M., Dillig, I.: Cartesian hoare logic for verifying k-safety properties. In: ACM SIGPLAN Notices, vol. 51, pp. 57–69. ACM (2016)
25. Sousa, M., Dillig, I., Vytiniotis, D., Dillig, T., Gkantsidis, C.: Consolidation of queries with user-defined functions. In: ACM SIGPLAN Notices, vol. 49, pp. 554–564. ACM (2014)
26. Terauchi, T., Aiken, A.: Secure information flow as a safety problem. In: Hankin, C., Siveroni, I. (eds.) SAS 2005. LNCS, vol. 3672, pp. 352–367. Springer, Heidelberg (2005). https://doi.org/10.1007/11547662_24
27. Vardi, M.Y., Wolper, P.: Reasoning about infinite computations. Inf. Comput. **115**(1), 1–37 (1994)
28. Yang, H.: Relational separation logic. Theor. Comput. Sci. **375**(1–3), 308–334 (2007)

10

Verifying Hyperliveness

Norine Coenen[1]([✉]), Bernd Finkbeiner[1],
César Sánchez[2], and Leander Tentrup[1]

[1] Reactive Systems Group, Saarland University,
Saarbrücken, Germany
`coenen@react.uni-saarland.de`
[2] IMDEA Software Institute, Madrid, Spain

Abstract. HyperLTL is an extension of linear-time temporal logic for the specification of hyperproperties, i.e., temporal properties that relate multiple computation traces. HyperLTL can express information flow policies as well as properties like symmetry in mutual exclusion algorithms or Hamming distances in error-resistant transmission protocols. Previous work on HyperLTL model checking has focussed on the alternation-free fragment of HyperLTL, where verification reduces to checking a standard trace property over an appropriate self-composition of the system. The alternation-free fragment does, however, not cover general hyperliveness properties. Universal formulas, for example, cannot express the secrecy requirement that for every possible value of a secret variable there exists a computation where the value is different while the observations made by the external observer are the same. In this paper, we study the more difficult case of hyperliveness properties expressed as HyperLTL formulas with quantifier alternation. We reduce existential quantification to strategic choice and show that synthesis algorithms can be used to eliminate the existential quantifiers automatically. We furthermore show that this approach can be extended to reactive system synthesis, i.e., to automatically construct a reactive system that is guaranteed to satisfy a given HyperLTL formula.

1 Introduction

HyperLTL [6] is a temporal logic for *hyperproperties* [7], i.e., for properties that relate multiple computation traces. Hyperproperties cannot be expressed in standard linear-time temporal logic (LTL), because LTL can only express *trace properties*, i.e., properties that characterize the correctness of individual computations. Even branching-time temporal logics like CTL and CTL*, which quantify over computation paths, cannot express hyperproperties, because quantifying over a second path automatically means that the subformula can no longer refer to the previously quantified path. HyperLTL addresses this limitation with quantifiers over trace variables, which allow the subformula to refer to all previously chosen traces. For example, *noninterference* [21] between a secret input h and a public output o can be specified in HyperLTL by requiring that all pairs of traces π and π' that always have the same inputs except for h (i.e., all inputs in $I \setminus \{h\}$ are equal on π and π') also have the same output o at all times:

$$\forall \pi. \forall \pi'. \ \Box \Big(\bigwedge_{i \in I \setminus \{h\}} i_\pi = i_{\pi'} \Big) \ \Rightarrow \ \Box (o_\pi = o_{\pi'})$$

This formula states that a change in the secret input h alone cannot cause any difference in the output o.

For certain properties of interest, the additional expressiveness of HyperLTL comes at no extra cost when considering the model checking problem. To check a property like noninterference, which only has universal trace quantifiers, one simply builds the self-composition of the system, which provides a separate copy of the state variables for each trace. Instead of quantifying over all pairs of traces, it then suffices to quantify over individual traces of the self-composed system, which can be done with standard LTL. Model checking universal formulas is NLOGSPACE-complete in the size of the system and PSPACE-complete in the size of the formula, which is precisely the same complexity as for LTL.

Universal HyperLTL formulas suffice to express hypersafety properties like noninterference, but not hyperliveness properties that require, in general, quantifier alternation. A prominent example is *generalized noninterference* (GNI) [27], which can be expressed as the following HyperLTL formula:

$$\forall \pi. \forall \pi'. \exists \pi''. \ \Box (h_\pi = h_{\pi''}) \ \wedge \ \Box (o_{\pi'} = o_{\pi''})$$

This formula requires that for every pair of traces π and π', there is a third trace π'' in the system that agrees with π on h and with π' on o. The existence of an appropriate trace π'' ensures that in π and π', the value of o is not determined by the value of h. Generalized noninterference stipulates that low-security outputs may not be altered by the injection of high-security inputs, while permitting nondeterminism in the low-observable behavior. The existential quantifier is needed to allow this nondeterminism. GNI is a hyperliveness property [7] even though the underlying LTL formula is a safety property. The reason for that is that we can extend any set of traces that violates GNI into a set of traces that satisfies GNI, by adding, for each offending pair of traces π, π', an appropriate trace π''.

Hyperliveness properties also play an important role in applications beyond security. For example, *robust cleanness* [9] specifies that significant differences in the output behavior are only permitted after significant differences in the input:

$$\forall \pi. \forall \pi'. \exists \pi''. \ \Box \big(i_{\pi'} = i_{\pi''} \big) \ \wedge \ \big(\hat{d}(o_\pi, o_{\pi''}) \leq \kappa_o \ W \ \hat{d}(i_\pi, i_{\pi''}) > \kappa_i \big)$$

The differences are measured by a distance function $\hat{d}$ and compared to constant thresholds κ_i for the input and κ_o for the output. The formula specifies the existence of a trace π'' that globally agrees with π' on the input and where the difference in the output o between π and π'' is bounded by κ_o, unless the difference in the input i between π and π'' was greater than κ_i. Robust cleanness, thus, forbids unexpected jumps in the system behavior that are, for example, due to software doping, while allowing for behavioral differences due to nondeterminism.

With quantifier alternation, the model checking problem becomes much more difficult. Model checking HyperLTL formulas of the form $\forall^*\exists^*\varphi$, where φ is a quantifier-free formula, is PSPACE-complete in the size of the system and EXPSPACE-complete in the formula. The only known model checking algorithm replaces the existential quantifier with the negation of a universal quantifier over the negated subformula; but this requires a complementation of the system behavior, which is completely impractical for realistic systems.

In this paper, we present an alternative approach to the verification of hyperliveness properties. We view the model checking problem of a formula of the form $\forall\pi.\exists\pi'.\ \varphi$ as a game between the $\forall$-player and the $\exists$-player. While the $\forall$-player moves through the state space of the system building trace π, the $\exists$-player must match each move in a separate traversal of the state space resulting in a trace π' such that the pair π, π' satisfies φ. Clearly, the existence of a winning strategy for the $\exists$-player implies that $\forall\pi.\exists\pi'.\ \varphi$ is satisfied. The converse is not necessarily true: Even if there always is a trace π' that matches the universally chosen trace π, the $\exists$-player may not be able to construct this trace, because she only knows about the choices made by the $\forall$-player in the finite prefix of π that has occurred so far, and not the choices that will be made by the $\forall$-player in the infinite future. We address this problem by introducing *prophecy variables* into the system. Without changing the behavior of the system, the prophecy variables give the $\exists$-player the information about the future that is needed to make the right choice after seeing only the finite prefix. Such prophecy variables can be provided manually by the user of the model checker to provide a lookahead on future moves of the $\forall$-player.

This game-theoretic approach provides an opportunity for the user to reduce the complexity of the model checking problem: If the user provides a strategy for the $\exists$-player, then the problem reduces to the cheaper model checking problem for universal properties. We show that such strategies can also be constructed automatically using synthesis. Beyond model checking, the game-theoretic approach also provides a method for the synthesis of systems that satisfy a conjunction of hypersafety and hyperliveness properties. Here, we do not only synthesize the strategy, but also construct the system itself, i.e., the game graph on which the model checking game is played. While the synthesis from $\forall^*\exists^*$ hyperproperties is known to be undecidable in general, we show that the game-theoretic approach can naturally be integrated into bounded synthesis, which checks for the existence of a correct system up to a bound on the number of states.

Related Work. While the verification of general HyperLTL formulas has been studied before [6,17,18], there has been, so far, no practical model checking algorithm for HyperLTL formulas with quantifier alternation. The existing algorithm involves a complementation of the system automaton, which results in an exponential blow-up of the state space [18]. The only existing model checker for HyperLTL, MCHYPER [18], was therefore, so far, limited to the alternation-free fragment. Although some hyperliveness properties lie in this fragment, quantifier alternation is needed to express general hyperliveness properties like GNI. In this paper, we present a technique to model check these hyperliveness properties and extend MCHYPER to formulas with quantifier alternation.

· The situation is similar in the area of reactive synthesis. There is a synthesis algorithm that automatically constructs implementations from HyperLTL specifications [13] using the bounded synthesis approach [20]. This algorithm is, however, also only applicable to the alternation-free fragment of HyperLTL. In this paper, we extend the bounded synthesis approach to HyperLTL formulas with quantifier alternation. Beyond the model checking and synthesis problems, the satisfiability [11,12,14] and monitoring [15,16,22] problems of HyperLTL have also been studied in the past.

For certain information-flow security policies, there are verification techniques that use methods related to our model checking and synthesis algorithms. Specifically, the self-composition technique [2,3], a construction based on the product of copies of a system, has been tailored for various trace-based security definitions [10,23,28]. Unlike our algorithms, these techniques focus on specific information-flow policies, not on a general logic like HyperLTL.

The use of prophecy variables [1] to make information about the future accessible is a known technique in the verification of trace properties. It is, for example, used to establish simulation relations between automata [26] or in the verification of CTL* properties [8].

In our game-theoretic view on the model checking problem for $\forall^*\exists^*$ hyperproperties the $\exists$-player has an infinite lookahead. There is some work on *finite* lookahead on trace languages [24]. We use the idea of finite lookahead as an approximation to construct existential strategies and give a novel synthesis construction for strategies with delay based on bounded synthesis [20].

2 Preliminaries

For tuples $x \in X^n$ and $y \in X^m$ over set X, we use $x \cdot y \in X^{n+m}$ to denote the concatenation of x and y. Given a function $f \colon X \to Y$ and a tuple $x \in X^n$, we define by $f \circ x \in Y^n$ the tuple $(f(x[1]), \ldots, f(x[n]))$. Let AP be a finite set of atomic propositions and let $\Sigma = 2^{\mathrm{AP}}$ be the corresponding alphabet. A *trace* $t \in \Sigma^\omega$ is an infinite sequence of elements of Σ. We denote a set of traces by $Tr \subseteq \Sigma^\omega$. We define $t[i, \infty]$ to be the suffix of t starting at position $i \geq 0$.

HyperLTL. HyperLTL [6] is a temporal logic for specifying hyperproperties. It extends LTL by quantification over trace variables π and a method to link atomic propositions to specific traces. Let $\mathcal{V}$ be an infinite set of trace variables. Formulas in HyperLTL are given by the grammar

$$\varphi ::= \forall \pi. \varphi \mid \exists \pi. \varphi \mid \psi \ , \text{ and}$$
$$\psi ::= a_\pi \mid \neg \psi \mid \psi \vee \psi \mid \bigcirc \psi \mid \psi \mathcal{U} \psi \ ,$$

where $a \in \text{AP}$ and $\pi \in \mathcal{V}$. We allow the standard boolean connectives $\wedge$, $\rightarrow$, $\leftrightarrow$ as well as the derived LTL operators release $\varphi \, \mathcal{R} \, \psi \equiv \neg(\neg\varphi \, \mathcal{U} \, \neg\psi)$, eventually $\Diamond \varphi \equiv \text{true} \, \mathcal{U} \, \varphi$, globally $\Box \varphi \equiv \neg \Diamond \neg \varphi$, and weak until $\varphi \, \mathcal{W} \, \psi \equiv \Box \varphi \vee (\varphi \, \mathcal{U} \, \psi)$.

We call a $\mathcal{Q}^+ \mathcal{Q}'^+ \varphi$ HyperLTL formula (for $\mathcal{Q}, \mathcal{Q}' \in \{\forall, \exists\}$ and quantifier-free formula φ) *alternation-free* iff $\mathcal{Q} = \mathcal{Q}'$. Further, we say that $\mathcal{Q}^+ \mathcal{Q}'^+ \varphi$ has *one quantifier alternation* (or lies in the *one-alternation fragment*) iff $\mathcal{Q} \neq \mathcal{Q}'$.

The semantics of HyperLTL is given by the satisfaction relation $\models_{Tr}$ over a set of traces $Tr \subseteq \Sigma^\omega$. We define an assignment $\Pi : \mathcal{V} \rightarrow \Sigma^\omega$ that maps trace variables to traces. $\Pi[\pi \mapsto t]$ updates Π by assigning variable π to trace t.

$$
\begin{aligned}
&\Pi, i \models_{Tr} a_\pi && \text{iff} && a \in \Pi(\pi)[i] \\
&\Pi, i \models_{Tr} \neg\varphi && \text{iff} && \Pi, i \not\models_{Tr} \varphi \\
&\Pi, i \models_{Tr} \varphi \vee \psi && \text{iff} && \Pi, i \models_{Tr} \varphi \text{ or } \Pi, i \models_{Tr} \psi \\
&\Pi, i \models_{Tr} \bigcirc \varphi && \text{iff} && \Pi, i+1 \models_{Tr} \varphi \\
&\Pi, i \models_{Tr} \varphi \, \mathcal{U} \, \psi && \text{iff} && \exists j \geq i. \, \Pi, j \models_{Tr} \psi \wedge \forall i \leq k < j. \, \Pi, k \models_{Tr} \varphi \\
&\Pi, i \models_{Tr} \exists \pi. \varphi && \text{iff} && \text{there is some } t \in Tr \text{ such that } \Pi[\pi \mapsto t], i \models_{Tr} \varphi \\
&\Pi, i \models_{Tr} \forall \pi. \varphi && \text{iff} && \text{for all } t \in Tr \text{ it holds that } \Pi[\pi \mapsto t], i \models_{Tr} \varphi
\end{aligned}
$$

We write $Tr \models \varphi$ for $\{\}, 0 \models_{Tr} \varphi$ where $\{\}$ denotes the empty assignment.

Every hyperproperty is an intersection of a hypersafety and a hyperliveness property [7]. A *hypersafety* property is one where there is a finite set of finite traces that is a bad prefix, i.e., that cannot be extended into a set of traces that satisfies the hypersafety property. A *hyperliveness* property is a property where every finite set of finite traces can be extended to a possibly infinite set of infinite traces such that the resulting trace set satisfies the hyperliveness property.

Transition Systems. We use transition systems as a model of computation for reactive systems. Transition systems consume sequences over an input alphabet by transforming their internal state in every step. Let I and O be a finite set of input and output propositions, respectively, and let $\Upsilon = 2^I$ and $\Gamma = 2^O$ be the corresponding finite alphabets. A Γ-labeled Υ-*transition system* $\mathcal{S}$ is a tuple $\langle S, s_0, \tau, l \rangle$, where S is a finite set of states, $s_0 \in S$ is the designated initial state, $\tau : S \times \Upsilon \rightarrow S$ is the transition function, and $l : S \rightarrow \Gamma$ is the state-labeling function. We write $s \xrightarrow{\upsilon} s'$ or $(s, \upsilon, s') \in \tau$ if $\tau(s, \upsilon) = s'$. We generalize the transition function to sequences over Υ by defining $\tau^* : \Upsilon^* \rightarrow S$ recursively as $\tau^*(\epsilon) = s_0$ and $\tau^*(\upsilon_0 \cdots \upsilon_{n-1} \upsilon_n) = \tau(\tau^*(\upsilon_0 \cdots \upsilon_{n-1}), \upsilon_n)$ for $\upsilon_0 \cdots \upsilon_{n-1} \upsilon_n \in \Upsilon^+$. Given an infinite word $\upsilon = \upsilon_0 \upsilon_1 \ldots \in \Upsilon^\omega$, the transition system produces an infinite sequence of outputs $\gamma = \gamma_0 \gamma_1 \gamma_2 \ldots \in \Gamma^\omega$, such that $\gamma_i = l(\tau^*(\upsilon_0 \ldots \upsilon_{i-1}))$ for every $i \geq 0$. The resulting *trace* ρ is $(\upsilon_0 \cup \gamma_0)(\upsilon_1 \cup \gamma_1) \ldots \in \Sigma^\omega$ where we have $\text{AP} = I \cup O$. The set of traces generated by $\mathcal{S}$ is denoted by $traces(\mathcal{S})$. Furthermore, we define $\varepsilon = \langle \{s\}, s, \tau_\varepsilon, l_\varepsilon \rangle$ as the transition system over $I = O = \emptyset$ that has only a single trace, that is $traces(\varepsilon) = \{\emptyset^\omega\}$. For this transition system, $\tau_\varepsilon(s, \emptyset) = s$ and $l_\varepsilon(s) = \emptyset$. Given two transition systems $\mathcal{S} = \langle S, s_0, \tau, l \rangle$ and $\mathcal{S}' = \langle S', s_0', \tau', l' \rangle$, we define $\mathcal{S} \times \mathcal{S}' = \langle S \times S', (s_0, s_0'), \tau'', l'' \rangle$ as the Γ^2-labeled Υ^2-transition system where $\tau''((s, s'), (\upsilon, \upsilon')) = (\tau(s, \upsilon), \tau'(s', \upsilon'))$ and $l''((s, s')) = (l(s), l'(s'))$. A transition system $\mathcal{S}$ satisfies a general HyperLTL formula φ, if, and only if, $traces(\mathcal{S}) \models \varphi$.

Automata. An alternating parity automaton $\mathcal{A}$ over a finite alphabet Σ is a tuple $\langle Q, q_0, \delta, \alpha \rangle$, where Q is a finite set of states, $q_0 \in Q$ is the designated initial state, $\delta \colon Q \times \Sigma \to \mathbb{B}^+(Q)$ is the transition function, and $\alpha \colon Q \to C$ is a function that maps states of $\mathcal{A}$ to a finite set of colors $C \subset \mathbb{N}$. For $C = \{0, 1\}$ and $C = \{1, 2\}$, we call $\mathcal{A}$ a co-Büchi and Büchi automaton, respectively, and we use the sets $F \subseteq Q$ and $B \subseteq Q$ to represent the rejecting ($C = 1$) and accepting ($C = 2$) states in the respective automaton (as a replacement of the coloring function α). A safety automaton is a Büchi automaton where every state is accepting. The transition function δ maps a state $q \in Q$ and some $a \in \Sigma$ to a positive Boolean combination of successor states $\delta(q, a)$. An automaton is *non-deterministic* or *universal* if δ is purely disjunctive or conjunctive, respectively.

A run of an alternating automaton is a Q-labeled tree. A tree T is a subset of $\mathbb{N}_{>0}^*$ such that for every node $n \in \mathbb{N}_{>0}^*$ and every positive integer $i \in \mathbb{N}_{>0}$, if $n \cdot i \in T$ then (i) $n \in T$ (i.e., T is prefix-closed), and (ii) for every $0 < j < i$, $n \cdot j \in T$. The root of T is the empty sequence ϵ and for a node $n \in T$, $|n|$ is the length of the sequence n, in other words, its distance from the root. A run of $\mathcal{A}$ on an infinite word $\rho \in \Sigma^\omega$ is a Q-labeled tree (T, r) such that $r(\epsilon) = q_0$ and for every node $n \in T$ with children $n_1, \ldots, n_k$ the following holds: $1 \le k \le |Q|$ and $\{r(n_1), \ldots, r(n_k)\} \models \delta(q, \rho[i])$, where $q = r(n)$ and $i = |n|$. A path is accepting if the highest color appearing infinitely often is even. A run is accepting if all its paths are accepting. The language of $\mathcal{A}$, written $\mathcal{L}(\mathcal{A})$, is the set $\{\rho \in \Sigma^\omega \mid \mathcal{A} \text{ accepts } \rho\}$. A transition system $\mathcal{S}$ is accepted by an automaton $\mathcal{A}$, written $\mathcal{S} \models \mathcal{A}$, if $traces(\mathcal{S}) \subseteq \mathcal{L}(\mathcal{A})$.

Strategies. Given two disjoint finite alphabets Υ and Γ, a strategy $\sigma \colon \Upsilon^* \to \Gamma$ is a mapping from finite histories of Υ to Γ. A transition system $\mathcal{S} = \langle S, s_0, \tau, l \rangle$ *generates* the strategy σ if $\sigma(v) = l(\tau^*(v))$ for every $v \in \Upsilon^*$. A strategy σ is called *finite-state* if there exists a transition system that generates σ.

In the following, we use finite-state strategies to modify the inputs of transition systems. Let $\mathcal{S} = \langle S, s_0, \tau, l \rangle$ be a transition system over input and output alphabets Υ and Γ and let $\sigma \colon (\Upsilon')^* \to \Upsilon$ be a finite-state strategy. Let $\mathcal{S}' = \langle S', s_0', \tau', l' \rangle$ be the transition system implementing σ, then $\mathcal{S} \parallel \sigma = \mathcal{S} \parallel \mathcal{S}'$ is the transition system $\langle S \times S', (s_0, s_0'), \tau^{\parallel}, l^{\parallel} \rangle$ where $\tau^{\parallel} \colon (S \times S') \times \Upsilon' \to (S \times S')$ is defined as $\tau^{\parallel}((s, s'), v') = (\tau(s, l'(s')), \tau'(s', v'))$ and $l^{\parallel} \colon (S \times S') \to \Gamma$ is defined as $l^{\parallel}(s, s') = l(s)$ for every $s \in S$, $s' \in S'$, and $v' \in \Upsilon'$.

Model Checking HyperLTL. We recap the model checking of universal Hyper-LTL formulas. This case, as well as the dual case of only existential quantifiers, is well-understood and, in fact, efficiently implemented in the model checker MCHYPER [18]. The principle behind the model checking approach is *self-composition*, where we check a standard trace property on a composition of an appropriate number of copies of the given system.

Let *zip* denote the function that maps an n-tuple of sequences to a single sequence of n-tuples, for example, $zip([1, 2, 3], [4, 5, 6]) = [(1, 4), (2, 5), (3, 6)]$, and let *unzip* denote its inverse. Given $\mathcal{S} = \langle S, s_0, \tau, l \rangle$, the n-fold self-composition of $\mathcal{S}$ is the transition system $\mathcal{S}^n = \langle S^n, s_0', \tau_n, l_n \rangle$, where $s_0' := (s_0, \ldots, s_0) \in S^n$, $\tau_n(s, v) := \tau \circ zip(s, v)$ and $l_n(s) := l \circ s$ for every $s \in S^n$ and $v \in \Upsilon^n$. If $traces(\mathcal{S})$

is the set of traces generated by $\mathcal{S}$, then $\{ zip(\rho_1, \ldots, \rho_n) \mid \rho_1, \ldots, \rho_n \in traces(\mathcal{S}) \}$ is the set of traces generated by $\mathcal{S}^n$. We use the notation $zip(\varphi, \pi_1, \pi_2, \ldots, \pi_n)$ for some HyperLTL formula φ to combine the trace variables $\pi_1, \pi_2, \ldots, \pi_n$ (occurring free in φ) into a fresh trace variable π^*.

Theorem 1 (Self-composition for universal HyperLTL formulas [18]). *For a transition system $\mathcal{S}$ and a HyperLTL formula of the form $\forall \pi_1. \forall \pi_2. \ldots \forall \pi_n.\ \varphi$ it holds that $\mathcal{S} \vDash \forall \pi_1. \forall \pi_2. \ldots \forall \pi_n.\ \varphi$ iff $\mathcal{S}^n \vDash \forall \pi^*. zip(\varphi, \pi_1, \pi_2, \ldots, \pi_n)$.*

Theorem 2 (Complexity of model checking universal formulas [18]). *The model checking problem for universal HyperLTL formulas is PSPACE-complete in the size of the formula and NLOGSPACE-complete in the size of the transition system.*

The complexity of verifying universal HyperLTL formulas is exactly the same as the complexity of verifying LTL formulas. For HyperLTL formulas with quantifier alternations, the model checking problem is significantly more difficult.

Theorem 3 (Complexity of model checking formulas with one quantifier alternation [18]). *The model checking problem for HyperLTL formulas with one quantifier alternation is in EXPSPACE in the size of the formula and in PSPACE in the size of the transition system.*

One way to circumvent this complexity is to fix the existential choice and strengthen the formula to the universal fragment [9, 13, 18]. While avoiding the complexity problem, this transformation requires deep knowledge of the system, is prone to errors, and cannot be verified automatically as the problem of checking implications becomes undecidable [11]. In the following section, we present a technique that circumvents the complexity problem while still inheriting strong correctness guarantees. Further, we provide a method that can, under certain restrictions, derive a strategy for the existential choice automatically.

3   Model Checking with Quantifier Alternations

3.1   Model Checking with Given Strategies

Our first goal is the verification of HyperLTL formulas with one quantifier alternation, i.e., formulas of the form $\forall^* \exists^* \varphi$ or $\exists^* \forall^* \varphi$, where φ is a quantifier-free formula. Note that the presented techniques can, similar to skolemization, be extended to more than one quantifier alternation. Quantifier alternation introduces dependencies between the quantified traces. In a $\forall^* \exists^* \varphi$ formula, the choices of the existential quantifiers depend on the choices of the universal quantifiers preceding them. In a formula of the form $\exists^* \forall^* \varphi$, however, there has to be a single choice for the existential quantifiers that works for all choices of the universal quantifiers. In this case, the existentially quantified variables do not depend on the universally quantified variables. Hence, the witnesses for the existential quantifiers are traces rather than functions that map tuples of traces to traces. As established above, the model checking problem for HyperLTL formulas with quantifier alternation is known to be significantly more difficult than the model checking problem for universal formulas.

Our verification technique for formulas with quantifier alternation is to substitute strategic choice for existential choice. As discussed in the introduction, the existence of a strategy implies the existence of a trace.

Theorem 4 (Substituting Strategic Choice for Existential Choice). *Let $\mathcal{S}$ be a transition system over input alphabet Υ.*
It holds that $\mathcal{S} \vDash \forall \pi_1 \forall \pi_2 \ldots \forall \pi_n. \exists \pi'_1 \exists \pi'_2 \ldots \exists \pi'_m. \varphi$ if there is a strategy $\sigma : (\Upsilon^n)^* \to \Upsilon^m$ such that $\mathcal{S}^n \times (\mathcal{S}^m \parallel \sigma) \vDash \forall \pi^*. zip(\varphi, \pi_1, \pi_2, \ldots \pi_n, \pi'_1, \pi'_2, \ldots, \pi'_m).$
It holds that $\mathcal{S} \vDash \exists \pi_1 \exists \pi_2 \ldots \exists \pi_m. \forall \pi'_1 \forall \pi'_2 \ldots \forall \pi'_n. \varphi$ if there is a strategy $\sigma : (\Upsilon^0)^* \to \Upsilon^m$ such that $(\mathcal{S}^m \parallel \sigma) \times \mathcal{S}^n \vDash \forall \pi^*. zip(\varphi, \pi_1, \pi_2, \ldots \pi_m, \pi'_1, \pi'_2, \ldots, \pi'_n).$

Proof. Let σ be such a strategy, then we define a witness for the existential trace quantifiers $\exists \pi'_1 \exists \pi'_2 \ldots \exists \pi'_m$ as the sequence of inputs $\upsilon = \upsilon_0 \upsilon_1 \ldots \in (\Upsilon^m)^\omega$ such that $\upsilon_i = \sigma(\upsilon'_0 \upsilon'_1 \ldots \upsilon'_{i-1})$ for every $i \geq 0$ and every $\upsilon'_i \in \Upsilon^n$; analogously, we define a witness for the existential trace quantifiers $\exists \pi_1 \exists \pi_2 \ldots \exists \pi_m$ as the sequence of inputs $\upsilon = \upsilon_0 \upsilon_1 \ldots \in (\Upsilon^m)^\omega$ such that $\upsilon_i = \sigma(\upsilon'_0 \upsilon'_1 \ldots \upsilon'_{i-1})$ for every $i \geq 0$ and every $\upsilon'_i \in \Upsilon^0$. □

An application of the theorem reduces the verification problem of a HyperLTL formula with one quantifier alternation to the verification problem of a universal HyperLTL formula. If a sufficiently small strategy can be found, the reduction in complexity is substantial:

Corollary 1 (Model checking with Given Strategies). *The model checking problem for HyperLTL formulas with one quantifier alternation and given strategies for the existential quantifiers is in PSPACE in the size of the formula and NLOGSPACE in the size of the product of the strategy and the system.*

Note that the converse of Theorem 4 is not in general true. The satisfaction of a $\forall^* \exists^*$ HyperLTL formula does not imply the existence of a strategy, because at any given point in time the strategy only knows about a finite prefix of the universally quantified traces. Consider the formula $\forall \pi \exists \pi'. \bigcirc a_\pi \leftrightarrow a_{\pi'}$ and a system that can produce arbitrary sequences of a and $\neg a$. Although the system satisfies the formula, it is not possible to give a strategy that allows us to prove this fact. Whatever choice our strategy makes, the next move of the $\forall$-player can make sure that the strategy's choice was wrong. In the following, we present a method that addresses this problem.

Prophecy Variables. A classic technique for resolving future dependencies is the introduction of *prophecy variables* [1]. Prophecy variables are auxiliary variables that are added to the system without affecting the behavior of the system. Such variables can be used to make predictions about the future.

We use prophecy variables to define strategies that depend on the future. In the example discussed above, $\forall \pi \exists \pi'. \bigcirc a_\pi \leftrightarrow a_{\pi'}$, the choice of the value of $a_{\pi'}$ in the first position depends on the value of a_π in the second position. We introduce a prophecy variable p that predicts in the first position whether a_π is true in the second position. With the prophecy variable, there exists a strategy that correctly assigns the value of p whenever the prediction is correct: The strategy chooses to set $a_{\pi'}$ if, and only if, p holds.

Technically, the proof technique introduces a set of fresh input variables P into the system. For a Γ-labeled Υ-transition system $\mathcal{S} = \langle S, s_0, \tau, l \rangle$, we define the Γ-labeled $(\Upsilon \cup P)$-transition system $\mathcal{S}^P = \langle S, s_0, \tau^P, l \rangle$ including the inputs P where $\tau^P \colon S \times (\Upsilon \cup P) \to S$. For all $s \in S$ and $v^P \in \Upsilon \cup P$, $\tau^P(s, v^P) = \tau(s, v)$ for $v \in \Upsilon$ obtained by removing the variables in P from v^P (i.e., $v =_{\backslash P} v^P$). Moreover, the proof technique modifies the specification so that the original property only needs to be satisfied if the prediction is actually correct. We obtain the modified specification $\forall \pi \exists \pi'.(p_\pi \leftrightarrow \bigcirc a_\pi) \to (\bigcirc a_\pi \leftrightarrow a_{\pi'})$ in our example. The following theorem describes the general technique for one prophecy variable.

Theorem 5 (Model checking with Prophecy Variables). *For a transition system $\mathcal{S}$ and a quantifier-free formula φ, let ψ be a quantifier-free formula over the universally quantified trace variables $\pi_1, \pi_2 \ldots \pi_n$ and let p be a fresh atomic proposition. It holds that $\mathcal{S} \models \forall \pi_1 \forall \pi_2 \ldots \forall \pi_n. \exists \pi_1' \exists \pi_2' \ldots \exists \pi_m'. \varphi$ if, and only if, $\mathcal{S}^{\{p\}} \models \forall \pi_1 \forall \pi_2 \ldots \forall \pi_n. \exists \pi_1' \exists \pi_2' \ldots \exists \pi_m'.\Box(p_{\pi_1} \leftrightarrow \psi) \to \varphi$.*

Note that ψ is restricted to refer only to *universally* quantified trace variables. Without this restriction, the method would not be sound. In our example, $\psi = a_{\pi'}$ would lead to the modified formula $\forall \pi \exists \pi'.(p_\pi \leftrightarrow a_{\pi'}) \to (\bigcirc a_\pi \leftrightarrow a_{\pi'})$, which could be satisfied with the strategy that assigns $a_{\pi'}$ to *true* iff p_π is *false*, and thus falsifies the assumption that the prediction is correct, rather than ensuring that the original formula is true.

Proof. It is easy to see that the original specification implies the modified specification, since the original formula is the conclusion of the implication. Assume that the modified specification holds. Since the prophecy variable p is a fresh atomic proposition, and ψ does not refer to the existentially chosen traces, we can, for every choice of the universally quantified traces, always choose the value of p such that it guesses correctly, i.e., that p is true whenever ψ holds. In this case, the conclusion and therefore the original specification must be true. $\Box$

Unfortunately, prophecy variables do not provide a complete proof technique. Consider a system allowing arbitrary sequences of a and b and this specification:

$$\forall \pi \exists \pi'. b_{\pi'} \wedge \Box(b_{\pi'} \leftrightarrow \bigcirc \neg b_{\pi'})$$
$$\wedge (a_{\pi'} \to (a_\pi \, \mathcal{W} \, (b_{\pi'} \wedge \neg a_\pi)))$$
$$\wedge (\neg a_{\pi'} \to (a_\pi \, \mathcal{W} \, (\neg b_{\pi'} \wedge \neg a_\pi)))$$

Intuitively, π' has to be able to predict whether π will stop outputting a at an even or odd position of the trace. There is no HyperLTL formula to be used as ψ in Theorem 5, because, like LTL, HyperLTL can only express non-counting properties. It is worth noting that in our practical experiments, the incompleteness was never a problem. In many cases, it is not even necessary to add prophecy variables at all. The presented proof technique is, thus, practically useful despite this incompleteness result.

3.2 Model Checking with Synthesized Strategies

We now extend the model checking approach with the automatic synthesis of the strategies for the existential quantifiers. For a given HyperLTL formula of the form $\forall^n \exists^m \varphi$ and a transition system $\mathcal{S}$, we search for a transition system $\mathcal{S}_\exists = \langle X, x_0, \mu, l_\exists \rangle$, where X is a set of states, $x_0 \in X$ is the designated initial state, $\mu \colon X \times \Upsilon^n \to X$ is the transition function, and $l_\exists \colon X \to \Upsilon^m$ is the labeling function, such that $\mathcal{S}^n \times (\mathcal{S}^m \parallel \mathcal{S}_\exists) \models zip(\varphi)$. (Since for formulas of the form $\exists^m \forall^n \varphi$ the problem only differs in the input of $\mathcal{S}_\exists$, we focus on $\forall \exists$ HyperLTL.)

Theorem 6. *The strategy realizability problem for $\forall^* \exists^*$ formulas is* 2ExpTime-*complete.*

Proof (Sketch). We reduce the strategy synthesis problem to the problem of synthesizing a distributed reactive system with a single black-box process. This problem is decidable [19] and can be solved in 2ExpTime. The lower bound follows from the LTL realizability problem [30]. □

The decidability result implies that there is an upper bound on the size of $\mathcal{S}_\exists$ that is doubly exponential in φ. Thus, the bounded synthesis approach [20] can be used to search for increasingly larger implementations, until a solution is found or the maximal bound is reached, yielding an efficient decision procedure for the strategy synthesis problem. In the following, we describe this approach in detail.

Bounded Synthesis of Strategies. We transform the synthesis problem into an SMT constraint satisfaction problem, where we leave the representation of strategies uninterpreted and challenge the solver to provide an interpretation. Given a HyperLTL formula $\forall^n \exists^m \varphi$ where φ is quantifier-free, the model checking is based on the product of the n-fold self composition of the transition system $\mathcal{S}$, the m-fold self-composition of $\mathcal{S}$ where the strategy $\mathcal{S}_\exists$ controls the inputs, and the universal co-Büchi automaton $\mathcal{A}_\varphi$ representing the language $\mathcal{L}(\varphi)$ of φ.

For a quantifier-free HyperLTL formula φ, we construct the universal co-Büchi automaton $\mathcal{A}_\varphi$ such that $\mathcal{L}(\mathcal{A}_\varphi)$ is the set of words w such that $unzip(w) \models \varphi$, i.e., the tuple of traces satisfies φ. We get this automaton by dualizing the non-deterministic Büchi automaton for $\neg \psi$ [6], i.e., changing the branching from non-deterministic to universal and the acceptance condition from Büchi to co-Büchi. Hence, $\mathcal{S}$ satisfies a universal HyperLTL formula $\forall \pi_1 \ldots \forall \pi_n. \varphi$ if the traces generated by the self-composition $\mathcal{S}^n$ are a subset of $\mathcal{L}(\mathcal{A}_\varphi)$.

In more detail, the algorithm searches for a transition system $\mathcal{S}_\exists = \langle X, x_0, \mu, l_\exists \rangle$ such that the run graph of $\mathcal{S}^n$, $\mathcal{S}^m \parallel \mathcal{S}_\exists$, and $\mathcal{A}_\varphi$, written $\mathcal{S}^n \times (\mathcal{S}^m \parallel \mathcal{S}_\exists) \times \mathcal{A}_\varphi$, is accepting. Formally, given a Γ-labeled Υ-transition system $\mathcal{S} = \langle S, s_0, \tau, l \rangle$ and a universal co-Büchi automaton $\mathcal{A}_\varphi = \langle Q, q_0, \delta, F \rangle$, where $\delta \colon Q \times \Upsilon^{n+m} \times \Gamma^{n+m} \to 2^Q$, the run graph $\mathcal{S}^n \times (\mathcal{S}^m \parallel \mathcal{S}_\exists) \times \mathcal{A}_\varphi$ is the directed graph (V, E), with the set of vertices $V = S^n \times S^m \times X \times Q$, initial vertex $v_{init} = ((s_0, \ldots, s_0), (s_0, \ldots, s_0), x_0, q_0)$ and the edge relation $E \subseteq V \times V$ satisfying $((\boldsymbol{s_n}, \boldsymbol{s_m}, x, q), (\boldsymbol{s_n'}, \boldsymbol{s_m'}, x', q')) \in E$ if, and only if

$$\exists \boldsymbol{v} \in \Upsilon^n. \; \left(\boldsymbol{s_n} \xrightarrow[\tau_n]{v} \boldsymbol{s_n'} \right) \wedge \left(\boldsymbol{s_m} \xrightarrow[\tau_m]{l_\exists(x)} \boldsymbol{s_m'} \right) \wedge \left(x \xrightarrow[\mu]{v} x' \right)$$

$$\wedge \; q' \in \delta(q, \boldsymbol{v} \cdot l_\exists(x), l_n(\boldsymbol{s_n}) \cdot l_m(\boldsymbol{s_m})).$$

Theorem 7. *Given $\mathcal{S}$, $\mathcal{S}_\exists$, and a HyperLTL formula $\forall^n \exists^m \varphi$ where φ is quantifier-free. Let $\mathcal{A}_\varphi$ be the universal co-Büchi automaton for φ. If the run graph $\mathcal{S}^n \times (\mathcal{S}^m \parallel \mathcal{S}_\exists) \times \mathcal{A}_\varphi$ is accepting, then $\mathcal{S} \vDash \forall^n \exists^m \varphi$.*

Proof. Follows from Theorem 4 and the fact that $\mathcal{A}_\varphi$ represents $\mathcal{L}(\varphi)$. $\qquad\square$

The acceptance of a run graph is witnessed by an annotation $\lambda \colon V \to \mathbb{N} \cup \{\bot\}$ which is a function mapping every reachable vertex $v \in V$ in the run graph to a natural number $\lambda(v)$, i.e., $\lambda(v) \neq \bot$. Intuitively, $\lambda(v)$ returns the number of visits to rejecting states on any path from the initial vertex v_{init} to v. If we can bound this number for every reachable vertex, the annotation is *valid* and the run graph is accepting. Formally, an annotation λ is valid, if (1) the initial state is reachable ($\lambda(v_{init}) \neq \bot$) and (2) for every $(v, v') \in E$ with $\lambda(v) \neq \bot$ it holds that $\lambda(v') \neq \bot$ and $\lambda(v) \rhd \lambda(v')$ where $\rhd$ is $>$ if v' is rejecting and $\geq$ otherwise. Such an annotation exists if, and only if, the run graph is accepting [20].

We encode the search for $\mathcal{S}_\exists$ and the annotation λ as an SMT constraint system. Therefore, we use uninterpreted function symbols to encode $\mathcal{S}_\exists$ and λ. A transition system $\mathcal{S}$ is represented in the constraint system by two functions, the transition function $\tau \colon S \times \Upsilon \to S$ and the labeling function $l \colon S \to \Gamma$. The annotation is split into two parts, a reachability constraint $\lambda^{\mathbb{B}} \colon V \to \mathbb{B}$ indicating whether a state in the run graph is reachable and a counter $\lambda^{\#} \colon V \to \mathbb{N}$ that maps every reachable vertex v to the maximal number of rejecting states $\lambda^{\#}(v)$ visited by any path from the initial vertex to v. The resulting constraint asserts that there is a transition system $\mathcal{S}_\exists$ with an accepting run graph. Note, that the functions representing the system $\mathcal{S}$ ($\tau \colon S \times \Upsilon \to S$ and $l \colon S \to \Gamma$) are given, that is, they are interpreted.

$$\exists \lambda^{\mathbb{B}} \colon S^n \times S^m \times X \times Q \to \mathbb{B}. \, \exists \lambda^{\mathbb{N}} \colon S^n \times S^m \times X \times Q \to \mathbb{N}.$$

$$\exists \mu \colon X \times \Upsilon^n \to X. \, \exists l_\exists \colon X \to \Upsilon^m$$

$$\forall \boldsymbol{v} \in \Upsilon^n. \, \forall \boldsymbol{s_n}, \boldsymbol{s_n'} \in S^n. \, \forall \boldsymbol{s_m}, \boldsymbol{s_m'} \in S^m. \, \forall q, q' \in Q. \, \forall x, x' \in X.$$

$$\lambda^{\mathbb{B}}((s_0, \ldots, s_0), (s_0, \ldots, s_0), x_0, q_0) \wedge$$

$$\left(\lambda^{\mathbb{B}}(\boldsymbol{s_n}, \boldsymbol{s_m}, x, q) \wedge q' \in \delta(q, (\boldsymbol{v} \cdot l_\exists(x)), (l \circ (\boldsymbol{s_n} \cdot \boldsymbol{s_m}))) \wedge x' = \mu(x, \boldsymbol{v}) \right.$$

$$\left. \wedge \; \boldsymbol{s_n'} = \tau_n(\boldsymbol{s_n}, \boldsymbol{v}) \wedge \boldsymbol{s_m'} = \tau_m(\boldsymbol{s_m}, l_\exists(x)) \right)$$

$$\Rightarrow \lambda^{\mathbb{B}}(\boldsymbol{s_n'}, \boldsymbol{s_m'}, x', q') \wedge \lambda^{\mathbb{N}}(\boldsymbol{s_n}, \boldsymbol{s_m}, x, q) \rhd \lambda^{\mathbb{N}}(\boldsymbol{s_n'}, \boldsymbol{s_m'}, x', q')$$

where $\trianglerighteq$ is $>$ if $q' \in F$ and $\geq$ otherwise. The *bounded synthesis algorithm* increases the bound of the strategy $\mathcal{S}_\exists$ until either the constraints system becomes satisfiable, or a given upper bound is reached. In the case the constraint system is satisfiable, we can extract interpretations for the functions μ and $l_\exists$ using a solver that is able to produce models. These functions then represent the synthesized transition system $\mathcal{S}_\exists$.

Corollary 2. *Given $\mathcal{S}$ and a HyperLTL formula $\forall^*\exists^*\varphi$ where φ is quantifier-free. If the constraint system is satisfiable for some bound on the size of $\mathcal{S}_\exists$ then $\mathcal{S} \models \forall^*\exists^*\varphi$.*

Proof. Follows immediately by Theorem 7. $\qquad\qquad\qquad\qquad\qquad\qquad$ $\square$

As the decision problem is decidable, we know that there is an upper bound on the size of a realizing $\mathcal{S}_\exists$ and, thus, the bounded synthesis approach is a decision procedure for the strategy realizability problem.

Corollary 3. *The bounded synthesis algorithm decides the strategy realizability problem for $\forall^*\exists^*$ HyperLTL.*

Proof. The existence of such an upper bound follows from Theorem 6. $\qquad$ $\square$

Approximating Prophecy. We introduce a new parameter to the strategy synthesis problem to approximate the information about the future that can be captured using prophecy variables. This bound represents a constant *lookahead* into future choices made by the environment. In other words, for a given $k \geq 0$, the strategy $\mathcal{S}_\exists$ is allowed to depend on choices of the $\forall$-player in the next k steps. While constant lookahead is only an approximation of infinite clairvoyance, it suffices for many practical situations as shown by prior case studies [9,18].

We present a solution to synthesizing transition systems with constant lookahead for $k \geq 0$ using bounded synthesis. To simplify the presentation, we present the stand-alone problem with respect to a specification given as a universal co-Büchi automaton. The integration into the constraint system for the $\forall^*\exists^*$ HyperLTL synthesis as presented in the previous section is then straightforward. First, we present an extension to the transition system model that incorporates the notion of constant lookahead. The idea of this extension is to replace the initial state s_0 by a function $init \colon \Upsilon^k \to S$ that maps input sequences of length k to some state. Thus, the transition system observes the first k inputs, chooses some initial state based on those inputs, and then progresses with the same pace as the input sequence. Next, we define the run graph of such a system $\mathcal{S}_k = \langle S, init, \tau, l \rangle$ and an automaton $\mathcal{A} = \langle Q, q_0, \delta, F \rangle$, where $\delta \colon Q \times \Upsilon \times \Gamma \to Q$, as the directed graph (V, E) with the set of vertices $V = S \times Q \times \Upsilon^k$, the initial vertices $(s, q_0, \boldsymbol{v}) \in V$ such that $s = init(\boldsymbol{v})$ for every $\boldsymbol{v} \in \Upsilon^k$, and the edge relation $E \subseteq V \times V$ satisfying $((s, q, v_1 v_2 \cdots v_k), (s', q', v_1' v_2' \cdots v_k')) \in E$ if, and only if

$$\exists v_{k+1} \in \Upsilon. \, s \xrightarrow{v_{k+1}} s' \wedge q' \in \delta(q, v_1, l(s)) \wedge \bigwedge_{1 \leq i \leq k} v_i' = v_{i+1}.$$

Lemma 1. *Given a universal co-Büchi automaton $\mathcal{A}$ and a k-lookahead transition system $\mathcal{S}_k$. $\mathcal{S}_k \vDash \mathcal{A}$ if, and only if, the run graph $\mathcal{S}_k \times \mathcal{A}$ is accepting.*

Finally, synthesis amounts to solving the following constraint system:

$$\exists \lambda^{\mathbb{B}} \colon S \times Q \times \Upsilon^k \to \mathbb{B}. \, \exists \lambda^{\mathbb{N}} \colon S \times Q \times \Upsilon^k \to \mathbb{N}.$$

$$\exists init \colon \Upsilon^k \to S. \, \exists \tau \colon S \times \Upsilon \to S. \, \exists l \colon S \to \Gamma.$$

$$(\forall \boldsymbol{v} \in \Upsilon^k. \, \lambda^{\mathbb{B}}(init(\boldsymbol{v}), q_0, \boldsymbol{v})) \, \wedge$$

$$\forall v_1 v_2 \cdots v_{k+1} \in \Upsilon^{k+1}. \, \forall s, s' \in S. \, \forall q, q' \in Q.$$

$$\left(\lambda^{\mathbb{B}}(s, q, v_1 \cdots v_k) \wedge s' = \tau(s, v_{k+1}) \wedge q' \in \delta(q, v_1, l(s)) \right)$$

$$\Rightarrow \lambda^{\mathbb{B}}(s', q', v_2 \cdots v_{k+1}) \wedge \lambda^{\mathbb{N}}(s, q, v_1 \cdots v_k) \unrhd \lambda^{\mathbb{N}}(s', q', v_2 \cdots v_{k+1})$$

Corollary 4. *Given some $k \geq 0$, if the constraint system is satisfiable for some bound on the size of $\mathcal{S}_k$ then $\mathcal{S}_k \vDash \mathcal{A}$.*

4 Synthesis with Quantifier Alternations

We now build on the introduced techniques to solve the *synthesis* problem for HyperLTL with quantifier alternation, that is, we search for implementations that satisfy the given properties. In previous work [13], the synthesis problem for $\exists^* \forall^*$ HyperLTL was solved by a reduction to the distributed synthesis problem. We present an alternative synthesis procedure that (1) introduces the necessary concepts for the synthesis of the $\forall^* \exists^*$ fragment and that (2) strictly decomposes the choice of the existential trace quantifier from the implementation.

Fix a formula of the form $\exists^m \forall^n \varphi$. We again reduce the verification problem to the problem of determining whether a run graph is accepting. As the existential quantifiers do not depend on the universal ones, there is no future dependency and thus no need for prophecy variables or bounded lookahead. Formally, $\mathcal{S}_\exists$ is a tuple $\langle X, x_0, \mu, l_\exists \rangle$ such that X is a set of states, $x_0 \in X$ is the designated initial state, $\mu \colon X \to X$ is the transition function, and $l_\exists \colon X \to \Upsilon^m$ is the labeling function. $\mathcal{S}_\exists$ produces infinite sequences of $(\Upsilon^m)^\omega$, without having any knowledge about the behavior of the universally quantified traces. The run graph is then $(\mathcal{S}^m \, \| \, \mathcal{S}_\exists) \times \mathcal{S}^n \times \mathcal{A}_\varphi$. The constraint system is built analogously to Sect. 3.2, with the difference that the representation of the system $\mathcal{S}$ is now also uninterpreted. In the resulting SMT constraint system, we have two bounds, one for the size of the implementation $\mathcal{S}$ and one for the size of $\mathcal{S}_\exists$.

Corollary 5. *The bounded synthesis algorithm decides the realizability problem for $\exists^* \forall^1$ HyperLTL and is a semi-decision procedure for $\exists^* \forall^{>1}$ HyperLTL.*

The synthesis problem for formulas in the $\forall^* \exists^*$ HyperLTL fragment uses the same reduction to a constraint system as the strategy synthesis in Sect. 3.2, with the only difference that the transition system $\mathcal{S}$ itself is uninterpreted. In the resulting SMT constraint systems, we have three bounds, the size of the implementation $\mathcal{S}$, the size of the strategy $\mathcal{S}_\exists$, and the lookahead k.

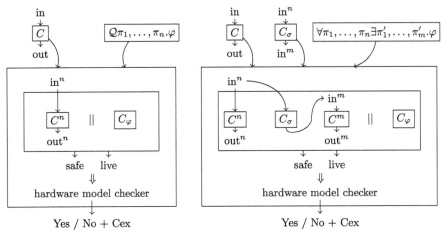

(a) Alternation-free model check-   (b) One-alternation model checking with
ing with self-composition   given strategy (case $\forall^n \exists^m$ HyperLTL)

Fig. 1. HyperLTL model checking with MCHYPER

Corollary 6. *Given a HyperLTL formula $\forall^n \exists^m \varphi$ where φ is quantifier-free. $\forall^n \exists^m \varphi$ is realizable if the SMT constraint system corresponding to the run graph $\mathcal{S}^n \times (\mathcal{S}^m \parallel \mathcal{S}_\exists) \times \mathcal{A}_\varphi$ is satisfiable for some bounds on $\mathcal{S}$, $\mathcal{S}_\exists$, and lookahead k.*

5   Implementations and Experimental Evaluation

We have integrated the model checking technique with a manually provided strategy into the HyperLTL hardware model checker MCHYPER[1]. For the synthesis of strategies and reactive systems from hyperproperties, we have developed a separate bounded synthesis tool based on SMT-solving. In the following, we describe these implementations and report on experimental results. All experiments ran on a machine with dual-core Core i7, 3.3 GHz, and 16 GB memory.

Hardware Model Checking with Given Strategies. We have extended the model checker MCHYPER [18] from the alternation-free fragment to formulas with one quantifier alternation. The input to MCHYPER is a circuit description as an And-Inverter-Graph in the AIGER format and a HyperLTL formula. Figures 1a and 1 show the model checking process in MCHYPER without and with quantifier alternation, respectively. For formulas with quantifier alternation, the model checker now also accepts a strategy as an additional AIGER circuit C_σ. Based on this strategy, MCHYPER creates a new circuit where only the inputs of the universal system copies are exposed and the inputs of the existential system

---

[1] Try the online tool interface with the latest version of MCHYPER.

Table 1. Experimental results for MCHYPER on the software doping and mutual exclusion benchmarks. All experiments used the IC3 option for ABC. Model and property names correspond to the ones used in [9] and [18].

Model	#Latches	Property	Time[s]
EC 0.05	17	$(10.a) + (10.b)$	1.8
EC 0.00625	23	$(10.a) + (10.b)$	53.4
AEC 0.05	19	$(\neg 10.a) + (\neg 10.b)$	2.8
AEC 0.00625	25	$(\neg 10.a) + (\neg 10.b)$	160.1
Bakery.a.n.s	47	Sym5	50.6
		Sym6	27.5
Bakery.a.n.s.5proc	90	Sym7	461.3
		Sym8	472.3

copies are determined by the strategy. The new circuit is then model checked as described in [18] with ABC [4].

We evaluate our extension of MCHYPER on formulas with quantifier alternation based on benchmarks from software doping [9] and symmetry in mutual exclusion algorithms [18]. Both considered problems have previously been analyzed with MCHYPER; however, since the properties in both problems require quantifier alternation, we were previously limited to a (manually obtained) approximation of the properties as universal formulas. The correctness of manual approximations is not given but has to be shown separately. By directly model checking the formula with quantifier alternation we know that we are checking the correct formula without needing any additional proof of correctness.

Software Doping. D'Argenio et al. [9] examined a clean and a doped version of an emission control program of a car and used the previous version of MCHYPER to formally verify approximations of these properties. Robust cleanness is expressed in the one-alternation fragment using two $\forall^2 \exists^1$ HyperLTL formulas (given in Prop. 19 in [9], cf. Sect. 1). In [9], the formulas were strengthened into alternation-free formulas that imply the original properties. Despite the quantifier alternation, Table 1 shows that the new version of MCHYPER verifies the precise formulas in roughly the same time as the alternation-free approximations [9] while giving stronger correctness guarantees.

Symmetry in Mutual Exclusion Protocols. $\forall^* \exists^*$ HyperLTL allows us to specify symmetry for mutual exclusion protocols. In such protocols, we wish to guarantee that every request is eventually answered, and the grants are mutually exclusive. In our experiments, we used an implementation of the Bakery protocol [25]. Table 1 shows the verification results for the precise $\forall^1 \exists^1$ properties. Comparing these results to the performance on the approximations of the symmetry properties [18], we, again, observe that the verification times are similar. However, we gain the additional correctness guarantees as described above.

Strategy and System Synthesis. For the synthesis of strategies for existential quantifiers and for the synthesis of reactive systems from hyperproperties, we have developed a separate bounded synthesis tool based on SMT-solving with z3 [29]. Our evaluation is based on two benchmark families, the *dining cryptographers* problem [5] and a simplified version of the symmetry problem in mutual exclusion protocols discussed previously. The results are shown in Table 2. Obviously, synthesis operates at a vastly smaller scale than model checking with given strategies. In the dining cryptographers example, z3 was unable to find an implementation for the full synthesis problem, but could easily synthesize strategies for the existential trace quantifiers when provided with an implementation. With the progress of constraint solver that employ quantification over Boolean functions [31] we expect scalability improvements of our synthesis approach.

Table 2. Summary of the experimental results on the benchmarks sets described in Sect. 5. When no hyperproperty is given, only the LTL part is used.

Instance	Hyperproperty	$|\mathcal{S}|$	$|\mathcal{S}_\exists|$	Time [s]
Dining cryptographers	distributed + deniability			TO
	distributed + deniability with given $\mathcal{S}$	(1)	1	1.2
Mutex	—	2	–	<1
	symmetry	3	1	3.4
Mutex w/o spurious grants	—	3	–	<1
	symmetry	3	1	3.9
	wait-free	3	3	46
	symmetry + wait-free	3	1 + 3	840

6 Conclusions

We have presented model checking and synthesis techniques for hyperliveness properties expressed as HyperLTL formulas with quantifier alternation. The alternation makes it possible to specify hyperproperties such as generalized noninterference, symmetry, and deniability. Our approach is the first method for the synthesis of reactive systems from HyperLTL formulas with quantifier alternation and the first practical method for the verification of such specifications.

The approach is based on a game-theoretic view of existential quantifiers, where the $\exists$-player reacts to decisions of the $\forall$-player. The key advantage is that the complementation of the system automaton is avoided (cf. [18]). Instead, a strategy must be found for the $\exists$-player. Since this can be done either manually or through automatic synthesis, the user of the model checking or synthesis tool has the opportunity to trade some automation for a significant gain in performance.

Acknowledgements. We would like to thank Sebastian Biewer for providing the software doping models and formulas, Marvin Stenger for his advice on our synthesis experiments, and Jana Hofmann for her helpful comments on a draft of this paper.

References

1. Abadi, M., Lamport, L.: The existence of refinement mappings. Theor. Comput. Sci. **82**(2), 253–284 (1991). https://doi.org/10.1016/0304-3975(91)90224-P

2. Barthe, G., Crespo, J.M., Kunz, C.: Beyond 2-safety: asymmetric product programs for relational program verification. In: Artemov, S., Nerode, A. (eds.) LFCS 2013. LNCS, vol. 7734, pp. 29–43. Springer, Heidelberg (2013). https://doi.org/10.1007/978-3-642-35722-0_3

3. Barthe, G., D'Argenio, P.R., Rezk, T.: Secure information flow by self-composition. In: Proceedings of CSFW, pp. 100–114. IEEE Computer Society (2004). https://doi.org/10.1109/CSFW.2004.17

4. Brayton, R., Mishchenko, A.: ABC: an academic industrial-strength verification tool. In: Touili, T., Cook, B., Jackson, P. (eds.) CAV 2010. LNCS, vol. 6174, pp. 24–40. Springer, Heidelberg (2010). https://doi.org/10.1007/978-3-642-14295-6_5

5. Chaum, D.: Security without identification: transaction systems to make big brother obsolete. Commun. ACM **28**(10), 1030–1044 (1985). https://doi.org/10.1145/4372.4373

6. Clarkson, M.R., Finkbeiner, B., Koleini, M., Micinski, K.K., Rabe, M.N., Sánchez, C.: Temporal logics for hyperproperties. In: Abadi, M., Kremer, S. (eds.) POST 2014. LNCS, vol. 8414, pp. 265–284. Springer, Heidelberg (2014). https://doi.org/10.1007/978-3-642-54792-8_15

7. Clarkson, M.R., Schneider, F.B.: Hyperproperties. J. Comput. Secur. **18**(6), 1157–1210 (2010). https://doi.org/10.3233/JCS-2009-0393

8. Cook, B., Khlaaf, H., Piterman, N.: On automation of CTL* verification for infinite-state systems. In: Kroening, D., Păsăreanu, C.S. (eds.) CAV 2015. LNCS, vol. 9206, pp. 13–29. Springer, Cham (2015). https://doi.org/10.1007/978-3-319-21690-4_2

9. D'Argenio, P.R., Barthe, G., Biewer, S., Finkbeiner, B., Hermanns, H.: Is your software on dope? - formal analysis of surreptitiously "enhanced" programs. In: Yang, H. (ed.) ESOP 2017. LNCS, vol. 10201, pp. 83–110. Springer, Heidelberg (2017). https://doi.org/10.1007/978-3-662-54434-1_4

10. D'Souza, D., Holla, R., Raghavendra, K.R., Sprick, B.: Model-checking trace-based information flow properties. J. Comput. Secur. **19**(1), 101–138 (2011). https://doi.org/10.3233/JCS-2010-0400

11. Finkbeiner, B., Hahn, C.: Deciding hyperproperties. In: Proceedings of CONCUR. LIPIcs, vol. 59, pp. 13:1–13:14. Schloss Dagstuhl - Leibniz-Zentrum fuer Informatik (2016). https://doi.org/10.4230/LIPIcs.CONCUR.2016.13

12. Finkbeiner, B., Hahn, C., Hans, T.: MGHYPER: checking satisfiability of HyperLTL formulas beyond the $\exists^*\forall^*$ fragment. In: Lahiri, S.K., Wang, C. (eds.) ATVA 2018. LNCS, vol. 11138, pp. 521–527. Springer, Cham (2018). https://doi.org/10.1007/978-3-030-01090-4_31

13. Finkbeiner, B., Hahn, C., Lukert, P., Stenger, M., Tentrup, L.: Synthesizing reactive systems from hyperproperties. In: Chockler, H., Weissenbacher, G. (eds.) CAV 2018. LNCS, vol. 10981, pp. 289–306. Springer, Cham (2018). https://doi.org/10.1007/978-3-319-96145-3_16

14. Finkbeiner, B., Hahn, C., Stenger, M.: EAHyper: satisfiability, implication, and equivalence checking of hyperproperties. In: Majumdar, R., Kunčak, V. (eds.) CAV 2017. LNCS, vol. 10427, pp. 564–570. Springer, Cham (2017). https://doi.org/10.1007/978-3-319-63390-9_29

15. Finkbeiner, B., Hahn, C., Stenger, M., Tentrup, L.: Monitoring hyperproperties. In: Lahiri, S., Reger, G. (eds.) RV 2017. LNCS, vol. 10548, pp. 190–207. Springer, Cham (2017). https://doi.org/10.1007/978-3-319-67531-2_12

16. Finkbeiner, B., Hahn, C., Stenger, M., Tentrup, L.: RVHyper: a runtime verification tool for temporal hyperproperties. In: Beyer, D., Huisman, M. (eds.) TACAS 2018. LNCS, vol. 10806, pp. 194–200. Springer, Cham (2018). https://doi.org/10.1007/978-3-319-89963-3_11

17. Finkbeiner, B., Hahn, C., Torfah, H.: Model checking quantitative hyperproperties. In: Chockler, H., Weissenbacher, G. (eds.) CAV 2018. LNCS, vol. 10981, pp. 144–163. Springer, Cham (2018). https://doi.org/10.1007/978-3-319-96145-3_8

18. Finkbeiner, B., Rabe, M.N., Sánchez, C.: Algorithms for model checking Hyper-LTL and HyperCTL*. In: Kroening, D., Păsăreanu, C.S. (eds.) CAV 2015. LNCS, vol. 9206, pp. 30–48. Springer, Cham (2015). https://doi.org/10.1007/978-3-319-21690-4_3

19. Finkbeiner, B., Schewe, S.: Uniform distributed synthesis. In: Proceedings of LICS, pp. 321–330. IEEE Computer Society (2005). https://doi.org/10.1109/LICS.2005.53

20. Finkbeiner, B., Schewe, S.: Bounded synthesis. STTT **15**(5–6), 519–539 (2013). https://doi.org/10.1007/s10009-012-0228-z

21. Goguen, J.A., Meseguer, J.: Security policies and security models. In: Proceedings of S&P, pp. 11–20. IEEE Computer Society (1982). https://doi.org/10.1109/SP.1982.10014

22. Hahn, C., Stenger, M., Tentrup, L.: Constraint-based monitoring of hyperproperties. In: Vojnar, T., Zhang, L. (eds.) TACAS 2019. LNCS, vol. 11428, pp. 115–131. Springer, Cham (2019). https://doi.org/10.1007/978-3-030-17465-1_7

23. Huisman, M., Worah, P., Sunesen, K.: A temporal logic characterisation of observational determinism. In: Proceedings of CSFW, p. 3. IEEE Computer Society (2006). https://doi.org/10.1109/CSFW.2006.6

24. Klein, F., Zimmermann, M.: How much lookahead is needed to win infinite games? In: Halldórsson, M.M., Iwama, K., Kobayashi, N., Speckmann, B. (eds.) ICALP 2015. LNCS, vol. 9135, pp. 452–463. Springer, Heidelberg (2015). https://doi.org/10.1007/978-3-662-47666-6_36

25. Lamport, L.: A new solution of Dijkstra's concurrent programming problem. Commun. ACM **17**(8), 453–455 (1974). https://doi.org/10.1145/361082.361093

26. Lynch, N.A., Vaandrager, F.W.: Forward and backward simulations: I. untimed systems. Inf. Comput. **121**(2), 214–233 (1995). https://doi.org/10.1006/inco.1995.1134

27. McCullough, D.: Noninterference and the composability of security properties. In: Proceedings of S&P, pp. 177–186. IEEE Computer Society (1988). https://doi.org/10.1109/SECPRI.1988.8110

28. van der Meyden, R., Zhang, C.: Algorithmic verification of noninterference properties. Electr. Notes Theor. Comput. Sci. **168**, 61–75 (2007). https://doi.org/10.1016/j.entcs.2006.11.002

29. de Moura, L., Bjørner, N.: Z3: an efficient SMT solver. In: Ramakrishnan, C.R., Rehof, J. (eds.) TACAS 2008. LNCS, vol. 4963, pp. 337–340. Springer, Heidelberg (2008). https://doi.org/10.1007/978-3-540-78800-3_24

30. Pnueli, A., Rosner, R.: On the synthesis of a reactive module. In: Proceedings of POPL, pp. 179–190. ACM Press (1989). https://doi.org/10.1145/75277.75293
31. Tentrup, L., Rabe, M.N.: Clausal abstraction for DQBF. In: Janota, M., Lynce, I. (eds.) SAT 2019. LNCS, vol. 11628, pp. 388–405. Springer, Cham (2019). https://doi.org/10.1007/978-3-030-24258-9_27

Abstraction Refinement Algorithms for Timed Automata

Victor Roussanaly, Ocan Sankur,
and Nicolas Markey(✉)

Univ Rennes, Inria, CNRS, IRISA, Rennes, France
nmarkey@irisa.fr

Abstract. We present abstraction-refinement algorithms for model checking safety properties of timed automata. The abstraction domain we consider abstracts away zones by restricting the set of clock constraints that can be used to define them, while the refinement procedure computes the set of constraints that must be taken into consideration in the abstraction so as to exclude a given spurious counterexample. We implement this idea in two ways: an enumerative algorithm where a lazy abstraction approach is adopted, meaning that possibly different abstract domains are assigned to each exploration node; and a symbolic algorithm where the abstract transition system is encoded with Boolean formulas.

1 Introduction

Model checking [4,10,12,26] is an automated technique for verifying that the set of behaviors of a computer system satisfies a given property. Model-checking algorithms explore finite-state automata (representing the system under study) in order to decide if the property holds; if not, the algorithm returns an explanation. These algorithms have been extended to verify real-time systems modelled as timed automata [2,3], an extension of finite automata with clock variables to measure and constrain the amount of time elapsed between occurrences of transitions. The state-space exploration can be done by representing clock constraints efficiently using convex polyhedra called *zones* [8,9]. Algorithms based on this data structure have been implemented in several tools such as Uppaal [7], and have been applied in various industrial cases.

The well-known issue in the applications of model checking is the *state-space explosion* problem: the size of the state space grows exponentially in the size of the description of the system. There are several sources for this explosion: the system might be made of the composition of several subsystems (such as a distributed system), it might contain several discrete variables (such as in a piece of software), or it might contain a number of real-valued clocks as in our case.

Numerous attempts have been made to circumvent this problem. Abstraction is a generic approach that consists in simplifying the model under study, so as to make it easier to verify [13]. *Existential* abstraction may only add extra behaviors, so that when a safety property holds in an abstracted model, it also holds in the original model; if on the other hand a safety property fails to hold, the model-checking algorithms return a witness trace exhibiting the non-safe behaviour: this either invalidates the property on the original model, if the trace exists in that model, or gives information about how to automatically refine the abstraction. This approach, named CEGAR (counter-example guided abstraction refinement) [11], was further developed and used, for instance, in software verification (BLAST [20], SLAM [5], ...).

The CEGAR approach has been adapted to timed automata, e.g. in [14, 18], but the abstractions considered there only consist in removing clocks and discrete variables, and adding them back during refinement. So for most well-designed models, one ends up adding all clocks and variables which renders the method useless. Two notable exceptions are [22], in which the zone extrapolation operators are dynamically adapted during the exploration, and [29], in which zones are refined when needed using interpolants. Both approaches define "exact" abstractions in the sense that they make sure that all traces discovered in the abstract model are feasible in the concrete model at any time.

In this work, we consider a more general setting and study *predicate abstractions* on clock variables. Just like in software model checking, we define abstract state spaces using these predicates, where the values of the clocks and their relations are approximately represented by these predicates. New predicates are generated if needed during the refinement step. We instantiate our approach by two algorithms. The first one is a zone-based enumerative algorithm inspired by the *lazy abstraction* in software model checking [19], where we assign a possibly different abstract domain to each node in the exploration. The second algorithm is based on binary decision diagrams (BDD): by exploiting the observation that a small number of predicates was often sufficient to prove safety properties, we use an efficient BDD encoding of zones similar to one introduced in early work [28].

Let us explain the abstract domains we consider. Assume there are two clock variables x and y. The abstraction we consider consists in restricting the clock

(a) Abstraction of zone $1 \leq x, y \leq 2$ (b) Abstraction of zone $y \leq 1 \wedge 1 \leq x - y \leq 2$

Fig. 1. The abstract domain is defined by the clock constraints shown in thick red lines. In each example, the abstraction of the zone shown on the left (shaded area) is the larger zone on the right. (Color figure online)

constraints that can be used when defining zones. Assume that we only allow to compare x with 2 or 3; that y can only be compared with 2, and $x - y$ can only be compared with -1 or 2. Then any conjunction of constraints one might obtain in this manner will be delimited by the thick red lines in Fig. 1; one cannot define a finer region under this restriction. The figure shows the abstraction process: given a "concrete" zone, its abstraction is the smallest zone which is a superset and is definable under our restriction. For instance, the abstraction of $1 \leq x, y \leq 2$ is $0 \leq x, y \leq 2 \wedge -1 \leq x - y$ (cf. Fig. 1a).

Related Works. We give more detail on zone abstractions in timed automata. Most efforts in the literature have been concentrated in designing zone abstraction operators that are exact in the sense that they preserve the reachability relation between the locations of a timed automaton; see [6]. The idea is to determine bounds on the constants to which a given clock can be compared to in a given part of the automaton, since the clock values do not matter outside these bounds. In [21,22], the authors give an algorithm where these bounds are dynamically adapted during the exploration, which allows one to obtain coarser abstractions. In [29], the exploration tree contains pairs of zones: a concrete zone as in the usual algorithm, and a coarser abstract zone. The algorithm explores all branches using the coarser zone and immediately refines the abstract zone whenever an edge which is disabled in the concrete zone is enabled. In [17], a CEGAR loop was used to solve timed games by analyzing strategies computed for each abstract game. The abstraction consisted in collapsing locations.

Some works have adapted the abstraction-refinement paradigm to timed automata. In [14], the authors apply "localization reduction" to timed automata within an abstraction-refinement loop: they abstract away clocks and discrete variables, and only introduce them as they are needed to rule out spurious counterexamples. A more general but similar approach was developed in [18]. In [31], the authors adapt the trace abstraction refinement idea to timed automata where a finite automaton is maintained to rule out infeasible edge sequences.

The CEGAR approach was also used recently in the LinAIG framework for verifying linear hybrid automata [1]. In this work, the backward reachability algorithm exploits *don't-cares* to reduce the size of the Boolean circuits representing the state space. The abstractions consist in enlarging the size of *don't-cares* to reduce the number of linear predicates used in the representation.

2 Timed Automata and Zones

2.1 Timed Automata

Given a finite set of clocks $\mathcal{C}$, we call *valuations* the elements of $\mathbb{R}_{\geq 0}^{\mathcal{C}}$. For a clock valuation v, a subset $R \subseteq \mathcal{C}$, and a non-negative real d, we denote with $v[R \leftarrow d]$ the valuation w such that $w(x) = v(x)$ for $x \in \mathcal{C} \setminus R$ and $w(x) = d$ for $x \in R$, and with $v + d$ the valuation w' such that $w'(x) = v(x) + d$ for all $x \in \mathcal{C}$. We extend these operations to sets of valuations in the obvious way. We write $\mathbf{0}$ for the valuation that assigns 0 to every clock. An *atomic guard* is a formula of the form $x \prec k$ or $x - y \prec k$ with $x, y \in \mathcal{C}$, $k \in \mathbb{N}$, and $\prec \in \{<, \leq, >, \geq\}$. A *guard* is a conjunction of atomic guards. A valuation v satisfies a guard g, denoted $v \models g$, if all atomic guards hold true when each $x \in \mathcal{C}$ is replaced with $v(x)$. Let $\llbracket g \rrbracket = \{v \in \mathbb{R}_{\geq 0}^{\mathcal{C}} \mid v \models g\}$ denote the set of valuations satisfying g. We write $\Phi_{\mathcal{C}}$ for the set of guards built on $\mathcal{C}$.

A *timed automaton* $\mathcal{A}$ is a tuple $(\mathcal{L}, \mathsf{Inv}, \ell_0, \mathcal{C}, E)$, where $\mathcal{L}$ is a finite set of locations, $\mathsf{Inv} \colon \mathcal{L} \to \Phi_{\mathcal{C}}$ defines location invariants, $\mathcal{C}$ is a finite set of clocks, $E \subseteq \mathcal{L} \times \Phi_{\mathcal{C}} \times 2^{\mathcal{C}} \times \mathcal{L}$ is a set of edges, and $\ell_0 \in \mathcal{L}$ is the initial location. An edge $e = (\ell, g, R, \ell')$ is also written as $\ell \xrightarrow{g, R} \ell'$. For any location ℓ, we let $E(\ell)$ denote the set of edges leaving ℓ.

A *configuration* of $\mathcal{A}$ is a pair $q = (\ell, v) \in \mathcal{L} \times \mathbb{R}_{\geq 0}^{\mathcal{C}}$ such that $v \models \mathsf{Inv}(\ell)$. A *run* of $\mathcal{A}$ is a sequence $q_1 e_1 q_2 e_2 \ldots q_n$ where for all $i \geq 1$, $q_i = (\ell_i, v_i)$ is a configuration, and either $e_i \in \mathbb{R}_{>0}$, in which case $q_{i+1} = (\ell_i, v_i + e_i)$, or $e_i = (\ell_i, g_i, R_i, \ell_{i+1}) \in E$, in which case $v_i \models g_i$ and $q_{i+1} = (\ell_{i+1}, v_i[R_i \leftarrow 0])$. A *path* is a sequence of edges with matching endpoint locations.

2.2   Zones and DBMs

Several tools for timed automata implement algorithms based on *zones*, which are particular polyhedra definable with clock constraints. Formally, a zone Z is a subset of $\mathbb{R}_{\geq 0}^{\mathcal{C}}$ definable by a guard in $\Phi_{\mathcal{C}}$.

We recall a few basic operations defined on zones. First, the intersection $Z \cap Z'$ of two zones Z and Z' is clearly a zone. Given a zone Z, the set of time-successors of Z, defined as $Z{\uparrow} = \{v + t \in \mathbb{R}_{\geq 0}^{\mathcal{C}} \mid t \in \mathbb{R}_{\geq 0}, \ v \in Z\}$, is easily seen to be a zone; similarly for time-predecessors $Z{\downarrow} = \{v \in \mathbb{R}_{\geq 0}^{\mathcal{C}} \mid \exists t \geq 0. \ v + t \in Z\}$. Given $R \subseteq \mathcal{C}$, we let $\mathsf{Reset}_R(Z)$ be the zone $\{v[R \leftarrow 0] \in \mathbb{R}_{\geq 0}^{\mathcal{C}} \mid v \in Z\}$, and $\mathsf{Free}_x(Z) = \{v' \in \mathbb{R}_{\geq 0}^{\mathcal{C}} \mid \exists v \in Z, d \in \mathbb{R}_{\geq 0}, v' = v[x \leftarrow d]\}$.

Zones can be represented as *difference-bound matrices (DBM)* [8, 15]. Let $\mathcal{C}_0 = \mathcal{C} \cup \{0\}$, where 0 is an extra symbol representing a special clock variable whose value is always 0. A DBM is a $|\mathcal{C}_0| \times |\mathcal{C}_0|$-matrix taking values in $(\mathbb{Z} \times \{<, \leq\}) \cup \{(+\infty, <)\}$. Intuitively, cell (x, y) of a DBM M stores a pair $(d, \prec)$ representing an upper bound on the difference $x - y$. For any DBM M, we let $\llbracket M \rrbracket$ denote the zone it defines.

While several DBMs can represent the same zone, each zone admits a *canonical* representation, which is obtained by storing the tightest clock constraints defining the zone. This canonical representation can be obtained by computing shortest paths in a graph where the vertices are clocks and the edges weighted by clock constraints, with natural addition and comparison of elements of $(\mathbb{Z} \times \{<, \leq\}) \cup \{(+\infty, <)\}$. This graph has a negative cycle if, and only if, the associated DBM represents the empty zone.

All the operations on zones can be performed efficiently (in $O(|\mathcal{C}_0|^3)$) on their associated DBMs while maintaining reduced form. For instance, the intersection $N = Z \cap Z'$ of two canonical DBMs Z and Z' can be obtained by first computing the DBM $M = \min(Z, Z')$ such that $M(x, y) = \min\{Z(x, y), Z'(x, y)\}$ for all $(x, y) \in \mathcal{C}_0{}^2$, and then turning M into canonical form. We refer to [8] for full details. By a slight abuse of notation, we use the same notations for DBMs as for zones, writing e.g. $M' = M\uparrow$, where M and M' are reduced DBMs such that $[\![M']\!] = [\![M]\!]\uparrow$. Given an edge $e = (\ell, g, R, \ell')$, and a zone Z, we define $\mathsf{Post}_e(Z) = \mathsf{Inv}(\ell') \cap (g \cap \mathsf{Reset}_R(Z))\uparrow$, and $\mathsf{Pre}_e(Z) = (g \cap \mathsf{Free}_R(\mathsf{Inv}(\ell') \cap Z))\downarrow$. For a path $\rho = e_1 e_2 \ldots e_n$, we define Post_ρ and Pre_ρ by iteratively applying Post_{e_i} and Pre_{e_i} respectively.

2.3 Clock-Predicate Abstraction and Interpolation

For all clocks x and y in $\mathcal{C}_0$, we consider a finite set $\mathcal{D}_{x,y} \subseteq \mathbb{N} \times \{\leq, <\}$, and gather these in a table $\mathcal{D} = (\mathcal{D}_{x,y})_{x,y \in \mathcal{C}_0}$. $\mathcal{D}$ is the *abstract domain* which restricts zones to be defined only using constraints of the form $x - y \prec k$ with $(k, \prec) \in \mathcal{D}_{x,y}$, as seen earlier. Let us call $\mathcal{D}$ the *concrete domain* if $\mathcal{D}_{x,y} = \mathbb{N} \times \{\leq, <\}$ for all $x, y \in \mathcal{C}_0$. A zone Z is $\mathcal{D}$-definable if there exists a DBM D such that $Z = [\![D]\!]$ and $D(x, y) \in \mathcal{D}_{x,y}$ for all $x, y \in \mathcal{C}_0$. Note that we do not require this witness DBM D to be reduced; the reduction of such a DBM might introduce additional values. We say that domain $\mathcal{D}'$ is a *refinement* of $\mathcal{D}$ if for all $x, y \in \mathcal{C}_0$, we have $\mathcal{D}_{x,y} \subseteq \mathcal{D}'_{x,y}$.

An abstract domain $\mathcal{D}$ induces an *abstraction function* $\alpha_\mathcal{D} \colon 2^{\mathbb{R}^\mathcal{C}_{\geq 0}} \to 2^{\mathbb{R}^\mathcal{C}_{\geq 0}}$ where $\alpha_\mathcal{D}(Z)$ is the smallest $\mathcal{D}$-definable zone containing Z. For any reduced DBM D, $\alpha_\mathcal{D}([\![D]\!])$ can be computed by setting $D'(x, y) = \min\{(k, \prec) \in \mathcal{D}_{x,y} \mid D(x, y) \leq (k, \prec)\}$ (with $\min \emptyset = (\infty, <)$).

An *interpolant* for a pair of zones (Z_1, Z_2) with $Z_1 \cap Z_2 = \emptyset$ is a zone Z_3 with $Z_1 \subseteq Z_3$ and $Z_3 \cap Z_2 = \emptyset$[1] [29]. We use interpolants to refine our abstractions; in order not to add too many new constraints when refining, our aim is to find *minimal interpolants*: define the density of a DBM D as $d(D) = \#\{(x, y) \in \mathcal{C}_0{}^2 \mid D(x, y) \neq (\infty, <)\}$. Notice that while any pair of disjoint convex polyhedra can be separated by hyperplanes, not all pairs of disjoint zones admit interpolants of density 1; this is because not all (half-spaces delimited by) hyperplanes are zones. Still, we can bound the density of a minimal interpolant:

Lemma 1. *For any pair of disjoint, non-empty zones (A, B), there exists an interpolant of density less than or equal to $|\mathcal{C}_0|/2$.*

By adapting the algorithm of [29] for computing interpolants, we can compute minimal interpolants efficiently:

Proposition 2. *Computing a minimal interpolant can be performed in $O(|\mathcal{C}|^4)$.*

3 Enumerative Algorithm

The first type of algorithm we present is a zone-based enumerative algorithm based on the clock-predicate abstractions. Let us first describe the overall

---

[1] It is sometimes also required that the interpolant only involves clocks that have non-trivial constraints in both Z_1 and Z_2. We do not impose this requirement in our definition, but it will hold true in the interpolants computed by our algorithm.

algorithm in Algorithm 1, which is a typical abstraction-refinement loop. We then explain how the abstract reachability and refinement procedures are instantiated.

Algorithm 1. Enumerative algorithm checking the reachability of a target location ℓ_T.

Input: $\mathcal{A} = (\mathcal{L}, \mathsf{Inv}, \ell_0, \mathcal{C}, E)$, ℓ_T

1   Initialize $\mathcal{D}_0$;
2   wait$:= \{\mathsf{node}(\ell_0, \mathbf{0}\!\uparrow, \mathcal{D}_0)\}$;
3   passed$:= \emptyset$;
4   **while do**
5      $\pi := \mathsf{AbsReach}(\mathcal{A}, \mathsf{wait}, \mathsf{passed}, \ell_T)$;
6   **if** $\pi = \emptyset$ **then**
7   **return** Not reachable;
8   **else**
9   **if** *trace π is feasible* **then**
10   **return** Reachable;
11   **else**
            Refine$(\pi, \mathsf{wait}, \mathsf{passed})$;

12 **return** Not reachable;

Algorithm 2. AbsReach

Input: $(\mathcal{L}, \mathsf{Inv}, l_0, \mathcal{C}, E)$, wait, passed, ℓ_T

1   **while** wait $\neq \emptyset$ **do**
2     $n := \mathsf{wait}.pop()$;
3   **if** $n.\ell = \ell_T$ **then**
4   **return** Trace from root to n;
5   **if** $\exists n' \in \mathsf{passed}$ *such that* $n.\ell = n'.\ell \wedge n.Z \subseteq n'.Z$ **then**
6        $n.\mathsf{covered} := n'$;
7   **else**
8        $n.Z := \alpha(n.Z, n)$;
9        $\mathsf{passed}.add(n)$;
10   **for** $e = (\ell, g, R, \ell') \in E(n.\ell)$ *s.t.* $Z' := \mathsf{Post}_e(n.Z) \neq \emptyset$ **do**
11           $\mathcal{D}' := \mathsf{choose\text{-}dom}(n, e)$;
12           $n' := \mathsf{node}(\ell', Z', \mathcal{D}')$;
13           $n'.\mathsf{parent} := n$;
14           $\mathsf{wait}.add(n')$;

15 **return** $\emptyset$;

The initialization at line 1 chooses an abstract domain for the initial state, which can be either empty (thus the coarsest abstraction) or defined according to some heuristics. The algorithm maintains the wait and passed lists that are used in the forward exploration. As usual, the wait list can be implemented as a stack, a queue, or another priority list that determines the search order. The algorithm also uses covering nodes. Indeed if there are two node n and n', with $n \in$ passed, $n' \in$ wait, $n.\ell = n'.\ell$, and $n'.z \subseteq n.Z$, then we know that every location reachable from n' is also reachable from n. Since we have already explored n and we generated its successors, there is no need to explore the successors of n'. The algorithm explicitly creates an exploration tree: line 2 creates a node containing location ℓ_0, zone $\mathbf{0}\!\uparrow$, and the abstract domain $\mathcal{D}_0$ as the root of our tree, and adds this to the wait list. More details on the tree are given in the next subsection. Procedure AbsReach then looks for a trace to the target location ℓ_T. If such a trace exists, line 9 checks its feasibility. Here π is a sequence of node and edges of $\mathcal{A}$. The feasibility check is done by computing predecessors with zones starting from the final state, without using the abstraction function. If the last zone intersects our initial zone, this means that the trace is feasible. More details are given in Sect. 3.2.

3.1 Abstract Forward Reachability: AbsReach

We give a generic algorithm independently from the implementations of the abstraction functions and the refinement procedure.

Algorithm 2 describes the reachability procedure under a given abstract domain $\mathcal{D}$. It is similar to the standard forward reachability algorithm using a wait-list and a passed-list. We explicitly create an exploration tree where the leaves are nodes in wait, covered nodes, or nodes that have no non-empty successors. Each node n contains the fields ℓ, Z which are labels describing the current location and zone; field covered points to a node covering the current node (it is undefined if the current node is not (known to be) covered); field parent points to the parent node in the tree (it is undefined for the root); and field $\mathcal{D}$ is the abstract domain associated with the node. Thus, the algorithm uses a possibly different abstract domain for each node in the exploration tree.

The difference of our algorithm w.r.t. the standard reachability can be seen at lines 8 and 11. At line 8, we apply the abstraction function to the zone taken from the wait-list before adding it to the passed-list. The abstraction function α is a function of a zone Z and a node n. This allows one to define variants with different dependencies; for instance, α might depend on the abstract domain $n.\mathcal{D}$ at the current node, but it can also use other information available in n or on the path ending in n. For now, it is best to think of α simply as $Z \mapsto \alpha_{n.\mathcal{D}}(Z)$. At line 11, the function choose-dom chooses an abstract domain for the node n'. The domain could be chosen global for all nodes, or local to each node. A good trade-off, which we used in our experiments, is to have domains associated with locations of the timed automaton.

Remark 1. Note that we use the abstraction function when the node is inserted in the passed list. This is because we want the node to contain the smallest zone possible when we test whether the node is covered. We only need to use the abstracted zone when we compute its successor and when we test whether the node is covering. This allows us to store a unique zone.

As a first step towards proving correctness of our algorithm, we show that the following property is preserved by Algorithm AbsReach:

> For all nodes n in passed, for all edges e from $n.\ell$, if $\mathsf{Post}_e(n.Z) \neq \emptyset$, then n has a child n' such that $\mathsf{Post}_e(n.Z) \subseteq n'.Z$. If n' is in passed, then we also have $\alpha_{n'.\mathcal{D}}(\mathsf{Post}_e(n.Z)) \subseteq n'.Z$.   (1)

Lemma 3. *Algorithm* AbsReach *preserves Property* (1).

Note that although we use inclusion in Property (1), AbsReach would actually preserve equality of zones, but we will not always have equality before running AbsReach. This is because Refine might change the zones of some nodes without updating the zones of all their descendants.

3.2   Refinement: Refine

We now describe our refinement procedure Refine. Let us now assume that AbsReach returns $\pi = A_1 \xrightarrow{\sigma_1} A_2 \xrightarrow{\sigma_2} \ldots \xrightarrow{\sigma_{k-1}} A_k$, and write $\mathcal{D}_i$ for the domain associated with each A_i. We write C_1 for the initial concrete zone, and for $i < k$, we define $C_{i+1} = \mathsf{Post}_{\sigma_i}(A_i)$. We also note $Z_k = A_k$ and for $i < k$, $Z_i = \mathsf{Pre}_{\sigma_i}(Z_{i+1}) \cap A_i$. Then π is not feasible if, and only if, $\mathsf{Post}_{\sigma_1 \ldots \sigma_k}(C_1) = \emptyset$, or equivalently $\mathsf{Pre}_{\sigma_1 \ldots \sigma_k}(A_k) \cap C_1 = \emptyset$. Since for all $i < k$, it holds $C_i \subseteq A_{i+1}$, we have that π is not feasible if, and only if, $\exists i \leq k.\ C_i \cap Z_i = \emptyset$. We illustrate this on Fig. 2.

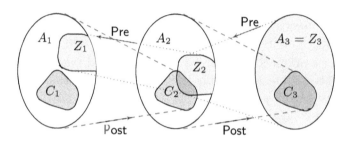

Fig. 2. Spurious counter-example: $Z_1 \cap C_1 = \emptyset$

Let us assume that π is not feasible. Let us denote by i_0 the maximal index such that $C_{i_0} \cap Z_{i_0} = \emptyset$. This index also has the property that for all $j < i_0$, we have $Z_j = \emptyset$ and $Z_{i_0} \neq \emptyset$. Once we have identified this trace as spurious by computing the Z_j, we have two possibilities:

- if $Z_{i_0} \cap \alpha_{\mathcal{D}_{i_0}}(C_{i_0}) \neq \emptyset$: this means that we can reach A_k from $\alpha_{\mathcal{D}_{i_0}}(C_{i_0})$ but not from C_{i_0}. In other words, our abstraction is too coarse and we must add some values to $\mathcal{D}_{i_0}$ so that $Z_{i_0} \cap \alpha_{\mathcal{D}_{i_0}}(C_{i_0}) = \emptyset$. Those values are found by computing the interpolant of Z_{i_0} and C_{i_0}
- Otherwise it means that $\alpha_{\mathcal{D}_{i_0}}(C_{i_0})$ cannot reach A_k and the only reason the trace exists is because either $\mathcal{D}_{i_0}$ or A_{i_0-1} has been modified at some point and A_{i_0} was not modified accordingly.

We can then update the values of C_i for $i > i_0$ and repeat the process until we reach an index j_0 such that $C_{j_0} = \emptyset$. We then have modified the nodes $n_{i_0}, \ldots, n_{j_0}$ and knowing that $n_{j_0}.Z = \emptyset$, we can delete it and all of its descendants. Since some of the descendants of n_{i_0} have not been modified, this might cause some refinements of the first type in the future. In order to ensure termination, we sometimes have to cut a subtree from a node in $n_{i_0}, \ldots, n_{j_0-1}$ and reinsert it in the wait list to restart the exploration from there. We call this action cut, and we can use several heuristics to decide when to use it. In the rest of this paper we will use the following heuristics: we perform cut on the first node of $n_{i_0} \ldots n_{j_0}$ that is covered by some other node. Since this node is covered, we know that we will not restart the exploration from this node, or that the node was covered by one of its descendant. If none of these nodes are covered, we delete n_{j_0} and its descendants. Other heuristics are possible, for instance applying cut on n_{i_0}. We found that the above heuristics was the most efficient in our experiments.

Lemma 4. *Pick a node n, and let $Y = n.Z$. Then after running* Refine, *either node n is deleted, or it holds $n.Z \subseteq Y$. In other words, the zone of a node can only be reduced by* Refine.

It follows that Refine also preserves Property (1), so that:

Lemma 5. *Algorithm 1 satisfies Property* (1).

We can then prove that our algorithm correctly decides the reachability problem and always terminates.

Theorem 6. *Algorithm 1 terminates and is correct.*

4 Symbolic Algorithm

4.1 Boolean Encoding of Zones

We now present a symbolic algorithm that represents abstract states using Boolean formulas. Let $\mathbb{B} = \{0, 1\}$, and $\mathcal{V}$ be a set of variables. A Boolean formula f that uses variables from set $X \subseteq \mathcal{V}$ will be written $f(X)$ to make the dependency explicit; we sometimes write $f(X, Y)$ in place of $f(X \cup Y)$. Such a formula represents a set $[\![f]\!] = \{v \in \mathbb{B}^{\mathcal{V}} \mid v \models f\}$. We consider primed versions of all variables; this will allow us to write formulas relating two valuations. For any subset $X \subseteq \mathcal{V}$, we define $X' = \{p' \mid p \in X\}$.

A *literal* is either p or $\neg p$ for a variable p. Given a set X of variables, an X-*minterm* is the conjunction of literals where each variable of X appears exactly once. X-minterms can be seen as elements of $\mathbb{B}^X$. Given a vector of Boolean formulas $Y = (Y_x)_{x \in X}$, formula $f[Y/X]$ is the *substitution of X by Y in f*, obtained by replacing each $x \in X$ with the formula Y_x. The positive cofactor of $f(X)$ by x is $\exists x. (x \wedge f(X))$, and its negative cofactor is $\exists x. (\neg x \wedge f(X))$.

Let us define a generic operator post that computes successors of a set $S(X, Y)$ given a relation $R(X, X')$ (here, Y designates any set of variables on which S might depend outside of X): $\text{post}_R(S(X, Y)) = (\exists X. S(X, Y) \wedge R(X, X'))[X/X']$. Similarly, we set $\text{pre}_R(S(X, Y)) = (\exists X'. S(X, Y)[X'/X] \wedge R(X, X'))$, which computes the predecessors of $S(X, Y)$ by the relation R [24].

Clock Predicate Abstraction. We fix a total order $\lhd$ on $\mathcal{C}_0$. In this section, abstract domains are defined as $\mathcal{D} = (\mathcal{D}_{x,y})_{x \lhd y \in \mathcal{C}_0}$, that is only for pairs $x \lhd y$. In fact, constraints of the form $x - y \leq k$ with $x \rhd y$ are encoded using the negation of $y - x < -k$ since $(x - y \leq k) \Leftrightarrow \neg(y - x < -k)$. We thus define $\mathcal{D}_{x,y} = -\mathcal{D}_{y,x}$ for all $x \rhd y$.

For $x, y \in \mathcal{C}_0$, let $\mathcal{P}_{x,y}$ denote the set of *clock predicates* associated to $\mathcal{D}_{x,y}$:

$$\mathcal{P}_{x,y}^{\mathcal{D}} = \{P_{x-y \prec k} \mid (k, \prec) \in \mathcal{D}_{x,y}\}.$$

Let $\mathcal{P}^{\mathcal{D}} = \cup_{x,y \in \mathcal{C}_0} \mathcal{P}_{x,y}$ denote the set of all clock predicates associated with $\mathcal{D}$ (we may omit the superscript $\mathcal{D}$ when it is clear). For all $(x, y) \in \mathcal{C}_0^2$ and $(k, \prec) \in \mathcal{D}_{x,y}$, we denote by $p_{x-y \prec k}$ the literal $P_{x-y \prec k}$ if $x \lhd y$, and $\neg P_{y-x \prec^{-1} -k}$ otherwise (where $\leq^{-1} = <$ and $<^{-1} = \leq$). We also consider a set $\mathcal{B}$ of Boolean variables used to encode locations. Overall, the state space is described using Boolean formulas on these two types of variables, so states are elements of $\mathbb{B}^{\mathcal{P} \cup \mathcal{B}}$.

Our Boolean encoding of clock constraints and semantic operations follow those of [28] for a concrete domain. We define these however for abstract domains, and show how successor computation and refinement operations can be performed.

Let us define the *clock semantics* of predicate $P_{x-y \preceq k}$ as $[\![P_{x-y \preceq k}]\!]_{\mathcal{C}_0} = \{\nu \in \mathbb{R}_{\geq 0}^{\mathcal{C}_0} \mid \nu(x) - \nu(y) \preceq k\}$. Since the set $\mathcal{C}$ of clocks is fixed, we may omit the subscript and just write $[\![P_{x-y \preceq k}]\!]$. We define the conjunction, disjunction, and negation as intersection, union, and complement, respectively. Given a $\mathcal{P}$-minterm $v \in \mathbb{B}^{\mathcal{P}}$, we define $[\![v]\!]_{\mathcal{D}} = \bigcap_{p \text{ s.t. } v(p)} [\![p]\!]_{\mathcal{D}} \cap \bigcap_{p \text{ s.t. } \neg v(p)} [\![p]\!]_{\mathcal{D}}^{c}$. Thus, negation of a predicate encodes its complement. For a Boolean formula $F(\mathcal{P})$, we set $[\![F]\!] = \bigcup_{v \in \text{Minterms}(F)} [\![v]\!]_{\mathcal{D}}$. Intuitively, the minterms of $\mathcal{P}$ define smallest zones of $\mathbb{R}_{\geq 0}^{\mathcal{C}}$ definable using $\mathcal{P}$. A minterm $v \in \mathbb{B}^{\mathcal{B} \cup \mathcal{P}}$ defines a pair $[\![v]\!]_{\mathcal{D}} = (l, Z)$ where l is encoded by $v_{|\mathcal{B}}$ and $Z = [\![v_{|\mathcal{P}}]\!]_{\mathcal{D}}$. A Boolean formula F on $\mathcal{B} \cup \mathcal{P}$ defines a set $[\![F]\!]_{\mathcal{D}} = \bigcup_{v \in \text{Minterms}(F)} [\![v]\!]_{\mathcal{D}}$ of such pairs. A minterm v is *satisfiable* if $[\![v]\!]_{\mathcal{D}} \neq \emptyset$.

An abstract domain $\mathcal{D}$ induces an *abstraction function* $\alpha_{\mathcal{D}} \colon 2^{\mathbb{R}_{\geq 0}^{\mathcal{C}}} \to 2^{\mathbb{B}^{\mathcal{P}}}$ with $\alpha_{\mathcal{D}}(Z) = \{v \mid v \in \mathbb{B}^{\mathcal{P}} \text{ and } [\![v]\!]_{\mathcal{D}} \cap Z \neq \emptyset\}$, from the set of zones to the set of subsets of Boolean valuations on $\mathcal{P}$. We define the *concretization function* as $[\![\cdot]\!]_{\mathcal{D}} \colon 2^{\mathbb{B}^{\mathcal{P}}} \to 2^{\mathbb{R}_{\geq 0}^{\mathcal{C}}}$. The pair $(\alpha_{\mathcal{D}}, [\![\cdot]\!]_{\mathcal{D}})$ is a Galois connection, and $[\![\alpha_{\mathcal{D}}(Z)]\!]_{\mathcal{D}}$ is the most precise abstraction of Z in the domain induced by $\mathcal{D}$. Notice that $\alpha_{\mathcal{D}}$ is non-convex in general: for instance, if the clock predicates are $x \leq 2, y \leq 2$, then the set defined by the constraint $x = y$ maps to $(p_{x \leq 2} \wedge p_{y \leq 2}) \vee (\neg p_{x \leq 2} \wedge \neg p_{y \leq 2})$.

4.2 Reduction and Successor Computation

We now define the reduction operation, which is similar to the reduction of DBMs. The idea is to eliminate unsatisfiable minterms from a given Boolean formula. For example, we would like to make sure that in all minterms, if $p_{x-y \leq 1}$ holds, then so does $p_{x-y \leq 2}$, when both are available predicates. Another issue is to eliminate minterms that are unsatisfiable due to triangle inequality. This is similar to the shortest path computation used to turn DBMs in canonical form.

Example 1. Given predicates $\mathcal{P} = \{p_{x-y \leq 1}, p_{y-z \leq 1}, p_{x-z \leq 2}\}$, the formula $p_{x-y \leq 1} \wedge p_{y-z \leq 1}$ is not reduced since it contains the unsatisfiable minterm

$p_{x-y\leq 1} \wedge p_{y-z\leq 1} \wedge \neg p_{x-z\leq 2}$. However, the same formula is reduced if $\mathcal{P} = \{p_{x-y\leq 1}, p_{y-z\leq 1}\}$.

In this paper, we use limited reduction, since reductions are the most expensive operations in our algorithms. The following formula corresponds to 2-reduction, which intuitively amounts to applying shortest paths for paths of lengths 1 and 2:

$$\bigwedge_{\substack{(x,y)\in\mathcal{C}_0{}^2 \\ (k,\prec)\in\mathcal{D}_{x,y}}} \left[p_{x-y\prec k} \leftarrow \left(\bigvee_{\substack{(l_1,\prec_1)\in\mathcal{D}_{x,y} \\ (l_1,\prec_1)\leq(k,\prec)}} p_{x-y\prec_1 l_1} \vee \bigvee_{\substack{z\in\mathcal{C}_0,(l_1,\prec_1)\in\mathcal{D}_{x,z}, \\ (l_2,\prec_2)\in\mathcal{D}_{z,y} \\ (l_1,\prec_1)+(l_2,\prec_2)\leq(k,\prec)}} p_{x-z\prec l} \wedge p_{z-y\prec' l'} \right) \right]$$

Lemma 7. *For all formulas $S(\mathcal{P})$, we have $[\![S]\!]_\mathcal{D} = [\![\mathsf{reduce}_\mathcal{D}^2(S)]\!]_\mathcal{D}$ and all minterms of $\mathsf{reduce}_\mathcal{D}^2(S)$ are 2-reduced.*

Since 2-reduction des not consider shortest paths of all lengths, there are, in general, 2-reduced unsatisfiable minterms. Nevertheless, any abstraction can be refined so that the updated 2-reduction eliminates a given unsatisfiable minterm:

Lemma 8. *Let $v \in \mathbb{B}^{\mathcal{P}^\mathcal{D}}$ be a minterm such that $v \models \mathsf{reduce}_\mathcal{D}^2$ and $[\![v]\!] = \emptyset$. One can compute in polynomial time a refinement $\mathcal{D}' \supset \mathcal{D}$ such that $v \not\models \mathsf{reduce}_{\mathcal{D}'}^2$.*

We now explain how successor computation is realized in our encoding. For a guard g, assume we have computed an abstraction $\alpha_\mathcal{D}(g)$ in the present abstract domain. For each transition $\sigma = (\ell_1, g, R, \ell_2)$, let us define the formula $T_\sigma = \ell_1 \wedge \alpha_\mathcal{D}(g)$. We show how each basic operation on zones can be computed in our BDD encoding. In our algorithm, all formulas $A(\mathcal{B},\mathcal{P})$ representing sets of states are assumed to be reduced, that is, $A(\mathcal{B},\mathcal{P}) \subseteq \mathsf{reduce}_\mathcal{D}^2(A(\mathcal{B},\mathcal{P}))$.

The intersection operation is simply logical conjunction:

Lemma 9. *For all reduced formulas $A(\mathcal{P})$ and $B(\mathcal{P})$, we have $A(\mathcal{P}) \wedge B(\mathcal{P}) = \alpha_\mathcal{D}([\![A(\mathcal{P})]\!]_\mathcal{D} \cap [\![B(\mathcal{P})]\!]_\mathcal{D})$.*

For the time successors, we define $\mathsf{Up}(A(\mathcal{B},\mathcal{P})) = \mathsf{reduce}(\mathsf{post}_{S_{\mathsf{Up}}}(A(\mathcal{B},\mathcal{P})))$ where

$$S_{\mathsf{Up}} = \bigwedge_{\substack{x\in\mathcal{C} \\ (k,\prec)\in\mathcal{D}_{x,0}}} (\neg p_{x-0\prec k} \rightarrow \neg p'_{x-0\prec k}) \bigwedge_{\substack{x,y\in\mathcal{C}_0, x\neq 0 \\ (k,\prec)\in\mathcal{D}_{x,y}}} (p'_{x-y\prec k} \leftrightarrow p_{x-y\prec k}).$$

Lemma 10. *For any Boolean formula $A(\mathcal{B},\mathcal{P})$, $\alpha_\mathcal{D}([\![A]\!]\!\uparrow) \subseteq \mathsf{Up}(A)$. Moreover, if $\mathcal{D}$ is the concrete domain and A is reduced, then this holds with equality.*

Following similar ideas, we handle clock resets by defining $\mathsf{Reset}_z(A) = \mathsf{reduce}(\mathsf{post}_{S_{\mathsf{Reset}_z}}(A))$, for a (complex) relation S_{Reset_z} to encode how predicates evolve (see the long version [27] of this article for more detailled explanations).

We get:

Lemma 11. *For any Boolean formula $A(\mathcal{B},\mathcal{P})$, and any clock $z \in \mathcal{C}$, we have $\alpha_\mathcal{D}(\mathsf{Reset}_z([\![A]\!]_\mathcal{D})) \subseteq \mathsf{Reset}_z(A)$. Moreover, if $\mathcal{D}$ is the concrete domain, and A is reduced, then the above holds with equality.*

Algorithm 3. Algorithm SymReach that checks the reachability of a target location l_T in a given abstract domain $\mathcal{D}$.

Input: $\mathcal{A} = (\mathcal{L}, \mathsf{Inv}, \ell_0, \mathcal{C}, E)$, ℓ_T, $\mathcal{D}$

1 ;
2 next := $\mathsf{enc}(l_0) \wedge \alpha_{\mathcal{D}}(\wedge_{x \in \mathcal{C}} x = 0)$;
3 layers := $[]$;
4 reachable := false;
5 **while** $(\neg\mathsf{reachable} \wedge \mathsf{next}) \neq$ false **do**
6   reachable := reachable $\vee$ next;
7   next := $\mathsf{ApplyEdges}(\mathsf{Up}(\mathsf{next})) \wedge \neg\mathsf{reachable}$;
8   layers.$push$(next);
9   **if** $(\mathsf{next} \wedge \mathsf{enc}(l_T)) \neq$ false **then**
10   **return** ExtractTrace (layers);
11 **return** Not reachable;

4.3 Model-Checking Algorithm

Algorithm 3 shows how to check the reachability of a target location given an abstract domain. The list layers contains, at position i, the set of states that are reachable in i steps. The function ApplyEdges computes the disjunction of immediate successors by all edges. It consists in looping over all edges $e = (l_1, g, R, l_2)$, and gathering the following image by e:

$$\mathsf{enc}(\ell_2) \wedge \mathsf{Reset}_{r_k}(\mathsf{Reset}_{r_{k-1}}(\ldots(\mathsf{Reset}_{r_1}((((\exists \mathcal{B}.A(\mathcal{B}, \mathcal{P}) \wedge \mathsf{enc}(\ell_1)) \wedge \alpha_{\mathcal{D}}(g)))))))),$$

where $R = \{r_1, \ldots, r_k\}$. We thus use a partitioned transition relation and do not compute the monolithic transition relation.

When the target location is found to be reachable, ExtractTrace(layers) returns a trace reaching the target location. This is standard and can be done by computing backwards from the last element of layers, by finding which edge can be applied to reach the current state. Since both reset and time successor operations are defined using relations, predecessors in our abstract system can be easily computed using the operator pre_R. As it is standard, we omit the precise definition of this function (the reader can refer to the implementation) but assume that it returns a trace of the form $A_1 \xrightarrow{\sigma_1} A_2 \xrightarrow{\sigma_2} \ldots \xrightarrow{\sigma_{n-1}} A_n$, where the $A_i(\mathcal{B}, \mathcal{P})$ are minterms and the σ_i belong to the trace alphabet $\Sigma = \{\mathsf{up}, r_\emptyset\} \cup \{r(x)\}_{x \in \mathcal{C}}$, with the following meaning:

- if $A_i \xrightarrow{\mathsf{up}} A_{i+1}$ then $A_{i+1} = \mathsf{Up}(A_i)$;
- if $A_i \xrightarrow{r_\emptyset} A_{i+1}$ then $A_{i+1} = A_i$;
- if $A_i \xrightarrow{r(x)} A_{i+1}$ then $A_{i+1} = \mathsf{Reset}_x(A_i)$.

The feasibility of such a trace is easily checked using DBMs.

The overall algorithm then follows a classical CEGAR scheme. We initialize $\mathcal{D}$ by adding the clock constraints that appear syntactically in $\mathcal{A}$, which is often a good heuristic. We run the reachability check of Algorithm 3. If no trace is found, then the target location is not reachable. If a trace is found, then we check for feasibility. If it is feasible, then the counterexample is confirmed. Otherwise, the trace is spurious and we run the refinement procedure described in the next subsection, and repeat the analysis.

4.4 Abstraction Refinement

Since we initialize $\mathcal{D}$ with all clock constraints appearing in guards, we can assume that all guards are represented exactly in the considered abstractions. Note that the algorithm can be easily extended to the general case; but this simplifies the presentation.

The abstract transition relation we use is not the most precise abstraction of the concrete transition relation. Therefore, it is possible to have abstract transitions $A_1 \xrightarrow{a} A_2$ for some action a while no concrete transition exists between $[\![A_1]\!]$ and $[\![A_2]\!]$. This requires care and is not a direct application of the standard refinement technique from [11]. A second difficulty is due to incomplete reduction of the predicates using $\mathsf{reduce}_{\mathcal{D}}^2$. In fact, some reachable states in our abstract model will be unsatisfiable. Let us explain how we refine the abstraction in each of these cases.

Consider an algorithm interp which returns an interpolant of given zones Z_1, Z_2. In what follows, by the *refinement of* $\mathcal{D}$ *by* $\mathsf{interp}(Z_1, Z_2)$, we mean the domain $\mathcal{D}'$ obtained by adding $(k, \prec)$ to $\mathcal{D}_{x,y}$ for all constraints $x - y \prec k$ of $\mathsf{interp}(Z_1, Z_2)$. Observe that $\alpha_{\mathcal{D}'}(Z_1) \cap \alpha_{\mathcal{D}'}(Z_2) = \emptyset$ in this case.

We define concrete successor and predecessor operations for the actions in Σ. For each $a \in \Sigma$, let Pre_a^c denote the concrete predecessor operation on zones defined straightforwardly, and similarly for Post_a^c.

Consider domain $\mathcal{D}$ and the induced abstraction function $\alpha_{\mathcal{D}}$. Assume that we are given a spurious trace $\pi = A_1 \xrightarrow{\sigma_1} A_2 \xrightarrow{\sigma_1} \ldots \xrightarrow{\sigma_{n-1}} A_n$. Let $B_1 \ldots B_n$ be the sequence of concrete states visited along π in $\mathcal{A}$, that is, B_1 is the concrete initial state, and for all $2 \leq i \leq n$, let $B_i = \mathsf{Post}_{\pi_{i-1}}^c(B_{i-1})$. This sequence can be computed using DBMs.

The trace is *realizable* if $B_n \neq \emptyset$, in which case the counterexample is confirmed. Otherwise it is *spurious*. We show how to refine the abstraction to eliminate a spurious trace π.

Let i_0 be the maximal index such that $B_{i_0} \neq \emptyset$. There are three possible reasons explaining why B_{i_0+1} is empty:

1. first, if the abstract successor A_{i_0+1} is unsatisfiable, that is, if it contains contradictory predicates; in this case, $[\![A_{i_0+1}]\!] = \emptyset$, and the abstraction is refined by Lemma 8 to eliminate this case by strengthening $\mathsf{reduce}_{\mathcal{D}}^k$.
2. if there are predecessors of A_{i_0+1} inside A_{i_0} but none of them are in B_{i_0}, i.e., $\mathsf{Pre}_{\pi_{i_0}}^c([\![A_{i_0+1}]\!]) \cap [\![A_{i_0}]\!] \neq \emptyset$; in this case, we refine the domain by separating these predecessors from the rest of A_{i_0} using $\mathsf{interp}(\mathsf{Pre}_{\pi_{i_0}}^c([\![A_{i_0+1}]\!]), B_{i_0-1})$, as in [11].

3. otherwise, there are no predecessors of A_{i_0+1} inside A_{i_0}: we refine the abstraction according to the type of the transition from step i_0 to $i_0 + 1$:
   (a) if $\pi_{i_0} = $ up: refine $\mathcal{D}$ by $\mathsf{interp}([\![A_{i_0}]\!]\!\uparrow, [\![A_{i_0+1}]\!]\!\downarrow)$.
   (b) if $\pi_{i_0} = r(x)$: refine $\mathcal{D}$ by $\mathsf{interp}(\mathsf{Free}_x([\![A_{i_0}]\!]), \mathsf{Free}_x([\![A_{i_0+1}]\!]))$.

Note that the case $\pi_{i_0} = r_\emptyset$ is not possible since this induces the identity function both in the abstract and concrete systems.

Given abstraction $\alpha_{\mathcal{D}}$ and spurious trace π, let $\mathsf{refine}(\alpha_{\mathcal{D}}, \pi)$ denote the refined abstraction $\alpha_{\mathcal{D}'}$ obtained as described above.

The following two lemmas justify the two subcases of the third case above. They prove that the detected spurious transition disappears after refinement. The reset and up operations depend on the abstraction, so we make this dependence explicit below by using superscripts, as in Reset_x^α and Up^α, in order to distinguish the operations before and after a refinement.

Lemma 12. *Consider* $(A_1, A_2) \in \mathsf{Up}^\alpha$ *with* $[\![A_1]\!]\!\uparrow \cap [\![A_2]\!] = \emptyset$. *Then* $[\![A_1]\!]\!\uparrow \cap [\![A_2]\!]\!\downarrow = \emptyset$. *Moreover, if* α' *is obtained by refinement of* α *by* $\mathsf{interp}([\![A_1]\!]\!\uparrow, [\![A_2]\!]\!\downarrow)$, *then for all* $(A_1', A_2') \in \mathsf{Up}^{\alpha'}$, $[\![A_1']\!] \subseteq [\![A_1]\!]$ *implies* $[\![A_2']\!] \cap [\![A_2]\!] = \emptyset$.

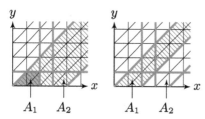
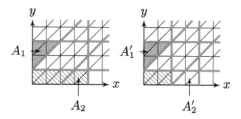

(a) Refinement for the time successors operation. The interpolant that separates $[\![A_1]\!]\!\uparrow$ from $[\![A_2]\!]\!\downarrow$ contains the constraint $x = y + 2$. When this is added to the abstract domain, the set A_2' (which is A_2 in the new abstraction) is no longer reachable by the time successors operation.

(b) Refinement for the reset operation. The interpolant that separates $\mathsf{Free}_y(A_1)$ from $\mathsf{Free}_y(A_2)$ contains the constraint $x < 2$. When this is added to the abstract domain, the set A_2' (which is A_2 in the new abstraction) is no longer reachable by the reset operation.

Lemma 13. *Consider* $x \in \mathcal{C}$, *and* $(A_1, A_2) \in \mathsf{Reset}_x^\alpha$ *such that* $[\![A_1]\!][x \leftarrow 0] \cap [\![A_2]\!] = \emptyset$. *Then* $\mathsf{Free}_x([\![A_1]\!]) \cap \mathsf{Free}_x([\![A_2]\!]) = \emptyset$. *Moreover, if* α' *is obtained by refinement of* α *by* $\mathsf{interp}(\mathsf{Free}_x([\![A_1]\!]), \mathsf{Free}_x([\![A_2]\!]))$, *then for all* $(A_1', A_2') \in \mathsf{Reset}_x^{\alpha'}$ *with* $[\![A_1']\!] \subseteq [\![A_1]\!]$, *we have* $[\![A_2']\!] \cap [\![A_2]\!] = \emptyset$.

5 Experiments

We implemented both algorithms. The symbolic version was implemented in OCaml using the CUDD library[2]; the explicit version was implemented in C++ within an existing model checker using Uppaal DBM library. Both prototypes

---

[2] http://vlsi.colorado.edu/~fabio/.

take as input networks of timed automata with invariants, discrete variables, urgent and committed locations. The presented algorithms are adapted to these features without difficulty.

We evaluated our algorithms on three classes of benchmarks we believe are significant. We compare the performance of the algorithm with that of Uppaal [7] which is based on zones, as well as the BDD-based model checker engine of PAT [25]. We were unable to compare with RED [30] which is not maintained anymore and not open source, and with which we failed to obtain correct results. The tool used in [16] was not available either. We thus only provide a comparison here with two well-maintained tools.

Two of our benchmarks are variants of schedulability-analysis problems where task execution times depend on the internal states of executed processes, so that an analysis of the state space is necessary to obtain a precise answer.

Monoprocess Scheduling Analysis. In this variant, a single process sequentially executes tasks on a single machine, and the execution time of each cycle depends on the state of the process. The goal is to determine a bound on the maximum execution time of a single cycle. This depends on the semantics of the process since the bound depends on the reachable states.

More precisely, we built a set of benchmarks where the processes are defined by synchronous circuit models taken from the Synthesis Competition (http://www.syntcomp.org). We assume that each latch of the circuit is associated with a resource, and changing the state of the resource takes some amount of time. So a subset of the latches have clocks associated with them, which measure the time elapsed since the latest value change (latest moment when the value changed from 0 to 1, or from 1 to 0). We provide two time positive bounds ℓ_0 and ℓ_1 for each latch, which determine the execution time as follows: if the value of latch ℓ changes from 0 to 1 (resp. from 1 to 0), then the execution time of the present cycle cannot be less than ℓ_1 (resp. ℓ_0). The execution time of the step is then the minimum that satisfies these constraints.

Multi-process Stateful Scheduling Analysis. In this variant, three processes are scheduled on two machines with a round-robin policy. Processes schedule tasks one after the other without any delay. As in the previous benchmarks, a process executing a task (on any machine) corresponds to a step of the synchronous circuit model. Each task is described by a tuple (C_1, C_2, D) which defines the minimum and maximum execution times, and the relative deadline. When a task finishes, the next task arrives immediately. The values in the tuple depend on the state of the process. The goal is to check the absence of any deadline miss. Processes are also instantiated with AIG circuits from http://www.syntcomp.org.

Asynchronous Computation. We consider an asynchronous network of "threshold gates", defined as follows: each gate is characterized by a tuple $(n, \theta, [l, u])$ where n is the number of inputs, $0 \leq \theta \leq n$ is the threshold, and $l \leq u$ are lower and upper bounds on activation time. Each gate has an output which is initially undefined. The gate becomes active during the time period $[l, u]$.

During this time, if all inputs are defined, and if at least θ of the inputs have value 1, then it sets its output to 1. At the end of the time period, it becomes deactivated and the output becomes undefined again, until the next period, which starts l time units after the deactivation. The goal is to check whether the given gate can output 1 within a given time bound T.

Results. Figure 3 displays the results of our experiments. All algorithms were given 8 GB of memory and a timeout of 30 min, and the experiments were run on laptop with an Intel i7@3.2 Ghz processor running Linux. The symbolic algorithm performs best among all on the monoprocess and multiprocess scheduling benchmarks. Uppaal is the second best, but does not solve as many benchmarks as our algorithm. Our enumerative algorithm quickly fails on these benchmarks, often running out of memory. On asynchronous computation benchmarks, our enumerative algorithm performs remarkably well, beating all other algorithms. We ran our tools on the CSMA/CD benchmarks (with 3 to 12 processes); Uppaal performs the best but our enumerative algorithm is slightly behind. The symbolic algorithm does not scale, while PAT fails to terminate in all cases.

The tool used for the symbolic algorithm is open source and can be found at https://github.com/osankur/symrob along with all the benchmarks.

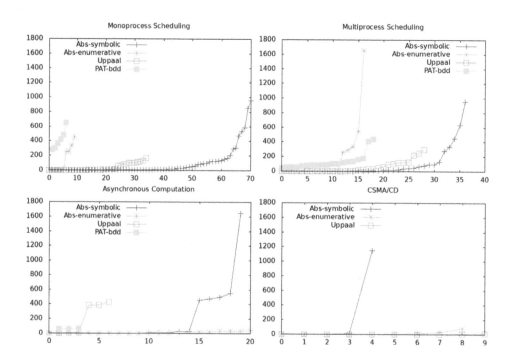

Fig. 3. Comparison of our enumerative and symbolic algorithms (referred to as Absenumerative and Abs-symbolic) with Uppaal and PAT. Each figure is a cactus plot for the set of benchmarks: a point (X, Y) means X benchmarks were solved within time bound Y.

6 Conclusion and Future Work

There are several ways to improve the algorithm. Since the choice of interpolants determines the abstraction function and the number of refinements, we assumed that taking the minimal interpolant should be preferable as it should keep the abstractions as coarse as possible. But it might be better to predict which interpolant is the most adapted for the rest of the computation in order to limit future refinements. The number of refinement also depends on the search order, and although it has already been studied in [23], it could be interesting to study it in this case. Generally speaking, it is worth noting that we currently cannot predict which (variant of) our algorithms is better suited for which model.

Several extensions of our algorithms could be developed, *e.g.* combining our algorithms with other methods based on finer abstractions as in [22], integrating predicate abstraction on discrete variables, or developing SAT-based versions of our algorithms.

References

1. Althaus, E., et al.: Verification of linear hybrid systems with large discrete statespaces using counterexample-guided abstraction refinement. Sci. Comput. Program. **1**(48), 123–160 (2017)
2. Alur, R., Courcoubetis, C., Dill, D.L.: Model-checking in dense real-time. Inf. Comput. **104**(1), 2–34 (1993)
3. Alur, R., Dill, D.: Automata for modeling real-time systems. In: Paterson, M.S. (ed.) ICALP 1990. LNCS, vol. 443, pp. 322–335. Springer, Heidelberg (1990). https://doi.org/10.1007/BFb0032042
4. Baier, Ch., Katoen, J.-P.: Principles of Model-Checking. MIT Press, Cambridge (2008)
5. Ball, T., Rajamani, S.K.: The SLAM toolkit. In: Berry, G., Comon, H., Finkel, A. (eds.) CAV 2001. LNCS, vol. 2102, pp. 260–264. Springer, Heidelberg (2001). https://doi.org/10.1007/3-540-44585-4_25
6. Behrmann, G., Bouyer, P., Larsen, K.G., Pelánek, R.: Lower and upper bounds in zone based abstractions of timed automata. In: Jensen, K., Podelski, A. (eds.) TACAS 2004. LNCS, vol. 2988, pp. 312–326. Springer, Heidelberg (2004). https://doi.org/10.1007/978-3-540-24730-2_25
7. Behrmann, G.: Uppaal 4.0. In: Proceedings of the 3rd International Conference on Quantitative Evaluation of Systems (QEST 2006), pp. 125–126. IEEE Computer Society Press, September 2006
8. Bengtsson, J., Yi, W.: Timed automata: semantics, algorithms and tools. In: Desel, J., Reisig, W., Rozenberg, G. (eds.) ACPN 2003. LNCS, vol. 3098, pp. 87–124. Springer, Heidelberg (2004). https://doi.org/10.1007/978-3-540-27755-2_3
9. Berthomieu, B., Menasche, M.: An enumerative approach for analyzing time Petri nets. In: Mason, R.E.A. (eds.) Information Processing–Proceedings of the 9th IFIP World Computer Congress (WCC 1983), pp. 41–46. North-Holland/IFIP, September 1983
10. Clarke, E.M., Emerson, E.A.: Design and synthesis of synchronization skeletons using branching time temporal logic. In: Kozen, D. (ed.) Logic of Programs 1981. LNCS, vol. 131, pp. 52–71. Springer, Heidelberg (1982). https://doi.org/10.1007/BFb0025774

11. Clarke, E.M., Grumberg, O., Jha, S., Lu, Y., Veith, H.: Counterexample-guided abstraction refinement for symbolic model checking. J. ACM **50**(5), 752–794 (2003)
12. Clarke, E.M., Grumberg, O., Peled, D.A.: Model Checking. MIT Press, Cambridge (2000)
13. Cousot, P., Cousot, R.: Abstract interpretation: a unified lattice model for static analysis of programs by construction or approximation of fixpoints. In: Conference Record of the 4th ACM Symposium on Principles of Programming Languages (POPL 1977), pp. 238–252. ACM Press, January 1977
14. Dierks, H., Kupferschmid, S., Larsen, K.G.: Automatic abstraction refinement for timed automata. In: Raskin, J.-F., Thiagarajan, P.S. (eds.) FORMATS 2007. LNCS, vol. 4763, pp. 114–129. Springer, Heidelberg (2007). https://doi.org/10.1007/978-3-540-75454-1_10
15. Dill, D.L.: Timing assumptions and verification of finite-state concurrent systems. In: Sifakis, J. (ed.) CAV 1989. LNCS, vol. 407, pp. 197–212. Springer, Heidelberg (1990). https://doi.org/10.1007/3-540-52148-8_17
16. Ehlers, R., Fass, D., Gerke, M., Peter, H.-J.: Fully symbolic timed model checking using constraint matrix diagrams. In: Proceedings of the 31st IEEE Symposium on Real-Time Systems (RTSS 2010), pp. 360–371. IEEE Computer Society Press, November 2010
17. Ehlers, R., Mattmüller, R., Peter, H.-J.: Combining symbolic representations for solving timed games. In: Chatterjee, K., Henzinger, T.A. (eds.) FORMATS 2010. LNCS, vol. 6246, pp. 107–121. Springer, Heidelberg (2010). https://doi.org/10.1007/978-3-642-15297-9_10
18. He, F., Zhu, H., Hung, W.N.N., Song, X., Gu, M.: Compositional abstraction refinement for timed systems. In: 2010 4th IEEE International Symposium on Theoretical Aspects of Software Engineering, pp. 168–176, August 2010
19. Henzinger, T.A., Jhala, R., Majumdar, R., Sutre, G.: Lazy abstraction. In: Conference Record of the 29th ACM SIGPLAN-SIGACT Symposium on Principles of Programming Languages (POPL 2002). ACM Press, January 2002. ACM SIGPLAN Notices **37**(1), 58–70
20. Henzinger, T.A., Jhala, R., Majumdar, R., Sutre, G.: Software verification with BLAST. In: Ball, T., Rajamani, S.K. (eds.) SPIN 2003. LNCS, vol. 2648, pp. 235–239. Springer, Heidelberg (2003). https://doi.org/10.1007/3-540-44829-2_17
21. Herbreteau, F., Kini, D., Srivathsan, B., Walukiewicz, I.: Using non-convex approximations for efficient analysis of timed automata. In: Chakraborty, S., Kumar, A. (eds.) Proceedings of the 31st Conference on Foundations of Software Technology and Theoretical Computer Science (FSTTCS 2011), volume 13 of Leibniz International Proceedings in Informatics, pp. 78–89. Leibniz-Zentrumfür Informatik, December 2011
22. Herbreteau, F., Srivathsan, B., Walukiewicz, I.: Lazy abstractions for timed automata. In: Sharygina, N., Veith, H. (eds.) CAV 2013. LNCS, vol. 8044, pp. 990–1005. Springer, Heidelberg (2013). https://doi.org/10.1007/978-3-642-39799-8_71
23. Herbreteau, F., Tran, T.-T.: Improving search order for reachability testing in timed automata. In: Sankaranarayanan, S., Vicario, E. (eds.) FORMATS 2015. LNCS, vol. 9268, pp. 124–139. Springer, Cham (2015). https://doi.org/10.1007/978-3-319-22975-1_9
24. McMillan, K.L.: Symbolic model checking—an approach to the state explosion problem. Ph.D. thesis, Carnegie Mellon University, Pittsburgh, Pennsylvania, USA (1993)

25. Nguyen, T.K., Sun, J., Liu, Y., Dong, J.S., Liu, Y.: Improved BDD-based discrete analysis of timed systems. In: Giannakopoulou, D., Méry, D. (eds.) FM 2012. LNCS, vol. 7436, pp. 326–340. Springer, Heidelberg (2012). https://doi.org/10.1007/978-3-642-32759-9_28

26. Pnueli, A.: The temporal logic of programs. In: Proceedings of the 18th Annual Symposium on Foundations of Computer Science (FOCS 1977), pp. 46–57. IEEE Computer Society Press, October–November 1977

27. Roussanaly, V., Sankur, O., Markey, N.: Abstraction refinement algorithms for timed automata. Technical report arXiv:1905.07365 arXiv, May 2019

28. Seshia, S.A., Bryant, R.E.: Unbounded, fully symbolic model checking of timed automata using boolean methods. In: Hun Jr., W.A., Somenzi, F. (eds.) CAV 2003. LNCS, vol. 2725, pp. 154–166. Springer, Heidelberg (2003). https://doi.org/10.1007/978-3-540-45069-6_16

29. Tóth, T., Majzik, I.: Lazy reachability checking for timed automata using interpolants. In: Abate, A., Geeraerts, G. (eds.) FORMATS 2017. LNCS, vol. 10419, pp. 264–280. Springer, Cham (2017). https://doi.org/10.1007/978-3-319-65765-3_15

30. Wang, F.: Symbolic verification of complex real-time systems with clock-restriction diagram. In: Kim, M., Chin, B., Kang, S., Lee, D. (eds.) Proceedings of the 21st IFIP TC6/WG6.1 International Conference on Formal Techniques for Networked and Distributed Systems (FORTE 2001), volume 197 of IFIP Conference Proceedings, pp. 235–250. Chapman & Hall, August 2001

31. Wang, W., Jiao, L.: Trace abstraction refinement for timed automata. In: Cassez, F., Raskin, J.-F. (eds.) ATVA 2014. LNCS, vol. 8837, pp. 396–410. Springer, Cham (2014). https://doi.org/10.1007/978-3-319-11936-6_28

Overfitting in Synthesis: Theory and Practice

Saswat Padhi[1](✉), Todd Millstein[1], Aditya Nori[2], and Rahul Sharma[3]

[1] University of California, Los Angeles, USA
{padhi,todd}@cs.ucla.edu
[2] Microsoft Research, Cambridge, UK
adityan@microsoft.com
[3] Microsoft Research, Bengaluru, India
rahsha@microsoft.com

Abstract. In syntax-guided synthesis (SyGuS), a synthesizer's goal is to automatically generate a program belonging to a grammar of possible implementations that meets a logical specification. We investigate a common limitation across state-of-the-art SyGuS tools that perform counterexample-guided inductive synthesis (CEGIS). We empirically observe that as the expressiveness of the provided grammar increases, the performance of these tools degrades significantly.

We claim that this degradation is not only due to a larger search space, but also due to *overfitting*. We formally define this phenomenon and prove *no-free-lunch* theorems for SyGuS, which reveal a fundamental tradeoff between synthesizer performance and grammar expressiveness.

A standard approach to mitigate overfitting in machine learning is to run multiple learners with varying expressiveness in parallel. We demonstrate that this insight can immediately benefit existing SyGuS tools. We also propose a novel single-threaded technique called *hybrid enumeration* that interleaves different grammars and outperforms the winner of the 2018 SyGuS competition (`Inv` track), solving more problems and achieving a 5× mean speedup.

1 Introduction

The *syntax-guided synthesis* (SyGuS) framework [3] provides a unified format to describe a program synthesis problem by supplying **(1)** a logical specification for the desired functionality, and **(2)** a grammar of allowed implementations. Given these two inputs, a SyGuS tool searches through the programs that are permitted by the grammar to generate one that meets the specification. Today, SyGuS is at the core of several state-of-the-art program synthesizers [5, 14, 23, 24, 29], many of which compete annually in the SyGuS competition [1, 4].

We demonstrate empirically that five state-of-the-art SyGuS tools are very sensitive to the choice of grammar. Increasing grammar expressiveness allows the tools to solve some problems that are unsolvable with less-expressive grammars. However, it also causes them to fail on many problems that the tools are able to solve with a less expressive grammar. We analyze the latter behavior both theoretically and empirically and present techniques that make existing tools much more robust in the face of increasing grammar expressiveness.

We restrict our investigation to a widely used approach [6] to SyGuS called *counterexample-guided inductive synthesis* (CEGIS) [37, §5]. In this approach, the synthesizer is composed of a learner and an oracle. The learner iteratively identifies a candidate program that is consistent with a given set of examples (initially empty) and queries the oracle to either prove that the program is *correct*, i.e., meets the given specification, or obtain a counterexample that demonstrates that the program does not meet the specification. The counterexample is added to the set of examples for the next iteration. The iterations continue until a correct program is found or resource/time budgets are exhausted.

Overfitting. To better understand the observed performance degradation, we instrumented one of these SyGuS tools (Sect. 2.2). We empirically observe that for a large number of problems, the performance degradation on increasing grammar expressiveness is often accompanied by a significant increase in the number of counterexamples required. Intuitively, as grammar expressiveness increases so does the number of *spurious* candidate programs, which satisfy a given set of examples but violate the specification. If the learner picks such a candidate, then the oracle generates a counterexample, the learner searches again, and so on.

In other words, increasing grammar expressiveness increases the chances for *overfitting*, a well-known phenomenon in machine learning (ML). Overfitting occurs when a learned function explains a given set of observations but does not generalize correctly beyond it. Since SyGuS is indeed a form of function learning, it is perhaps not surprising that it is prone to overfitting. However, we identify its specific source in the context of SyGuS—the spurious candidates induced by increasing grammar expressiveness—and show that it is a significant problem in practice. We formally define the *potential for overfitting* (Ω), in Definition 7, which captures the number of spurious candidates.

No Free Lunch. In the ML community, this tradeoff between expressiveness and overfitting has been formalized for various settings as *no-free-lunch* (NFL) theorems [34, §5.1]. Intuitively such a theorem says that for every learner there exists a function that cannot be efficiently learned, where efficiency is defined by the number of examples required. We have proven corresponding NFL theorems for the CEGIS-based SyGuS setting (Theorems 1 and 2).

A key difference between the ML and SyGuS settings is the notion of *m-learnability*. In the ML setting, the learned function may differ from the true function, as long as this difference (expressed as an error probability) is relatively small. However, because the learner is allowed to make errors, it is in turn required to learn given an arbitrary set of m examples (drawn from some distribution). In contrast, the SyGuS learning setting is *all-or-nothing*—either the tool synthesizes a program that meets the given specification or it fails. Therefore, it would be overly strong to require the learner to handle an arbitrary set of examples.

Instead, we define a much weaker notion of m-learnability for SyGuS, which only requires that there *exist* a set of m examples for which the learner succeeds. Yet, our NFL theorem shows that even this weak notion of learnability can always be thwarted: given an integer $m \geq 0$ and an expressive enough (as a function of m) grammar, for every learner there exists a SyGuS problem that cannot be learned without access to more than m examples. We also prove that overfitting is inevitable with an expressive enough grammar (Theorems 3 and 4) and that the potential for overfitting increases with grammar expressiveness (Theorem 5).

Mitigating Overfitting. Inspired by *ensemble methods* [13] in ML, which aggregate results from multiple learners to combat overfitting (and underfitting), we propose PLEARN—a black-box framework that runs multiple parallel instances of a SyGuS tool with different grammars. Although prior SyGuS tools run multiple instances of learners with different random seeds [7,20], to our knowledge, this is the first proposal to explore multiple grammars as a means to improve the performance of SyGuS. Our experiments indicate that PLEARN significantly improves the performance of five state-of-the-art SyGuS tools—CVC4 [7,33], EUSOLVER [5], LOOPINVGEN [29], SKETCHAC [20,37], and STOCH [3, III F].

However, running parallel instances of a synthesizer is computationally expensive. Hence, we also devise a white-box approach, called *hybrid enumeration*, that extends the enumerative synthesis technique [2] to efficiently interleave exploration of multiple grammars in a single SyGuS instance. We implement hybrid enumeration within LOOPINVGEN[1] and show that the resulting single-threaded learner, LOOPINVGEN+HE, has negligible overhead but achieves performance comparable to that of PLEARN for LOOPINVGEN. Moreover, LOOPINVGEN+HE significantly outperforms the winner [28] of the invariant-synthesis (Inv) track of 2018 SyGuS competition [4]—a variant of LOOPINVGEN specifically tuned for the competition—including a $5\times$ mean speedup and solving two SyGuS problems that no tool in the competition could solve.

Contributions. In summary, we present the following contributions:

(Section 2) We empirically observe that, in many cases, increasing grammar expressiveness degrades performance of existing SyGuS tools due to *overfitting*.

(Section 3) We formally define overfitting and prove *no-free-lunch* theorems for the SyGuS setting, which indicate that overfitting with increasing grammar expressiveness is a fundamental characteristic of SyGuS.

(Section 4) We propose two mitigation strategies – **(1)** a black-box technique that runs multiple parallel instances of a synthesizer, each with a different grammar, and **(2)** a single-threaded enumerative technique, called *hybrid enumeration*, that interleaves exploration of multiple grammars.

(Section 5) We show that incorporating these mitigating measures in existing tools significantly improves their performance.

---

[1] Our implementation is available at https://github.com/SaswatPadhi/LoopInvGen.

2   Motivation

In this section, we first present empirical evidence that existing SyGuS tools are sensitive to changes in grammar expressiveness. Specifically, we demonstrate that as we increase the expressiveness of the provided grammar, every tool starts failing on some benchmarks that it was able to solve with less-expressive grammars. We then investigate one of these tools in detail.

2.1   Grammar Sensitivity of SyGuS Tools

We evaluated 5 state-of-the-art SyGuS tools that use very different techniques:

- SKETCHAC [20] extends the SKETCH synthesis system [37] by combining both explicit and symbolic search techniques.
- STOCH [3, III F] performs a stochastic search for solutions.
- EUSOLVER [5] combines enumeration with unification strategies.
- Reynolds et al. [33] extend CVC4 [7] with a refutation-based approach.
- LOOPINVGEN [29] combines enumeration and Boolean function learning.

We ran these five tools on 180 invariant-synthesis benchmarks, which we describe in Sect. 5. We ran the benchmarks with each of the six grammars of quantifier-free predicates, which are shown in Fig. 1. These grammars correspond to widely used abstract domains in the analysis of integer-manipulating programs— Equalities, Intervals [11], Octagons [25], Polyhedra [12], algebraic expressions (Polynomials) and arbitrary integer arithmetic (Peano) [30]. The $*_s$ operator denotes scalar multiplication, e.g., $(*_s\ 2\ x)$, and $*_N$ denotes nonlinear multiplication, e.g., $(*_N\ x\ y)$.

In Fig. 2, we report our findings on running each benchmark on each tool with each grammar, with a 30-minute wall-clock timeout. For each $\langle tool, grammar \rangle$ pair, the y-axis shows the number of failing benchmarks that the same tool is able to solve with a less-expressive grammar. We observe that, for each tool, the number of such failures increases with the grammar expressiveness. For instance, introducing the scalar multiplication operator $(*_s)$ causes CVC4 to fail on 21 benchmarks that it is able to solve with Equalities $(4/21)$, Intervals $(18/21)$, or Octagons $(10/21)$. Similarly, adding nonlinear multiplication causes LOOPINVGEN to fail on 10 benchmarks that it can solve with a less-expressive grammar.

$\langle b \rangle \models$ true $|$ false $|$ $\langle$Bool variables$\rangle$
  $|$ (not b) $|$ (or b b) $|$ (and b b)
$\langle i \rangle \models \langle$Int constants$\rangle$ $|$ $\langle$Int variables$\rangle$

► Additional rule in Equalities grammar:
  $\langle b \rangle \stackrel{+}{\models}$ (= i i)

► Additional rules in Intervals grammar:
  $\langle b \rangle \stackrel{+}{\models}$ (> i i) $|$ (>= i i)
    $|$ (< i i) $|$ (<= i i)

► Additional rules in Octagons grammar:
  $\langle i \rangle \stackrel{+}{\models}$ (+ i i) $|$ (- i i)

► Additional rule in Polyhedra grammar:
  $\langle i \rangle \stackrel{+}{\models}$ ($*_S$ i i)

► Additional rule in Polynomials grammar:
  $\langle i \rangle \stackrel{+}{\models}$ ($*_N$ i i)

► Additional rule in Peano grammar:
  $\langle i \rangle \stackrel{+}{\models}$ (div i i) $|$ (mod i i)

Fig. 1. Grammars of quantifier-free predicates over integers (We use the $\stackrel{+}{\models}$ operator to append new rules to previously defined nonterminals.)

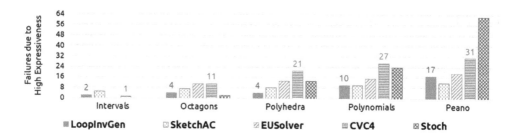

Fig. 2. For each grammar, each tool, the ordinate shows the number of benchmarks that *fail* with the grammar but are solvable with a less-expressive grammar.

	Increase (↑)	Unchanged (=)	Decrease (↓)
Expressiveness↑ ∧ Time↑ → Rounds?	27 %	67 %	6 %
Expressiveness↑ ∧ Rounds↑ → Time?	79 %	6 %	15 %

Fig. 3. Observed correlation between synthesis time and number of rounds, upon increasing grammar expressiveness, with LoopInvGen [29] on 180 benchmarks

2.2 Evidence for Overfitting

To better understand this phenomenon, we instrumented LoopInvGen [29] to record the candidate expressions that it synthesizes and the number of CEGIS iterations (called *rounds* henceforth). We compare each pair of successful runs of each of our 180 benchmarks on distinct grammars.[2] In 65 % of such pairs, we observe performance degradation with the more expressive grammar. We also report the correlation between performance degradation and number of rounds for the more expressive grammar in each pair in Fig. 3.

In 67 % of the cases with degraded performance upon increased grammar expressiveness, the number of rounds remains unaffected—indicating that this slowdown is mainly due to a larger search space. However, there is significant evidence of performance degradation due to *overfitting* as well. We note an increase in the number of rounds for 27 % of the cases with degraded performance. Moreover, we notice performance degradation in 79 % of all cases that required more rounds on increasing grammar expressiveness.

Thus, a more expressive grammar not only increases the search space, but also makes it more likely for LoopInvGen to overfit—select a spurious expression, which the oracle rejects with a counterexample, hence requiring more rounds. In the remainder of this section, we demonstrate this overfitting phenomenon on the verification problem shown in Fig. 4, an example by Gulwani and Jojic [17], which is the fib_19 benchmark in the Inv track of SyGuS-Comp 2018 [4].

---

[2] We ignore failing runs since they require an unknown number of rounds.

For Fig. 4, we require an inductive invariant that is strong enough to prove that the assertion on line 6 always holds. In the SyGuS setting, we need to synthesize a predicate $\mathcal{I}\colon \mathbb{Z}^4 \to \mathbb{B}$ defined on a symbolic state $\sigma = \langle m, n, x, y \rangle$, that satisfies $\forall \sigma \colon \varphi(\mathcal{I}, \sigma)$ for the specification φ:[3]

```
1  assume (0 ≤ n ∧ 0 ≤ m ≤ n)
2  assume (x = 0 ∧ y = m)
3  while (x < n) do
4      x ← x + 1
5      if (x > m) then y ← y + 1
6  assert (y = n)
```

Fig. 4. The `fib_19` benchmark [17]

$$\varphi(\mathcal{I}, \sigma) \stackrel{\text{def}}{=} \big(0 \leq n \wedge 0 \leq m \leq n \wedge x = 0 \wedge y = m\big) \implies \mathcal{I}(\sigma) \qquad \text{(precondition)}$$
$$\wedge \; \forall \sigma' \colon \big(\mathcal{I}(\sigma) \wedge T(\sigma, \sigma')\big) \implies \mathcal{I}(\sigma') \qquad \text{(inductiveness)}$$
$$\wedge \; \big(x \geq n \wedge \mathcal{I}(\sigma)\big) \implies y = n \qquad \text{(postcondition)}$$

where $\sigma' = \langle m', n', x', y' \rangle$ denotes the new state after one iteration, and T is a transition relation that describes the loop body:

$$T(\sigma, \sigma') \stackrel{\text{def}}{=} (x < n) \wedge (x' = x + 1) \wedge (m' = m) \wedge (n' = n)$$
$$\wedge \big[(x' \leq m \wedge y' = y) \vee (x' > m \wedge y' = y + 1) \big]$$

	Increasing expressiveness →				
Equalities	**Intervals**	**Octagons**	**Polyhedra**	**Polynomials**	**Peano**
×	0.32 s	2.49 s	2.48 s	55.3 s	68.0 s
FAIL	(19 rounds)	(57 rounds)	(57 rounds)	(76 rounds)	(88 rounds)

(a) Synthesis time and number of CEGIS iterations (rounds) with various grammars

16: $(x \geq n) \vee (x + 1 < n) \vee (m \geq x \wedge m = y)$

28: $(x = y) \vee (y + m - n = x) \vee (x + 2 < n)$

57: $(m = y) \vee (x \geq m \wedge x \geq y)$

(b) Sample predicates with Polyhedra

16: $(x \geq n) \vee (x + 1 < n) \vee (2y = n) \vee (y(m - 1) = m)$

28: $(y = 1) \vee (y = 0) \vee (m < 1) \vee (x^2 y > 1)$

57: $(x + 1 \geq n) \vee (x + 2 < n) \vee ((m - n)(x - y) = 1)$

(c) Sample predicates with Peano

Solution in both grammars: $(n \geq y) \wedge (y \geq x) \wedge ((m = y) \vee (x \geq m \wedge x \geq y))$

Fig. 5. Performance of LoopInvGen [29] on the `fib_19` benchmark (Fig. 4). In **(b)** and **(c)**, we show predicates generated at various rounds (numbered in **bold**).

In Fig. 5(a), we report the performance of LoopInvGen on `fib_19` (Fig. 4) with our six grammars (Fig. 1). It succeeds with all but the least-expressive grammar. However, as grammar expressiveness increases, the number of rounds increase significantly—from 19 rounds with Intervals to 88 rounds with Peano.

LoopInvGen converges to the *exact same* invariant with both Polyhedra and Peano but requires 30 more rounds in the latter case. In Figs. 5(b) and (c), we list some expressions synthesized with Polyhedra and Peano respectively. These expressions are solutions to intermediate subproblems—the final loop invariant is a conjunction of a subset of these expressions [29, §3.2]. Observe that the expressions generated with the Peano grammar are quite complex and unlikely to generalize well. Peano's extra expressiveness leads to more spurious candidates, increasing the chances of overfitting and making the benchmark harder to solve.

---

[3] We use $\mathbb{B}$, $\mathbb{N}$, and $\mathbb{Z}$ to denote the sets of all Boolean values, all natural numbers (positive integers), and all integers respectively.

3 SyGuS Overfitting in Theory

In this section, first we formalize the *counterexample-guided inductive synthesis* (CEGIS) approach [37] to SyGuS, in which examples are iteratively provided by a verification oracle. We then state and prove *no-free-lunch* theorems, which show that there can be no optimal learner for this learning scheme. Finally, we formalize a natural notion of *overfitting* for SyGuS and prove that the potential for overfitting increases with grammar expressiveness.

3.1 Preliminaries

We borrow the formal definition of a SyGuS problem from prior work [3]:

Definition 1 (SyGuS Problem). *Given a background theory* $\mathbb{T}$, *a function symbol* $f\colon X \to Y$, *and constraints on* f: *(1)* *a semantic constraint, also called a* specification, $\phi(f, x)$ *over the vocabulary of* $\mathbb{T}$ *along with* f *and a symbolic input* x, *and (2)* *a syntactic constraint, also called a* grammar, *given by a (possibly infinite) set* $\mathcal{E}$ *of expressions over the vocabulary of the theory* $\mathbb{T}$; *find an expression* $e \in \mathcal{E}$ *such that the formula* $\forall x \in X\colon \phi(e, x)$ *is valid modulo* $\mathbb{T}$.

We denote this SyGuS problem as $\langle f_{X \to Y} \mid \phi, \mathcal{E} \rangle_{\mathbb{T}}$ *and say that it is* satisfiable *iff there exists such an expression* e, *i.e.,* $\exists e \in \mathcal{E}\colon \forall x \in X\colon \phi(e, x)$. *We call* e *a* satisfying expression *for this problem, denoted as* $e \models \langle f_{X \to Y} \mid \phi, \mathcal{E} \rangle_{\mathbb{T}}$.

Recall, we focus on a common class of SyGuS learners, namely those that learn from examples. First we define the notion of input-output (IO) examples that are consistent with a SyGuS specification:

Definition 2 (Input-Output Example). *Given a specification* ϕ *defined on* $f\colon X \to Y$ *over a background theory* $\mathbb{T}$, *we call a pair* $\langle x, y \rangle \in X \times Y$ *an input-output (IO) example for* ϕ, *denoted as* $\langle x, y \rangle \succeq_{\mathbb{T}} \phi$ *iff it is satisfied by some valid interpretation of* f *within* $\mathbb{T}$, *i.e.,*

$$\langle x, y \rangle \succeq_{\mathbb{T}} \phi \;\overset{\text{def}}{=}\; \exists e_* \in \mathbb{T}\colon e_*(x) = y \;\wedge\; \big(\forall x \in X\colon \phi(e_*, x)\big)$$

The next two definitions respectively formalize the two key components of a CEGIS-based SyGuS tool: the verification oracle and the learner.

Definition 3 (Verification Oracle). *Given a specification* ϕ *defined on a function* $f\colon X \to Y$ *over theory* $\mathbb{T}$, *a verification oracle* $\mathcal{O}_\phi$ *is a partial function that given an expression* e, *either returns* $\bot$ *indicating* $\forall x \in X\colon \phi(e, x)$ *holds, or gives a counterexample* $\langle x, y \rangle$ *against* e, *denoted as* $e \rightsquigarrow\!\!\times_\phi \langle x, y \rangle$, *such that*

$$e \rightsquigarrow\!\!\times_\phi \langle x, y \rangle \;\overset{\text{def}}{=}\; \neg \phi(e, x) \;\wedge\; e(x) \neq y \;\wedge\; \langle x, y \rangle \succeq_{\mathbb{T}} \phi$$

We omit ϕ from the notations $\mathcal{O}_\phi$ and $\rightsquigarrow\!\!\times_\phi$ when it is clear from the context.

Definition 4 (CEGIS-based Learner). *A CEGIS-based learner $\mathcal{L}^{\mathcal{O}}(q, \mathcal{E})$ is a partial function that given an integer $q \geq 0$, a set $\mathcal{E}$ of expressions, and access to an oracle $\mathcal{O}$ for a specification ϕ defined on $f\colon X \to Y$, queries $\mathcal{O}$ at most q times and either fails with $\bot$ or generates an expression $e \in \mathcal{E}$. The trace*

$$\left[e_0 \rightsquigarrow \langle x_0, y_0 \rangle, \ \ldots, \ e_{p-1} \rightsquigarrow \langle x_{p-1}, y_{p-1} \rangle, \ e_p \right] \qquad \text{where } 0 \leq p \leq q$$

summarizes the interaction between the oracle and the learner. Each e_i denotes the ith candidate for f and $\langle x_i, y_i \rangle$ is a counterexample e_i, i.e.,

$$\left(\forall j < i \colon e_i(x_j) = y_j \land \phi(e_i, x_j) \right) \ \land \ \left(e_i \rightsquigarrow_\phi \langle x_i, y_i \rangle \right)$$

Note that we have defined oracles and learners as (partial) functions, and hence as *deterministic*. In practice, many SyGuS tools are deterministic and this assumption simplifies the subsequent theorems. However, we expect that these theorems can be appropriately generalized to randomized oracles and learners.

3.2 Learnability and No Free Lunch

In the machine learning (ML) community, the limits of learning have been formalized for various settings as *no-free-lunch* theorems [34, §5.1]. Here, we provide a natural form of such theorems for CEGIS-based SyGuS learning.

In SyGuS, the learned function must conform to the given grammar, which may not be fully expressive. Therefore we first formalize grammar expressiveness:

Definition 5 (k-Expressiveness). *Given a domain X and range Y, a grammar $\mathcal{E}$ is said to be k-expressive iff $\mathcal{E}$ can express exactly k distinct $X \to Y$ functions.*

A key difference from the ML setting is our notion of *m-learnability*, which formalizes the number of examples that a learner requires in order to learn a desired function. In the ML setting, a function is considered to m-learnable by a learner if it can be learned using an *arbitrary* set of m i.i.d. examples (drawn from some distribution). This makes sense in the ML setting since the learned function is allowed to make errors (up to some given bound on the error probability), but it is much too strong for the *all-or-nothing* SyGuS setting.

Instead, we define a much weaker notion of m-learnability for CEGIS-based SyGuS, which only requires that there *exist* a set of m examples that allows the learner to succeed. The following definition formalizes this notion.

Definition 6 (CEGIS-based m-Learnability). *Given a SyGuS problem $S = \langle f_{X \to Y} \mid \phi, \mathcal{E} \rangle_{\mathbb{T}}$ and an integer $m \geq 0$, we say that S is m-learnable by a CEGIS-based learner $\mathcal{L}$ iff there exists a verification oracle $\mathcal{O}$ under which $\mathcal{L}$ can learn a satisfying expression for S with at most m queries to $\mathcal{O}$, i.e., $\exists \mathcal{O} \colon \mathcal{L}^{\mathcal{O}}(m, \mathcal{E}) \models S$.*

Finally we state and prove the no-free-lunch (NFL) theorems, which make explicit the tradeoff between grammar expressiveness and learnability. Intuitively, given an integer m and an expressive enough (as a function of m) grammar, for every learner there exists a SyGuS problem that cannot be solved without access to at least $m + 1$ examples. This is true despite our weak notion of learnability.

Put another way, as grammar expressiveness increases, so does the number of examples required for learning. On one extreme, if the given grammar is 1-expressive, i.e., can express exactly one function, then all satisfiable SyGuS problems are 0-learnable—no examples are needed because there is only one function to learn—but there are *many* SyGuS problems that cannot be satisfied by this function. On the other extreme, if the grammar is $|Y|^{|X|}$-expressive, i.e., can express all functions from X to Y, then for every learner there exists a SyGuS problem that requires *all* $|X|$ *examples* in order to be solved.

Below we first present the NFL theorem for the case when the domain X and range Y are finite. We then generalize to the case when these sets may be countably infinite. We provide the proofs of these theorems in the extended version of this paper [27, Appendix A.1].

Theorem 1 (NFL in CEGIS-based SyGuS on Finite Sets). *Let X and Y be two arbitrary finite sets, $\mathbb{T}$ be a theory that supports equality, $\mathcal{E}$ be a grammar over $\mathbb{T}$, and m be an integer such that $0 \leq m < |X|$. Then, either:*

- $\mathcal{E}$ *is not k-expressive for any $k > \sum_{i=0}^{m} \frac{|X|! \ |Y|^i}{(|X|-i)!}$, or*
- *for every CEGIS-based learner $\mathcal{L}$, there exists a satisfiable SyGuS problem $S = \langle f_{X \to Y} \mid \phi, \mathcal{E} \rangle_{\mathbb{T}}$ such that S is not m-learnable by $\mathcal{L}$. Moreover, there exists a different CEGIS-based learner for which S is m-learnable.*

Theorem 2 (NFL in CEGIS-based SyGuS on Countably Infinite Sets). *Let X be an arbitrary countably infinite set, Y be an arbitrary finite or countably infinite set, $\mathbb{T}$ be a theory that supports equality, $\mathcal{E}$ be a grammar over $\mathbb{T}$, and m be an integer such that $m \geq 0$. Then, either:*

- $\mathcal{E}$ *is not k-expressive for any $k > \aleph_0$, where $\aleph_0 \stackrel{\text{def}}{=} |\mathbb{N}|$, or*
- *for every CEGIS-based learner $\mathcal{L}$, there exists a satisfiable SyGuS problem $S = \langle f_{X \to Y} \mid \phi, \mathcal{E} \rangle_{\mathbb{T}}$ such that S is not m-learnable by $\mathcal{L}$. Moreover, there exists a different CEGIS-based learner for which S is m-learnable.*

3.3 Overfitting

Last, we relate the above theory to the notion of *overfitting* from ML. In the context of SyGuS, overfitting can potentially occur whenever there are multiple candidate expressions that are consistent with a given set of examples. Some of these expressions may not generalize to satisfy the specification, but the learner has no way to distinguish among them (using just the given set of examples) and so can "guess" incorrectly. We formalize this idea through the following measure:

Definition 7 (Potential for Overfitting). *Given a problem $S = \langle f_{X \to Y} \mid \phi, \mathcal{E} \rangle_{\mathbb{T}}$ and a set Z of IO examples for ϕ, we define the potential for overfitting Ω as the number of expressions in $\mathcal{E}$ that are consistent with Z but do not satisfy S, i.e.,*

$$\Omega(S, Z) \stackrel{\text{def}}{=} \begin{cases} |\{e \in \mathcal{E} \mid e \not\models S \land \forall \langle x, y \rangle \in Z : e(x) = y\}| & \forall z \in Z : z \approx_{\mathbb{T}} \phi \\ \bot \quad \text{(undefined)} & \text{otherwise} \end{cases}$$

Intuitively, a zero potential for overfitting means that overfitting is not possible on the given problem with respect to the given set of examples, because there is no spurious candidate. A positive potential for overfitting means that overfitting is possible, and higher values imply more spurious candidates and hence more potential for a learner to choose the "wrong" expression.

The following theorems connect our notion of overfitting to the earlier NFL theorems by showing that overfitting is inevitable with an expressive enough grammar. The proofs of these theorems can be found in the extended version of this paper [27, Appendix A.2].

Theorem 3 (Overfitting in SyGuS on Finite Sets). *Let X and Y be two arbitrary finite sets, m be an integer such that $0 \leq m < |X|$, $\mathbb{T}$ be a theory that supports equality, and $\mathcal{E}$ be a k-expressive grammar over $\mathbb{T}$ for some $k > \dfrac{|X|! \, |Y|^m}{m! \, (|X| - m)!}$. Then, there exists a satisfiable SyGuS problem $S = \langle f_{X \to Y} \mid \phi, \mathcal{E} \rangle_{\mathbb{T}}$ such that $\Omega(S, Z) > 0$, for every set Z of m IO examples for ϕ.*

Theorem 4 (Overfitting in SyGuS on Countably Infinite Sets). *Let X be an arbitrary countably infinite set, Y be an arbitrary finite or countably infinite set, $\mathbb{T}$ be a theory that supports equality, and $\mathcal{E}$ be a k-expressive grammar over $\mathbb{T}$ for some $k > \aleph_0$. Then, there exists a satisfiable SyGuS problem $S = \langle f_{X \to Y} \mid \phi, \mathcal{E} \rangle_{\mathbb{T}}$ such that $\Omega(S, Z) > 0$, for every set Z of m IO examples for ϕ.*

Finally, it is straightforward to show that as the expressiveness of the grammar provided in a SyGuS problem increases, so does its potential for overfitting.

Theorem 5 (Overfitting Increases with Expressiveness). *Let X and Y be two arbitrary sets, $\mathbb{T}$ be an arbitrary theory, $\mathcal{E}_1$ and $\mathcal{E}_2$ be grammars over $\mathbb{T}$ such that $\mathcal{E}_1 \subseteq \mathcal{E}_2$, ϕ be an arbitrary specification over $\mathbb{T}$ and a function symbol $f : X \to Y$, and Z be a set of IO examples for ϕ. Then, we have*

$$\Omega\big(\langle f_{X \to Y} \mid \phi, \mathcal{E}_1 \rangle_{\mathbb{T}}, Z \big) \;\leq\; \Omega\big(\langle f_{X \to Y} \mid \phi, \mathcal{E}_2 \rangle_{\mathbb{T}}, Z \big)$$

4   Mitigating Overfitting

Ensemble methods [13] in machine learning (ML) are a standard approach to reduce overfitting. These methods aggregate predictions from several learners to make a more accurate prediction. In this section we propose two approaches, inspired by ensemble methods in ML, for mitigating overfitting in SyGuS. Both are based on the key insight from Sect. 3.3 that synthesis over a subgrammar has a smaller potential for overfitting as compared to that over the original grammar.

4.1   Parallel SyGuS on Multiple Grammars

Our first idea is to run multiple parallel instances of a synthesizer on the same SyGuS problem but with grammars of varying expressiveness. This framework, called PLEARN, is outlined in Algorithm 1. It accepts a synthesis tool $\mathcal{T}$, a SyGuS

Algorithm 1. The PLEARN framework for SyGuS tools.

---

1 **func** PLEARN $(\mathcal{T}: \text{Synthesis Tool}, \langle f_{X \to Y} \mid \phi, \mathcal{E} \rangle_{\mathbb{T}}: \text{Problem}, \mathcal{E}_{1...p}: \text{Subgrammars})$

2 ▸ **Requires:** $\forall \mathcal{E}_i \in \mathcal{E}_{1...p}: \mathcal{E}_i \subseteq \mathcal{E}$

3   **parallel for** $i \leftarrow 1, \ldots, p$ **do**

4          $\mathsf{S}_i \leftarrow \langle f_{X \to Y} \mid \phi, \mathcal{E}_i \rangle_{\mathbb{T}}$

5          $e_i \leftarrow \mathcal{T}(\mathsf{S}_i)$

6   **if** $e_i \neq \bot$ **then return** e_i

7   **return** $\bot$

---

problem $\langle f_{X \to Y} \mid \phi, \mathcal{E} \rangle_{\mathbb{T}}$, and subgrammars $\mathcal{E}_{1...p}$,[4] such that $\mathcal{E}_i \subseteq \mathcal{E}$. The **parallel for** construct creates a new thread for each iteration. The loop in PLEARN creates p copies of the SyGuS problem, each with a different grammar from $\mathcal{E}_{1...p}$, and dispatches each copy to a new instance of the tool $\mathcal{T}$. PLEARN returns the first solution found or $\bot$ if none of the synthesizer instances succeed.

Since each grammar in $\mathcal{E}_{1...p}$ is subsumed by the original grammar $\mathcal{E}$, any expression found by PLEARN is a solution to the original SyGuS problem. Moreover, from Theorem 5 it is immediate that PLEARN indeed reduces overfitting.

Theorem 6 (PLEARN Reduces Overfitting). *Given a SyGuS problem* $\mathsf{S} = \langle f_{X \to Y} \mid \phi, \mathcal{E} \rangle_{\mathbb{T}}$, *if* PLEARN *is instantiated with* S *and subgrammars* $\mathcal{E}_{1...p}$ *such that* $\forall \mathcal{E}_i \in \mathcal{E}_{1...p}: \mathcal{E}_i \subseteq \mathcal{E}$, *then for each* $\mathsf{S}_i = \langle f_{X \to Y} \mid \phi, \mathcal{E}_i \rangle_{\mathbb{T}}$ *constructed by* PLEARN, *we have that* $\Omega(\mathsf{S}_i, Z) \leq \Omega(\mathsf{S}, Z)$ *on any set* Z *of IO examples for* ϕ.

A key advantage of PLEARN is that it is agnostic to the synthesizer's implementation. Therefore, existing SyGuS learners can immediately benefit from PLEARN, as we demonstrate in Sect. 5.1. However, running p parallel SyGuS instances can be prohibitively expensive, both computationally and memory-wise. The problem is worsened by the fact that many existing SyGuS tools already use multiple threads, e.g., the SKETCHAC [20] tool spawns 9 threads. This motivates our *hybrid enumeration* technique described next, which is a novel synthesis algorithm that interleaves exploration of multiple grammars in a single thread.

4.2 Hybrid Enumeration

Hybrid enumeration extends the *enumerative synthesis* technique, which enumerates expressions within a given grammar in order of size and returns the first candidate that satisfies the given examples [2]. Our goal is to simulate the behavior of PLEARN with an enumerative synthesizer in a single thread. However, a straightforward interleaving of multiple PLEARN threads would be highly inefficient because of redundancies – enumerating the same expression (which is contained in multiple grammars) multiple times. Instead, we propose a technique that **(1)** enumerates each expression at most once, and **(2)** reuses previously enumerated expressions to construct larger expressions.

---

[4] We use the shorthand $X_{1,...,n}$ to denote the sequence $\langle X_1, \ldots, X_n \rangle$.

To achieve this, we extend a widely used [2, 15, 31] synthesis strategy, called *component-based synthesis* [21], wherein the grammar of expressions is induced by a set of components, each of which is a typed operator with a fixed arity. For example, the grammars shown in Fig. 1 are induced by integer components (such as 1, +, mod, =, etc.) and Boolean components (such as true, and, or, etc.). Below, we first formalize the grammar that is implicit in this synthesis style.

Definition 8 (Component-Based Grammar). *Given a set $\mathscr{C}$ of typed components, we define the component-based grammar $\mathcal{E}$ as the set of all expressions formed by well-typed component application over $\mathscr{C}$, i.e.,*

$$\mathcal{E} = \{ c(e_1, \ldots, e_a) \mid (c : \tau_1 \times \cdots \times \tau_a \to \tau) \in \mathscr{C} \land e_{1 \ldots a} \subset \mathcal{E}$$
$$\land\, e_1 : \tau_1 \land \cdots \land e_a : \tau_a \}$$

where $e : \tau$ denotes that the expression e has type τ.

We denote the set of all components appearing in a component-based grammar $\mathcal{E}$ as components($\mathcal{E}$). Henceforth, we assume that components($\mathcal{E}$) is known (explicitly provided by the user) for each $\mathcal{E}$. We also use values($\mathcal{E}$) to denote the subset of nullary components (variables and constants) in components($\mathcal{E}$), and operators($\mathcal{E}$) to denote the remaining components with positive arities.

The closure property of component-based grammars significantly reduces the overhead of tracking which subexpressions can be combined together to form larger expressions. Given a SyGuS problem over a grammar $\mathcal{E}$, hybrid enumeration requires a sequence $\mathcal{E}_{1 \ldots p}$ of grammars such that each $\mathcal{E}_i$ is a component-based grammar and that $\mathcal{E}_1 \subset \cdots \subset \mathcal{E}_p \subseteq \mathcal{E}$. Next, we explain how the subset relationship between the grammars enables efficient enumeration of expressions.

Given grammars $\mathcal{E}_1 \subset \cdots \subset \mathcal{E}_p$, observe that an expression of size k in $\mathcal{E}_i$ may only contain subexpressions of size $\{1, \ldots, (k-1)\}$ belonging to $\mathcal{E}_{1 \ldots i}$. This allows us to enumerate expressions in an order such that each subexpression e is synthesized (and cached) before any expressions that have e as a subexpression. We call an enumeration order that ensures this property a *well order*.

Definition 9 (Well Order). *Given arbitrary grammars $\mathcal{E}_{1 \ldots p}$, we say that a strict partial order $\lhd$ on $\mathcal{E}_{1 \ldots p} \times \mathbb{N}$ is a well order iff*

$$\forall \mathcal{E}_a, \mathcal{E}_b \in \mathcal{E}_{1 \ldots p} : \ \forall k_1, k_2 \in \mathbb{N} : [\mathcal{E}_a \subseteq \mathcal{E}_b \land k_1 < k_2] \implies (\mathcal{E}_a, k_1) \lhd (\mathcal{E}_b, k_2)$$

Motivated by Theorem 5, our implementation of hybrid enumeration uses a particular well order that incrementally increases the expressiveness of the space of expressions. For a rough measure of the expressiveness (Definition 5) of a pair $(\mathcal{E}, k)$, i.e., the set of expressions of size k in a given grammar $\mathcal{E}$, we simply overapproximate the number of syntactically distinct expressions:

Theorem 7. *Let $\mathcal{E}_{1 \ldots p}$ be component-based grammars and $\mathscr{C}_i = $ components($\mathcal{E}_i$). Then, the following strict partial order $\lhd_*$ on $\mathcal{E}_{1 \ldots p} \times \mathbb{N}$ is a well order*

$$\forall \mathcal{E}_a, \mathcal{E}_b \in \mathcal{E}_{1 \ldots p} : \ \forall m, n \in \mathbb{N} : (\mathcal{E}_a, m) \lhd_* (\mathcal{E}_b, n) \iff |\mathscr{C}_a|^m < |\mathscr{C}_b|^n$$

We now describe the main hybrid enumeration algorithm, which is listed in Algorithm 2. The HENUM function accepts a SyGuS problem $\langle f_{X \to Y} \mid \phi, \mathcal{E} \rangle_{\mathbb{T}}$, a set $\mathcal{E}_{1...p}$ of component-based grammars such that $\mathcal{E}_1 \subset \cdots \subset \mathcal{E}_p \subseteq \mathcal{E}$, a well order $\lhd$, and an upper bound $q \geq 0$ on the size of expressions to enumerate. In lines 4–8, we first enumerate all values and cache them as expressions of size one. In general $C[j, k][\tau]$ contains expressions of type τ and size k from $\mathcal{E}_j \setminus \mathcal{E}_{j-1}$. In line 9 we sort (grammar, size) pairs in some total order consistent with $\lhd$. Finally, in lines 10–20, we iterate over each pair $(\mathcal{E}_j, k)$ and each operator from $\mathcal{E}_{1...j}$ and invoke the DIVIDE procedure (Algorithm 3) to carefully choose the operator's argument subexpressions ensuring **(1)** *correctness* – their sizes sum up to $k - 1$, **(2)** *efficiency* – expressions are enumerated at most once, and **(3)** *completeness* – all expressions of size k in $\mathcal{E}_j$ are enumerated.

The DIVIDE algorithm generates a set of locations for selecting arguments to an operator. Each location is a pair (x, y) indicating that any expression from $C[x, y][\tau]$ can be an argument, where τ is the argument type required by the operator. DIVIDE accepts an arity a for an operator o, a size budget q, the index l of the least-expressive grammar containing o, the index j of the least-expressive grammar that should contain the constructed expressions of the form $o(e_1, \ldots, e_a)$, and an accumulator α that stores the list of argument locations. In lines 7–9, the size budget is recursively divided among $a - 1$ locations. In each recursive step, the upper bound $(q - a + 1)$ on v ensures that we have a size budget of at least $q - (q - a + 1) = a - 1$ for the remaining $a - 1$ locations. This results in a call tree such that the accumulator α at each leaf node contains the locations from which to select the last $a - 1$ arguments, and we are left with some size budget $q \geq 1$ for the first argument e_1. Finally in lines 4–5, we carefully select the locations for e_1 to ensure that $o(e_1, \ldots, e_a)$ has not been synthesized before—either $o \in \mathsf{components}(\mathcal{E}_j)$ or at least one argument belongs to $\mathcal{E}_j \setminus \mathcal{E}_{j-1}$.[5]

We conclude by stating some desirable properties satisfied by HENUM. Their proofs are provided in the extended version of this paper [27, Appendix A.3].

Theorem 8 (HENUM is Complete up to Size q). *Given a SyGuS problem $S = \langle f_{X \to Y} \mid \phi, \mathcal{E} \rangle_{\mathbb{T}}$, let $\mathcal{E}_{1...p}$ be component-based grammars over theory $\mathbb{T}$ such that $\mathcal{E}_1 \subset \cdots \subset \mathcal{E}_p = \mathcal{E}$, $\lhd$ be a well order on $\mathcal{E}_{1...p} \times \mathbb{N}$, and $q \geq 0$ be an upper bound on size of expressions. Then, $\mathrm{HENUM}(S, \mathcal{E}_{1...p}, \lhd, q)$ will eventually find a satisfying expression if there exists one with size $\leq q$.*

Theorem 9 (HENUM is Efficient). *Given a SyGuS problem $S = \langle f_{X \to Y} \mid \phi, \mathcal{E} \rangle_{\mathbb{T}}$, let $\mathcal{E}_{1...p}$ be component-based grammars over theory $\mathbb{T}$ such that $\mathcal{E}_1 \subset \cdots \subset \mathcal{E}_p \subseteq \mathcal{E}$, $\lhd$ be a well order on $\mathcal{E}_{1...p} \times \mathbb{N}$, and $q \geq 0$ be an upper bound on size of expressions. Then, $\mathrm{HENUM}(S, \mathcal{E}_{1...p}, \lhd, q)$ will enumerate each distinct expression at most once.*

---

[5] We use $\diamond$ as the `cons` operator for sequences, e.g., $x \diamond \langle y, z \rangle = \langle x, y, z \rangle$.

Algorithm 2. *Hybrid enumeration* to combat overfitting in SyGuS

---

1   **func** HENUM $(\langle f_{X \to Y} \mid \phi, \mathcal{E} \rangle_{\mathbb{T}}$: Problem, $\mathcal{E}_{1...p}$: Grammars, $\lhd$: WO, q: Max. Size)

2   ▶ **Requires: component-based grammars** $\mathcal{E}_1 \subset \cdots \subset \mathcal{E}_p \subseteq \mathcal{E}$ **and** v **as the input variable**

3       $C \leftarrow \{\}$

4   **for** $i \leftarrow 1$ **to** p **do**

5           $V \leftarrow$ **if** $i = 1$ **then** values$(\mathcal{E}_1)$ **else** $[\,$values$(\mathcal{E}_i) \setminus$ values$(\mathcal{E}_{i-1})\,]$

6   **for each** $(e : \tau) \in V$ **do**

7               $C[i, 1][\tau] \leftarrow C[i, 1][\tau] \cup \{e\}$

8   **if** $\forall x \in X : \phi(\lambda v.\, e, x)$ **then return** $\lambda v.\, e$

9       $R \leftarrow$ SORT$(\lhd, \mathcal{E}_{1...p} \times \{2, \ldots, q\})$

10   **for** $i \leftarrow 1$ **to** $|R|$ **do**

11          $(\mathcal{E}_j, k) \leftarrow R[i]$

12   **for** $l \leftarrow 1$ **to** j **do**

13              $O \leftarrow$ **if** $l = 1$ **then** operators$(\mathcal{E}_1)$ **else** $[\,$operators$(\mathcal{E}_l) \setminus$ operators$(\mathcal{E}_{l-1})\,]$

14   **for each** $(o : \tau_1 \times \cdots \times \tau_a \to \tau) \in O$ **do**

15                  $L \leftarrow$ DIVIDE$(a, \ k - 1, \ l, \ j, \ \langle\rangle)$

16   **for each** $\langle (x_1, y_1), \ldots, (x_a, y_a) \rangle \in L$ **do**

17   **for each** $e_{1 \ldots a} \in C[x_1, y_1][\tau_1] \times \cdots \times C[x_a, y_a][\tau_a]$ **do**

18                          $e \leftarrow o(e_1, \ldots, e_a)$

19                          $C[j, k][\tau] \leftarrow C[j, k][\tau] \cup \{e\}$

20   **if** $\forall x \in X : \phi(\lambda v.\, e, x)$ **then return** $\lambda v.\, e$

21   **return** $\perp$

Algorithm 3. An algorithm to divide a given size budget among subexpressions [5]

---

1   **func** DIVIDE $(a$: Arity, q: Size, l: Op. Level, j: Expr. Level, α: Accumulated Args.)

2   ▶ **Requires:** $1 \leq a \leq q \ \wedge \ l \leq j$

3   **if** $a = 1$ **then**

4   **if** $l = j \ \vee \ \exists \langle x, y \rangle \in \alpha : x = j$ **then return** $\{(1, q) \diamond \alpha, \ldots, (j, q) \diamond \alpha\}$

5   **return** $\{(j, q) \diamond \alpha\}$

6       $L = \{\}$

7   **for** $u \leftarrow 1$ **to** j **do**

8   **for** $v \leftarrow 1$ **to** $(q - a + 1)$ **do**

9               $L \leftarrow L \ \cup \ $DIVIDE$(a - 1, \ q - v, \ l, \ j, \ (u, v) \diamond \alpha)$

10   **return** L

---

5   Experimental Evaluation

In this section we empirically evaluate PLEARN and HENUM. Our evaluation uses a set of 180 synthesis benchmarks,[6] consisting of all 127 official benchmarks from the Inv track of 2018 SyGuS competition [4] augmented with benchmarks from the 2018 Software Verification competition (SV-Comp) [8] and challenging verification problems proposed in prior work [9,10]. All these synthesis tasks are

---

[6] All benchmarks are available at https://github.com/SaswatPadhi/LoopInvGen.

defined over integer and Boolean values, and we evaluate them with the six grammars described in Fig. 1. We have omitted benchmarks from other tracks of the SyGuS competition as they either require us to construct $\mathcal{E}_{1...p}$ (Sect. 4) by hand or lack verification oracles. All our experiments use an 8-core Intel® Xeon® E5 machine clocked at 2.30 GHz with 32 GB memory running Ubuntu® 18.04.

5.1 Robustness of PLEARN

For five state-of-the-art SyGuS solvers – (a) LoopInvGen [29], (b) CVC4 [7,33], (c) Stoch [3, III F], (d) SketchAC [8,20], and (e) EUSolver [5] – we have compared the performance across various grammars, with and without the PLEARN framework (Algorithm 1). In this framework, to solve a SyGuS problem with the pth expressiveness level from our six integer-arithmetic grammars (see Fig. 1), we run p independent parallel instances of a SyGuS tool, each with one of the first p grammars. For example, to solve a SyGuS problem with the Polyhedra grammar, we run four instances of a solver with the Equalities, Intervals, Octagons and Polyhedra grammars. We evaluate these runs for each tool, for each of the 180 benchmarks and for each of the six expressiveness levels.

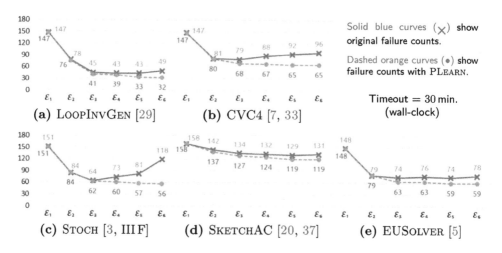

Fig. 6. The number of failures on increasing grammar expressiveness, for state-of-the-art SyGuS tools, with and without the PLEARN framework (Algorithm 1)

Figure 6 summarizes our findings. Without PLEARN the number of failures initially decreases and then increases across all solvers, as grammar expressiveness increases. However, with PLEARN the tools incur fewer failures at a given level of expressiveness, and there is a trend of *decreased* failures with increased expressiveness. Thus, we have demonstrated that PLEARN is an effective measure to mitigate overfitting in SyGuS tools and significantly improve their performance.

5.2   Performance of Hybrid Enumeration

To evaluate the performance of hybrid enumeration, we augment an existing synthesis engine with HENUM (Algorithm 2). We modify our LOOPINVGEN tool [29], which is the best-performing SyGuS synthesizer from Fig. 6. Internally, LOOP-INVGEN leverages ESCHER [2], an enumerative synthesizer, which we replace with HENUM. We make no other changes to LOOPINVGEN. We evaluate the performance and resource usage of this solver, LOOPINVGEN+HE, relative to the original LOOPINVGEN with and without PLEARN (Algorithm 1).

Performance. In Fig. 7(a), we show the number of failures across our six grammars for LOOPINVGEN, LOOPINVGEN+HE and LOOPINVGEN with PLEARN, over our 180 benchmarks. LOOPINVGEN+HE has a significantly lower failure rate than LOOPINVGEN, and the number of failures decreases with grammar expressiveness. Thus, hybrid enumeration is a good proxy for PLEARN.

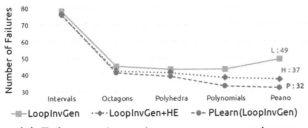

Grammar	$M\left[\frac{\tau[P]}{\tau[H]}\right]$	$M\left[\frac{\tau[H]}{\tau[L]}\right]$
Equalities	1.00	1.00
Intervals	1.91	1.04
Octagons	2.84	1.03
Polyhedra	3.72	1.01
Polynomials	4.62	1.00
Peano	5.49	0.97

(a) Failures on increasing grammar expressiveness   (b) Median(M) overhead

Fig. 7. **L** = LOOPINVGEN, **H** = LOOPINVGEN+HE, **P** = PLEARN (LOOPINVGEN). **H** is not only significantly robust against increasing grammar expressiveness, but it also has a smaller total-time cost (τ) than **P** and a negligible overhead over **L**.

Resource Usage. To estimate how computationally expensive each solver is, we compare their *total-time cost* (τ). Since LOOPINVGEN and LOOPINVGEN+HE are single-threaded, for them we simply use the wall-clock time for synthesis as the total-time cost. However, for PLEARN with p parallel instances of LOOPINVGEN, we consider the total-time cost as p times the wall-clock time for synthesis.

In Fig. 7(b), we show the median overhead (ratio of τ) incurred by PLEARN over LOOPINVGEN+HE and LOOPINVGEN+HE over LOOPINVGEN, at various expressiveness levels. As we move to grammars of increasing expressiveness, the total-time cost of PLEARN increases significantly, while the total-time cost of LOOPINVGEN+HE essentially matches that of LOOPINVGEN.

5.3   Competition Performance

Finally, we evaluate the performance of LOOPINVGEN+HE on the benchmarks from the Inv track of the 2018 SyGuS competition [4], against the official winning solver, which we denote LIG [28]—a version of LOOPINVGEN [29] that has been extensively tuned for this track. In the competition, there are some invariant-synthesis problems where the postcondition itself is a satisfying expression.

LIG starts with the postcondition as the first candidate and is extremely fast on such programs. For a fair comparison, we added this heuristic to LOOPINVGEN +HE as well. No other change was made to LOOPINVGEN+HE.

LOOPINVGEN solves 115 benchmarks in a total of 2191 seconds whereas LOOPINVGEN+HE solves 117 benchmarks in 429 seconds, for a mean speedup of over 5×. Moreover, no entrants to the competition could solve [4] the two additional benchmarks (`gcnr_tacas08` and `fib_20`) that LOOPINVGEN+HE solves.

6 Related Work

The most closely related work to ours investigates overfitting for verification tools [36]. Our work differs from theirs in several respects. First, we address the problem of overfitting in CEGIS-based synthesis. Second, we formally define overfitting and prove that all synthesizers must suffer from it, whereas they only observe overfitting empirically. Third, while they use cross-validation to combat overfitting in tuning a specific hyperparameter of a verifier, our approach is to search for solutions at different expressiveness levels.

The general problem of efficiently searching a large space of programs for synthesis has been explored in prior work. Lee et al. [24] use a probabilistic model, learned from known solutions to synthesis problems, to enumerate programs in order of their likelihood. Other approaches employ type-based pruning of large search spaces [26, 32]. These techniques are orthogonal to, and may be combined with, our approach of exploring grammar subsets.

Our results are widely applicable to existing SyGuS tools, but some tools fall outside our purview. For instance, in programming-by-example (PBE) systems [18, §7], the specification consists of a set of input-output examples. Since any program that meets the given examples is a valid satisfying expression, our notion of overfitting does not apply to such tools. However in a recent work, Inala and Singh [19] show that incrementally increasing expressiveness can also aid PBE systems. They report that searching within increasingly expressive grammar subsets requires significantly fewer examples to find expressions that generalize better over unseen data. Other instances where the synthesizers can have a free lunch, i.e., always generate a solution with a small number of counterexamples, include systems that use grammars with limited expressiveness [16, 21, 35].

Our paper falls in the category of formal results about SyGuS. In one such result, Jha and Seshia [22] analyze the effects of different kinds of counterexamples and of providing bounded versus unbounded memory to learners. Notably, they do not consider variations in "concept classes" or "program templates," which are precisely the focus of our study. Therefore, our results are complementary: we treat counterexamples and learners as opaque and instead focus on grammars.

7 Conclusion

Program synthesis is a vibrant research area; new and better synthesizers are being built each year. This paper investigates a general issue that affects all

CEGIS-based SyGuS tools. We recognize the problem of overfitting, formalize it, and identify the conditions under which it must occur. Furthermore, we provide mitigating measures for overfitting that significantly improve the existing tools.

Acknowledgement. We thank Guy Van den Broeck and the anonymous reviewers for helpful feedback for improving this work, and the organizers of the SyGuS competition for making the tools and benchmarks publicly available.

This work was supported in part by the National Science Foundation (NSF) under grants CCF-1527923 and CCF-1837129. The lead author was also supported by an internship and a PhD Fellowship from Microsoft Research.

References

1. The SyGuS Competition (2019). http://sygus.org/comp/. Accessed 10 May 2019
2. Albarghouthi, A., Gulwani, S., Kincaid, Z.: Recursive program synthesis. In: Sharygina, N., Veith, H. (eds.) CAV 2013. LNCS, vol. 8044, pp. 934–950. Springer, Heidelberg (2013). https://doi.org/10.1007/978-3-642-39799-8_67
3. Alur, R., et al.: Syntax-guided synthesis. In: Formal Methods in Computer-Aided Design, FMCAD, pp. 1–8. IEEE (2013). http://ieeexplore.ieee.org/document/6679385/
4. Alur, R., Fisman, D., Padhi, S., Singh, R., Udupa, A.: SyGuS-Comp 2018: Results and Analysis. CoRR abs/1904.07146 (2019). http://arxiv.org/abs/1904.07146
5. Alur, R., Radhakrishna, A., Udupa, A.: Scaling enumerative program synthesis via divide and conquer. In: Legay, A., Margaria, T. (eds.) TACAS 2017. LNCS, vol. 10205, pp. 319–336. Springer, Heidelberg (2017). https://doi.org/10.1007/978-3-662-54577-5_18
6. Alur, R., Singh, R., Fisman, D., Solar-Lezama, A.: Search-based program synthesis. Commun. ACM **61**(12), 84–93 (2018). https://doi.org/10.1145/3208071
7. Barrett, C., et al.: CVC4. In: Gopalakrishnan, G., Qadeer, S. (eds.) CAV 2011. LNCS, vol. 6806, pp. 171–177. Springer, Heidelberg (2011). https://doi.org/10.1007/978-3-642-22110-1_14
8. Beyer, D.: Software verification with validation of results. In: Legay, A., Margaria, T. (eds.) TACAS 2017. LNCS, vol. 10206, pp. 331–349. Springer, Heidelberg (2017). https://doi.org/10.1007/978-3-662-54580-5_20
9. Bounov, D., DeRossi, A., Menarini, M., Griswold, W.G., Lerner, S.: Inferring loop invariants through gamification. In: Proceedings of the 2018 CHI Conference on Human Factors in Computing Systems, CHI, p. 231. ACM (2018). https://doi.org/10.1145/3173574.3173805
10. Bradley, A.R., Manna, Z., Sipma, H.B.: The polyranking principle. In: Caires, L., Italiano, G.F., Monteiro, L., Palamidessi, C., Yung, M. (eds.) ICALP 2005. LNCS, vol. 3580, pp. 1349–1361. Springer, Heidelberg (2005). https://doi.org/10.1007/11523468_109
11. Cousot, P., Cousot, R.: Static determination of dynamic properties of generalized type unions. In: Language Design for Reliable Software, pp. 77–94 (1977). https://doi.org/10.1145/800022.808314
12. Cousot, P., Halbwachs, N.: Automatic Discovery of Linear Restraints Among Variables of a Program. In: Conference Record of the Fifth Annual ACM Symposium on Principles of Programming Languages. pp. 84–96. ACM Press (1978), https://doi.org/10.1145/512760.512770

13. Dietterich, T.G.: Ensemble methods in machine learning. In: Kittler, J., Roli, F. (eds.) MCS 2000. LNCS, vol. 1857, pp. 1–15. Springer, Heidelberg (2000). https://doi.org/10.1007/3-540-45014-9_1

14. Ezudheen, P., Neider, D., D'Souza, D., Garg, P., Madhusudan, P.: Horn-ICE learning for synthesizing invariants and contracts. PACMPL **2**(OOPSLA), 131:1–131:25 (2018). https://doi.org/10.1145/3276501

15. Feng, Y., Martins, R., Geffen, J.V., Dillig, I., Chaudhuri, S.: Component-based synthesis of table consolidation and transformation tasks from examples. In: Proceedings of the 38th ACM SIGPLAN Conference on Programming Language Design and Implementation, PLDI, pp. 422–436. ACM (2017). https://doi.org/10.1145/3062341.3062351

16. Godefroid, P., Taly, A.: Automated synthesis of symbolic instruction encodings from I/O samples. In: ACM SIGPLAN Conference on Programming Language Design and Implementation, PLDI, pp. 441–452. ACM (2012). https://doi.org/10.1145/2254064.2254116

17. Gulwani, S., Jojic, N.: Program verification as probabilistic inference. In: Proceedings of the 34th ACM SIGPLAN-SIGACT Symposium on Principles of Programming Languages, POPL, pp. 277–289. ACM (2007). https://doi.org/10.1145/1190216.1190258

18. Gulwani, S., Polozov, O., Singh, R.: Program synthesis. Found. Trends Program. Lang. **4**(1–2), 1–119 (2017). https://doi.org/10.1561/2500000010

19. Inala, J.P., Singh, R.: WebRelate: Integrating Web Data with Spreadsheets using Examples. PACMPL **2**(POPL), 2:1–2:28 (2018). https://doi.org/10.1145/3158090

20. Jeon, J., Qiu, X., Solar-Lezama, A., Foster, J.S.: Adaptive concretization for parallel program synthesis. In: Kroening, D., Păsăreanu, C.S. (eds.) CAV 2015. LNCS, vol. 9207, pp. 377–394. Springer, Cham (2015). https://doi.org/10.1007/978-3-319-21668-3_22

21. Jha, S., Gulwani, S., Seshia, S.A., Tiwari, A.: Oracle-guided component-based program synthesis. In: Proceedings of the 32nd ACM/IEEE International Conference on Software Engineering. ICSE, vol. 1, pp. 215–224. ACM (2010). https://doi.org/10.1145/1806799.1806833

22. Jha, S., Seshia, S.A.: A theory of formal synthesis via inductive learning. Acta Informatica **54**(7), 693–726 (2017). https://doi.org/10.1007/s00236-017-0294-5

23. Le, X.D., Chu, D., Lo, D., Le Goues, C., Visser, W.: S3: syntax- and semantic-guided repair synthesis via programming by examples. In: Proceedings of the 11th Joint Meeting on Foundations of Software Engineering. ESEC/FSE, pp. 593–604. ACM (2017). https://doi.org/10.1145/3106237.3106309

24. Lee, W., Heo, K., Alur, R., Naik, M.: Accelerating search-based program synthesis using learned probabilistic models. In: Proceedings of the 39th ACM SIGPLAN Conference on Programming Language Design and Implementation, PLDI 2018, pp. 436–449. ACM (2018). https://doi.org/10.1145/3192366.3192410

25. Miné, A.: The octagon abstract domain. In: Proceedings of the Eighth Working Conference on Reverse Engineering, WCRE, p. 310. IEEE Computer Society (2001). https://doi.org/10.1109/WCRE.2001.957836

26. Osera, P., Zdancewic, S.: Type-and-example-directed program synthesis. In: Proceedings of the 36th ACM SIGPLAN Conference on Programming Language Design and Implementation, PLDI, pp. 619–630. ACM (2015). https://doi.org/10.1145/2737924.2738007

27. Padhi, S., Millstein, T., Nori, A., Sharma, R.: Overfitting in Synthesis: Theory and Practice. CoRR abs/1905.07457 (2019). https://arxiv.org/pdf/1905.07457

28. Padhi, S., Sharma, R., Millstein, T.: LoopInvGen: A Loop Invariant Generator based on Precondition Inference. CoRR abs/1707.02029 (2018). http://arxiv.org/abs/1707.02029
29. Padhi, S., Sharma, R., Millstein, T.D.: Data-driven precondition inference with learned features. In: Proceedings of the 37th ACM SIGPLAN Conference on Programming Language Design and Implementation, PLDI, pp. 42–56. ACM (2016). https://doi.org/10.1145/2908080.2908099
30. Peano, G.: Calcolo geometrico secondo l'Ausdehnungslehre di H. Grassmann: preceduto dalla operazioni della logica deduttiva, vol. 3. Fratelli Bocca (1888)
31. Perelman, D., Gulwani, S., Grossman, D., Provost, P.: Test-driven synthesis. In: ACM SIGPLAN Conference on Programming Language Design and Implementation, PLDI, pp. 408–418. ACM (2014). https://doi.org/10.1145/2594291.2594297
32. Polikarpova, N., Kuraj, I., Solar-Lezama, A.: Program synthesis from polymorphic refinement types. In: Proceedings of the 37th ACM SIGPLAN Conference on Programming Language Design and Implementation, PLDI, pp. 522–538. ACM (2016). https://doi.org/10.1145/2908080.2908093
33. Reynolds, A., Deters, M., Kuncak, V., Tinelli, C., Barrett, C.: Counterexample-guided quantifier instantiation for synthesis in SMT. In: Kroening, D., Păsăreanu, C.S. (eds.) CAV 2015. LNCS, vol. 9207, pp. 198–216. Springer, Cham (2015). https://doi.org/10.1007/978-3-319-21668-3_12
34. Shalev-Shwartz, S., Ben-David, S.: Understanding Machine Learning: From Theory to Algorithms. Cambridge University Press, Cambridge (2014)
35. Sharma, R., Gupta, S., Hariharan, B., Aiken, A., Liang, P., Nori, A.V.: A data driven approach for algebraic loop invariants. In: Felleisen, M., Gardner, P. (eds.) ESOP 2013. LNCS, vol. 7792, pp. 574–592. Springer, Heidelberg (2013). https://doi.org/10.1007/978-3-642-37036-6_31
36. Sharma, R., Nori, A.V., Aiken, A.: Bias-variance tradeoffs in program analysis. In: The 41st Annual ACM SIGPLAN-SIGACT Symposium on Principles of Programming Languages, POPL, pp. 127–138. ACM (2014). https://doi.org/10.1145/2535838.2535853
37. Solar-Lezama, A.: Program sketching. STTT **15**(5–6), 475–495 (2013)

Permissions

All chapters in this book were first published by Springer; hereby published with permission under the Creative Commons Attribution License or equivalent. Every chapter published in this book has been scrutinized by our experts. Their significance has been extensively debated. The topics covered herein carry significant findings which will fuel the growth of the discipline. They may even be implemented as practical applications or may be referred to as a beginning point for another development.

The contributors of this book come from diverse backgrounds, making this book a truly international effort. This book will bring forth new frontiers with its revolutionizing research information and detailed analysis of the nascent developments around the world.

We would like to thank all the contributing authors for lending their expertise to make the book truly unique. They have played a crucial role in the development of this book. Without their invaluable contributions this book wouldn't have been possible. They have made vital efforts to compile up to date information on the varied aspects of this subject to make this book a valuable addition to the collection of many professionals and students.

This book was conceptualized with the vision of imparting up-to-date information and advanced data in this field. To ensure the same, a matchless editorial board was set up. Every individual on the board went through rigorous rounds of assessment to prove their worth. After which they invested a large part of their time researching and compiling the most relevant data for our readers.

The editorial board has been involved in producing this book since its inception. They have spent rigorous hours researching and exploring the diverse topics which have resulted in the successful publishing of this book. They have passed on their knowledge of decades through this book. To expedite this challenging task, the publisher supported the team at every step. A small team of assistant editors was also appointed to further simplify the editing procedure and attain best results for the readers.

Apart from the editorial board, the designing team has also invested a significant amount of their time in understanding the subject and creating the most relevant covers. They scrutinized every image to scout for the most suitable representation of the subject and create an appropriate cover for the book.

The publishing team has been an ardent support to the editorial, designing and production team. Their endless efforts to recruit the best for this project, has resulted in the accomplishment of this book. They are a veteran in the field of academics and their pool of knowledge is as vast as their experience in printing. Their expertise and guidance has proved useful at every step. Their uncompromising quality standards have made this book an exceptional effort. Their encouragement from time to time has been an inspiration for everyone.

The publisher and the editorial board hope that this book will prove to be a valuable piece of knowledge for researchers, students, practitioners and scholars across the globe.

List of Contributors

Paul Gastin
LSV, ENS Paris-Saclay, CNRS, Université Paris-Saclay, Cachan, France

Sayan Mukherjee and B. Srivathsan
Chennai Mathematical Institute, Chennai, India

Victor Roussanaly, Ocan Sankur and Nicolas Markey
Univ Rennes, Inria, CNRS, IRISA, Rennes, France

Loris D'Antoni
University of Wisconsin–Madison, Madison, WI 53706-1685, USA

Tiago Ferreira, Matteo Sammartino and Alexandra Silva
University College London, Gower Street, London WC1E 6BT, UK

Julien Lange
University of Kent, Canterbury, UK

Nobuko Yoshida
Imperial College London, London, UK

Suguman Bansal and Moshe Y. Vardi
Rice University, Houston, TX 77005, USA

Saeid Tizpaz-Niari, Pavol Černý and Ashutosh Trivedi
University of Colorado Boulder, Boulder, USA

Norine Coenen, Bernd Finkbeiner and Leander Tentrup
Reactive Systems Group, Saarland University, Saarbrücken, Germany

César Sánchez
IMDEA Software Institute, Madrid, Spain

Mahmoud Elfar, Yu Wang and Miroslav Pajic
Duke University, Durham, NC 27708, USA

Azadeh Farzan and Anthony Vandikas
University of Toronto, Toronto, Canada

Miriam García Soto, Thomas A. Henzinger, Christian Schilling and Luka Zeleznik
IST Austria, Klosterneuburg, Austria

Samuel Drews, Aws Albarghouthi and Loris D'Antoni
University of Wisconsin-Madison, Madison, USA

Saswat Padhi and Todd Millstein
University of California, Los Angeles, USA

Aditya Nori
Microsoft Research, Cambridge, UK

Rahul Sharma
Microsoft Research, Bengaluru, India

Index

A

Abstract Domain, 194, 197-199, 202-204, 230

Abstraction Function, 197-199, 202, 205, 209

Abstraction Refinement

Algorithms, 193, 211

Algorithm, 2-16, 19, 31-34, 38, 40-42, 45-49, 51-53, 55-57, 71, 74, 88-89, 122-123, 125-128, 137, 145-146, 148-150, 152, 155-156, 164-172, 176-177, 201, 203-205, 207-209, 222, 224-226

Arithmetic Formula, 41, 118

Artificial Intelligence, 116, 134

Asynchronous Switching Specification, 46

Automata Library, 80, 96

B

Binary Decision Diagrams, 194

Boolean Constraints, 117, 132

Boolean Formula, 201-203

Boolean Operations, 79, 95

Boolean Variable, 119

C

Clock Constraints, 193-194, 196, 202, 204-205

Clock Variables, 193-194

Component-based Grammars, 223-225

Computational Learning Theory, 121-122, 124-125, 134

Computer System, 193

Computer-aided Design, 173, 229

Concrete Domain, 197, 202-203

Continuous Dynamics, 42, 52

Convex Polyhedra, 47, 193, 197

Counterexample-guided Inductive Synthesis, 212-213, 218

Counterexample-guided Refinement Loop, 156, 164

Current Node, 199

Cyclic-linear Hybrid Automaton, 42, 55

D

Data Extraction, 117, 134

Data Wrangling, 117, 134

Decision-making Model, 117

Delayed-action Games, 20-21, 25

Diagonal Constraints, 1-4, 7-12, 14-19

Discrete Variables, 193-195, 207, 209

E

Enumerative Algorithm, 193-194, 197-198, 208

Error Probability, 213, 219

Extrapolation Operators, 2, 6, 194

F

Finite-state Automata, 144, 193

Functional Specification, 119-120, 125-126, 129, 131, 133

G

Grammar Expressiveness, 212-220, 226-227

H

Hybrid Enumeration, 212, 214, 222-225, 227

I

Information, 7, 20-21, 23, 25-26, 32, 37, 39, 42, 64, 86, 89, 97, 102-103, 111, 113-116, 132, 168-169, 172-174, 176-177, 185, 190, 194, 199, 209

Input Probability, 117, 119

Input/output Traces, 42, 57

Invariants, 40-42, 46, 48-49, 155, 196, 207, 229-231

L

Less-expressive Grammars, 212, 215

Low-level Code, 117

M

Machine Learning, 113, 212-213, 219, 230-231

Model Checking, 17-18, 20, 36, 76, 152-153, 165, 174-177, 179-183, 187-189, 191, 193-194, 210-211

N

No-free-lunch, 212-214, 218-219

O
Open-source, 80, 91
Operator, 7, 23, 27, 32, 201, 204, 215, 223-224

P
Parallel Programs, 170, 172
Polyhedra Library, 53, 56
Probabilistic Constraints, 117, 133
Probabilistic Postcondition, 119
Probabilistic Specifications, 132
Probabilistic Synthesis Problem, 117-118
Procedure Membership, 49-50
Product Programs, 170-172, 190
Program Synthesis, 117, 132, 134, 212, 228-231
Programming Languages, 58, 73-74, 114, 134-135, 210, 229-231
Proof Checking Algorithm, 156, 167, 169-171
Proof Construction, 156, 169-170

R
Reachable Switching Set, 47, 49-52
Real-time Systems, 19, 38, 193, 209-211
Refinement Procedure, 193, 199-200, 205
Refinement Rounds, 170

S
Sequential Benchmarks, 169-170
Software Engineering, 153, 210, 230
Source Code, 99, 108, 112-113
Stochastic Satisfiability, 133
Subsection, 46, 127, 198, 205
Supergame, 34-36
Symbolic Algorithm, 193, 201, 208
Synchronous Switching Specification, 45
Syntax-guided Synthesis, 153, 212, 229
Synthesis Framework, 20-21, 31, 37
Synthesized Programs, 117, 120

T
Technology, 1, 57, 210
Timed Automata, 1-4, 6-7, 11, 14-19, 42, 57, 73, 193-196, 207, 209-211
Transition System, 4-5, 27, 61, 66, 71-72, 83, 178-186, 193

V
Verification Oracle, 218-219
Vertices, 43, 46-47, 184-185, 196

Printed in the USA
CPSIA information can be obtained
at www.ICGtesting.com
JSHW051358221024
72173JS00006B/1311